Applying Communication Theory for Professional Life

Fourth Edition

Sara Miller McCune founded SAGE Publishing in 1965 to support the dissemination of usable knowledge and educate a global community. SAGE publishes more than 1000 journals and over 800 new books each year, spanning a wide range of subject areas. Our growing selection of library products includes archives, data, case studies and video. SAGE remains majority owned by our founder and after her lifetime will become owned by a charitable trust that secures the company's continued independence.

Los Angeles | London | New Delhi | Singapore | Washington DC | Melbourne

Applying Communication Theory for Professional Life

A Practical Introduction

Fourth Edition

Marianne Dainton
La Salle University

Elaine D. Zelley
La Salle University

Los Angeles | London | New Delhi
Singapore | Washington DC | Melbourne

FOR INFORMATION:

SAGE Publications, Inc.
2455 Teller Road
Thousand Oaks, California 91320
E-mail: order@sagepub.com

SAGE Publications Ltd.
1 Oliver's Yard
55 City Road
London EC1Y 1SP
United Kingdom

SAGE Publications India Pvt. Ltd.
B 1/I 1 Mohan Cooperative Industrial Area
Mathura Road, New Delhi 110 044
India

SAGE Publications Asia-Pacific Pte. Ltd.
3 Church Street
#10-04 Samsung Hub
Singapore 049483

Acquisitions Editor: Terri Accomazzo
Editorial Assistant: Erik Helton
Production Editor: Myleen Medina
Copy Editor: Michelle Ponce
Typesetter: C&M Digitals (P) Ltd.
Proofreader: Rae-Ann Goodwin
Cover Designer: Anupama Krishnan
Marketing Manager: Allison Henry

Printed in the United States of America

Library of Congress Cataloging-in-Publication Data

Names: Dainton, Marianne author. | Zelley, Elaine D. author.

Title: Applying communication theory for professional life : a practical introduction / Marianne Dainton, La Salle University ; Elaine D. Zelley, La Salle University.

Description: Fourth edition. | Los Angeles : SAGE, 2019. | Includes bibliographical references and index.

Identifiers: LCCN 2017039906 | ISBN 9781506315478 (pbk. : alk. paper)

Subjects: LCSH: Communication—Philosophy.

Classification: LCC P90 .D245 2018 | DDC 302.2/01—dc23
LC record available at https://lccn.loc.gov/2017039906

This book is printed on acid-free paper.

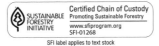

Certified Chain of Custody
SUSTAINABLE FORESTRY INITIATIVE
Promoting Sustainable Forestry
www.sfiprogram.org
SFI-01268
SFI label applies to text stock

18 19 20 21 22 10 9 8 7 6 5 4 3 2 1

BRIEF CONTENTS

DETAILED CONTENTS

ACKNOWLEDGMENTS

We would like to thank the reviewers for this edition, as well as the faculty members who have e-mailed us with their compliments and recommendations. We are very appreciative of their support and feedback, and we hope we have done justice to your recommendations.

We also would like to thank several of our graduate students, whose workplace stories serve as the foundation for some of our cases in this and previous cases. Specifically, we thank Tiffany Mercer-Robbins, Michele Langley, Vincent Haas, Maryam Ashfar, Janet Donovan, Lauren Zane-Virostek, Cristina Tosti, and Julie Pompizzi (all names and organizations listed in the case studies are pseudonyms).

We also would like to thank our students and colleagues at La Salle University. Our students continue to challenge us with the "so what" question, and we are pleased most of them are persuaded by our answers. Our colleagues in the communication department also deserve acknowledgment; they not only serve as outstanding instructor role models but also continue to greet our work with enthusiasm and provide us with much-needed social support. We particularly thank Katie Neary Dunleavy for her advice and support.

It often goes without saying (but shouldn't!) that we thank our family members and friends for their ongoing support. Both Marianne and Elaine are especially grateful to their husbands, Scott and Bryan, for serving as sounding boards and providing insight from the corporate world. More than a few of their experiences have made it into this text.

CHAPTER ONE

INTRODUCTION TO COMMUNICATION THEORY

There are almost 600,000 web pages devoted to explaining that "communication is easy" (go ahead and search it!) and over 7 million YouTube hits for the same phrase. Of course, if mastering the communication process really only required viewing a 4-minute video, we would all be maestros of getting our messages understood. Unfortunately, much of popular culture tends to minimize the challenges associated with the communication process. Yes, in the 21st century, we believe communication skill is important—you need only to peruse the content of talk shows, dating apps, advice columns, and organizational performance reviews to recognize that communication skills can make or break an individual's personal and professional life. Companies want to hire and promote people with excellent communication skills (Beaton, 2017). Divorces occur because spouses believe they "no longer communicate" (Dutihl, 2012). Communication is perceived as a magical elixir, one that can ensure a happy long-term relationship and guarantee organizational success. Yet, despite lauding communication as the *sine qua non* of contemporary success, the secret to that success is treated superficially at best in our modern information environment. Clearly, popular culture holds paradoxical views about communication: It is easy to do yet powerful in its effects, simultaneously simple and magical.

We believe the communication process is complex. "Good" communication means different things to different people in different situations. Accordingly, simply adopting a set of particular skills is not going to guarantee success. Genuinely good communicators are those who understand the underlying principles behind communication and are able to enact, appropriately and effectively, particular communication skills as the situation warrants. This book seeks to provide the foundation for those sorts of decisions. We focus on communication theories that can be applied in your personal and professional lives. Understanding these theories—including their underlying assumptions and the predictions they make—can make you a more competent communicator.

Learning Objectives

After reading this chapter, you will be able to do the following:

1. Analyze a definition of communication, articulating the definition's level of observation, intentionality, and normative judgment

2. Recognize the various contexts in which communication takes place

3. Differentiate a communication theory from a concept and a model

4. Discriminate between commonsense, working, and scholarly theories

5. Use criteria for evaluating theory to determine the relative usefulness of a communication theory

WHAT IS COMMUNICATION?

This text is concerned with communication theory, so it is important to be clear about the term *communication*. The everyday view of communication is quite different from the view of communication taken by communication scholars. In the business world, for example, a popular view is that communication is synonymous with information. Thus, the communication process is the flow of information from one person to another (Axley, 1984). Communication is viewed as simply one activity among many others, such as planning, controlling, and managing (Deetz, 1994). It is *what* we do in organizations.

Communication scholars, on the other hand, recognize communication as more than just the flow of information. In a simplified world in which a short YouTube clip could explain to viewers why communication is "easy,"-we could handily provide you with a one-sentence definition of the term *communication*. Based on that simple definition, we would all understand the meaning of the term, and we would all use the term in exactly the same way. However, scholars disagree as to the scope of the process, whether a source or receiver orientation should be taken, and whether message exchange need be successful to count as communication.

DANCE'S DEFINITIONS OF COMMUNICATION

Fundamentally, communication is a complex process associated with sending, receiving, and interpreting messages. Beyond that, however, the concept of **communication** is just not that easy to delineate. Back in 1976, Dance and Larson reported 126 published definitions of the term *communication*. The variations in the definitions were profound. Table 1.1 highlights the ways the definitions varied.

In looking at the multitude of definitions of communication, Dance (1970) identified three variations. First, Dance argued that definitions varied based on the **level of observation**, which he described as the scope of what is included in the definition. For example, Dance (1967, as reported in Dance & Larson, 1976, Appendix A) defined communication as "eliciting a response through verbal symbols." This definition limits what is considered communication in two ways. First, it limits communication to only that which elicits a response. Consider an example where you instruct a coworker to fill out a particular form. If that coworker doesn't respond in any way, by this definition, communication hasn't occurred. The second way this definition limits communication is in saying communication is only verbal. So, if your coworker gives you the "okay" gesture when you've asked her to fill out the report, her response to your request would not be considered communication, as it was purely nonverbal. Definitions that make such limitations are said to have a relatively narrow level of observation; only specific types of message exchanges "count" as communication. These types of definitions might suggest messages that don't meet the requirements to be considered communication are *informative* rather than *communicative*.

Other definitions, however, try to be very inclusive about behaviors that might be considered communication. To illustrate, another definition identified by Dance and Larson (1976) says communication is "all of the procedures by which one mind can affect another" (Weaver, 1949, as cited in Dance & Larson, Appendix A). Notice that this definition does not give any indication of whether the mind is of a human, an animal, or even an alien (if there are such things). More importantly, it suggests *all* behavior can count as communication. Such definitions are considered to have a broad level of observation. As such, the first way to differentiate between theories is to consider what "counts" as communication.

A second distinction made by Dance (1970) is the stance the definition takes on **intentionality**. Some definitions explicitly indicate that for communication to occur, the exchange of messages has to be on purpose. For example, Miller (1966) defined communication as "those situations in which a source transmits a message to a receiver with conscious intent to affect the latter's behaviors" (as cited in Dance & Larson, 1976, Appendix A). Definitions such as this one are said to take a **source orientation**. So, for example, if your boss were to yawn while you gave a presentation, this definition would not consider the yawn as communication if your boss did not yawn on purpose (i.e., if she yawned as a physiological response to tiredness rather than to suggest you were boring her).

However, other definitions take a **receiver orientation** to communication. Such definitions buy into the notion that "you cannot not communicate"; anything you say or do is potentially communicative, regardless of whether you intended to send a message or not (see Watzlawick, Bavelas, & Jackson, 1967). For example, Ruesch and Bateson (1961, as cited in Dance & Larson, 1976, Appendix A) say that "communication does not refer to verbal, explicit, and intentional transmission of messages alone. . . . The concept of communication would include all those processes by which people influence one another." In this case, if you (as the receiver) were to interpret your boss's yawn as a message of boredom, it should be considered communication, regardless of whether the boss intended to send that message or not.

The final way Dance (1970) argues that definitions of communication vary is **normative judgment**, which is a focus on whether the definition requires an indication of success or accuracy. Some definitions would suggest that even if people misunderstand each other, communication has still occurred. Berelson and Steiner (1964), for example, say communication is "the transmission of information, ideas, emotions, skills, etc., by the use of—symbols—words, pictures, figures, graphs, etc. It is the act or process of transmission that is called communication" (as cited in Dance & Larson, 1976, Appendix A). In this case, it is the transmission that is important, not the understanding. So, if a student has no idea what a teacher is talking about, by this definition, communication has still occurred, it just may not have been very effective communication. Definitions like this are said to be nonevaluative.

Other definitions limit communication to only those situations where the receiver and the source share the same understanding after the communicative effort. These definitions, identified as being evaluative, require shared meaning in order to be considered communication; unsuccessful messages are not considered to be communication. To illustrate, Gode (1959, as cited in Dance & Larson, 1976, Appendix A) defines communication as "a process that makes common to two or several what was the monopoly of one or some." This definition suggests that if the message has not resulted in a common understanding, communication has not occurred. In the example of student-teacher interaction described earlier, if the student doesn't understand the teacher, then by this definition the teacher has not communicated. She or he may have lectured, cajoled, or presented, but she or he has not communicated.

Table 1.1	Ways Definitions Vary		
Differences in Definitions		**Stance**	**Taken**
Level of observation: *Are there limitations on what counts as communication?*		**Narrow** Yes	**Broad** No
Intentionality: *Do only messages sent consciously and on purpose count?*		**Source** Yes	**Receiver** No
Normative judgment: *Does the message have to be successfully received to count as communication?*		**Evaluative** Yes	**Nonevaluative** No

By now you understand some of the complexities of the nature of communication. Throughout the book, different theorists likely use different definitions of communication. Sometimes these variations in definition will be obvious, sometimes they will be less so. For example, systems theory (see Chapter 9) spends a great deal of time articulating the nature of communication. In so doing, it becomes clear that this theory takes a broad level of observation, a receiver orientation, and is nonevaluative. However, other theories only imply what they mean by communication. Poole and colleagues, in their adaptive structuration approach (see Chapter 8), never articulate their definition of communication. Because the theory is grounded in Giddens's sociological approach, however, we can assume they define communication in a similar fashion to Giddens, who defines communication as "a basis for understanding and bridging experiences, a way of creating social reality" (Giddens, 1976, as cited in Putnam, 1983, p. 51). As such, this theory also takes a broad level of observation, but the focus is more on intentional acts (source orientation), and by stressing the notion of understanding, it is more evaluative in nature.

CONTEXTS OF COMMUNICATION

Although we hesitate to provide a single definition of communication, we can identify some specific **contexts of communication**. In fact, we have organized this book around these specific contexts. The first context that requires consideration is the cognitive context, by which we mean the influence our thoughts have on the way we communicate. Relatedly, the second context is the individual differences context. Here we consider the nature-nurture debate. In so doing, we continue to consider how individual differences and social roles play a role in the communication process. Third is the interpersonal context, which refers to the interactions between two individuals, who most often have a relationship with each other. Fourth is the intercultural context, which focuses on interpersonal communication when two people are from different cultures. The fifth context is not specifically focused on a setting for communication but on a particular type of communication: the persuasive context. Readers should know that persuasion actually takes place in a variety of settings, ranging from inside one person's mind to the mass media. The sixth and seventh contexts are closely aligned

Table 1.2 Contexts of Communication

Context	Theories
Cognitive	• Attribution theory • Uncertainty reduction theory • Expectancy violations theory • Cognitive dissonance
Individual and social	• Social role theory of gender • Emotional intelligence • Message design logics • An interactional perspective on workplace generations
Interpersonal	• Politeness • Social exchange theory • Dialectical perspective • Privacy management theory
Intercultural	• Hofstede's cultural dimensions • Communication accommodation theory • Anxiety/uncertainty management theory • Face negotiation theory
Persuasive	• Elaboration likelihood model • Theory of reasoned action/theory of planned behavior • Inoculation theory • Narrative paradigm
Group	• Functional group decision making • Groupthink • Adaptive structuration theory • Symbolic convergence theory
Organizational	• Organizational culture • Organizational assimilation • Organizational identification and control • Organizing theory

(Continued)

Table 1.2 (Continued)	
Context	**Theories**
Mediated	• Diffusion of innovations
	• Social network analysis
	• Media richness theory
	• Uses and gratifications theory
Mass communication	• Agenda-setting theory
	• Cultivation theory
	• Social cognitive theory
	• Encoding/decoding theory

with the world of work: the group context and the organizational context. Finally, the eighth context is the mediated context, which is concerned with how technology influences our interpersonal, group, and organizational communication. The ninth and final context is the mass communication context, which focuses on the influence of mass-mediated messages. Table 1.2 provides an overview of these contexts and the theories covered in this text that are associated with each context.

COMMUNICATION COMPETENCE

Because we believe one of the goals of studying communication theory is to make you a better communicator, we should articulate more clearly the nature of **communication competence**. Research indicates that communication competence is most often understood as achieving a successful balance between effectiveness and appropriateness (Spitzberg & Cupach, 1989). *Effectiveness* is the extent to which you achieve your goals in an interaction. Did you get the raise? Were you able to convince a subordinate that timeliness is important? Did you persuade your spouse to clean the bathroom? *Appropriateness* refers to fulfilling social expectations for a particular situation. Did you assertively ask for the raise, or was it a meek inquiry? Were you insistent or wishy-washy when discussing your employee's tardiness? Was your interaction with your spouse demonstrative, or did you passive-aggressively pile dirty towels on the floor? Many times, a person is effective without being appropriate; consider a job applicant who lies on a resume to get a job for which he or she is unqualified. That person might be very effective in getting the job, but is such deceit appropriate? On the other hand, many times people are appropriate to the point of failing to achieve their goals. For example, a person who doesn't wish to take on an additional task at work, but says nothing because he or she fears causing conflict, might be sacrificing effectiveness for appropriateness. The key is that when faced with communicative decisions, the competent communicator considers how to be both effective *and* appropriate. We believe the theories described in this book will help you achieve your communication goals by providing an indication of both what should be done as well as how you should do it.

CONCEPTS, MODELS, AND THEORIES

The term ***theory*** is often intimidating to students. We hope by the time you finish reading this book you will find working with theory to be less daunting than you might have expected. The reality is that you have been working with theories of communication all of your life, even if they haven't been labelled as such. Theories simply provide an abstract understanding of the communication process (Miller, 2002). As an abstract understanding, they move beyond describing a single event by providing a means by which all such events can be understood. To illustrate, a theory of customer service can help you understand the poor customer service you received from your cable company this morning. Likewise, the same theory can also help you understand a good customer service encounter you had last week at a favorite restaurant. In a professional context, the theory can assist your organization in training and developing customer service personnel.

At their most basic level, theories provide us with a lens by which to view the world. Think of theories as a pair of glasses. Corrective lenses allow wearers to observe more clearly, but they also affect vision in unforeseen ways. For example, they can limit the span of what you see, especially when you try to look peripherally outside the range of the frames. Similarly, lenses can also distort the things you see, making objects appear larger or smaller than they really are. You can also try on lots of pairs of glasses until you finally pick a pair that works best for your lifestyle. Theories operate in a similar fashion. A theory can illuminate an aspect of your communication so you understand the process much more clearly; theory also can hide things from your understanding or distort the relative importance of things.

We consider a communication theory to be any systematic summary about the nature of the communication process. Certainly, theories can do more than summarize. Other functions of theories are to focus attention on particular concepts, clarify observations, predict communication behavior, and generate personal and social change (Littlejohn, 1989). We do not believe, however, that all of these functions are necessary for a systematic summary of communication processes to be considered a theory.

Although similar to at least two other terms, we want to be careful to differentiate theories from other abstract notions. First, a **concept** refers to an agreed-upon aspect of reality. For example, *time* is a concept, as is *love*, the color *orange*, and a *bitter* taste. All of these notions are abstract, meaning they can be applied to a variety of individual experiences or objects and can be understood in different ways. That is, you might love your cat in a different way than you love your mother; you might think time drags when in a class you don't much like but that it speeds up over the weekend; and you might hate the color orange and love the bitterness of certain foods. However, in and of themselves these concepts are not theories; they represent an effort to define or classify something, but they do not provide insights into how or why we experience them in a particular way.

Typically, theories provide a way to predict or understand one or more concepts. So, a definition of communication described earlier is a concept, but how that definition is used to explain the communication process is a theory.

A second term you might confuse with theory is a **model**. Part of the confusion you might experience is because the term *model* is used in at least four ways (Gabrenya, 2003; Goldfarb & Ratner, 2008): as a synonym to the term *theory*, as a precursor to a theory (a model is developed and eventually becomes a theory), as a physical representation of a theory (i.e., a diagram such as the one that appears for expectancy violations theory in Chapter 3), or as a specific—often mathematical—application of predication (e.g., a researcher might develop a mathematical model to predict which job categories are going to be in high demand in upcoming years). Because of these varying ways of understanding a model, we believe the term *theory* is preferable when talking about systematic summaries of the communication process.

THREE TYPES OF THEORY

Of central interest is the importance of theory for people in communication, business, and other professions. Our definition of theory suggests that any time you say a communication strategy *usually* works this way at your workplace, or that a specific approach is *generally* effective with your boss, or that certain types of communication are *typical* for particular media organizations, you are in essence providing a theoretical explanation. Most of us make these types of summary statements on a regular basis. The difference between this sort of theorizing and the theories provided in this book centers on the term *systematic* in the definition. Table 1.3 presents an overview of three types of theory.

The first summary statements in the table describe what is known as **commonsense theory**, or theory-in-use. This type of theory is often created by an individual's own personal experiences or developed from helpful hints passed on from family members, friends, or colleagues. Commonsense theories are useful because they are often the basis for our decisions about how to communicate. Sometimes, however, our commonsense backfires. For example, think about common knowledge regarding deception. Most people believe that liars don't look the person they are deceiving in the eyes, yet research indicates this is not the case (DePaulo, Stone, & Lassiter, 1985). Let's face it: If we engage in deception, we will work very hard at maintaining eye contact simply *because* we believe liars don't make eye contact! In this case, commonsense theory is not supported by research into the phenomenon.

A second type of theory is known as **working theory**. These are generalizations made in particular professions about the best techniques for doing something. Journalists work using the "inverted pyramid" of story construction (most important information to least important information). Filmmakers operate using specific camera shots to evoke particular emotions in the audience, so close-ups are used when a filmmaker wants the audience to place particular emphasis on the object in the shot. Giannetti (1982), for example, describes a scene in Hitchcock's *Notorious* in which the heroine realizes she is being poisoned by her coffee, and the audience "sees" this realization through a close-up of the coffee cup. Working theories are more systematic than commonsense theories because they represent agreed-on ways of doing things for a particular profession. In fact, these working theories may very well be based on scholarly theories. However,

Table 1.3	Three Types of Theory
Type of Theory	**Example**
Commonsense theory	• Never date someone you work with—it will always end badly. • The squeaky wheel gets the grease. • The more incompetent you are, the higher you get promoted.
Working theory	• Audience analysis should be done prior to presenting a speech. • To get a press release published, it should be newsworthy and written in journalistic style.
Scholarly theory	• Effects of violations of expectations depend on the reward value of the violator (expectancy violations theory). • The media do not tell us what to think but what to think about (agenda-setting theory).

working theories more closely represent guidelines for behavior rather than systematic representations. These types of theories are typically taught in content-specific courses (such as public relations, media production, or public speaking).

The type of theory we focus on in this book is known as **scholarly theory**. Students often assume (incorrectly!) that because a theory is labeled as *scholarly* it is not useful for people in business and the professions. Instead, the term *scholarly* indicates that the theory has undergone systematic research. Accordingly, scholarly theories provide more thorough, accurate, and abstract explanations for communication than do commonsense or working theories. The downside is that scholarly theories are typically more complex and difficult to understand than commonsense or working theories. If you are genuinely committed to improving your understanding of the communication process, however, scholarly theory will provide a strong foundation for doing so.

EVALUATING THEORY

Earlier we suggested that all theories have strengths and weaknesses; they reveal certain aspects of reality and conceal others. An important task students and scholars face is to evaluate the theories available to them. We are not talking about evaluation in terms of "good" versus "bad" but evaluating the *usefulness* of the theory. Each of you is likely to find some of the theories presented in this text more useful than others. Such a determination is likely due at least in part to your own background and experiences, as well as your profession. We would like to challenge you to broaden your scope and consider not just the usefulness of each theory to you personally but the usefulness of the theory for people's personal and professional lives in general.

A number of published standards can be used to evaluate theories (e.g., Griffin, Ledbetter, & Sparks, 2015; West & Turner, 2017). All are appropriate and effective tools for comparing the relative usefulness of a given theory. Because this text is geared toward working professionals, however (or those who wish to soon be working in the profession of their choice), we believe the following five criteria outlined in Table 1.4 best capture the way to assess the relative usefulness of communication theories in the communication, business, and related professions. Note that we are talking about the *relative* usefulness of the theory. We are not talking about either/or, good or bad, weak or strong. Instead, we hope you look at these distinctions as continua that range from very useful at one end to not particularly useful at the other end.

The first area of focus is **accuracy**. Simply put, the best theories correctly summarize the way communication actually works. Recall, however, that we are referring to scholarly theories. As such, we do not mean accuracy in terms of whether the theory accurately reflects your own personal experience (although we would hope that it does!). Instead, when we use the term *accuracy*, we are suggesting that systematic research supports the explanations provided by the theory. Thus, in assessing this quality, you should look at research studies that have used the theory to see whether the research supports or fails to support it.

A second way to evaluate theories is **practicality**. The best theories can be used to address real-world communication problems; in fact, Lewin (1951) said, "There is nothing so practical as a good theory" (p. 169). Clearly, some profound theories have changed the way we understand the world even though they aren't actually *used* by most people on a daily basis (Einstein's theory of relativity or Darwin's theory of evolution, for example). In terms of communication theories, however, theories that are accurate but can't be used in everyday life are not as good as theories that have great practical utility. For example, a theory that can help a person make better communicative decisions in his or her interactions with coworkers is better than a theory so abstract that it cannot be used by an individual in daily communication. Thus, a theory with more applications is better than a theory without practical uses. In assessing this criterion, you should look not only for how the theory has been used in the research literature but also whether the theory has made the leap to professional practice.

Succinctness is the third way to evaluate a good business or professional communication theory. *Succinctness* refers to whether or not a theory's explanation or description is sufficiently concise. Importantly, succinctness does not mean the theory is necessarily easy to understand or has only a few short steps; because the world is complex, theories trying to explain it are often fairly complex as well. Instead, what we mean by succinctness is whether the theory is formulated using as few steps as possible. The "three bears" analogy works here. Theories that have extra steps or include variables that don't help us understand real-world experiences would be considered overly complex. Theories that do not have enough steps, that don't delve beneath the surface, or that don't have enough variables to understand real-world problems are too simple. Theories that include no more and no less than necessary to understand a phenomenon thoroughly are considered just right; they are appropriately succinct. The best way to think of succinctness is to compare how much of the communication situation is explained by the theory in proportion to how many concepts are being used to explain it. The larger the situation and the smaller the number of necessary steps or concepts, the more succinct the theory.

The fourth way to evaluate a theory is to consider its **consistency**. The most useful theories have both internal and external consistency. By **internal consistency**, we mean the ideas of the theory are logically built on one another. A theory that proposes at one point that cooperation among team members guarantees success and at a different point proposes that competition is more effective than cooperation has a logical flaw. Similarly, theories that "skip" steps do not have much internal consistency. A theory predicting that age is related to the experience of jealousy and that one's expression of jealousy affects the future of the relationship, but then fails to tell us how the experience of jealousy is related to the expression of jealousy, has a logical gap. As such, it does not have strong internal consistency.

External consistency, on the other hand, refers to the theory's coherence with other widely held theories. If we presume that widely held theories are true, then the theory under evaluation that disagrees with those believed supported theories also presents a logical problem. As such, the notion of consistency, whether internal or external, is concerned with the logic of the theory. The most useful theories are those that have a strong logical structure.

The final area for evaluation is **acuity**. *Acuity* refers to the ability of a theory to provide insight into an otherwise intricate issue. Earlier we said theories evaluated as "succinct" are not necessarily easy to understand because the real world is often complicated. A theory that explains an intricate problem, however, is of greater value than a theory that explains something less complex. Think of acuity as the "wow" factor. If, after understanding the theory, you think "wow, I never considered that!" the theory has acuity. If, on the other hand, you think "no duh," the theory does not demonstrate acuity. To illustrate, a theory that explains a complex problem, such as how organizational cultures can influence employee retention, is a more useful theory than a theory that explains a relatively straightforward problem, such as how to gain attention in a speech. Those theories that explain difficult problems show acuity; those that focus on fairly obvious problems demonstrate superficiality.

Table 1.4 Criteria for Evaluating Theory	
Area of Evaluation	**What to Look For**
Accuracy	Has research supported that the theory works the way it says it does?
Practicality	Have real-world applications been found for the theory?
Succinctness	Has the theory been formulated with the appropriate number (fewest possible) of concepts or steps?
Consistency	Does the theory demonstrate coherence within its own premises and with other theories?
Acuity	To what extent does the theory make clear an otherwise complex experience?

SUMMARY

In this chapter, we discussed the popular perception of communication, which suggests that the communication process is paradoxically simple yet powerful. We identified three ways our understanding of communication can vary: the level of observation (what is included or not included in the definition), the role of intentionality (whether speaker intent is required), and normative judgment (whether success is required in order for an interaction to be considered communication). We then turned our attention to communication competence, indicating that competent communicators are those who can balance effectiveness and appropriateness. Next, we discussed the nature of theory. We differentiated between concepts, models, and theories. We also discussed the distinctions between commonsense theories, working theories, and scholarly theories. Finally, we provided a means by which scholarly theories of communication can be evaluated, namely accuracy, practicality, succinctness, consistency, and acuity.

KEY TERMS

Accuracy   10

Acuity   11

Commonsense theory   8

Communication   2

Communication
   competence   6

Concept   7

Consistency   11

Contexts of
   communication   4

External consistency   11

Intentionality   3

Internal consistency   11

Level of observation   2

Model   8

Normative judgment   3

Practicality   10

Receiver orientation   3

Scholarly theory   9

Source orientation   3

Succinctness   10

Theory   7

Working theory   8

CASE STUDY 1: EDUCATION AS ENTERTAINMENT

Imagine a new theory has been proposed, described shortly. This isn't a "real" theory: it has been created just so that you can apply the material from this chapter. We challenge you to think critically about the theory using the concepts you have learned.

In 1969, a radical new children's program appeared on television, one specifically designed to blend education with entertainment (characterproducts.com, 2004). *Sesame Street*, which has been on the air continuously for almost 50 years, uses puppets, live action, and cartoons in an effort to teach children basic skills such as identifying colors, the ABCs, and counting. The show itself is grounded in contemporary educational research, with a child psychologist in charge of evaluation of material that appears on the show (2004; McMullin, 2001). McMullin (2001) argues that *Sesame Street* is the "single largest educator of young children in the world" (¶ 2).

More than just a television show, *Sesame Street* has also branched into other media forms.

In addition to their website, *Sesame Street* currently produces 10 game apps, 6 story apps, over 75 electronic books, and 5 apps that are listed as "family tool kits" to assist children in coping with social issues like divorce and incarceration. Further, there is a subscription *Sesame Street* channel on YouTube that has more than 2 million subscribers and more than a billion hits per year (Folkenflik, 2016), as well as six other channels affiliated with *Sesame Street*, including a YouTube channel called Sesame Studios that features original digital content distinct from the popular *Sesame Street* puppets. "The idea is to create new content swiftly and inexpensively, reaching children where they consume media, just like adults, on smartphones, tablets and computers," (Folkneflik, 2016, ¶2).

Despite the popularity and success of the *Sesame Street* conglomerate, we propose education as entertainment theory (EET), which suggests there is a dark side to educational media such as *Sesame Street*. Specifically, the theory asserts that children exposed to screen media that blend education and entertainment become so accustomed to the idea that "learning is fun" that they are actually less motivated to learn when alternative instructional methods are used in a classroom setting. There are five key terms associated with this theory: *entertainment-education media*, *instructional style*, *expectations*, *motivation*, and *learning*.

Entertainment-education media. According to the American Academy of Pediatrics (2017), children spend an average of 7 hours per day in front of a screen. About 25% of children under the age of 8 regularly watch educational television, about 8% play educational games on a computer, and 7% access educational content on mobile devices (Heintz & Wartella, 2012). The common goal of these educational media forms is to engage children's attention so that they might learn. Yet, research has demonstrated a number of negative effects of screen time on young children, including childhood obesity, irregular sleep patterns, and social and behavioral issues (Summers, 2014). More importantly, research also indicates that use of digital media is associated with changes in early learning and development (Kates, 2016). EET argues that heavy consumption of entertainment-education content has a negative impact on children's later school performance because of the expectation that learning should always be fun. This leads to the second central idea, instructional style.

Instructional style. Instructional style refers to the techniques used in the education process. According to Forrest (2004), "A review of the research regarding learning processes suggests that instructors use a wide variety of teaching methods, believing that this affords all students an opportunity to gain the necessary knowledge, regardless of their learning styles" (p. 74).

The research makes a distinction between instructor-focused and student-focused teaching (Andersen, Nussbaum, Pecchioni, & Grant, 1999). Instructor-focused teaching is the traditional model, wherein the teacher is in charge of the pace and content of the class. Student-focused instruction encourages greater student participation, for example, cooperative learning (where students are put into groups or teams and teach and motivate each other) and class discussion (Andersen et al., 1999).

EET focuses on entertainment instructional style. This refers to efforts to make learning "fun." The entertainment instructional style relies on music, role-playing, games, and visual stimulation, among other things. The goal is to increase interest and reduce boredom. Efforts are made to have students participate in the learning in an informal style (Handfield-Jones, Nasmith, Steinert, & Lawn, 1993).

Expectations. Expectations are what we anticipate will happen. In the case of EET, we are

(Continued)

(Continued)

referring to expectations based on context, specifically, the learning context. According to Staton (1999), "Both instructors and students bring with them to the classroom certain expectations for the kind of speech that should and should not occur, for the kind of behavior that is and is not appropriate, for the roles that the instructor and students should and should not take, and for the nature of the social atmosphere that should and should not develop" (p. 35). In this case, we are specifically talking about expectations for entertaining instruction.

Motivation. Motivation refers to a student's desire for learning (Kerssen-Griep, Hess, & Trees, 2003). It is a drive for achievement in a particular course or content area. We presume that expectations influence motivation, such that when expectations are met, a student will be more motivated to learn. This is supported by research, which has found that instructional methods influence student motivation (Kerssen-Griep et al., 2003).

Learning. Learning is defined as "a process of progressive change from ignorance to knowledge, from inability to competence, and from indifference to understanding" (Fincher, 1994, as cited in Forrest, 2004, p. 74). According to Rubin (1999), learning is typically measured through assignments such as skills performance (e.g., a speech) or written assignments (exams, papers).

In summary, EET proposes that early childhood experiences with entertainment education media (such as *Sesame Street*) increase an individual's expectations for an entertainment

instructional style. If such expectations are met, the student will be more motivated and will learn more. If the expectations are not met, the student will be unmotivated and will therefore learn less. This can be illustrated as above.

Questions for Consideration

1. The theorists associated with EET have not formally defined communication. Where do you think "communication" occurs in this theory (hint: consider the contexts listed in Table 1.2)? Provide evidence from the theory that might indicate how the theorists' views of communication might be classified using Dance's three ways definitions of communication vary.

2. Using the definition of communication competence provided in this chapter, what role might communication competence play in the EET process?

3. What are the concepts associated with EET? Why are these concepts (rather than theories or models)?

4. Which of the four types of models described in the chapter is used by the theory?

5. Describe your initial reaction to EET. Then, critically reflect on EET. How might EET fare if you evaluated its usefulness by using the criteria described in the chapter?

CHAPTER TWO

THEORY DEVELOPMENT

In Chapter 1, we defined theory as "any systematic summary about the nature of the communication process." We further introduced the topic of scholarly theory, which is different from other forms of theory because it has been carefully researched. The focus of this chapter is on the methods by which scholarly theories are created, developed, and modified. Our first concern is the nature of how theory and research are related.

THEORY–RESEARCH LINK

As much as we would like to provide a simple answer to how theory and research are linked, we can't easily articulate the connection because of debate about the theory–research relationship akin to the classic question, "Which came first, the chicken or the egg?" In this case, scholars disagree as to what starts the process: theory or research.

Some scholars argue that research comes before theory. This approach is known as **inductive theory**. Scholars using inductive theory, also known as grounded theory, believe the best theories emerge from the results of systematic study (Glaser & Strauss, 1967). That is, these scholars observe or examine a particular topic, and, based on patterns that emerge over time, they develop a theory; the research comes *before* the theory. If someone wanted to develop a theory about how management style affects employee performance, then that person would study management style and employee performance in great depth before proposing a theory. Preliminary theories may be proposed, but the data continue to be collected and analyzed until adding new data brings little to the researcher's understanding of the phenomenon or situation.

Learning Objectives

After reading this chapter, you will be able to do the following:

1. Describe the differences between inductive theory and deductive theory, especially in terms of the theory development process

2. Explain the major research methods used by communication theorists, including what they reveal and what they conceal about the communication process

3. Articulate why a particular research method is the appropriate method to answer a research question

4. Recognize the differences between humanistic and social scientific approaches to communication study

5. Summarize the ways theories change and grow

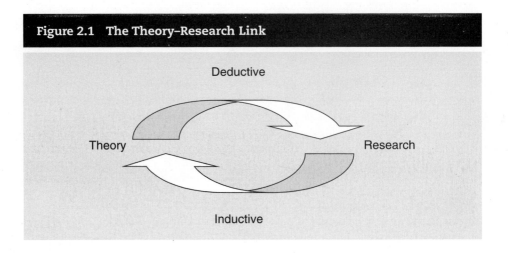

Figure 2.1   The Theory–Research Link

Deductive

Theory

Research

Inductive

On the other hand, some scholars believe in **deductive theory**. Deductive theory is generally associated with the scientific method (Reynolds, 1971). The deductive approach requires that a hypothesis, or working theory, be developed before any research is conducted. Once the theory has been developed, the theorist then collects data to test or refine the theory (i.e., to support or reject the hypothesis). What follows is a constant set of adjustments to the theory with additional research conducted until evidence in support of the theory is overwhelming. The resulting theory is known as a law (Reynolds, 1971). In short, deductive theory development starts with the theory and then looks at data. As an example, a researcher might start with the idea that supportive management styles lead to increased employee performances. The researcher would then seek to confirm his or her theory by collecting data about those variables.

As indicated earlier, these two approaches represent different starting points to what is in essence a "chicken or the egg" argument. But neither approach advocates a single cycle of theorizing or research. Instead, both approaches suggest theories are dynamic—they are modified as the data suggest, and data are reviewed to adjust the theory. Consider the model depicted in Figure 2.1. We believe this is the most accurate illustration of the link between theory and research. In this model, the starting points are different, but the reality of a repetitive loop between theory and research is identified.

WHAT IS RESEARCH?

Because research is a fundamental part of theory development, we must turn our attention to the question of what counts as research. Frey, Botan, and Kreps (2002) described research as "disciplined inquiry that involves studying something in a planned manner and reporting it so that other inquirers can potentially replicate the process if they choose" (p. 13). Accordingly, we do not mean informal types of research, such as reflections on personal experience, off-the-cuff interviews with acquaintances, or casual viewing of communication media. When we refer to research, we mean the methodical gathering of data as well as the careful reporting of the results of the data analysis.

Note that *how* the research is reported differentiates two categories of research. **Primary research** is reported by the person who conducted it. It is typically published in peer-reviewed academic journals. **Secondary research** is reported by someone other than the person who conducted it. This is research reported in newspapers, popular or trade magazines, handbooks and textbooks, and, frequently, the Internet. Certainly, there is value to the dissemination of research through these media. Textbooks, for example, can summarize hundreds of pages of research in a compact and understandable fashion. The Internet can reach millions of people. Trade magazines can pinpoint the readers who may benefit most from the results of the research. Regardless of whether the source is popular or academic, however, primary research is typically valued more than secondary research as a source of information. With secondary research, readers risk the chance that the writers have misunderstood or inadvertently distorted the results of the research. Similar to the childhood game of "whisper down the lane," the message typically becomes more vague and less accurate as it gets passed from person to person—or website to website.

RESEARCH METHODS IN COMMUNICATION

Every 60 seconds almost 4 million texts are sent, Google translates nearly 70,000,000 words, Facebook users "like" a post over 4 million times, and almost a million Tinder users swipe left or right (Dieker, 2016). Those figures are for *every* minute of *every* day. Millennials are estimated to consume approximately 17.8 hours of media every day (Taylor, 2014). This is an astonishing number, but to put it into perspective, many of these media forms are consumed simultaneously. It is clear that we are inundated with information. But what value does this information have? The proliferation of verifiably fake news (i.e., flagrant untruths), as well as hyper-partisan stories intended to pander to readers' preexisting beliefs, makes information literacy more important than ever. Even if you never conduct a research study in your life, knowing which information has been methodically collected and reported accurately will undoubtedly help you make more informed personal and professional decisions. This section focuses on the four research methods commonly used in the development of scholarly communication theory. When reading about these methods, pay particular attention to the types of information revealed and concealed by each method. This approach will allow you to be a better consumer of research.

Experiments

When people think of experiments, they often have flashbacks to high school chemistry classes. People are often surprised that communication scholars also use experiments, even though there isn't a Bunsen burner or beaker in sight. What makes something an experiment has nothing to do with the specific equipment or instruments involved; rather, experimentation is ultimately concerned with causation and control.

It is important to emphasize that an **experiment** is the *only* research method that allows researchers to conclude that one thing causes another. For example, if you are interested in determining whether friendly customer service causes greater customer satisfaction, whether advertisers' use of bright colors produces higher sales, or whether sexuality in film leads to a more promiscuous society, the only way to determine these things is through experimental research.

Experimental research allows researchers to determine causality because experiments are so controlled. In experimental research, the researcher is concerned with two variables. A **variable** is simply any concept that has two or more values (Frey et al., 2002). Sex is a variable, because we have men and women. Note that just looking at maleness is not a variable because there is only one value associated with it; it doesn't *vary*, so it isn't a *variable*. Masculinity is considered a variable, however, because you can be highly masculine, moderately masculine, nonmasculine, and so on.

Returning to our discussion of experimental research, then, the research is concerned with two variables. One of the variables is the presumed cause. This is known as the **independent variable**. The other is the presumed effect. This is known as the **dependent variable**. If you are interested in knowing whether bright colors in advertisements cause increased sales, your independent variable is the color (bright versus dull), and the dependent variable is the amount of sales dollars (more, the same, or less). The way the researcher determines causality is by carefully controlling the study participants' exposure to the independent variable. This control is known as **manipulation**, a term that commonly conjures negative connotations but in the research world is imperative to establishing causality. In the study of advertisements just described, the researcher would expose some people to an advertisement that used bright colors and other people to an advertisement that used dull colors, and she or he would observe the effects on sales based on these manipulations.

Experiments take place in two settings. A **laboratory experiment** takes place in a controlled setting so the researcher might better control efforts at manipulation. In the communication field, laboratories often simulate living rooms or conference rooms. Typically, however, they have two-way mirrors and cameras mounted on the walls to record what happens. For example, John Gottman has a mini "apartment" at the University of Washington. He has married couples "move in" to the apartment during the course of a weekend, and he observes all of their interaction during that weekend.

Some experiments don't take place in the laboratory but in participants' natural surroundings; these are called **field experiments**. These experiments often take place in public places, such as shopping malls, libraries, or schools, but they might take place in private areas as well. In all cases, participants must agree to be a part of the experiment to comply with ethical standards set by educational and research institutions.

Surveys

The most common means of studying communication is through the use of surveys. Market research, audience analysis, and organizational audits all make use of surveys. Unlike experiments, the use of surveys does not allow researchers to claim one thing causes another. The strength of **survey research** is that it is the *only* way to find out how someone thinks, feels, or intends to behave. In other words, surveys capture people's perception. If you want to know what people think about your organization, how they feel about a social issue, or whether they intend to buy a product after viewing an advertising spot you created, you need to conduct a survey.

In general, there are two types of survey research. An **interview** asks participants to respond orally. It might take place face-to-face or over the phone. One special type of interview is a **focus group**, which is when the interviewer (called a facilitator) leads a small group of people in a discussion about a specific product or program (Frey et al., 2002). A **questionnaire** asks participants to respond in writing. It can be distributed by mail, via the Internet, or administered with the researcher present. Some research is more suited for interviews than questionnaires. Interviews allow the researcher to ask more complex questions because he or she can clarify misunderstandings through probing questions. Questionnaires, however, might be more appropriate for the collection of sensitive information because they provide more anonymity to the respondent (Salant & Dillman, 1994).

The key concepts associated with either type of survey research are questioning and sampling. First, the purpose of a survey is quite simple: to ask questions of a group of people to understand their thoughts, feelings, and behaviors. Questions might take two forms. **Open-ended questions** allow respondents to answer in their own words, giving as much (or as little) information as they would like. For example, a market researcher might ask study participants to describe what they like about a particular product. Or an interviewer might ask someone to respond to a hypothetical situation. **Closed-ended questions** require respondents to use set answers. In this case, a market researcher might say something like "Respond to the following statement: Product X is a useful product. Would you say you strongly agree, agree, neither agree nor disagree, disagree, or strongly disagree?" Neither method is better than the other; the two types of questions simply provide different kinds of data that are analyzed using different means.

The second key concept associated with survey research is **sampling**. Researchers are typically concerned with large groups of people when they conduct surveys. These groups are known as a **population**, which means all people who possess a particular characteristic (Frey et al., 2002). For example, marketing firms want to study all possible consumers of a product. Newspaper publishers want to gather information from all readers. Pharmaceutical industries want to study everyone with a particular ailment. The size of these groups makes it difficult to study everyone of interest. Even if every member of the population could be identified, which isn't always the case, studying all of them can be extremely expensive.

Instead, survey researchers study a sample, or a small number of people in the population of interest. According to a basic premise in statistics known as the law of large numbers (LLN), if a sample is well selected and of sufficient size, the survey's results are likely also to hold true for the entire group. A **random sample**, in which every member of the target group has an equal chance of being selected, is better than a **nonrandom sample**, such as volunteers, a convenience sample (college students), or a purposive sample (people who meet a particular requirement, such as age, sex, or race). Essentially, a random sample of consumers is more likely to give representative information about brand preferences than a convenience sample, such as stopping people at the mall on a particular day to answer a few questions.

Textual Analysis

The third method used frequently by communication scholars is textual analysis. A text is any written or recorded message (Frey et al., 2002). A website, a transcript of a medical encounter, and an employee newsletter can all be considered texts. **Textual analysis** is used to uncover the content, nature, or structure of messages. It can also be used to evaluate messages, focusing on their strengths, weaknesses, effectiveness, or even ethicality. So textual analysis can be used to study the amount of violence on television, how power dynamics play out during doctor–patient intake evaluations, or even the strategies used to communicate a corporate mission statement.

There are three distinct forms textual analyses take in the communication discipline. **Rhetorical criticism** refers to "a systematic method for describing, analyzing, interpreting, and evaluating the persuasive force of messages" (Frey et al., 2002, p. 229). There are numerous types of rhetorical criticism, including historical criticism (how history shapes messages), genre criticism (evaluating particular types of messages, such as political speeches or corporate image restoration practices), and feminist criticism (how beliefs about gender are produced and reproduced in messages).

Content analysis seeks to identify, classify, and analyze the occurrence of particular types of messages (Frey et al., 2002). It was developed primarily to study mass-mediated messages, although it is also used in numerous other areas of the discipline. For example, public relations professionals often seek to assess the type of coverage given to a client. Typically, content analysis involves four steps: the selection of a particular text (e.g., newspaper articles), the development of content categories (e.g., "favorable organizational coverage," "neutral organizational coverage," "negative organizational coverage"), placing the content into categories, and an analysis of the results. In our example, the results of this study would be able to identify whether a particular newspaper has a pronounced slant when covering the organization. One modern derivation of this type of research is **text mining**, also known as **data mining**. Data mining is the use of advanced "data analysis tools to discover previously unknown, valid patterns and relationships in large data sets" (Seifert, 2007, p. 2). Given the immense amount of information available on the Internet, organizations can use complex programs to sift through enormous amounts of data to uncover the frequency and uses of particular words or ideas.

The third type of textual analysis typically conducted by communication scholars is **interaction analysis** (also known as **conversation analysis**). These approaches typically focus on interpersonal or group communication interactions that have been recorded, with a specific emphasis on the nature or structure of interaction. The strength of this type of research is that it captures the natural give-and-take that is part of most communication experiences. The weakness of rhetorical criticism, content analysis, and interaction analysis is that *actual* effects on the audience can't be determined solely by focusing on texts.

Ethnography

Ethnography is the final research method used by scholars of communication. First used by anthropologists, **ethnography** typically involves the researcher immersing himself or herself into a particular culture or context to understand communication rules and meanings for that culture or context. For example, an ethnographer might study an organizational culture, such as Johnson & Johnson's corporate culture, or a particular context, such as communication in hospital emergency rooms. The key to this type of research is that it is naturalistic and emergent, which means it must take place in the natural environment for the group under study and the particular methods used adjusted on the basis of what is occurring in that environment.

Typically, those conducting ethnographies need to decide on the role they will play in the research. A **complete participant** is fully involved in the social setting, and the participants do not know the researcher is studying them (Frey et al., 2002). This approach, of course, requires the researcher to know enough about the environment to be able to fit in. Moreover, there are numerous ethical hurdles the researcher must overcome. Combined, these two challenges prevent much research from being conducted in this fashion. Instead, **participant–observer** roles are more frequently chosen. In this case, the researcher becomes fully involved with the culture or context, but he or she has admitted his or her research agenda before entering the environment. In this way, knowledge is gained firsthand by the researcher, but extensive knowledge about the culture is not necessarily a prerequisite (Frey et al., 2002). Researchers choosing this strategy may also elect which to emphasize more: participation or observation. Finally, a researcher may choose to be a **complete observer**. Complete observers do not interact with the members of the culture or context, which means they do not interview any of the members of the group under study. As such, this method allows for the greatest objectivity in recording data, while simultaneously limiting insight into participants' own meanings of the observed communication.

Communication scholars use four primary research methods: experiments, which focus on causation and control; surveys, which focus on questioning and sampling; textual analysis, which focuses on the content, nature, or structure of messages; and ethnography, which focuses on the communication rules and meanings in a particular culture or context. A summary of the strengths and weaknesses of each of the four methods is summarized in Table 2.1.

Because this textbook is oriented toward students who are likely to use theory and research in the professional realm, we wish to make clear that people who work in the professions also use research, although that research is not used to develop scholarly theory (although it might be used to develop or refine a working theory). Marketing and public relations professionals, human resources executives, and managers in many industries conduct research as part of the creation and assessment of campaigns, for strategic planning, and for decision making. Like academics, professionals also use experiments (typically for product testing), surveys (especially focus groups), textual analysis (especially media monitoring), and ethnographies of a sort (typically observations of how customers use a product).

SOCIAL SCIENCE AND THE HUMANITIES

Thus far, we have talked about the central role research plays in the development of theories and how research comes either before creating the theory (in the case of inductive theory development) or after (in the case of deductive theory development). The reason for these differing approaches can be traced back to philosophical divisions within the field of communication. Communication has been described as both an art and a science (Dervin, 1993). On one hand, we respect the power of a beautifully crafted and creatively designed advertisement. On the other hand, we look to hard numbers to support decisions about the campaign featuring that advertisement. Although art and science are integrally related in the everyday practice of communication, in the more abstract realm of theory the two are often considered distinct pursuits. This concept can be traced to distinctions between the academic traditions of the humanities (which includes the arts) and the social sciences.

You might have some ideas about the terms *humanistic* and *social scientific* because most college students are required to take some courses in each of these areas. The distinctions between the humanities and social science are based on more than just tradition, however; they are based on very different philosophical beliefs. The interpretation of meaning is of central concern in the humanities (Littlejohn, 2002). Meaning is presumed to be subjective and unique to the individual, even though meaning is likely influenced by social processes. For individuals trained in the **humanistic approach**, **subjectivity** is a hallmark; one's own **interpretation** is of interest. Think about the study of English literature, a discipline at the heart of the humanities. English scholars study the interpretation of texts in an effort to understand the meaning of the object of study.

On the other hand, **objectivity** is a central feature of social science. Social scientists believe that through careful standardization (i.e., objectivity), researchers can observe patterns of communication that can hold true for all (or most) people, all (or most) of the time. These patterns that hold true across groups, time, and place are known as **generalizations**. To illustrate, psychology is a discipline rooted in the social sciences. As such, psychology scholars seek to explain general principles of how the human mind functions. These principles are intended to explain all people, all over the world, throughout history.

Because the humanities and social sciences have different areas of interest, they treat theory and research differently. Table 2.2 seeks to identify some of those distinctions. The first area of difference is the philosophical commitment to understanding the nature of human beings and the extent of their free will. Certainly, no one believes human beings are mere puppets who have no choice in how they behave. Communication theorists vary, however, in the extent to which they believe people *act* versus *react* to communication. For example, social scientists tend to follow **determinism**, which means they believe past experience, personality predispositions, and a number of other antecedent conditions *cause* people to behave in certain ways. Accordingly, deterministic approaches to human interaction propose that people in general tend to react to situations. Social scientists tend to look at the causes and effects of communication, such as what causes a marriage to fail or the effects of a particular marketing campaign.

Conversely, most humanists believe people have control over their behavior and make conscious choices to communicate to meet their goals. Theorists taking this stance are called pragmatists because they believe people are practical and plan their behavior. **Pragmatism** believes human beings are not passive reactors to situations but dynamic actors. Humanists, then, tend to focus on the choices people (or organizations) make, such as United Airlines' ineffective public relations response to a series of videos depicting callous—and violent—treatment of passengers.

A second way to differentiate between humanistic and social scientific scholarship is through a focus on *why* theories are developed. For example, the goal of social scientific theory is to both understand and predict communication processes. Because social science is interested in generalizations, the ability to predict is paramount. If a theorist understands the general pattern at the heart of a social scientific theory, she or he should be able to predict how any one individual might communicate. Those in the humanities, however, believe interpretations are always subjective; they are unique to the individual. Accordingly, humanists believe theorists can never actually predict how a person will behave; all that can be done is to try to understand human communication.

Although not directly related to the distinction between social science and the humanities, we note that some theories strive to do more than simply predict or understand. A special group of theories, called critical approaches, seeks to improve the world through social change. The goal of critical theory is to empower people in their professional and personal lives. For more information on critical communication theory, see Craig (1999).

The third difference between social science and the humanities is the process of theory development. Recall our discussion of the theory–research link discussed earlier in the chapter. Deductive theory is based on the scientific method, so it should be no surprise that the **social scientific approach** to theory development is *deductive*. Those in the humanities, however, tend to start with data and subsequently develop theory. For example, scholars of English literature would start with reading Shakespeare's plays before developing a theory about them. Thus, those in the humanities tend to use inductive theory development.

Finally, the focus and methods of research also vary in the social scientific and humanistic approaches. The focus of research for the social scientific method is on standardization and control. Because of these objectives, social scientists incrementally study narrowly defined areas at a time, believing the whole picture will be uncovered eventually. This approach is known as **particularism**. Humanists, on the other hand, believe in looking at the big picture; they propose that all pieces of the puzzle contribute to an understanding of the problem. Accordingly, they use holism, looking at the situation in its entirety, as the focal point of research.

Given the different areas of focus, it's not a surprise that the final difference between social scientists and humanists is the research methods they use. Earlier in this chapter, we discussed the four research methods used by communication scholars. Of the four, one is clearly social scientific, and one is clearly humanistic. Experimental methods, with their concern for causation and control, are uniquely suited for the social sciences. Remember that social science seeks to make predictions, and the best way to do that is to have research that supports particular causes and effects. Similarly, ethnography is uniquely suited for humanistic research. Ethnography leans to the understanding of communication in contexts and cultures, which is appropriate for theory that uses holism in its quest for interpretation of communicative events.

The uses of survey research and textual analysis cannot be easily classified. Instead of the methods themselves being associated with either social science or the humanities, the specific way data are analyzed determines whether the method is social scientific or humanistic. The two methods of data analysis are quantitative and qualitative. Quantitative methods are adapted from those used in the hard sciences, such as chemistry and biology. Accordingly, quantitative methods are associated with social science. Qualitative methods are those that have historically been used by the humanities.

Quantitative methods typically rely on numbers or statistics as the data source (Reinard, 1998). These data and statistics are generally explanatory and comprehensive; they seek to predict what will happen for large groups of people. To accomplish this, researchers control the study by identifying the variables of interest before data collection takes place and trying to prevent extraneous influences from affecting the data. As described earlier, these commitments allow social scientists to make generalizations.

Qualitative methods reject the limitations on individual interpretation that control requires. Moreover, qualitative research eschews the use of numbers and uses verbal descriptions of communicative phenomena. Typically, the data are in the form of extended quotes or transcripts of communication. Finally, qualitative research typically centers on a description or critique of communication rather than on generalizations (Reinard, 1998).

Social scientists tend to use quantitative surveys or textual analyses. For example, they'll collect data about how many people prefer a new formulation of a product versus

Table 2.1 Four Methods of Communication Research

Research Method	What It Reveals	What It Conceals
Experiments	Cause and effect	Whether the cause–effect relationship holds true in less controlled environments
Surveys	Respondents' thoughts, feelings, and intentions	Cannot establish causality; cannot determine what people actually do
Textual analysis	The content, nature, and structure of messages	The effect of the message on receivers
Ethnography	Rules and meanings of communication in a culture or context	May provide a highly subjective (and therefore biased) view of the culture or context

Table 2.2   Differences Between Social Scientific and Humanistic Approaches to Communication

Issue	Social Science	Humanities
Belief about human nature	Determinism	Pragmatism
Goal of theory	Understand and predict	Understand only
Process of theory development	Deductive	Inductive
Focus of research	Particularism	Holism
Research methods	Experiments, quantitative survey, and textual analysis	Ethnography, qualitative survey, and textual analysis

a previous formulation of a product or how frequently a manager uses a particular communication strategy in interaction. Humanists tend to use qualitative surveys and textual analyses. They ask participants to respond at length to questions in their own words about a particular product, or they identify various communication themes evident in a corporate brochure.

A final note should be made about the distinctions between social science and the humanities. The purpose of talking about these two academic traditions is because communication is *both* social scientific and humanistic. As such, you shouldn't view these distinctions as dichotomies but as continua. Individual theories may be more or less social scientific or humanistic (not either/or), with elements borrowed from both traditions.

HOW THEORIES CHANGE AND GROW

Our final concern in this chapter is to be clear that once developed, theories continue to change and grow. As we indicated in Figure 2.1, whether a researcher starts with the theory or starts with research, theory development continues the loop between research and theory, refining, modifying, and extending the theory. Specifically, Kaplan (1964) argues that theories can change by extension or by intention. Growth by **extension** means the theory adds more concepts and builds on what was already established. For example, in 1959 Thibaut and Kelley created interdependence theory, which is described in Chapter 5. One central aspect of the theory is the prediction that relationship dependence (otherwise known as commitment) can be determined by examining an individual's satisfaction with the relationship, as well as his or her perception of the availability and quality of alternatives to the relationship. Caryl Rusbult (1980), a student of John Thibaut, continued working on the theory and presented an expanded version of the theory, which she called the investment model. Her model argues that looking at satisfaction and alternatives is not enough to predict commitment; one also has to examine how much an individual has invested in the relationship. That is, people who are unhappy in their relationship, and who believe they can find a better partner, might stay in the relationship because they have invested a great deal of time, money, or even love, and they don't want to "lose" their investment. Thus, we can conclude that interdependence theory has grown through extension because a new concept—investment—was added to the theory to make its predictions more robust.

Conversely, growth by **intension** means scholars gain a deeper and more nuanced understanding of the original concepts presented in the theory. For example, communication accommodation theory, which is described in Chapter 6, was originally called speech accommodation theory, as the focus was purely on how our dialects and word choice varied based on to whom an individual was speaking. However, researchers quickly realized that accommodation occurs in other areas of verbal and nonverbal communication, such as speaking rate, politeness, and listening (see Gallois, Ogay, & Giles, 2005, for a review). The theory has grown by intension; the same principles of accommodation are still acknowledged by the theory, and no new concepts were added. Instead, additional research has allowed scholars to understand more fully the complex ways accommodation occurs, adding to the scope of the theory.

SUMMARY

In this chapter, we looked at how theories are developed and changed. We looked at two ways to create theory: inductive and deductive theory development. We discussed the links between theory and research, and we differentiated between primary and secondary research. We also identified the four primary research methods used by communication scholars: experiments, surveys, textual analysis, and ethnography. In addition to describing the key elements of each of these methods, the chapter focused on what each reveals and conceals about communication. Next, we turned our attention to the differences between social scientific and humanistic approaches to theory and research, centering our discussion on beliefs about human nature, the goal of theory, the development of theory, the focus of research, and the research methods used. Finally, we talked about how theories change through the processes of extension and intention.

KEY TERMS

Closed-ended questions 21	Dependent variable 20	Field experiment 20
Complete observer 23	Determinism 24	Focus group 21
Complete participant 23	Ethnography 23	Generalization 24
Content analysis 22	Experiment 20	Humanistic approach 24
Deductive theory 18	Extension 27	Independent variable 20

CASE STUDY 2: EDUCATION AS ENTERTAINMENT RECONSIDERED

In Chapter 1 you were introduced to a theory called education as entertainment theory (EET). We want you to reconsider EET, relying on what you learned in this chapter, as well as the following additional information.

In order to test EET, we conducted a survey. We created a questionnaire, which asked about age, sex, the frequency of viewing Sesame Street and other educational media, and expectations for instructional style, motivation, and perceived learning. For the expectations for instructional style, motivation, and perceived learning, we asked survey respondents to respond to the four

teaching styles using a 1-to-5 Likert-type scale, with 1 representing "not at all" and 5 indicating "always."

Survey

On average, how often did you watch educational television (for example, *Sesame Street*) or use educational media (e.g., computer games, apps) when you were a child? (circle one) *Not at All | Very Little | Occasionally | Every Week | Every Day*

To what extent do you *expect* college professors to use the following teaching styles (check one for each style)?

	Not at All	Very Little	Occasionally	Frequently	Always
Lecture					
Class discussion					
Group activities					
Entertainment (e.g., films, games)					

(Continued)

(Continued)

To what extent would each style *motivate* you to want to learn (check one for each style)?

	Not at All	Very Little	Occasionally	Frequently	Always
Lecture					
Class discussion					
Group activities					
Entertainment (e.g., films, games)					

To what extent do you think you *actually* learn using the following styles (check one for each style)?

	Not at All	Very Little	Occasionally	Frequently	Always
Lecture					
Class discussion					
Group activities					
Entertainment (e.g., films, games)					

We distributed the questionnaire to 75 current college students and 75 adults over the age of 50. We choose age 50 because those individuals would have been in school already when *Sesame Street* appeared and before the advent of personal computer technology. There were 58 female and 17 male college students. There were 51 female and 14 male adults.

Our results showed that the average report of using educational media was 3.7 out of 5 for the college students, corresponding to frequent use of educational media. The average amount of using educational media was 2.2 for the adults, corresponding to very little use of educational media. Accordingly, the college students consumed more educational media than the adults did as children.

The remaining average answers are calculated in the following chart, with the instructional style listed in the far-left column and the mean expectation, motivation, and learning score for the two groups in the remaining columns.

Teaching Style	Expect College	Expect Adult	Motivate College	Motivate Adults	Learn College	Learn Adult
Lecture	4.7	4.8	2.4	3.2	4.1	4.2
Discussion	3.9	3.6	3.6	4.2	4.3	4.2
Group	3.4	3.2	2.9	3.2	2.6	3.2
Entertain	3.2	2.9	4.4	3.2	2.6	2.8

In looking at the chart, the only significant difference when considering entertainment education is in motivation, with college students reporting being motivated by entertainment education to a larger extent than adults. However, neither group seems to expect a whole lot of entertainment education, and neither group reports learning a lot from entertainment education. Thus, the predictions of EET are not fully supported.

Questions for Consideration

1. Based on what you read in Chapter 1 and the additional information just provided, was EET developed using an inductive or a deductive theory development process? Why?

2. What type of research (primary or secondary) was used in the development of EET? Was this a good choice?

3. Is EET social scientific or humanistic? Provide details from the information in Chapter 1 and this chapter to support your case.

4. Which research method was used to test the theory? Is this the best method? Why, or why not?

5. Discuss what ethical challenges researchers should consider when conducting this type of research. How do ethical challenges shift if the research method changes?

6. In what ways do you think EET should change or grow in the future? Be specific in detailing how it might change and why it should change in that manner.

CHAPTER THREE

COGNITION AND INTRAPERSONAL COMMUNICATION

Regardless of whether you take a source or receiver orientation to communication, messages have no meaning without an individual's interpretation. Everyone has to process every message internally while considering how best to make sense of these messages. In other words, meaning is derived only after an individual perceives a message and gives it meaning; meaning resides in our *interpretations* of words or actions, not in the words or behaviors themselves. Consequently, communication is also an intrapersonal process.

COGNITIVE PROCESS

The roots of communication as an intrapersonal process can be traced to one of the major debates in psychology in the 20th century. At the beginning of the 1900s, American psychology was dominated by a focus on **behaviorism** (Runes, 1984). Most of us are familiar with Pavlov and his studies of salivary production in dogs. By associating the ringing of a bell with food, Pavlov was able to experimentally cause dogs to salivate when hearing a bell, even if the food was not present. Such is a description of a behavioral approach—a focus on external cause and behavioral effect. Major psychological figures such as J. B. Watson and B. F. Skinner argued that because we cannot observe mental processes, we should focus only on these causes and effects (Runes, 1984).

However, in the middle part of the 1900s, psychologists began arguing for a **cognitive** approach to understanding human behavior. Rather than focusing solely on external causes (or stimuli) and behavioral effects, these scholars argued we should be concerned with the mental processes used to process stimuli and generate particular effects (Runes, 1984). A major proponent of this approach was Noam Chomsky, who spearheaded a significant critique of behaviorism. **Cognition**, then, includes the processes of reducing, elaborating, transforming, and storing stimuli (Neisser, 1967). It refers to what happens in the mind that causes us to behave in particular ways.

Learning Objectives

After reading this chapter, you will be able to do the following:

1. Make predictions about the intentionality of behavior using Kelley's covariation model (consensus, consistency, distinctiveness, and locus of control)

2. Identify types of, conditions, and communicative strategies for reducing uncertainty

3. Use the concepts of expectancy, violation valence, and communicator reward valence to predict whether someone will reciprocate or compensate a violation

4. Explain how, by increasing or decreasing the magnitude of dissonance between beliefs and behaviors, one can influence or prevent change

5. Compare and contrast the major theoretical approaches to intrapersonal communication

6. Provide systematic understanding of a professional situation by employing theories of intrapersonal communication

In this chapter, we explain four theories that examine the cognitive and intrapersonal aspects of communication. First, attribution theory explains the process by which individuals assign causation or motivation to their own and others' behavior. The second theory presented in this chapter, uncertainty reduction theory, strives to explain and predict initial encounters with people. In other words, what drives you to initiate communication, and how do you go about reducing your uncertainty in a new situation? Third, expectancy violations theory seeks to predict and explain people's behavior when their expectations about what will happen are breached. The fourth theory presented, cognitive dissonance theory, explains and predicts how persuasion may be understood as a self-induced, intrapersonal event.

Altogether these theories emphasize the internal processes that serve as antecedents to the highly personalized creation of meaning, and each perspective applies to numerous communication contexts. From making judgments about a coworker based on her behavior as compared to others (i.e., attribution theory) to determining how best to reduce one's uncertainty during a job transfer (i.e., uncertainty reduction theory), each of the theories presented illustrates the internally driven process necessary to bring individual meaning to various messages.

ATTRIBUTION THEORY

According to attribution theorists, human beings often work like naïve detectives, continually trying to understand and make sense of what inspired various events, personal mannerisms, and individuals' conduct. Just as a crime scene investigator pieces together clues in an effort to determine a suspect's motive, you, too, go through life picking up clues and making judgments about what you believe influenced your own and others' behavior. These judgments and conclusions that provide reasons for behavior are called **attributions**. Attribution theory, then, explains the cognitive process one uses when trying to make causal explanations for behavior.

Attributions as Naïve Psychology

Attribution theory is not a new concept; researchers have long studied the ways in which people process events and then derive explanations for them. In the mid-1950s, however, Heider (1958) focused his attention on the process of drawing inferences—the assumptions individuals make regarding the causes of behavior as well as the judgments made about who is responsible for that behavior. According to Heider, individuals act as "naïve psychologists." When you see a person act, you immediately make judgments about the causal nature of the conduct. Specifically, Heider found that individuals try to determine whether a behavior in question was caused by dispositional or situational factors. **Dispositional factors** refer to internal or personal features, such as one's personality, character, or biological traits. These factors are relatively stable and unique to each individual. Conversely, **situational factors** refer to external dynamics that are relatively uncontrollable and determined by the environment or circumstance at hand. External factors obviously vary to a much greater extent than do internal factors because they are inherently based on the context of a given situation, not on more stable personality traits.

For example, if, at your monthly staff meeting, Ron's presentation of current sales figures appears disjointed and jumbled, you might attribute his awkwardness to the fact that his PowerPoint slides failed to upload properly onto the laptop. Here, the inference made suggests that because of the situation (i.e., defective software), Ron was forced to give the presentation from memory and without visual aids. Thus, you might attribute Ron's bumbled speech to a technological glitch, thereby making a situational attribution for his behavior. On the other hand, you might attribute Ron's poor presentation to his lack of preparation (i.e., a character flaw). Surely by now everyone knows not to rely solely on PowerPoint; Ron should have come prepared with a backup plan ready in case of technical difficulties. Looking at the situation this way, you might blame Ron's failed presentation on his lazy preparation—something within his personal control, thereby making an internal attribution.

Correspondent Inference Theory

Expanding Heider's work, Jones and Davis (1965) were concerned with the intentionality of dispositional (internally driven) behavior. They argued that when a perceiver attributes the cause of a behavior to dispositional factors, the perceiver also makes judgments about the actor's intentions. Jones and Davis referred to these judgments of intention as **correspondent inferences**.

As Texter (1995) noted, "Before we can draw correspondent inferences from observing a person's behavior, we must make a determination about the person's intention: Did the person intentionally act in a certain way, knowing the effects the behavior would have?" (p. 55). When a dispositional inference mirrors an action and the perceiver labels the disposition and the action similarly (e.g., lazy), these inferences are said to "correspond." For instance, you might infer the disposition of laziness or apathy from Ron's seemingly lazy preparation for the meeting.

Determining the intentionality of an act is not easy; however, there are several factors one can consider when determining the purpose of another's behavior: choice, assumed desirability, social role, prior expectations, hedonic relevance, and personalism (Jones & Davis, 1965). Beginning with choice, individuals can assess an actor's intention by examining whether the actor in question had any alternatives. If you perceive alternative courses of action, you are also likely to assume the "selected" behavior was deliberate. Second, you can assess intentions by focusing on the assumed **social desirability** of the actor's actions. That is, if a person behaves in a manner contrary to social conventions, you are more likely to infer that the behavior reflects the person's true character and not merely an attempt at social correctness. Similarly, an actor's social role, or public position, can help determine the intentionality of a behavior, particularly when this person behaves in a manner contrary to the prescribed role.

Just as one's position affects expectations and assumptions of intentionality, so do prior expectations of that individual. Thus, your previous encounters with an actor, or knowledge about the person's background, may influence your assessments about the actor's intentions. **Hedonic relevance**, or the degree to which you believe an actor's behavior directly affects you (either positively through rewards or negatively through punishment), also shapes your assessment of the actor's intentions. The greater you perceive the hedonic relevance, the more likely you are to view the actor's behavior as deliberate. Last, **personalism** refers to the belief that an actor specifically and intentionally behaves in ways to hurt or help you. Thus, if you assume a person's behavior changes when you are not present, you may imagine the actions are intentional. Notably, although each of these six factors can aid in assessing an actor's intentions, relying on any of these reasons may lead to biased judgments of an actor's disposition.

Kelley's Covariation Model

Perhaps a more holistic approach to attribution theory, Kelley's (1967, 1973) covariation model explains the causal nature of the complete attribution process. Specifically, this model has a greater scope than does Jones and Davis's correspondent inference theory because Kelley seeks to explain attributions overall, whereas Jones and Davis focused only on the intentionality of dispositional inferences.

According to Kelley (1967, 1973), individuals judge the causality of another's behavior by examining four factors: consensus, consistency, distinctiveness, and controllability. When the first three of these features are combined (i.e., consensus, consistency, distinctiveness), a perceiver can judge whether the actions were internally controlled (i.e., disposition) or externally controlled (i.e., situational). That is, you assign meaning based on perceived controllability—how much command an individual had over the behavior in question.

First, the perceiver determines if an actor's behavior demonstrates **consensus**, that is, would other people react similarly if placed in the same situation? The more you observe people behaving similarly, the greater the perception of consensus. If Rebecca storms out of the quarterly sales meeting in a huff and snarls at everyone in her path while the other members of the sales team leave the meeting with smiles and small talk, low consensus has occurred. If, however, everyone on the sales team heads out of the meeting sporting a grimace and a foul mood, then you have observed high consensus.

Second, the perceiver must determine whether the actor's behavior demonstrates consistency. **Consistency** refers to whether the person in question engages in similar behaviors over time. Comparable to consensus, the more you observe an actor engaging in the same behavior, the greater your perception of consistency. If Rebecca always seems to be angry and rude to colleagues, then you would say that her ill-tempered behavior after the sales meeting is highly consistent with her previous behavior. Conversely, if you typically view Rebecca as pleasant and enthusiastic, you would conclude that her sudden change of behavior has low consistency.

Third, a perceiver judges an actor's **distinctiveness**, that is, whether the person acts differently depending on the situation. Unlike consensus and consistency, which increase with others' conformity and number of observances over time, distinctiveness decreases when the actor behaves similarly across many situations. That is, a behavior is only labeled distinctive if it is "markedly different in one situation or task from others" (Texter, 1995, p. 60). Continuing with our example, if Rebecca speaks rudely and demonstrates hostility toward everyone in the company, to her friends, to her children, and to her neighbors, then Rebecca's offensive mannerisms have low distinctiveness because her rudeness is not unique. On the other hand, if Rebecca's anger and disrespectful tone occurred only after this one meeting and in no other meetings or situations, then you would conclude this behavior is highly distinctive because it appears contrary to the other circumstances in her life.

As mentioned earlier, by combining these judgments of consensus, consistency, and distinctiveness, the perceiver can determine the controllability of the actor's behavior. For example, you suppose an **interior locus of control** when you believe the actor could have controlled the behavior. Alternatively, you assume an **exterior locus of control** when the behavior appears to have been unavoidable.

Considered individually, predictions made using any single variable (i.e., consensus, consistency, or distinctiveness) may provide an incomplete picture. However, by combining the judgments of consensus, consistency, and distinctiveness, eight possible combinations result. It is the combination of variables that allow the perceiver to predict with greater accuracy the controllability of the actor's behavior as either internally or externally motivated (Kelley, 1973).

Specifically, an external (or situational) attribution is made about the individual when consensus is high, consistency is low, and distinctiveness is high. For example, if Rebecca and her entire team leave the sales meeting angry (high consensus), and Rebecca doesn't usually leave meetings in a huff (low consistency), and Rebecca is usually pleasant around the office, not bad-tempered (high distinctiveness), we will assume that something happened at the meeting (the situation) to cause the unpleasant mood. Conversely, an internal (or dispositional) attribution is made about another person when consensus is low, consistency is high, and distinctiveness is low. Returning to the previous example, if only Rebecca leaves the sales meeting angry while the rest of the team is jovial (low consensus), and Rebecca often leaves the sales meetings in a huff (high consistency), and Rebecca snaps at people at work, at home, and at church (low distinctiveness), we can assume that it's Rebecca's disposition influencing her behavior. A summary of the predictions of Kelley's covariation model are in Table 3.1.

Table 3.1 Types of Attributions Based on Kelley's Predictions	
Consensus	"Do other people act this **way**?" If **yes**, an external attribution is likely. If **no**, an internal attribution is likely.
Consistency	"Has this person behaved similarly **many times** before?" If **yes**, an internal attribution is likely. If **no**, an external attribution is likely.
Distinctiveness	"Has this person behaved similarly in **other types of situations**?" If **yes**, an internal attribution is likely. If **no**, an external attribution is likely.

To review, attribution theorists have emphasized various explanations for the attributions you make in assigning the causes and motivations of your own and others' behavior. Whereas Heider examined the causal location of dispositional and situational sources of behavior, Jones and Davis focused more narrowly on determining the perceived intent that drives dispositional behavior. Kelley broadened the scope of attribution theory by examining the interplay of consensus, consistency, and distinctiveness.

UNCERTAINTY REDUCTION THEORY

The second intrapersonal theory discussed here is uncertainty reduction theory (URT). Berger and Calabrese's (1975) URT holds that social life is filled with ambiguities. Not knowing what to wear on the first day at a new job (Should I wear a suit or go with business casual?), uncertainty as to how to greet a new boss (Should I call her Megan? Ms. Smith? Mrs. Smith? Dr. Smith?), and wondering whether you will get along with the new office mate who just transferred from another location (Will she bother me with questions? Will he gossip about team members?) are just a few typical concerns during an average workday. Guided by several assumptions and **axioms** of human behavior, URT seeks to explain and predict when, why, and how individuals use communication to minimize their doubts when interacting with others.

Three assumptions guide the uncertainty reduction framework. First, Berger and Calabrese (1975) maintained that the primary goal of communication is to minimize uncertainties humans have about the world and the people therein. Second, they proposed that individuals experience uncertainty on a regular basis and that the experience of uncertainty is an unpleasant one. Third, Berger and Calabrese assumed that communication is the primary vehicle for reducing uncertainty. Importantly, with so many uncertainties presented to you within a given 24-hour period, Berger (1979) admitted individuals couldn't possibly reduce uncertainty about all of these new people or situations. Instead, he argued there are three possible preceding conditions that influence whether people have the motivation necessary to reduce their uncertainty.

Reducing Uncertainty

Antecedent Conditions

Berger (1979) argued that individuals are motivated to reduce uncertainty only under one of three specific antecedent conditions. First, anticipation of future interaction suggests you are more motivated to reduce uncertainty about someone you are likely to see again. Thus, you are more inclined to use uncertainty reduction behaviors when a new office mate joins the team because you know you will be working with this person on a daily basis. The second condition, **incentive** value, includes the notion that you are prompted to learn more about someone when the individual in question has the potential to provide you with rewards or even punishments. In other words, what can this person do for you or to you? The third antecedent condition is **deviance**. If a person is odd, eccentric, bizarre, or unusual in some way that counters your expectations, URT suggests individuals will be more likely to reduce their uncertainty about the individual.

Types of Uncertainty

Beyond the antecedent conditions that prompt people to want to reduce uncertainty, Berger and Bradac (1982) argued there are two distinct variations, or types, of uncertainty. The first type, **behavioral uncertainty**, takes into account your insecurity about which actions are appropriate in a given situation. For example, when starting a job at a new company, there is often some ambiguity about the hours "required." Do employees of my position begin promptly at 9:00 a.m. and leave right at 5:00 p.m.? Or am I expected to arrive early and stay late? Should I work through lunch, eating at my desk, or do colleagues expect me to go out to lunch with them and socialize? These are all examples of typical behavioral uncertainty for a new employee not yet sure how to act within the new corporation.

The second type of uncertainty is **cognitive uncertainty**. Whereas individuals experiencing behavioral uncertainty question how they should act in a given situation, those who experience cognitive uncertainty are unsure as to what to think about someone or something. In other words, cognitive uncertainty emphasizes the doubts in your ability to pinpoint the attitudes and beliefs of others. When a colleague makes a comment about how "comfortable" you look on a casual Friday, you may wonder, was this a compliment? Or was the remark a subtle hint that you may be dressed in a manner that is too casual for the office? Should you even care what the person thinks of your attire? All of these questions emphasize cognitive uncertainty.

Axioms Explaining the Uncertainty Reduction Process

URT seeks to explain and predict the ways in which individuals use communication to reduce ambiguity. Specifically, the process of reducing uncertainty is predicated on eight axioms, or self-evident truths, established and supported in previous research (Berger & Calabrese, 1975). These axioms are summarized in Table 3.2.

As you can see, these axioms make sense; they are, after all, "self-evident truths." Unlike a commonsense theory, however, URT's axioms have been classified, paired together to create theorems, and tested systematically over time, thereby providing URT with scholarly credence. Moreover, the axioms presented in Table 3.2 supply only the backbone of the theory. In other words, to say that using friendly nonverbal behaviors reduces uncertainty is not enough to warrant a scholarly theory. Discussed next, communication strategies to reduce uncertainty provide additional substance to URT's axioms.

Uncertainty Reduction Strategies

When examining communication strategies for reducing uncertainty, it is important to remember Berger and Calabrese's (1975) original premise: Uncertainty reduction is central to all social relations. Likewise, Berger (1995, 1997) noted that much of social interaction is goal driven. In other words, you communicate for a reason, and you create cognitive plans that guide individuals' social interaction.

URT is related to Berger's (1995, 1997) notion of plan-based messages. Specifically, when seeking information about social realities, individuals create and use plans that vary in complexity. Individuals may vary widely in their relational goals and have a

Table 3.2 Axioms of Uncertainty Reduction Theory

Axiom 1	As your verbal communication with a communication partner increases, your level of uncertainty about that person decreases; as a result, verbal communication continues to increase.
Axiom 2	As welcoming nonverbal expressions increase, uncertainty decreases and vice versa.
Axiom 3	The greater your uncertainty, the more information-seeking behaviors you use. Conversely, as your uncertainty lessens, you seek less information.
Axiom 4	When uncertainty in a relationship is high, the intimacy level of communication content will be low. On the other hand, the reduction of uncertainty leads to greater intimacy.
Axiom 5	The more uncertain you are, the more you will use reciprocal communication strategies and vice versa.
Axiom 6	The more similarities you perceive to share with the target person(s), the more your uncertainty is reduced. Alternatively, perceiving dissimilarities leads to increased uncertainty.
Axiom 7	As uncertainty decreases, liking increases. Conversely, if your uncertainty rises, your liking of the person will decrease.
Axiom 8	Shared communication networks, or shared ties, lessen your uncertainty. On the other hand, if you share no common relations, your uncertainty intensifies.

Source: Axioms 1 through 7 are adapted from Berger and Calabrese, 1975. Axiom 8 is adapted from Parks and Adelman, 1983.

range of specific tactics available to cope with uncertainty. Despite these differences in goals, however, three overarching strategies typify most uncertainty-reduction communication: passive, active, and interactive.

Indicative of the passive strategy, individuals observe their surroundings and surreptitiously gather clues about which behaviors are appropriate as well as which attitudes and beliefs others hold. The passive approach is much like playing detective. The active strategy to uncertainty reduction involves seeking information from a third party. Rather than playing detective yourself, you go to someone else who may know more about the person or situation in question. Last, the **interactive strategy** is when you go straight to the source in question and ask for as much information as possible.

For example, imagine yourself in a new position at a new company. As the December holiday season approaches, you begin to wonder whether you should give a gift to your boss. You could wait to see if others give gifts (passive strategy), you could ask several peers what they do for their supervisors (active strategy), or you could directly ask your boss what the company culture is like and what he or she expects (interactive strategy). Clearly, there are many possible goals that would influence which plan to enact. If the overarching goal is to appear appropriate, effective, and appreciative, the active strategy is probably the best choice. By asking others in your position what they do, you can get a good sense of what your supervisor expects without offending or embarrassing him or her.

Beyond Initial Interactions

Uncertainty reduction theory was originally concerned with explaining and predicting the ambiguity associated with initial interactions (Berger, 1979; Berger & Calabrese, 1975). That is, research using URT emphasized when, why, and how individuals minimize doubt when in new situations or when meeting new people. Berger (1997) has since expanded his position on URT, however, noting that uncertainty exists in new and developing relationships as well as in long-term, ongoing relationships. For example, when Allen is suddenly laid off, Dan and Davida become (understandably) uncertain about their own job security. Even in the face of positive change, uncertainty is inevitable. Imagine you are promoted and will now manage some of your closest friends at work. This change in power—from peer to superior—will likely increase your uncertainty. All relationships are characterized by change and growth—both of which promote the rise of uncertainty. Furthermore, as discussed in Chapter 5, some researchers believe a little bit of uncertainty is actually necessary for maintaining a healthy relationship.

To review, URT focuses on when and why individuals use communication to reduce uncertainty about others. Uncertainty predictably decreases when nonverbal immediacy, verbal messages, self-disclosure, shared similarities, and shared social networks increase. People routinely use passive, active, and interactive information-seeking strategies to reduce their uncertainty when encountering others.

EXPECTANCY VIOLATIONS THEORY

Developed by Judee Burgoon (1978, 1994), expectancy violations theory (EVT) explains the meanings people attribute to the violation, or infringement, of their personal space. Importantly, whereas much of Burgoon's work emphasizes nonverbal violations of physical space (known as the study of proxemics), personal space can also refer to psychological or emotional space. Similar to URT, EVT is derived from a series of assumptions and axioms.

Assumptions

EVT builds on a number of communication axioms; most central to the understanding of EVT, however, is the assumption that humans have competing needs for personal space and for affiliation (Burgoon, 1978). Specifically, humans all need a certain amount of personal space, also thought of as distance or privacy; people also desire a certain amount of closeness with others, or affiliation. When you perceive that one of your needs has been compromised, EVT predicts you will try to do something about it. Thus, Burgoon's initial work focused on the realm of physical space—what happens when someone violates your expectations for appropriate physical distance or closeness.

Beyond explaining individuals' physical space and privacy needs, EVT also makes specific predictions as to how individuals will react to a given violation. Will you **reciprocate**, or return, someone's unexpected behavior, perhaps moving closer or turning toward the individual? Or will you **compensate**, or counteract, by doing the opposite of your partner's behavior? Before making a prediction about reciprocation or compensation, however, you must evaluate EVT's three core concepts: expectancy, violation valence, and communicator reward valence.

Core Concepts of Expectancy Violations Theory

First, **expectancy** refers to what an individual anticipates will happen in a given situation. Expectancy is similar to the idea of social norms and is based on three primary factors. The first factor associated with expectancy emphasizes the *context* of the behavior. In a formal business meeting, for example, hugging a colleague to show support may be inappropriate and may raise some eyebrows. If, however, you hug the same colleague while attending his mother's funeral, the gesture may be perfectly acceptable. A second factor, the *relationship* one has with the person in question, must be examined. If attending the funeral of your boss's mother, a hug may still be perceived as inappropriate, whereas if the funeral is for the mother of a colleague who is also a personal friend, a hug would likely be more suitable. The third factor, *communicator characteristics*, also fuels your expectations; you have beliefs about the way people of both sexes and of certain ages, ethnicities, socioeconomic status, and the like will communicate.

By examining the context, relationship, and communicator's characteristics, individuals arrive at a certain expectation for how a given person should and will likely behave. Changing even one of these expectancy variables might lead to a different expectation. Once you have determined, however, that someone's behavior was, in fact, a breach of expectation, you then judge the behavior in question. This breach is known as the **violation valence**—the positive or negative evaluation you make about a behavior you did not anticipate. Importantly, not all violations are evaluated negatively. Very often a person behaves in a way you might not have expected, but this surprising behavior is viewed positively. For example, a normally bad-tempered colleague brings coffee and muffins to the Monday morning staff meeting or the habitually shy intern actually makes eye contact with you and gives an opinion on a new project.

Notably, others' behavior can be confusing and hard to interpret. Therefore, the third element that must be addressed before predicting reciprocation or compensation involves assessing the person whose behavior is in question. Similar to the violation valence, the **communicator reward valence** (also called the rewardingness of partner) is an evaluation you make about the person who committed the violation. Specifically, how rewarding or interpersonally attractive do you perceive this person to be? If you view the person engaging in the violation to be likeable, charismatic, nice looking, and smart, then you will likely believe the person has a positive reward valence. Conversely, if you perceive the violator to be rude, stingy, unattractive, or conceited, you will likely judge this person as having a negative reward valence. Importantly, the same behavior can be interpreted positively if committed by someone with a positive communicator reward valence and negatively by someone with a negative reward valence. For example, let's say you make a flawless presentation to a difficult client. Afterward, a respected colleague congratulates you and gives an unexpected pat on the shoulder. You will likely judge this act positively and as a gesture of support. On the other hand, let's say it's a different colleague who gives the unexpected pat on the shoulder, one who is always grandstanding and trying to make the focus of attention all about him. In this second case, you will probably view the pat on the back as negative and patronizing. Thus, assessing the behavior itself is insufficient to make a reasonable prediction of how one will react to the violation. You need to take into account your relationship and view of the person performing the violation.

Predicting Reactions When Expectations Are Violated

After assessing expectancy, violation valence, and communicator reward valence of a given situation, it becomes possible to make rather specific predictions about whether the individual who perceived the violation will reciprocate or compensate for the behavior in question. These predictions are described in Figure 3.1.

Guerrero and Burgoon (1996; Guerrero, Jones, & Burgoon, 2000) noticed that predictable patterns develop when considering reward valence and violation valence together. Specifically, if the violation valence is perceived as positive, and the communicator reward valence is also perceived as positive, the theory predicts you will reciprocate the positive behavior. For example, your boss gives you a big smile after you've given a presentation. Guerrero and Burgoon would predict that you smile in return. Similarly, if you perceive the violation valence as negative and perceive the communicator reward valence as negative, the theory again predicts you reciprocate the negative behavior. Thus, if a disliked coworker is grouchy and unpleasant to you, you will likely reciprocate and be unpleasant in return.

Conversely, if you perceive a negative violation valence but view the communicator reward valence as positive, it is likely you will compensate for your partner's negative behavior. For example, one day your boss appears sullen and throws a stack of papers in front of you. Rather than grunt back, EVT predicts you will compensate for your boss's negativity, perhaps by asking if everything is okay (Guerrero & Burgoon, 1996). More difficult to predict, however, is the situation in which someone you view as having a negative reward valence violates you with a positive behavior. In this situation, you may reciprocate, giving the person the "benefit of the doubt." Alternatively, you may view the communicator as having suspicious motives, thereby compensating. For example, if the disliked coworker comes in one day and is very pleasant, you might be pleasant in return, but you also might treat the person with suspicion.

As evidenced, EVT focuses broadly on the infringement of one's expectations for "normal" behavior. Burgoon's research has chiefly emphasized the violation of nonverbal space; however, other expectations, such as behavioral norms, can also be violated. Notably, violations are not necessarily negative. One must evaluate the anticipated behavior, the communicator's characteristics, and the violation itself.

Figure 3.1   Predictions of Expectancy Violations Theory

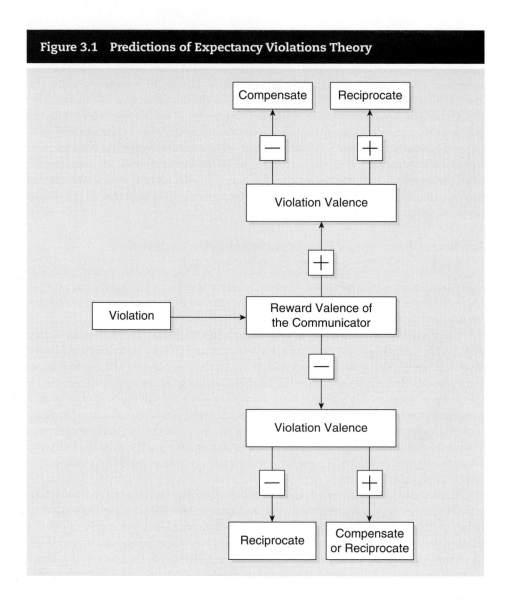

COGNITIVE DISSONANCE THEORY

The final intrapersonal theory featured in this chapter is cognitive dissonance theory—a way of understanding how persuasion may be understood as a cognitive event whereby an individual is motivated to create balance between one's own beliefs and behavior. Discussed in Chapter 7 along with other theories of persuasion, it is often assumed an outside source simply has to provide enough ammunition to change another's attitudes or beliefs. For example, public health campaigns often presume the best way to get a smoker to quit is to infuse the smoker with information about mortality rates, health problems, and the social stigma associated with smoking in order to change the person's attitude about cigarettes. If the smoker's attitude changes, surely he or she will stop smoking, right? After all, it doesn't make sense to engage in a habit known to cause premature aging and cancer and banned in many public places.

According to cognitive dissonance theory, however, this line of thinking may seem logical but is potentially incorrect, possibly explaining why there are so many smokers who acknowledge the health and social risks yet continue to indulge in the behavior. Cognitive dissonance theory (CDT) explains that persuasion is not simply the result of injecting new or refined beliefs into others. Instead, CDT predicts that influence is often an intrapersonal event, occurring when incongruence between our attitudes and behavior creates a tension resolved by altering either our beliefs or our behaviors, thereby effecting a change.

Schemata: Creating Familiarity or Discomfort

According to Festinger (1957, 1962), when presented with a new or unfamiliar stimulus, individuals use **schemata**—that is, cognitive structures for organizing new information. Essentially, for new information to be understood or useful, we must find schemata with which to link the new stimulus to previously understood experiences. For example, when trying frog legs for the first time, many people claim the dish tastes "just like chicken"; in this case, the previous experience of being familiar with the taste of chicken serves as schemata for relating the taste of frog legs.

Importantly, however, when newly presented information is inconsistent with our previously established beliefs (i.e., schemata), we experience an imbalance or dissonance (Festinger, 1957). It is this dissonance that becomes a highly persuasive tool because, according to Festinger, humans feel so uneasy with holding contradictory beliefs and actions that they will make every attempt to minimize the discomfort. In other words, when individuals behave in a manner incongruent with their beliefs, dissonance is created; dissonance creates discomfort. Because humans do not like to feel unnerved, individuals actively seek to change the situation to restore a balance between thought and action.

Relationship Between Beliefs and Behaviors

Three possible relationships between beliefs and behaviors exist: irrelevance, consonance, and dissonance (Festinger, 1957). Briefly stated, **irrelevance** simply refers to beliefs and behaviors that have nothing to do with each other. For example, Cory's beliefs about preserving the environment and his position on gun control are completely unrelated. Thus, irrelevance is the absence of both consonance and dissonance. Second, **consonance** occurs when two stimuli or pieces of information are in balance or achieve congruence. For example, if Cory believes recycling is an important way to maintain the environment, and he recycles everything from plastic bottles, to Styrofoam peanuts, to junk mail, it could be said Cory has consonance between his beliefs (recycling benefits the environment) and his actions (he avidly recycles household waste). According to

Festinger (1957), individuals prefer consonant relationships; that is, we strive to feel consistency between actions and beliefs.

Conversely, **dissonance** occurs when two stimuli or pieces of information contradict each other (Festinger, 1957). Continuing the previous example, if Cory believes the environment is a precious commodity that deserves protection, yet he drives an SUV for his 40-mile commute each day, he has created dissonance. Cory's beliefs (preserving the environment) and his actions (driving a gas-guzzling SUV) are incongruent. CDT predicts this dissonance will give Cory discomfort, at least until he can rationalize or augment the dissonance—either by shifting his belief (sure, the environment is important, but driving a car won't harm anyone) or by changing his behavior (trading in the SUV for an electric hybrid car).

Importantly, not all dissonance is created equally. That is, a **magnitude of dissonance** exists whereby some forms of incongruence produce greater discomfort than others (Zimbardo, Ebbesen, & Maslach, 1977). This magnitude of dissonance can be measured by three variables. First, the amount of dissonance one experiences is affected by the perceived importance of an issue. Recycling soda cans may not be as important an issue when compared with driving while intoxicated. Similarly, spending $5,000 on a beach rental that turns out to be a dilapidated shack is far more devastating than spending $100 to watch your favorite football team lose. Second, the **dissonance ratio** affects the amount of discomfort one feels. The dissonance ratio is simply the proportion of incongruent beliefs held in relation to the number of consonant beliefs. If you hold a greater number of incongruent beliefs and behaviors compared with consistent thoughts and actions, you will experience more discomfort. Third, one's ability to **rationalize**, or justify, the dissonance also affects the amount of discomfort experienced when faced with conflicting beliefs and behaviors. The more you can justify these contrasting attitudes and actions, the less discomfort you endure.

A related issue is perception. Specifically, the perceptual processes of selective exposure, attention, interpretation, and retention can help minimize dissonance. CDT argues that an individual selectively perceives various stimuli so as to minimize dissonance. For example, with **selective exposure**, a person actively avoids information inconsistent with previously established beliefs or behaviors. Thus, a prochoice supporter will likely avoid prolife demonstrations and vice versa. Similarly, **selective attention** suggests that if you have to expose yourself to a situation incongruent with your beliefs, you will only attend to information that reaffirms your beliefs, disregarding any information that fails to support your views. Thus, if prochoice supporters happen to come face-to-face with a prolife demonstration, they will likely only attend to those details that support their previously held beliefs, for example, that prolife supporters are religious "fanatics."

With regard to **selective interpretation**, CDT predicts individuals will carefully decipher ambiguous information so it is perceived to be consistent with their established beliefs. To illustrate, consider *Zero Dark Thirty*, a film that includes the explicit depiction of "enhanced interrogation techniques" used in the pursuit and killing of Osama Bin Laden. Individuals who support the use of torture in warfare are likely to have interpreted the film as providing evidence of the efficacy of the technique; those who do not support the use of torture may very well have interpreted the film as a condemnation of these techniques (Bruni, 2012).

Finally, CDT maintains individuals use **selective retention** to uphold their viewpoints while more easily dismissing or forgetting information that creates dissonance. Accordingly, we might remember all the good times we had in college and conveniently forget how stressful we found trying to balance the demands of schoolwork with the need to work to pay for college.

Persuasion Through Dissonance

By now it should be understood that CDT assumes humans prefer congruency between beliefs and behaviors. When we engage in an action that opposes our attitudes, we experience distress known as dissonance. Depending on the importance of the issue and the degree of our discomfort, we are motivated to change our beliefs or behaviors (i.e., be persuaded). CDT is often considered a **postdecision theory**, meaning individuals attempt to persuade themselves after a decision has been made or course of action has been enacted that the decision or behavior was okay (Gass & Seiter, 2003). The notion of buyer's remorse is an obvious example. After spending more than you feel comfortable with on a new home, car, vacation, or some other luxury item, you probably had to rationalize, or convince yourself, that the purchase was "worth" it. Thus, you try to reduce the dissonance created after making a decision to buy. Yet the question remains: How can communicators use CDT as a tool to persuade others?

Recall that, according to CDT, motivation results from an individual's internal struggle to change beliefs or behaviors to restore consonance (Festinger, 1957). Consequently, if a persuader can create or exploit dissonance while also offering a solution to minimize the disparity, it is likely the receiver will adopt these suggested new behaviors (or change beliefs).

In the case of buyer's remorse, sellers and real estate agents can capitalize on principles of CDT by reinforcing the wisdom of making certain choices. Realtors often encourage buyers to make a list of pros and cons before even looking for that new home with breathtaking views, a gourmet kitchen, or a sunken Jacuzzi tub (Light, 2002). This way, buyers can reduce dissonance that typically occurs after their bid is accepted by reinforcing their decision to purchase with the list of advantages. Home inspections and contingency clauses in the agreement of sale also help prospective buyers feel better about their decision to purchase.

Advertisers have also been using principles of CDT for decades, convincing consumers to buy their clients' products. For instance, the diet industry has made billions of dollars by preying on the average person's insecurities about his or her appearance and body image. Most adults know they should engage in exercise or physical activity on a daily basis, yet the majority of them don't. And although we may not be motivated enough to get off the couch and onto the treadmill, we are motivated to relieve the dissonance by purchasing so-called miracle products such as fat blockers, diet supplements, cellulite creams, and even cocktails formulated for skinny women. Thus, by presenting an easy alternative, these manufacturers help consumers to minimize their discomfort by realigning their beliefs and behaviors, if only on a temporary basis.

Within an organizational context, CDT predicts that by increasing employee commitments and loyalties, employee turnover could be reduced and satisfaction improved.

That is, "once we've invested our time and energy or poured our hearts and souls into a cause, a person, an idea, a project, or a group we find it too difficult to let go" (Gass & Seiter, 2003, p. 69). If you have already invested years, overcome financial burdens, or forged meaningful relationships with coworkers, you are much less likely to leave an organization—regardless of pay or other adverse circumstances. Instead, you suppress second thoughts about other career opportunities, rationalize your corporate loyalty, and may even intensify your efforts to prove to yourself and others that the job is worth it.

We would like to offer a few words of caution, however. Take care when trying to capitalize on others' inconsistencies as a persuasive strategy for changing receivers' beliefs or behaviors. As Gass and Seiter (2003) noted, if you create too much dissonance, the receivers may simply create balance by changing their attitudes so as not to like you. Likewise, ethical issues abound when individuals plot to exploit consumers' or employees' dissonance for material gain. We believe competent persuaders must think of each consumer or employee as an individual worthy of respect. If creating or magnifying another's dissonance strips that individual of self-worth, then such techniques should be avoided.

CDT focuses primarily on an individual's psychological response to inconsistencies in beliefs and actions. Because dissonance produces distress, human beings seek to maintain consonance or the appearance of consonance whenever possible. This adverse effect may mean changing one's behaviors or realigning one's beliefs through some type of rationalization or selective perception. Although often a postreactive approach, communicators can use this knowledge of CDT to better target their persuasive messages. By offering a solution, product, or course of action that bridges the gap between receivers' incongruent beliefs and behaviors, communicators may influence receivers to use these methods to create cognitive harmony.

SUMMARY AND RESEARCH APPLICATIONS

This chapter focused on cognition and communication, which refers to the way individuals assess others' behavior, attitudes, and messages to assign meaning. First, attribution theory focuses on how and why individuals assign causes to other peoples' behavior. Related to workplace communication, attribution theory has been applied to understanding how recipients of e-mail messages are interpreted by the sender when a response is not returned, as well as how recipients interpret their own behavior when a reply is not provided (Easton & Bommelje, 2011). Related to public relations and crisis communication, attribution theory has also been applied to media coverage of Toyota's 2010 global product recall, finding that media coverage of the crisis implied that the crisis was self-inflicted; that is, the media made internal attributions for the situation (Tennert, 2014). Second, URT states that when individuals encounter someone or something new, they experience uncertainty; uncertainty is uncomfortable, so people use communication strategies to reduce it. One application of URT is its usefulness in explaining how employees manage uncertainty in times of organizational change, with a particular focus on how this uncertainty influences employee satisfaction and performance (Cullen, Edwards, Casper, &

Gue, 2014). Next, EVT predicts whether people will reciprocate or compensate when their expectations are violated. Within organizational contexts, EVT has been used to explain varying responses to BP's oil spill crisis; individuals who viewed BP positively before the crisis responded more positively to public relations efforts than individuals who did not have a positive reward valence for the organization (Kim, 2014). Finally, cognitive dissonance theory explains persuasion as a cognitive response to inconsistencies in beliefs and actions, whereby individuals prefer to maintain consistency between their beliefs and behaviors. Intriguingly, Stoverink, Umphress, Gardner, and Miner (2014) found that supervisor mistreatment can actually result in greater team cohesiveness. They found that a leader's disrespectful and unfair behavior can threaten workers' self-concepts; to manage this dissonance, employees may behave in ways to increase team solidarity. This paradox explains why famously abusive leaders like Steve Jobs created a workplace noted for unity and solidarity.

KEY TERMS

Attribution   34

Axiom   38

Behavioral uncertainty   39

Behaviorism   33

Cognition   33

Cognitive   33

Cognitive uncertainty   39

Communicator reward
    valence   42

Compensate   42

Consensus   36

Consistency   36

Consonance   45

Correspondent inferences   35

Deviance   38

Dispositional factors   34

Dissonance   46

Dissonance ratio   46

Distinctiveness   36

Expectancy   42

Exterior locus of control   37

Hedonic relevance   36

Incentive   38

Interactive strategy   40

Interior locus of control   37

Irrelevance   45

Magnitude of dissonance   46

Personalism   36

Postdecision theory   47

Rationalize   46

Reciprocate   42

Schemata   45

Selective attention   46

Selective exposure   46

Selective interpretation   46

Selective retention   47

Situational factors   34

Social desirability   35

Violation valence   42

CASE STUDY 3: YOU'RE FIRED!

Lisa, Steve, and Chen were feeling triumphant. Just 3 months ago, their company, Ryan Project Systems, had merged with Gierig Strategien AG, a consulting firm headquartered in Germany. At the time, they were optimistic about the merger; the two companies were equivalent in size and mission, and the merger would allow for a stronger global reach. Ryan was already one of the top project management firms in the United States and Asia, and the merger with Gierig added most of Europe to the mix.

However, shortly after the merger, they were a bit less enthusiastic. It seemed that there were a lot of people on the Ryan side that

(Continued)

(Continued)

were being let go. Top management assured all employees that these personnel losses were simply a matter of reducing redundant positions—that the personnel changes that happened in the first month had "right-sized" the company and that the organization was now lean, competitive, and ready to become the premier project management organization in the world. Still, in their near daily conference calls, Steve (based in Charlotte, North Carolina) and Chen (based in Taiwan) frequently found time to catch up on the latest gossip of who was on the way out and who was on the way up. In one of their calls, Chen told Steve "Rumor has it Rajesh is being let go."

"Wow! He was one of the people who actually led the integration! Do you think he knew he was actually planning for his . . . uh . . . 'retirement'?," Steve asked.

"Well, Rajesh is pretty smart," Chen mused. "I can't imagine he didn't see this coming. He probably already has an exit plan. You know Rajesh, the next thing we know we'll be getting a LinkedIn notification that he is now a VP at some tech firm."

"I know we're pretty low on the totem pole, but do you think we're safe?" Steve asked.

"No one is safe," Chen snorted. "But we have some pretty strong evidence of our return on investment. Plus, Lisa has all sorts of political connections on both sides of the merger. She'll look out for us. We're a strong team."

Steve wanted to believe this, but his past experience had taught him to be wary. Just 5 years ago he had lost a position at a Fortune 500 company because of political maneuverings. One day he had a performance review that identified him as a high potential contributor, and the next day he was out of a job. He was lucky that he had strong networks, and Lisa created a position for him in her group because she knew what he was capable of.

Fast forward 3 months, and Lisa, Steve, and Chen had just completed a week-long consultation with a company in Barcelona. The Barcelona group was impressed with what the former Ryan employees could deliver, and the meeting concluded with a joint celebration that involved lots of *cava* and seafood. Lisa, Steve, and Chen were already planning their monthly visits as the project was completed, and they enthused that before the merger, their projects were more likely to bring them to boring cities in the American Midwest or polluted and poverty-stricken cities in India than the glittering cities of Europe.

After the trip, Steve returned to North Carolina, Chen returned to Taipei, and Lisa returned to New York. Just 3 days later, Steve received a phone call from Lisa. "We were wrong," Lisa said.

"Uh, I'm not sure what you are talking about," Steve replied.

"The decruitment is not over. More heads are rolling," she said calmly.

"Is it finally some of the folks from the Gierig side?" Steve asked. "Seriously, I don't know how they have such a large market share. So far I am not impressed with their processes."

"Nope, not Gierig," Lisa said. "Me."

Steve was stunned. Their group had just brought in a six-figure contract, and Lisa had negotiated a great deal for the company. "What could they possibly be thinking?" he mused. He didn't realize he had actually said it out loud until Lisa replied.

"They're threatened. We just walked onto their turf and showed them up. They aren't getting away with this," Lisa proclaimed. "I'm seeing a lawyer."

Steve was on the phone with Chen 5 minutes later. Chen was ready to resign right then and there.

"We're next," she intoned morosely.

"Maybe," Steve said, "But maybe not. We need to sit tight and see what happens next."

What happened next was an announcement that their group would now report to Konrad Aulbach, who was the director of corporate Development and a long-term Gierig employee.

In their first conference call, Konrad asked Steve and Chen to create a report detailing their current projects. It seemed reasonable, so they had a quick conference call to plan their attack.

Chen asked, "Do you think he wants a formal report or just a PowerPoint presentation?"

"He said a report, so I guess we should take him on his word," Steve replied.

"How much detail?"

"Well, he's coming from corporate development, so he probably doesn't know much about what we are doing on the ground. I'd rather give too much detail than too little," Steve responded. Chen agreed. The two worked tirelessly on providing a detailed report for each project, specifying their processes and including timelines, budgets, and current status.

They sent their report 3 days later. They were pretty proud that they were able to pull together such a comprehensive report so quickly and also were impressed with all that they were juggling. They felt certain that Konrad would see them for the valuable employees that they were.

They heard nothing for 3 days, and then they received a blistering e-mail from Konrad:

I asked you to update me on your projects. I don't have time to wade through all of this crap. I need you to tell me what you are actually working on right now.

Chen was annoyed, and Steve was frustrated. "If he just wanted an update, why did he ask for a report?" The two of them quickly conferred and sent back a joint e-mail that apologized for any misunderstanding and had bullet points for each of their current projects. Several days later they received another nasty e-mail:

I know what projects the company has under contract. What SPECIFICALLY are you doing? I don't see much work coming from either of you.

"Well, that's because we keep having to write reports for you," Steve thought angrily. But again, he decided to take the high road. He prided himself on being a hard worker who was able to work with anyone. He reached out to Konrad to clarify what he meant by "not seeing much work" coming from them.

"I'm hearing complaints that you aren't delivering on your promises," Konrad told Steve.

Steve was stunned. He knew his clients were enthusiastic supporters of his work, and he had e-mails to prove it. Who could possibly be saying that he wasn't delivering on his promises? As tough as it was, Steve swallowed his pride.

"I'm very surprised to hear that. Can you please let me know who is unhappy so I can reach out to them and rectify the problem?" Steve asked.

"It's not my job to babysit you," Konrad said. "If you can't even tell if your clients are dissatisfied, I'm not certain you have the skills to lead these sorts of projects."

"What the . . . !" Steve silently thought. "This guy has no clue what he is talking about!"

Konrad continued, "Let me spell this out to you. I need you to tell me how you are spending your days so I can determine if our investment in you makes sense."

Steve immediately called Chen after he got off the call with Konrad. He asked her if she had any intel on unhappy clients.

"I have no idea what he is talking about," she concurred. They spent the rest of the phone call discussing each individual client they had worked with in the past 6 months, and could think of no one who could be interpreted as dissatisfied.

(Continued)

(Continued)

"Do you think it might be Marjie Adams?" Steve asked. Marjie had been one of his clients nearly a year before. After the completion of the project, Marjie had a habit of calling Steve and Chen for answers to questions that they had already answered over and over again.

Steve decided that he would comply to Konrad's request by creating a log of billable hours, but he also compiled all of the e-mails he had received from happy clients. He sent an email to Konrad:

I have attached an Excel file of billable hours. If this assists you in keeping track of my activities, I would be glad to continue to do so every week. I also have attached a series of e-mails from previous clients expressing their evaluation of my work. I would be happy to discuss with you any patterns you see that might indicate client dissatisfaction.

For several weeks, there was silence from Konrad, so Steve thought he may have finally put his boss's misperceptions to rest. After all, in the tumultuous environment in which they worked, no news was good news, right? Nearly 2 months later, he received a request for a conference call with Konrad. They hadn't talked since the call in which Konrad had accused him of not meeting client expectations. The call was scheduled for 9 a.m. on a Friday.

Konrad said, "Steve, I want to let you know that human resources is on the phone with us right now. You are being terminated."

Steve was both surprised and not surprised at the same time.

"Might you tell me the cause for my termination?" Steve asked.

Konrad ignored him. "Human resources will inform you about the paperwork for your termination," he said and ended the call.

"What a gutmaggot," Steve thought. "This company is going down the tubes if this is the way they are going to run it."

Questions for Consideration

1. What attributions have Lisa, Steve, and Konrad made? Make sure to include information about consensus, consistency, and controllability.

2. What are the sources of uncertainty in the case? What strategies did Steve use to reduce his uncertainty?

3. Using examples for each of EVT's core components (expectancy, violation valence, and communicator reward valence), how does EVT explain Steve's response to Konrad?

4. Who experiences cognitive dissonance in the case, and why? Do you see any evidence that the characters have used selective exposure, selective attention, or selective interpretation?

5. What ethical issues arise in the case? Which theory or combination of theories might help to pinpoint or address any unethical behavior?

6. Which theory alone seems to provide the "best" explanation for the situation? Why do you believe this to be the case? What information might surface that would make a different theory or theories better at explaining the situation? How could you combine several theories to make for an even better explanation of the situation?

CHAPTER FOUR

INDIVIDUAL AND SOCIAL APPROACHES TO COMMUNICATION

NATURE VERSUS NURTURE

Nature versus nurture? One of the fundamental questions of philosophy is the extent to which human beings are shaped by their biology versus the environment in which they are raised. For example, are some people born liars, or is it the way people are raised and the social conditions in which they live that foster a tendency to engage in deceptive practices? The perception about whether a communication theory places an emphasis on nature or nurture has much to do with one's own view of the debate. Scholars on the nature side of the debate suggest the communication discipline historically has been focused on the nurture side of the debate. That is, they argue that much of communication scholarship has focused on how social rules and roles impact the communication process (Hickson & Neiva, 2002; Sherry, 2004). Conversely, those that firmly believe in the role of the environment tend to argue that the communication discipline suffers from placing too much emphasis on the individual rather than on the way interaction creates a social world (Leeds-Hurwitz, 1992).

On the nurture side of the debate, social approaches to communication focus on how lived experiences influence the individual. For example, a standpoint approach argues that expectations for communication are socially constructed. Developed first within philosophy to explain master–slave relationships (Hegel, 1807/1966) and later used in feminist scholarship (Hartsock, 1983), standpoint approaches build on the notion that you cannot understand others unless you walk a mile in their shoes. A **standpoint** is a position from which you view and understand the world; the point in time, the location, and the experiences you bring to an observation influence your standpoint. Groups of individuals who share similar viewpoints and understandings also share standpoints. Standpoint theory argues that differences in people's lives stem from imbalances in social, economic, and symbolic power (Wood, 1993).

Learning Objectives

After reading this chapter, you will be able to do the following:

1. Describe the communal and agentic stereotypes as well as the two types of prejudice central to role congruity theory

2. Explain how principles of emotional intelligence help to differentiate transactional leadership from transformational leadership

3. Articulate patterns of miscommunication between the three message design logics

4. Apply the axioms of the interactional perspective to generational conflicts in the workplace

5. Compare and contrast principles associated with individual and social approaches to communication

6. Provide systematic understanding of a professional situation by employing principles of individual and social approaches to communication

For example, many men and women have different standpoints because the two groups have different social, economic, and symbolic experiences as a result of gender expectations. Because boys and girls are socialized differently (Maccoby, 1990; Wood, 2015), they have different sets of rules, norms, goals, and meanings for their social experiences.

On the other hand, more and more communication scholars are recognizing the power evolutionary mechanisms, and especially genetics, play in communication practices. Beatty and McCroskey's (2001) **communibiological approach**, for example, is grounded in neuroscience. The approach argues that neurobiological structures create different temperaments or traits, that these temperaments and traits are genetic, and that temperament and traits are what cause variations in communication behavior. To illustrate, research suggests characteristics such as assertiveness, empathy, aggressiveness, and nurturing are inherited qualities passed on through genetics (McCroskey, 2006). However, McCroskey suggests that even though there is a genetic basis for these behaviors, our social environment does play some role. "Children do not learn to be aggressive or empathic. These and a large number of other trait orientations are what they are born with. How they respond to the genetically based temperamental demands, however, depends on a large number of other things. . . . Children learn culturally appropriate means of expressing (or not expressing) their genetically driven temperaments" (McCroskey, 2006, p. 34).

The theories in this chapter focus on the interplay of individual traits and social expectations in predicting or explaining communication activity. First, we consider social role theory, which argues that perceptions of men and women's behavior are always filtered through our stereotypes of how men and women should behave. We specifically apply this theory to research investigating women and leadership. Next, we describe emotional intelligence (EI), which suggests that personal and professional success might not be explained by an individual's intelligence quotient (IQ) but, rather, by the extent to which the individual is attuned to emotional experiences. We link EI to transformational leadership. The third theory we consider is message design logics, which proposes that variations in beliefs about communication explain problematic communication encounters. Finally, we describe the interactional perspective formulated by the Palo Alto Group. The tenets of this approach are used to explain why there is so much focus on the communication difficulties among members of different generations in the workplace.

SOCIAL ROLE THEORY OF GENDER

Examining sex and gender differences in communication is perhaps one of the most controversial and widely debated areas of communication research in recent decades (see Canary & Hause, 1993; Wood & Dindia, 1998). Despite the number of popular self-help books proclaiming the idea that men inhabit one planet while women occupy another (see Gray, 1992, 1997/2005) or alleging men and women "just don't understand" each other (see Tannen, 1990), there is actually very little communication theory—or research—to support these stereotypical claims of widespread sex differences (Anderson, 1998; Canary, Emmers-Sommer, & Faulker, 1997; Canary & Hause, 1993; Crawford, 2004).

Yet there has to be a reason why these books are bestsellers. According to social role theory, perhaps one of the reasons we find it so tempting to believe men and women are fundamentally different is because sex is the single easiest characteristic we can use to classify people into categories; it is easier, even, than using race, age, or other easily observable groupings (Eagly & Karau, 2002). Not only that, but stereotypes based on sex can be activated at very low levels of consciousness. Much like expectancy violations theory (EVT) described in Chapter 3, social role theory focuses on our expectations for behavior and how we respond when our expectations are violated. Unlike EVT, however, social role theory suggests that violations of our expectations almost always lead to negative responses.

Sex and Gender: What's the Difference?

"Not biology, but gender prescriptions for women and men account for most differences in priorities, behaviors, attitudes, feelings, and self-concepts of the sexes" (Julia Wood in a dialogue with Kathryn Dindia, see Wood & Dindia, 1998, p. 30). How often have you filled out a survey or questionnaire that asks for your gender and then has boxes for "male" or "female"? What the survey is probably trying to determine is your sex. You may scratch your head and wonder, "What's the difference?" The difference could be drastic or insignificant, depending on the context. When discussing messages and communication patterns between women and men, it is helpful to understand there is a substantial difference between sex and gender.

Social role theory assumes that **sex** is genetically determined; it is your biological makeup as either a male (with XY chromosomes) or a female (with XX chromosomes). Barring rare genetic abnormalities, sex is a dichotomous variable; you are one or the other, not both or neither. Whereas sex is a biological categorization determined at conception, gender is far more fluid. **Gender** is "the consensual beliefs about the attributes of women and men" (Eagly & Karau, 2002, p. 574). Importantly, all societies assign certain behaviors to each sex; in this way, gender is related to, but not equated with, sex. In Western culture, for instance, girls typically receive baby dolls and kitchen sets and are told to be "sugar and spice and everything nice," while their brothers typically receive trucks and toy guns and are told not to "cry like a girl." As adults, women are still expected to be primary caregivers, while men are expected to be primary breadwinners. When boys and girls and men and women behave outside of these prescriptions, eyebrows raise, a person's sexuality may be questioned (e.g., assuming male dancers are gay), and boundaries are pushed.

One of the central ways people stereotype women and men is in terms of communal and agentic qualities (Eagly, 1987). **Communal qualities** include behaviors that demonstrate concern for other people through the expression of affection and exhibiting sympathy, helpfulness, sensitivity, nurturance, and gentility. **Agentic qualities**, on the other hand, include being assertive, controlling, confident, ambitious, and forceful. Whereas communal attributes are stereotypically associated with women, agentic behaviors are stereotypically associated with men. Social role theory suggests people assume this connection between gender roles and individual dispositions. In other words, we expect a woman to show sympathy and helpfulness while we expect a man to demonstrate confidence and assertiveness. Even when faced with evidence to the contrary (e.g., a very dominant woman or a very nurturing man) people cling to social role expectations.

Role Congruity Theory and Leadership

Because leadership is most often described in masculine terms (i.e., leaders are supposed to be ambitious, assertive, and direct), social role theory has been extended to focus on sex differences in the realm of organizational leadership. Called role congruity theory, the theory suggests women in leadership positions are likely to experience two types of prejudice (Eagly & Karau, 2002). **Descriptive prejudice** refers to stereotypes that women have less leadership potential than men because they lack agentic qualities. **Prescriptive prejudice** (also called injunctive prejudice) refers to actual evaluations of women as less effective than men. Combined, these prejudices leave women in a **double bind**. "If they conform to their traditional gender role, women are not seen as having the potential for leadership; if they adopt the agentic characteristics associated with successful leaders, then they are evaluated negatively for behaving in an unfeminine manner" (Elsesser & Lever, 2011, p. 1557).

Eagly and Karau (2002; Koenig, Eagly, Mitchell, & Ristikari, 2011) predict that because of this role incongruity women are actually less likely to emerge as leaders in professional settings than are men. Of course, some might question whether the stereotypes might be based on reality. Research suggests this is not the case, however; even when women possess agentic qualities they are less likely to emerge as leaders in a mixed-sex group than are men (Offor, 2012; Ritter & Yoder, 2004). Unfortunately, these negative stereotypes can be exacerbated by the context of the workplace. Garcia-Retamero and López-Zafra (2006) found that people showed stronger prejudice against female leaders who worked in a stereotypically male industry (e.g., the auto industry as compared to the clothing industry) and that older individuals reported more prejudice against female leaders than did younger individuals.

Research has found some support for the predictions made by role congruity theory. Surveying over 60,000 workers, a recent study found evidence for a strong descriptive prejudice against female leaders (Elsesser & Lever, 2011). The good news is that competence ratings for actual male and female bosses were similar, and respondents did not view leaders who behaved in a counter stereotypical style (e.g., a sensitive male manager or a direct female manager) as less competent than those who behaved in a stereotypical fashion. However, although it appears prescriptive prejudices may be fading, the results suggested that a cross-sex preference might exist such that women reported having better relationships with male managers and vice versa.

What About Actual Differences in Communication?

Beyond the stereotypes we hold about men and women, and our evaluations of actual men and women because of these stereotypes, communication research shows little support for the notion that men and women differ with regard to their actual communication behavior simply because of their biological sex. In fact, research suggests we are more similar to the opposite sex than we are different. For example, Canary and Hause (1993) used a statistical procedure known as meta-analysis to compare more than 1,200 studies looking at sex differences in communication. When combined, they found that one's biological sex accounts for less than 1% of differences in communication behavior! This means that 99% of differences in communication behavior are likely created by something other than simply having XX or XY chromosomes.

On the other hand, there is support for the idea that gender roles influence communication styles. Regardless of biological sex, having a relationship partner who exhibits a feminine (i.e., communal) style of communication is positively related to romantic relationship satisfaction (Lamke, Sollie, Durbin, & Fitzpatrick, 1994), the use of positive and collaborative strategies for dealing with romantic relationship jealousy (Aylor & Dainton, 2001), and decreased loneliness among long-distance friends (Dainton, Aylor, & Zelley, 2002). Masculinity (i.e., engaging in agentic behavior) has been associated with more effective political campaign ads (Wadsworth et al., 1987) and more strategic uses of communication (Aylor & Dainton, 2004).

Despite little evidence of actual sex differences in communication, social role theory provides a way to understand how social expectations for behavior result in stereotypes. Although these stereotypes affect both men and women, they have a particularly insidious effect on women leaders, placing them in a double bind of being judged negatively regardless of the leadership style they adopt.

EMOTIONAL INTELLIGENCE AND TRANSFORMATIONAL LEADERSHIP

A second theory that focuses on the interplay of individual and social qualities is **emotional intelligence** (EI). In 1995, Daniel Goleman wrote a best-selling book on the topic that revolutionized the way people thought about career success. Building on the work of Salovey and Mayer (1989), Goleman wrote that emotional intelligence—the ability to monitor one's own and others' emotions—was more powerful than IQ and that "nearly 90% of the difference between star performers at work and average ones was due to EI" (Goleman, 1998, as cited in Mayer, Salovey & Caruso, 2008, p. 504). As the public face for emotional intelligence, Goleman himself has certainly provided support for the connection between the ability to recognize others' needs and public and financial recognition.

Aside from the popular culture version of EI, however, Salovey and Mayer have continued to carefully develop and refine their theory of emotional intelligence. They argue emotional intelligence is an ability that explains differences in individuals' problem solving and relationship maintenance. Specifically, they suggest EI is associated with the ability to monitor one's own and others' emotions, being able to carefully discriminate between emotions, and use emotional information strategically to make decisions and achieve goals. Despite other scholars' view that EI is a trait (see Bar-On, 2006), Salovey and Mayer assert that emotional intelligence is not based on personality types and claim that like other types of intelligence, EI changes and develops with age and experience (Caruso, Mayer, & Salovey, 2002; Mayer, Caruso, & Salovey, 1999).

Mayer and Salovey's (1997) theory suggests emotional intelligence is comprised of four branches arranged in a hierarchy from most basic to most complex. Further, within each branch abilities range from the very basic to the most intricate. Table 4.1 describes each branch from the least to most complex.

Although Salovey and Mayer are careful to distance themselves from Goleman's claim that high EI is a strong predictor of organizational success, research does support the notion that EI plays a role in the way an individual performs in an organizational setting (Mayer et al., 2008; Salovey, Caruso, & Mayer, 2004). One particularly intriguing connection links emotional intelligence to the use of a transformational leadership style (Gardner & Stough, 2002; Palmer, Walls, Burgess, & Stough, 2001; Sivanathan & Fekken, 2002; Wang & Huang, 2009). First described by Bass (1997), transformational leadership is the ability to change (i.e., "transform") employees and the organization through communication. Bass differentiates between two leadership styles—transactional and transformational—arguing that, although both can assist organizations in achieving goals, transformational leadership is superior in a contemporary business climate.

Transactional leadership seeks to achieve solid, consistent performance from subordinates through a process of bilateral exchange (Bass, 1985). Specifically, leaders fulfill the needs of the employee in exchange for the employee meeting performance expectations. To illustrate, there are three primary characteristics of transactional leaders. First, transactional leaders work with subordinates to develop clear and specific objectives. For example, a manager might meet with an employee to create performance standards jointly for an upcoming year. Second, transactional leaders exchange rewards and promises of rewards for employee effort. Accordingly, a leader might reward an employee on completion of a difficult task with an "Employee Excellence Award" or a financial bonus. Third, transactional leaders are responsive to the self-interests of workers, particularly if the workers' needs can be met while also getting the job done (Bass, 1985). For example, consider a single parent who receives a phone call that her child is sick. A transactional leader would be supportive of the employee going home to care for the sick child if acceptable arrangements can be made to ensure that the work would still be accomplished, for instance, working late another day or negotiating with a coworker to cover the required tasks. Transactional leadership is responsive to employees and offers clear and structured expectations. It is a natural result of bureaucratic systems. This leadership style focuses on meeting immediate needs as quickly and effectively as possible (Bass, 1985). Subordinates are respected and encouraged to participate in planning and decision making.

Transformational leadership, on the other hand, is founded on particular attitudes and behaviors that support organizational change (Bass, 1985). Whereas transactional leadership seeks to achieve reliable and stable functioning, transformational leadership seeks to inspire exceptional performance (Bryant, 2003). At the center of transformational leadership is the ability to use subordinates' ideas and actions as a catalyst for transformation—moving ideas and actions toward the greater good of the organization.

Bass (1985) identified four facets of transformational leadership. First, **idealized influence** refers to the fact that transformational leaders serve as role models for employees. Associated with charisma, idealized influence involves establishing trust, pride, and respect among all members of the organization. In so doing, the leader models ideal behavior for employees.

Second, **inspirational motivation** requires transformational leaders to present employees with a clear vision and desirable future. Followers are motivated by the attainment of this vision and receive encouragement and support for doing so. As such, employees' self-interest is subsumed to the interest of the greater good.

Third, transformational leaders provide **intellectual stimulation**. The status quo is not taken for granted; transformational leaders challenge their own assumptions and encourage new approaches. Differences of opinion are addressed openly and without fear; leaders willingly acknowledge their own mistakes and recognize the superior ideas of others. Followers are encouraged to reject tradition as a means for operating and to challenge their own thinking.

Fourth, **individualized consideration** is considered the hallmark of transformational leadership. The transformational leader considers each individual's needs and abilities, while supporting development and mentoring efforts. In this way, the confidence of followers is enhanced, and subordinates can turn their attention from simple existence (i.e., keeping the job) to achievement and growth. Effectiveness is preferred to efficiency, and equity (considering outputs relative to inputs) is preferred to equal exchange (i.e., everyone receiving the same rewards).

Both transactional and transformational leadership are associated with achievement of organizational goals (Bass, 1985). Moreover, any given leader can be both transactional and transformative. Research has consistently shown, however, that transformational leadership is associated with greater individual and organizational

Table 4.1 The Four-Branch Model of Emotional Intelligence

Component	Definition
Perceiving emotions	Ranges from the ability to accurately recognize one's own and others' emotions to the ability to discriminate between sincere and insincere expressions of feelings
Using emotions to assist thinking	Ranges from the ability to use emotions to direct attention to important information to the ability to use emotions to facilitate creativity or engage in inductive reasoning
Understanding and analyzing emotions	Ranges from the ability to recognize connections between emotions (e.g., envy and jealousy) to the ability to recognize emotional blends (e.g., fear and surprise) and transitions between emotions
Regulation of emotions	Ranges from the ability to be open to all feelings, including pleasant and unpleasant emotions, to the ability to manage one's own or others' emotional displays

outcomes (Bass, 1998). Research linking transformational leadership to EI suggests a leader's emotional intelligence predicts his or her use of transformational leadership, which in turn predicts employee satisfaction (Jimenez, 2017; Lam & O'Higgins, 2012).

Individuals high in EI have the ability to succeed in the workplace because they are able to recognize, manage, and use their own and others' emotions strategically. One important way individuals high in EI have an impact on organizations is through transformational leadership. As we will see shortly, other important qualities might explain positive (and problematic) interactions. Our third theory is message design logics.

MESSAGE DESIGN LOGICS

Everyone has been faced with the challenge of having to confront a coworker or subordinate who isn't pulling his or her weight. The dilemmas communicators confront when dealing with these sorts of situations can be understood by the theory of message design logics. According to O'Keefe (1988, 1997), because people think about communication differently, they also construct very different types of messages. A **message design logic** (MDL), then, is your belief about communication that, in turn, links thoughts to the construction of messages. Stated differently, people's views about the nature and function of communication affect their messages. Variation in message type is particularly evident when a person is faced with communication challenges such as trying to influence someone's behavior or dealing with a difficult coworker. According to O'Keefe (1997), there are three types of design logics from which people operate.

Three Message Design Logics

Building upon her previous work looking at impression management in persuasive interaction (O'Keefe & Delia, 1982) and ways in which individuals negotiate multiple goals in persuasive interaction (O'Keefe & Shepherd, 1987), O'Keefe (1988, 1997) developed her theory. Using an inductive approach, she analyzed the techniques people used to try to influence others. Despite a plethora of strategies that might be used, she found that individuals tended to rely on uniform techniques. Specifically, O'Keefe identified three distinct MDLs: expressive, conventional, and rhetorical. Each MDL emphasizes a different goal or combination of goals for communication.

The **expressive logic** is a sender-focused pattern (O'Keefe, 1988). That is, a person who relies on this pattern primarily values self-expression. The goal of communication is to convey the sender's thoughts and feelings. People who use the expressive MDL have a very difficult time holding back their thoughts; if it's in their heads, it's out their mouths. They appreciate openness, honesty, and clarity in communication and mistrust those who seem overly strategic in their communication. Such communicators pay little attention to context or what may be considered appropriate behavior. They feel a genuine obligation to say what is on their minds right there and then. When the situation calls for them to protect someone else's face or self-esteem, they typically accomplish this simply by editing their comments (e.g., replacing profanity with a euphemism) rather than through genuine efforts at politeness (see Chapter 5 for a discussion of politeness theory). For example, when faced with a colleague or employee who isn't pulling her or his weight, a person using an expressive MDL might respond in this way: "You are a real screw up. You have been given many chances to mend your ways, but you just don't seem to care. You come in late, you never work as hard as the rest of us. . . . You aren't going to get away with this. You're fired." (O'Keefe, 1988, p. 100).

Note that the content of this message is focused entirely on what the sender is feeling at the time. The sender might have made an effort to temper his or her anger by editing his or her language, but other than that, little effort is made to modify the expression of thoughts and feelings or to understand the other person's viewpoint.

Second, a person relying on **conventional logic** views communication as a rule-based game played cooperatively (O'Keefe, 1988). As such, those using a conventional MDL are primarily concerned with appropriateness; these individuals view communication contexts, roles, and relationships as having particular guidelines for behavior (O'Keefe, 1997). They are concerned about saying and doing the "right" thing in any given situation. To do the right thing, they follow the rules of politeness (see Chapter 5 for more on politeness theory). Keeping our example of dealing with a difficult employee, a person using a conventional MDL might respond like this: "You continue to be late returning from lunch. When you took this job all the rules and regulations were explained to you, and since then I've mentioned to you twice that we take our hours seriously in this office. In the future, please return from lunch promptly" (O'Keefe, 1988, p. 102).

In this case, the message sender makes several allusions to communication rules; not only does she or he point out that this behavior violates the office's "rules and regulations," but the speaker also throws in "please" as an attempt at politeness. The third MDL is **rhetorical**. Individuals using a rhetorical MDL view communication as a powerful tool used to create situations and negotiate multiple goals (O'Keefe, 1988). Instead of emphasizing self-expression (expressive logic) or social appropriateness (conventional logic), "those acting on the basis of a rhetorical design logic focus on the effect of messages on the recipient" (Bonito & Wolski, 2002, p. 256). This approach is noted for flexibility, as well as for its sophistication and depth of communication skill. Those using a rhetorical MDL pay close attention to other people's communication in an effort to figure out others' points of view. They try to anticipate and prevent problems by redefining situations to benefit all parties involved in the interaction. Unlike the expressive MDL, which is reactive and self-focused, the rhetorical MDL is proactive, flexible, and recognizes that words have relational consequences, now and in the future (O'Keefe, 1988). An example of a rhetorical MDL is as follows:

I understand that you have been making it a habit to return late from lunch. People have started to notice your behavior and comment on it. Since it is causing a lot of problems in the office, I think it would be better if you start coming back on time. If you need to be late and can tell me in advance, I'm sure we can work things out for you occasionally. (p. 103)

In this case, the manager seeks to balance his or her own goal (stopping the employee's lateness) with the employee's goal (maintaining face and protecting oneself against embarrassment). At the same time, the sender strives to maintain a good working relationship with the subordinate in the future. This is accomplished by redefining the situation from one of personal incompetence to that of off-setting office gossip. As well, the sender acknowledges his or her own flexibility by stating that occasional lateness for a good reason is okay. The sender attempts to show understanding for the other person's situation and lateness. By reframing the message, the rhetorical communicator has found "a common drama in which to play" (O'Keefe, 1988, p. 88).

Message Design Logics Preferences

Reading the three examples presented might give you insight into the MDL under which you tend to operate. More than likely, one of those messages is similar to something you might say in a situation you perceive as harassing, and the other message types might reflect something you would never say in a million years. Indeed, one of the challenges highlighted by this theory is the difficulty individuals have when dealing with others who use a different MDL. O'Keefe, Lambert, and Lambert (1997) argued that when two people use the same MDL, these individuals recognize that the problems are communication problems. When two parties use different MDLs, however, these individuals often do not realize they have communication problems; instead, they blame the difficulties on perceived bad intentions, mistaken beliefs, or undesirable personality characteristics (see attribution theory presented in Chapter 3). For example, a person who uses an expressive MDL tends to view those using a rhetorical MDL as dishonest because they "manipulate" their perception of the situation. Table 4.2 presents some forms of miscommunication due to differing MDLs.

Although individuals tend to prefer using one MDL to another, O'Keefe and colleagues have cautioned that MDLs are not the same as personality traits. Similar to EI, MDLs are not considered to be stable personality traits; instead, they can change and develop over an individual's life span. In fact, O'Keefe and Delia (1988) found that the three MDLs reflect a developmental process, with the expressive MDL the least developed and the rhetorical MDL the most developed pattern. However, O'Keefe et al. (1997) warned that this developmental trajectory should not imply that the rhetorical strategy is superior to others: "Every design logic provides a logically consistent and potentially satisfactory way for an individual to use language" (p. 49). They believe all communicators should recognize and accommodate diversity in MDLs. Knowing the variation is half the battle.

Again, O'Keefe's (1988, 1997) theory suggests that individuals tend to rely on one of the three MDLs, particularly when faced with conflict or attempts to influence. Users of expressive MDLs view communication primarily as a means of sharing their unique feelings, beliefs, and ideas. Those who rely on conventional MDLs perceive communication as a rules-based game; to play the "game" one must operate using social conventions for appropriateness. Last, a rhetorical MDL emphasizes a highly flexible approach to communication in which the speaker adapts to the situation, using self-expression or relying on social conventions as appropriate.

Table 4.2   Forms of Miscommunication Due to Message Design Logics

Message Producer	Message Recipient		
	Expressive MDL	**Conventional MDL**	**Rhetorical MDL**
Expressive MDL	Genuine differences in opinion prevent communicators from achieving any connection.	Expressive remarks perceived as embarrassing or crude due to inappropriateness.	Expressive person perceived as inconsiderate and uncooperative.
Conventional MDL	Ritualistic messages are taken literally by the expressive person (such as "Let's get together soon").	Differing views of appropriateness of the situation lead to perceived inappropriate behavior.	Conformity to appropriateness viewed as rigidity, overly conservative approach to interaction.
Rhetorical MDL	Messages viewed as unnecessarily elaborate and indirect; sender viewed as dishonest.	Failure to see coherence of complex messages because of focus on "correct" context.	Incompatible assumptions about goals can lead to misunderstanding of others' intent.

Source: O'Keefe, B. J., Lambert, B. L., & Lambert, C. A. (1997). Conflict and communication in a research and development unit. In B. D. Sypher (Ed.), *Case studies in organizational communication 2*, p. 42. New York, NY: Guilford Press.

INTERACTIONAL PERSPECTIVE ON WORKPLACE GENERATIONS

In 1967, a group of psychiatrists at the Mental Research Institute in Palo Alto, California, published a book called *Pragmatics of Human Communication*. Their focus was to uncover the reasons for schizophrenia, which they hypothesized had an environmental basis (we have since learned schizophrenia is much more on the "nature" than the "nurture" end of the continuum). However, Watzlawick, Bavelas, and Jackson (1967) presented a model for human communication grounded in a number of axioms, or assumptions, about the communication process. Called the interactional perspective, Watzlawick et al.'s view profoundly influenced our assumptions about communication and has been applied to everything from understanding foreign policy problems (Calhoun, 2008) to understanding brand relationships in advertising (Heath, Brandt, & Nairn, 2006).

According to the Palo Alto Group, there are five axioms of communication (Watzlawick et al., 1967). The first axiom is on the impossibility of not communicating.

Widely misinterpreted and debated, the axiom suggests all behavior has the potential to be communicative, regardless of whether the sender intended the behavior to be interpreted as a message. For example, according to this axiom, the "silent treatment" is indeed communicative because the recipient of the silent treatment is clearly receiving the message "I'm angry with you." Within a work setting, the person who is chronically tardy might be perceived as communicating his or her disinterest in the work activities. The group member who answers a cell phone in the middle of a meeting might be perceived as sending the message to his or her teammates that "I'm more important than you are." Intentionality is a complex issue in the field of communication, with scholars on both sides of the debate passionate about the role of intent (see Chapter 1). Regarding this debate, the Palo Alto Group is firmly committed to the belief that communication need not be intentional.

The second axiom is that all communication has both content and relationship levels (Watzlawick et al., 1967). When people interact with each other, they are sending particular messages, which are considered the **content level**. These messages may be verbal or nonverbal. At the same time, they are sending content, they are also sending additional information. The **relationship level** is characterized as how the content should be understood, particularly in terms of the relationship between the communicators. To illustrate, consider the following statements: "Peter, can you work on getting that brochure copy done?" and "Peter, get the brochure copy done." The content is virtually the same; however, the relationship level gives us quite different information in the two scenarios. The first statement can be understood as a request, whereas the second can be understood as a command. More than that, in the first situation, you understand that the two people are on equal footing and that their relationship is respectful. In the second situation, the speaker either has a legitimate superior status over the listener, or the speaker is trying to exert dominance over a status equal. The implications of this information are likely to affect the patterns of communication among everyone in the system.

The third axiom focuses on the tendency of communicators to punctuate sequences of behavior (Watzlawick et al., 1967). The grammatical definition of the term *punctuation* refers to the use of marks to separate sentences, clauses, and so forth. For example, the previous sentence has a capital *T* to indicate the beginning of the sentence, two commas to indicate pauses between a series, and a period to indicate the end of the sentence. Watzlawick et al.'s (1967) notion of punctuation is similar. They believe interaction is understood by the people involved in it as a series of beginnings and endings, of causes and effects. For example, in the example used for content and relationship levels, Peter might respond to the command by sarcastically responding, "Why yes, ma'am, right away ma'am, whatever you say, ma'am." Peter would likely view the perceived inappropriate command as the cause of his sarcasm, whereas the person who gave the command might view his flippant attitude as the reason why she had to give a command rather than a request in the first place. The point of this axiom is that although communicators tend to assign causes and effects to interactions, it is likely that interactants will view the same interaction as having different causes and effects; punctuation is always a matter of individual perception, with no perception being wholly correct or incorrect.

Moreover, Watzlawick et al. argue that differences in punctuation frequently lead to conflict among system members.

The fourth axiom is that communication entails both digital and analogic codes. According to Watzlawick et al. (1967), apart from a few exceptions, analogic communication "is virtually all nonverbal communication" (p. 43). Importantly, Watzlawick et al. emphasize the nonverbal communication is more than movement and gestures; it includes "posture, gesture, facial expression, voice inflection, the sequence, rhythm, and cadence of the words themselves" (p. 43). For example, holding two fingers up to indicate the number *2* is an analogue. Crying is an analogue to represent sadness; the tears are a physical representation of the emotion. Onomatopoeia, in which the word sounds like what it means (such as *buzz* or *click*), can also be considered examples of **analogic communication** because the tone or inflection of the word helps to define the word. The point is that analogic communication is rarely misunderstood because of the direct connection between the symbol and its meaning; even people from vastly different cultures can typically understand each other's analogic communication.

Digital communication refers to linguistic symbols that are arbitrarily linked to meaning—usually words (Watzlawick et al., 1967). Digital messages are more complex, more flexible, and more abstract than analogues. Digital messages rely on syntax and logic to convey meaning; they can refer to the past, present, or future, and the meanings of these symbols are culturally determined. Whereas a kiss from your significant other demonstrates analogic communication, having him or her say "I love you" exemplifies digital communication.

As with analogic communication, there are some exceptions to the rule. Some gestures, particularly emblems (which have dictionary-type definitions), can be considered digital. The OK symbol, wherein you make a circle with your thumb and forefinger, is an example of digital communication (which is why it has different meanings in different cultures). The challenge with digital communication is that two people operating from different digital codes (e.g., different language systems or different rules for nonverbal expression) likely don't understand that misunderstandings might be due to the nuances inherent in the use of digital codes.

The fifth and final axiom proposes that communication can be symmetrical or complementary. When communicators behave in the same manner, they are using a **symmetrical pattern**. For example, Mike is sarcastic to you, and you are sarcastic to Mike. Mike defers to you, and you defer to Mike. When the communicators behave in different ways, they are using a **complementary pattern**. For example, Mike commands, and you defer. Mike is sarcastic, and you whine. Notice that behaving in a complementary fashion does not mean interactants are behaving in an *opposite* fashion, just that the patterns of behavior are different. This axiom has most frequently been used to study control behaviors (Millar & Rogers, 1976).

Combined, these axioms explain the basis for a number of potential reasons for miscommunication. One increasingly popular context for investigating miscommunication in the workplace centers on differences in the values, beliefs, and behaviors of members of different generations. How many times have you heard an older person grouse about a younger person that "hasn't paid her dues"? How many times have you heard a younger person grumble that an older person is "completely rigid" when it comes to change? Popular books such as *Generations at Work: Managing the Clash of Boomers, Gen Xers, and Gen Yers in the Workplace* (Zemke, Raines, & Filipczak, 2013), *The Trophy Kids Grow Up* (Alsop, 2008), and Shaw's (2013) *Sticking Points: How to Get 4 Generations Working Together in the 12 Places They Come Apart*, all highlight potential age-based variations in professional settings. As of yet, no theories explain generational variations in communication behaviors at work, but we believe the interactional perspective can explain why miscommunication might occur between employees of different generations.

What Are the Generations?

Twenge and Campbell (2008) argued that each generation is influenced by specific events. Do you remember where you were when the Berlin Wall "fell"? When the events of 9/11 unfolded? When the stock market crashed in 2008? When same-sex marriage became a legal right in the United States? These cultural touchstones have influenced each generation in subtle ways.

> Just as people raised in Japan have different personality traits and attitudes (on average) from people raised in the USA, there are true differences among generations. Growing up in the 1990s was a fundamentally different experience from growing up in the 1970s or especially the 1950s. (Twenge & Campbell, 2008, p. 863)

Before addressing how an interactional perspective can explain intergenerational conflict, we need to identify generational differences in the United States. Most authors identify four generations in the contemporary workplace: Veterans (meaning WWII veterans), Baby Boomers, Generation X, and Millennials. Table 4.3 identifies the major characteristics associated with each of the groups.

Perhaps the strongest evidence to date comes from a cross-temporal meta-analysis. Twenge and Campbell's (2008) research reviewed hundreds of studies examining personality traits of college students over the span of 80 years and included more than 1.4 million people in their sample. Their results showed the current generation (Millennials) varies from previous generations in five ways that affect the workplace. First, they discovered a decreased need for social approval. That is, Millennials are less likely to follow rules simply because the rules exist. For organizations, implications include more informality in dress and communication styles. Second, Twenge and Campbell noted a simultaneous increase in both self-esteem and narcissism. After all, Millennials have been taught that they are "special" (Twenge, 2014). For Millennials at work, continued praise is expected, and criticism is often tough to swallow. Twenge recommends that managers of Millennials try using a "praise sandwich" (p. 273) in which criticism is situated between two praiseworthy behaviors.

Third, the meta-analysis determined that the current generation has an external locus of control (Twenge & Campbell, 2008). *Locus of control* refers to the tendency to explain the causes of events to either one's own effort (internal) or to the environment or outside forces (external). Millennials tend not to take responsibility for their own successes *or* failures, requiring their managers to push them harder in order to produce.

Interestingly, although the current generation does not feel as much individual responsibility as do previous generations, the fourth discovery made by Twenge and Campbell (2008) revealed that Millennials have higher levels of anxiety and depression than preceding generations, requiring organizations to provide more mental health services than ever before. Finally, the study found that women in the Millennial generation are more assertive. Twenge and Campbell concluded that this assertiveness will require organizations to provide more work–life balance, as female employees will simply demand it. Moreover, this balance isn't about working less; Twenge (2014) argues that flexibility for Millennials includes options to work remotely—from home or a coffee shop, for example, and that work hours should be whenever they want, so long as the deadlines are met.

Table 4.3 Generational Characteristics

Characteristics	Veterans	Baby Boomers	Generation X	Millennials
Date of birth	1922 to 1945	1946 to 1964	1965 to 1980	1980 to 2000
Core values	Respect, discipline	Optimism, involvement	Cynicism, informality	Clarity, flexibility
View of work	An obligation	Self-fulfillment	Entrepreneurship	A mechanism for success
Satisfaction comes from	A job well done	Making a difference	Changing the rules	Lots of recognition
Preferred rewards	Delayed and intrinsic (did their duty, private praise)	Primarily intrinsic (feeling good about self)	Extrinsic (recognition through time, money, and freedom)	Very extrinsic (recognition through immediate praise, opportunity, and status)
Communication style	Formal; letters and memos	Face-to-face discussion, meetings	Direct; comfortable with technology	Constant connection; heavy reliance on technology
Leadership style	Autocratic	Consensual	Confrontational	Passive-aggressive
Loyalty	High	High	Low	Low

Sources: Information synthesized from Busch, Venkitachalam, Richards, 2008; McGuire, Todnem By, and Hutchings, 2007; Smola and Sutton, 2002; Tomkiewicz and Bass, 2008; Twenge and Campbell, 2008; Twenge, Campbell, Hoffman, & Lance, 2010; Westermann and Yamamura, 2007.

Table 4.4 seeks to blend the axioms proposed by the interactional perspective with some of the implications for generational variations. Of course, thus far we have only sought to uncover potential areas of disagreement. The interactional perspective also provides possible solutions. Watzlawick, Weakland, and Fisch (1974) argue there are two types of change. **First-order change** refers to changing the behaviors of individuals in the system. In the case of patterns of behavior among those from different generations, first-order change would likely involve training and development, mentoring, or coaching efforts aimed at modifying communication styles. However, Watzlawick et al. (1974) caution that first-order change is analogous to treating the symptoms without curing the disease: Although communication between the generations might sound more polite and supportive, the underlying values and beliefs would still be at odds. Instead, they would recommend **second-order change**. Second-order change seeks to resolve underlying differences in perspective, most often through the process of reframing. Reframing is a process of intentionally seeking alternative perspectives to a problem. Interestingly, one way reframing might occur in the case of intergenerational conflict in the workplace might be to have members of each generation seek to understand each other's standpoint.

There is early evidence of generational differences in values and ways of behaving. However, scholars have only started to document these differences. As yet, we do not have a specific theory that can explain and predict why they occur, what they mean, and what might happen in the future, but the interactional view highlights some issues likely to emerge as well as some ways to manage those differences.

Table 4.4 Interactional Perspective Axioms and Implications for Generational Conflict

Axiom	Implication for Interpersonal Communication
The impossibility of not communicating	Members of different generations might not intend for their behaviors to cause workplace conflict, but those from different generations might interpret others' behavior as disrespectful or inappropriate.
Content and relationship levels	The content of communication might not be problematic, but the relationship dimension of messages might highlight disagreements about how workplace communication should be handled.
The problem of punctuation	Members of different generations are likely to see the cause of the perceived disrespect/inappropriateness as starting from the other generation.
Digital and analogic codes	The same word (e.g., *respect*) might be understood very differently by members of different generations.
Complementary and symmetrical communication	Within the workplace, complementary patterns are likely to emerge when members of different generations work together.

SUMMARY AND RESEARCH APPLICATIONS

In this chapter, we highlighted theories that seek to uncover how individual and social variations influence the communication process. First, we described the social role theory of gender, which highlights how assumptions of appropriate behavior for men and women influence our judgments about individual men and women in the workplace. In a recent meta-analysis of leadership effectiveness across 95 studies, researchers found partial support for social role theory (Paustian-Underdahl, Walker, & Woehr, 2014). Specifically, men were rated as more effective leaders in male-dominated organizations (government), whereas women were viewed as more effective in middle management positions and education. Women rated themselves as less effective leaders than did men. However, contrary to social role theory, when rated by others, women in senior management were viewed as more effective than their male counterparts. In a reverse application of the theory, Wallen, Mor, and Devine (2014) examined perceptions of men in the female-dominated job of nursing. Male nurses face contradictory expectations; on one hand, men are expected to be agentic, yet nursing requires communal skills typically associated with women. Wallen et al. found that male nurses' ability to integrate or reframe these contrary expectations "as compatible and overlapping" also perceived greater job satisfaction and organizational commitment than those who perceived their gender and professional identity as "conflicting and divided" (p. 311). This finding shows that, similar to women in male-dominated jobs, gender expectations challenge men in female-dominated professions. Second, we focused on the relationship between emotional intelligence and transformational leadership. In a recent study of 180 managers, Jimenez (2017) found that emotional intelligence was, in fact, positively correlated with a transformational leadership style. She recommended that organizations, and those experiencing organizational change in particular, would benefit from improving managers' awareness of EI and transformational leadership qualities.

The third theory explained was message design logics, which argues that because people have different beliefs about communication they communicate in notably different ways. Strekalova et al. (2016) employed an MDL framework to analyze nursing students' attempts to provide empathic responses. Expressive responses focused on the "you" pronoun and were more likely to overestimate a patient's health literacy, while nurses using conventional responses reported more "I" statements and indicated more sympathy toward the patient's condition (e.g., *"I'm sorry to hear that"*). Consistent with the MDL approach, nurses using rhetorical messages skillfully combined "I" and "you" statements to suggest that getting well was a joint endeavor.

Finally, we used the interactional perspective to analyze generational differences in the workplace. The axioms of communication highlight how and why miscommunication might occur and ways in which contemporary organizations might need to adapt their communication. In one experimental study of potential job seekers, researchers found that Millennials responded more favorably to job advertisements that specifically touted organizational initiatives to maintain a "psychologically healthy workplace" and that specified actions demonstrating corporate social responsibility (Catano & Hines, 2016). In other words, Millennials preferred organizations that showcased a positive work-life balance, similar to Twenge and Campbell's (2008) research suggesting that modern workplaces need to provide increased flexibility.

KEY TERMS

Agentic qualities   57

Analogic communication   67

Communal qualities   57

Communibiological approach   56

Complementary pattern   67

Content level   66

Conventional logic   63

Descriptive prejudice   58

CASE STUDY 4: CAUGHT IN BETWEEN

Two years out of college, Ashlee Mosteiller had recently joined the internal audit department of a large pharmaceutical company as a junior quality assurance analyst. As a team, these analysts conducted thousands of inspections to ensure that sales representatives complied with federal regulatory guidelines. It was a Monday afternoon, and Ashlee grabbed a seat at the weekly staff meeting. Her boss, Jim, sat at the head of the large conference room table, laptop open, ready to begin. Over the next hour, Jim previewed a new software application that he and a senior analyst, Erin, were implementing to help streamline and standardize the team's daily logging process.

A fit 45-year-old, Jim greeted the team and then jumped right to the point, "Look, we're not all looking into things with the same level of detail. Some of us are checking all voided cards looking for blanks. Others are looking at only a handful. We've gotta our act together." He explained that this type of inconsistency could leave the department open to liability issues and may be a problem in the department's yearly internal audit. "I just want to make sure everybody's on the same page," Jim explained. "Going forward, clean audits will mean a year-end bonus for the team. So, if you have any ideas about what should be included in the process,

let me know. I've set up an intranet thread to post your ideas or you can shoot me an e-mail. Erin and I are heading up this conversion project together so make sure to copy her, too." With that, as he did at each meeting, Jim asked each person at the table for an update and to bring forward any questions or other issues to discuss.

As soon as Ashlee got back to her desk after the meeting, Carol rushed into her cube, visibly angry. "What was THAT all about? Why don't they just replace us with robots! Can you even believe him?" Ashlee felt a twinge of discomfort; she had actually been one of the people who recognized that there was a large discrepancy in the analysts' process. She looked forward to using technology so that the logs were not only more uniform but also faster to process.

Before Ashlee could respond, Carol went on, "Why do we even need a computerized process? Is he really so sure I don't know how to do my own job? I've been in this department for 17 years! I think I know how to do an audit by now. Every day, I speak to senior VPs who are so far above his head, he couldn't even see them! Of course, with him being so short, that's not that difficult! I can't believe this!"

"Here we go again," Ashlee thought silently to herself. Although only a few months into the job, Ashlee had witnessed enough of Carol's vocal complaints to know that if left unchecked, she would go on and on. Ashlee again attempted to speak but was interrupted by Carol's rant, "We really need to discuss this as a team, in person, not over a discussion board and e-mail. I can't believe some smooth-talking GI Joe was hired to be my manager. He's such a phony! I'm supposed to respect his decision making? I can't. I won't. And why did he pick Erin? Probably just to be his little cheerleader. I have more seniority than both of them combined, even if my title doesn't reflect it! Puh-lease! It's a shame you weren't here before Jim got here, Ashlee. John respected us, trusted that we were doing a good job, and left us alone."

Ashlee didn't know how to respond. She shared flexible work space with Carol and didn't want to get on the woman's bad side. At the same time, Ashlee had gotten along well with Jim since he hired her a few months ago. Although she agreed that he could be abrupt at times, Ashlee appreciated his straightforward manner. Jim had been a captain in the U.S. Army, until a few years ago when he retired to civilian life. He came to this company a year ago after being recruited by another former Army vet, Mike, who had known Jim while stationed overseas. Ashlee had spoken privately with Jim a few times about his difficult transition from being in the military. Managing troops was confrontational, aggressive, and swift, unlike this organization, which encouraged a managerial style that seemed more about *how* the job got done than actually getting it done and making sure that employees had opportunities to develop and were satisfied with their positions. Sometimes, even now, Ashlee could tell that he had to stop and think about the "right" way to respond to a situation, instead of responding naturally, perhaps by yelling.

Complicating matters, Ashlee had learned from a coworker that Carol had applied for Jim's job but wasn't chosen. Knowing Mike's Army history with Jim, Ashlee assumed Mike had an interest in bringing in people with a military background to encourage more efficiency and group productivity. Carol, on the other hand, had chalked it up to nepotism via the old boys' club.

Ashlee could not imagine Carol as a manager. An attractive woman in her mid-50s, Carol was always meticulously put together. Twice divorced, Carol had a sarcastic, if caustic, sense of humor that had initially turned Ashlee off. Carol rarely held back from sharing her opinion as if it were the only correct one. Over the past few weeks, however, Ashlee's initial opinion had softened. From chatting with Carol, Ashlee learned that she had endured a lot early in life and, as a result, wasn't able to finish college. Starting as a secretary years before, Carol had slowly worked her way up the ranks, even without a degree. Although she really was good at her job, Ashlee noticed that Carol was rarely commended. Still, Ashlee was learning to take Carol's tirades about Jim with a grain of salt. Everyone else ignored her complaints as well.

Ashlee whispered quietly, so as not to be overheard, "Well, why didn't you raise any of your objections to the process in the meeting when Jim asked for feedback? He said he wanted to hear people's concerns."

"Are you freakin' kidding me?" Carol replied, in her regular speaking voice. "He only says he wants feedback because that's what he learned in some leadership class."

At that moment, Jim walked by on his way to Erin's office. Carol abruptly stopped talking and looked a little guilty. Ashlee sensed the tension, but knowing she had done nothing wrong, just smiled and greeted Jim as usual. She assumed Jim would smile and make a friendly joke as he normally did when he saw Ashlee. Instead, he curtly nodded his head in their direction and snapped, "How about more work and less chit

(Continued)

(Continued)

chat. Carol, when are you going to get me the digital referrals? I gave 'em to you days ago. If you're not comfortable with the technology yet, let me know; I can get Erin to help train you." Carol's face reddened, but she coolly replied, "I'll have them to you by day's end." Jim turned to Ashlee, smiled, and continued on his way.

Ashlee was taken aback; Jim had never spoken to her like he just had to Carol. Ashlee had recently submitted some digital referrals a day late herself, and Jim had reassured her that they were "no big deal, just more form-filling." Ashlee plopped down at her desk and sighed. "I'm staying out of this," she thought. "I'll just be nice to both of them and do my work." Ashlee wasn't planning on making this job her life's work anyway; she just wanted to get some experience in a Fortune 500 company that paid for graduate course credits so she could get her MBA in supply chain management.

Questions for Consideration

1. How might social role stereotypes explain the interaction? Is there any evidence of descriptive or prescriptive prejudices?

2. Discuss the extent to which Jim is able to use emotional intelligence to facilitate transformational leadership. Is he more of a transformational leader or transactional? What evidence do you have?

3. What message design logic does Ashlee rely on? Carol? How about Jim? Using Table 4.2 Forms of Miscommunication Due to MDL, analyze what might have happened between Jim, Carol, and Ashlee.

4. Assess the extent to which the axioms are present in the case. What generational variations might have played a role in the conflict?

5. What ethical dilemmas emerge? How can any of the theories help navigate these ethical issues?

6. Which theory seems to explain the situation better than the others? Why do you believe this to be the case? Are there other theories or a combination of theories that might explain what happened more fully?

Pixabay.com

CHAPTER FIVE

INTERPERSONAL COMMUNICATION

It's difficult to imagine a profession that doesn't require you to interact with other people. You likely use interpersonal communication every day—to handle complaints from a demanding client, to persuade your boss to give you some time off, or to comfort a friend dealing with a difficult relationship. This chapter explains a variety of interpersonal communication theories, including those that explain how relationships are initiated and developed, theories of how relationships are maintained over time, and theories that explain why and what to do when people behave in unexpected ways.

INTERPERSONAL COMMUNICATION DEFINED

Interpersonal communication (IPC) has been defined in many ways. Some scholars define IPC based on the situation and number of participants involved (see Miller, 1978). Using Miller's definition, IPC occurs between two individuals when they are in proximity, are able to provide immediate feedback, and use multiple senses. Others define IPC based on the degree of "personalness," or perceived quality, of a given interaction (see Peters, 1974). In Peters's view, IPC includes communication that is personal and occurring between people who are more than acquaintances. Another view of IPC is a goals approach; that is, IPC includes communication used to define or achieve personal goals through interaction with others (see Canary, Cody, & Manusov, 2008).

For the purpose of examining IPC theory, we argue that IPC encompasses a number of these definitions. IPC includes those messages between two interdependent persons, with a particular focus on how IPC messages are offered to initiate, define, maintain, or further a relationship. IPC is more than just saying a polite hello to the salesclerk in your favorite department store and then scurrying away never to be seen again. Instead, it refers both to the *content* and *quality* of messages relayed and the possibility of further

Learning Objectives

After reading this chapter, you will be able to do the following:

1. Explain the relationship between positive/negative face needs and strategies for engaging in face-threatening acts (FTAs)

2. Make predictions about a relationship's stability and satisfaction using principles of social exchange theory

3. Compare and contrast the central *internal* and *external* dialectics Baxter believes are inherent in close relationships

4. Articulate the complexities associated with information management using Petronio's six principles of privacy management

5. Compare and contrast the major theoretical approaches to interpersonal communication

6. Provide systematic understanding of a professional situation by employing theories of interpersonal communication

relationship development. We present four theories in this chapter critical to current understandings of IPC and the relationships that develop from these communications. First, politeness theory clarifies the strategies individuals use to maintain their "face," or sense of desired public image. Second, social exchange theory (SET) evaluates relationships on the basis of rewards and costs; this ratio of benefits to drawbacks explains whether a relationship will continue as well as whether partners will feel satisfied. Third, the dialectical perspective describes the contradictions individuals inevitably face within their personal relationships and explains how management of these contradictions can predict a relationship's success or failure. Finally, communication privacy management theory builds on these earlier theories and focuses on the decisions we make to reveal or conceal information.

POLITENESS THEORY

Described in Chapter 3, expectancy violations theory (EVT) presents an explanation and specific predictions about what individuals do when others behave in ways that contradict their assumptions—particularly assumptions and preferences for personal space. In a somewhat related vein, politeness theory (PT) explains how and why individuals try to promote, protect, or "save face," especially when embarrassing or shameful situations arise unexpectedly.

Developed by Brown and Levinson (1978, 1987), PT clarifies how we manage our own and others' identities through interaction, in particular, through the use of politeness strategies. Building on Goffman's (1967) notion of identity and facework, Brown and Levinson (1978, 1987) determined when, why, and how interpersonal interaction is constructed through (or in the absence of) politeness.

Assumptions of Politeness Theory

Three primary assumptions guide PT. First, PT assumes all individuals are concerned with maintaining face (Brown & Levinson, 1978, 1987). Simply put, **face** refers to your desired self-image, the identity you wish to present to others. Erving Goffman (1959) first proposed a dramaturgical approach to understand face, arguing that human interaction is akin to the theater. In different "scenes" and with different "actors," we often wear different "masks" either to highlight or deemphasize different aspects of our personality. Goffman wasn't suggesting we're all narcissistic phonies but rather that individuals are selective in revealing different aspects of themselves, in different contexts, and to different audiences. At the law office where she works, for example, Marta might want to project her image as intelligent, competent, and fair. With her young nieces and nephews, however, Marta might want to project the image of a caring and silly aunt who does cartwheels down the sidewalk. And with her new boyfriend, Marta might want to be viewed as caring, trustworthy, and romantic. All of these qualities are part of Marta's identity, but she is thoughtful about what part of her image is highlighted and with whom.

Not only does face refer to the image you want others to have for you, it also includes the recognition that your interactional partners have face needs of their own. Thus, Marta must recognize that her colleagues, family members, and significant other also each have self-images they want to maintain while at work, at home, and at play. Much like a dance, each party must help the other to uphold his or her desired image for face to work. If Marta's colleague, Rich, views her attempts to be seen as intelligent as pretentious and unsubstantiated, then Marta hasn't achieved the face she desires.

There are two dimensions to the concept of face: positive face and negative face (Brown & Levinson, 1978, 1987). **Positive face** includes a person's need to be liked, appreciated, and admired by select persons. Thus, maintaining positive face includes using behaviors to ensure these significant others continue to view you in an affirming fashion. **Negative face** assumes a person's desire to act freely, without constraints or imposition from others. It is difficult to achieve positive and negative face simultaneously— that is, acting in a way so that you gain others' approval often interferes with autonomous and unrestricted behavior.

Second, PT assumes human beings are rational and goal oriented, at least with respect to achieving face needs (Brown & Levinson, 1978, 1987). In other words, you have choices and make communicative decisions to achieve your relational and task-oriented goals within the context of maintaining face. Notably, Brown and Levinson (1978, 1987) posited that face management works best when everyone involved helps maintain the face of others. In other words, because "everyone's face depends on everyone else's [face] being maintained" (Brown & Levinson, 1987, p. 61), it is in your own best interest to make decisions that uphold this mutual, and rather vulnerable, construction of face.

The final assumption, despite the understanding of face as mutually constructed and maintained, is that some behaviors are fundamentally face threatening (Brown & Levinson, 1978, 1987). Inevitably, you will threaten someone else's face, just as another person will, at some point, threaten yours. These **face-threatening acts** (FTAs) include common behaviors such as apologies, compliments, criticisms, requests, and threats (Craig, Tracy, & Spisak, 1993).

PT, then, ties together these assumptions to explain and predict how, when, and where FTAs occur, as well as what individuals can do to restore face once endangered. Discussed next, we clarify strategies used to uphold and reclaim one's own face and present strategies that pertain to maintaining or threatening the face of others.

Preserving Face

As stated earlier, face is the self-image individuals desire to present to others as well as the acknowledgment that others have face needs of their own. To create and maintain this desired self-image, individuals must use **facework**—specific messages that thwart or minimize FTAs (Goffman, 1967). There are two categories of facework strategies related to politeness: preventive and corrective. **Preventive facework** includes communications used to help ourselves or others avoid FTAs (Cupach & Metts, 1994). For example, using disclaimers such as hedging or credentialing, avoiding certain topics, changing the subject, or pretending not to notice an FTA are all preventive facework strategies.

Similar to preventive facework, **corrective facework** consists of messages people use to restore their own face or to help others restore face after an FTA (Cupach & Metts, 1994). Corrective facework includes the use of strategies such as avoidance, humor, apologies, accounts or explanations of inappropriate actions, and physical remediation wherein one attempts to repair any physical damage from the FTA.

As noted earlier, your own face needs may conflict with your partner's face needs. How you manage this discrepancy between self and others' needs may instigate your use of an FTA. As you might imagine, behaving so as to gain others' approval (positive face) can obviously interfere with acting so as to appear self-sufficient and unrestricted (negative face). Sometimes, then, individuals need to choose between positive and negative face needs. Especially when your desire to appear unencumbered outweighs your desire to be liked, you may need to engage in an FTA.

According to PT, individuals can choose one of five suprastrategies when communicating in a manner that could potentially threaten the face of another (Brown & Levinson, 1978). Moving from most polite (and least direct) to least polite (and most direct), these suprastrategies include avoidance, going off-record, negative politeness, positive politeness, and bald-on-record. A speaker who uses **avoidance** simply chooses not to communicate in a way that would create embarrassment or a loss of face for another, whereas when a speaker is going **off-record**, he or she subtly hints of or indirectly mentions the face-threatening topic. Hinting or making indirect suggestions leaves the message open to interpretation, thereby minimizing any face threat. For example, Josephine works as a technician in a veterinary hospital where every fourth weekend she is expected to be on call for emergencies and to make daily rounds, checking in on the animals. If something comes up and Josephine wants to switch her weekend shift with a colleague, she can hint that "it really stinks that I have to work this weekend because my friends invited me to go to the beach for one of those last-minute weekend getaway specials." If Josephine's coworker picks up the hint, he may offer to cover her weekend shift. If the colleague doesn't pick up on her subtlety or doesn't want to work the weekend, he can simply take her disclosure at face value—Josephine wishes she were spending the weekend at a beach resort with friends.

A somewhat more direct approach, **negative politeness** occurs when the speaker makes an effort to recognize the other's negative face needs—that is, the receiver's need of freedom and lack of restraint. With negative politeness, you appeal to the receiver's negative face needs through apologies and self-effacement to make yourself appear vulnerable to the other, while also acknowledging that the FTA is impolite and inhibits the other's independence. For example, when Josephine attempts to get a coworker to cover her weekend shift, she might say, "I am so sorry to ask, but I need a huge favor. I know this is last minute, and I really hate to be such a pain, but could you cover my shift this weekend? I know this is really inconvenient, and I wouldn't ask if it weren't really important." By expressing such regret and making oneself appear self-conscious about committing an FTA, the speaker directly acknowledges the other person's discomfort and potential restriction, while still managing to engage in the FTA for which she claims to be so embarrassed.

An even more direct, yet less polite, strategy is that of **positive politeness**. Using positive politeness, the speaker emphasizes the receiver's need for positive face—that is, the need to be liked or appreciated. By ingratiating the receiver with flattery and compliments, you hope to camouflage your face-threatening behavior. For example, Josephine might attempt to "butter up" her colleague with praises before asking him to cover her weekend shift, saying, "Bill, you're the best coworker I've ever had. I feel like we are not only coworkers but friends. As a friend, would you cover my weekend shift?" Finally, the most direct and least polite strategy is **bald-on-record**. Using this strategy, the communicator makes no attempt to protect the other's face and simply commits the FTA. Continuing Josephine's predicament, then, she might simply demand Bill cover for her, saying, "Bill, I need you to cover my shift this weekend."

According to PT, people choose to engage in FTAs rather tactically. Specifically, there are a number of factors people use to decide how polite to be. These factors are described in Table 5.1. For example, when considering how polite to be, communicators determine whether the person has more or less **prestige** than they do, whether the communicator has **power** over them at the time, and whether what is going to be said runs the **risk** of hurting the other person (Brown & Levinson, 1987).

Each of the strategies for engaging in an FTA has positive and negative consequences. Going off-record to make a request, for example, leaves much room for ambiguity and a high chance the hint will be ignored. Conversely, using the bald-on-record approach will likely get you what you want but may cost you your own positive face in the process. Furthermore, PT predicts that because humans typically commit FTAs to achieve a desired goal (e.g., to obtain weekend shift coverage), individuals will not use strategies that are more polite than necessary because the cost of ambiguity is too great (Brown & Levinson, 1978).

Table 5.1   Factors Influencing Politeness Strategies

Consideration	Prediction
Prestige	If someone has more prestige than you (someone with an impressive title or a great deal of money), you will be more polite. If someone holds little or no prestige over you, you need not be so polite.
Power	If someone has power over you (your boss or even your auto mechanic if your car is not running), you will be more polite. If it is someone with little power over you, you need not be so polite.
Risk	If what you are going to say has a high chance of hurting someone (you are going to fire them or you are going to report that a spouse is cheating), you will be more polite. If it is not likely to hurt, you need not be so polite.

We should also underscore that the very understanding of face, both positive and negative, varies across cultures, within specific relationships, and even among individuals, to some degree. Thus, a person must carefully weigh each decision to commit an FTA, considering the anticipated payoff in relation to the context, culture, and individual communicator characteristics of a potential FTA target.

In brief, PT emphasizes the notion of face. Particularly in embarrassing or inappropriate situations, individuals typically try to balance their own positive and negative face while also attending to the other's face needs. When deliberately committing an FTA, individuals can save face using a variety of strategies.

SOCIAL EXCHANGE THEORY

Social exchange theory (SET) is a broad approach used to explain and predict relationship maintenance. Developed by Thibaut and Kelley (1959), SET clarifies when and why individuals continue and develop some personal relationships while ending others. Additionally, the theory takes into account how satisfied you will be with the relationships you choose to maintain.

As the name of the theory suggests, an exchange approach to social relationships is much like an economic theory based on the comparison of rewards and costs. Thibaut and Kelley's (1959) theory therefore looks at personal relationships in terms of costs versus benefits. What rewards do you receive from a given relationship, and what does it cost you to obtain those rewards? Before making specific predictions, however, certain assumptions must be understood.

Assumptions of SET

Three assumptions guide SET. First, Thibaut and Kelley (1959) argued that personal relationships are a function of comparing benefits gained versus costs to attain those benefits. Second, and intrinsically tied to the first assumption, people want to make the most of the benefits while lessening the costs. This is known as the **minimax principle**. Last, Thibaut and Kelley maintained that, by nature, humans are selfish. Thus, as a human being, you tend to look out for yourself first and foremost. Although these assumptions are sometimes difficult for students and the general public to accept, they become easier to recognize when explained more clearly within the frame of SET's three core components: outcome value, comparison level, and comparison level of alternatives.

Core Components of SET

Three core components make up SET. First, and prefaced in the previous paragraphs, to understand SET, we must acknowledge that social relationships bring both rewards and costs. The outcome of a relationship, therefore, is the ratio of rewards to costs in a given relationship; this can be represented by a simple mathematical equation: Rewards – Costs = Outcome (Thibaut & Kelley, 1959). Relational **rewards** include any benefits you perceive as enjoyable or that help you achieve specific aspirations.

For example, rewards between spouses might include companionship, affection, and sharing a joint savings account. Rewards between colleagues might be social support or task-related assistance. Relational **costs** are those drawbacks we perceive as unpleasant or that prevent us from pursuing or achieving an objective. For example, negotiating holiday visits with the in-laws, losing social independence, and having to put grad school on hold because of family obligations all could be potential costs for a married couple. In a professional setting, putting up with a colleague's endless complaining, having to share space with an untidy office mate, or coping with a perpetual text messenger might be viewed as costly.

What an individual perceives as a reward or cost in a given relationship will, of course, vary. The general idea is that people make mental notes of the rewards and costs associated with their relationships. One hopes the rewards outweigh the costs, resulting in a positive **outcome value**. If an individual perceives the relationship to yield more drawbacks than benefits, however, a negative outcome value will result. But the outcome value itself is not enough to predict whether a person will choose to stay in or leave a relationship. Rather, the outcome value becomes a benchmark used to help measure our relational rewards in comparison to our expectations and alternatives. Once the outcome value of a relationship is determined, individuals can begin to determine satisfaction with and stability of that relationship, as well as the likelihood of its continuing.

The second core element of SET is the **comparison level** (CL). The CL represents the rewards a person expects to receive in a particular relationship (Thibaut & Kelley, 1959). Expectations may be based on models for relationships (e.g., parents, friends), one's own experiences with relationships, television and other media representations of relationships, and the like. The importance of understanding what you expect in a relationship is this: SET maintains that individuals compare their current outcome value with their CL. In other words, if you perceive more rewards than costs in your relationship and this matches or exceeds your expectations for the relationship, SET predicts your satisfaction (Outcome > CL). Conversely, if you perceive more rewards than costs in a current relationship but expected to receive even more rewards than you currently have, a sense of dissatisfaction is predicted (CL > Outcome). Thus, predicting one's satisfaction with a relationship is based on a positive outcome value that also meets or exceeds one's expectations (CL).

The third and final component to SET is the **comparison level of alternatives** (CL_{alt}). Thibaut and Kelley (1959) recognized that simply determining one's satisfaction, or dissatisfaction, with a relationship is still not enough to predict whether the relationship will continue or end. Everyone knows a handful of individuals who are dissatisfied with any one of their personal relationships—whether it is a friendship, marriage, or work partnership—and yet, despite their unhappiness, these individuals remain in that relationship. Why?

SET holds that for any relationship to continue or end, individuals must also examine their CL_{alt} (Thibaut & Kelley, 1959). That is, what are your alternatives to staying in the relationship? Is ending it better or worse than the current situation? Only when you perceive the alternatives to be greater than your outcome and greater than your CL will you end a relationship. Even if satisfied with a current relationship (i.e., Outcome > CL),

Figure 5.1 Predictions Made by Social Exchange Theory

Outcome > Comparison Level (CL) = Satisfied

Outcome < CL = Dissatisfied

Outcome > Comparison Level of Alternatives (CL_{alt}) = Stay

Outcome < CL_{alt} = Terminate

you may perceive that your alternatives are even better, in which case SET predicts you will terminate the relationship (represented mathematically by CL_{alt} > Outcome > CL).

It should be obvious, then, that many scenarios are possible, depending on the perceptions of CL_{alt}—*Outcome*—*CL*. Only when individuals have knowledge of all three elements is it possible to make predictions about the state and status of a relationship. An overview of the specific predictions made is shown in Figure 5.1.

To review, SET explains and predicts an individual's decision to maintain or deescalate a particular relationship. Specifically, people evaluate the rewards and costs associated with remaining in their relationships while also considering their expectations and other alternatives.

DIALECTICAL PERSPECTIVE

The dialectical perspective is also useful for explaining and understanding how individuals sustain interpersonal relationships. Specifically, Baxter and Montgomery (1996; Baxter, 1988) argued that relationships are dynamic; these researchers believe it is impossible for a relationship to maintain a certain level of satisfaction or reach a constant status quo. Much like a spiraling trajectory, people continue to develop their relationships by managing a series of opposing, yet necessary, tensions or contradictions.

Assumptions of the Dialectical Perspective

Four primary assumptions guide a dialectical approach to relationship maintenance: praxis, change, contradiction, and totality (Baxter & Montgomery, 1996). First, **praxis** suggests the development of a relationship is neither linear (always moving forward) nor repetitive (cycling through the same things again and again). Instead, a dialectical perspective assumes relationships can become more intimate or less intimate over time (Canary & Zelley, 2000). Thus, relational partners act and react while their relationship's trajectory spirals—moving forward in time and therefore transforming reality.

Change, or motion, is the second assumption (Baxter, 1988; Baxter & Montgomery, 1996). A dialectical approach presumes the only guarantee in a relationship is that it will change. Viewed this way, it is virtually impossible to "maintain" a relationship because maintenance implies a steady state. Instead, Montgomery (1993) argued that relationships are "sustained," not maintained.

Third, a dialectical approach assumes relationships are grounded in interdependent, yet mutually negating, **contradictions** (Baxter, 1988; Baxter & Montgomery, 1996). Stated differently, within every relationship, both partners have essential, yet opposing, needs. Because these needs counteract each other such that you can't achieve both needs at the same time, ongoing tensions result. For example, spouses need to spend time together to sustain their marriage; on the other hand, both partners need to have some time to themselves, away from their partner and relational obligations. Both togetherness and independence are needed, but you can't have both at the same time. The dialectical perspective maintains that relationships are sustained based on partners' communication used to manage these ever-present contradictions.

The fourth and last assumption, **totality**, emphasizes interdependence between relationship partners (Baxter, 1988; Baxter & Montgomery, 1996). Dialectical approaches recognize that without interdependence a relationship cannot exist. Accordingly, a tension you feel will ultimately affect your relationship partner and vice versa, even if that person didn't initially feel the tension.

When these four assumptions are brought together, we reach a rather complex understanding of relationships. To sustain a relationship, therefore, means the relationship will constantly fluctuate, spiraling forward in time, while relational partners experience and try to satisfy **dialectical tensions**, or interdependent, yet opposing, needs.

Between any two relationship partners (e.g., husband/wife, boss/subordinate, friend/ friend, parent/child), three central tensions are thought to exist: autonomy–connection, openness–closedness, and predictability–novelty (Baxter, 1988). These tensions are known as **internal dialectics** because they exist within a dyad. With each pairing of internal tensions, you can see that each individual in a given relationship needs both elements, yet it is impossible to fulfill both needs simultaneously. The **autonomy–connection** dialectic refers to the tension between the desire to feel bonded to one's partner versus the desire to maintain a sense of independence. Similarly, the **openness–closedness** dialectic includes the pull between wanting to open up and self-disclose while also wanting to maintain one's privacy. Finally, the **predictability–novelty** dialectic is the tension between wanting stability or steadiness while also wanting opportunities for spontaneity. According to the dialectical perspective, then, relational partners continually vacillate between each of these three poles.

For example, Will and Vanessa have been married for 8 years. Both have demanding careers and are raising twin boys. To feel satisfied within this marriage while balancing two careers and a family, Will and Vanessa must make time to spend together. This might mean hiring a babysitter and going to dinner occasionally or making a point of staying up after the boys go to bed to discuss their day. In each case, however, the couple is trying to feel connected. At the same time, Will and Vanessa need to maintain a certain amount of independence, some time to pursue their own hobbies or just some quiet time to meditate or read a book.

It should be obvious that it is difficult, if not impossible, to have togetherness and independence simultaneously, hence the dialectical tension. Furthermore, these tensions become magnified when one partner desires connection while the other needs some autonomy. It is this constant struggle and balancing act that propels a relationship forward.

Just as internal tensions exist between two individuals in a relationship (e.g., between husband and wife), three tensions arise externally between the dyad and other people in their lives (e.g., between a couple and their children or their extended families). These tensions, or **external dialects**, mirror the internal dialectical tensions: inclusion–seclusion, revelation–concealment, and conventionality–uniqueness (Baxter, 1988). The key difference between internal and external tensions is that internal dialectics only involve the competing needs of the two people in the relationship. External dialectics appear when the pair interacts with other people in their lives (e.g., coworkers, friends, other family members). Figure 5.2 provides an illustration.

Again, note that it is both necessary and difficult to satisfy both poles of each contradiction simultaneously. The **inclusion–seclusion** dialectic emphasizes the tension partners as a unit experience when they want to spend time with friends, family, or coworkers versus wanting to spend their time alone together as a couple. The **revelation–concealment** dialectic involves the tension between relationship partners who want to disclose aspects of their relationship to the outside world while also wanting to keep some aspects of their relationship private. Last, the dialectic of **conventionality–uniqueness** emphasizes the tension partners feel between wanting to behave in ways considered normative or traditional versus wanting to emphasize their relationship's distinctiveness by doing something differently. Table 5.2 presents an overview of internal and external dialectics.

Returning to Will and Vanessa, they learn they are pregnant with their third child. Elated but also worried about the complications involved in the early stages of pregnancy, they aren't sure whether they should reveal their good news to their family or if they should wait until the first trimester passes. The struggle between deciding whether to disclose their news to friends and family (revelation) or to keep the pregnancy secret (concealment) until the second trimester is difficult, particularly if one partner wants to reveal and the other wants to conceal.

To manage or sustain a relationship, then, these tensions must be managed. Baxter and Montgomery (1996) identified four primary strategies used to handle the internal and external tensions: selection, cyclic or spiraling alteration, segmentation, and integration. The **selection** strategy involves favoring one pole or need at the expense of the other. For example, a couple who dates over long distance may eventually choose autonomy and break up because the tension between living an independent life versus making time to visit the other partner proves too difficult. Much like children playing on a seesaw, partners who use **cyclic alteration** (sometimes referred to as spiraling alteration) fulfill one pole or need now and shift to fulfill the other pole at a later time, creating a back-and-forth, back-and-forth strategy of coping.

The third strategy, **segmentation**, compartmentalizes the relationship such that certain issues coincide with one pole or need, and other issues are appropriate for the opposite pole. For example, if two close friends agree on mostly everything except for their bitter arguments about politics, a segmentation strategy would allow the friends to choose the closedness pole for politics but the openness pole for everything else. The fourth strategy, **integration**, includes several variations and is predicated on incorporating aspects of both poles so as to create a more fulfilling experience. For example, a couple who wants to integrate novelty and predictability might agree that Friday is date night—every Friday (predictability) they will get a babysitter and try a new restaurant (novelty). Obviously a more sophisticated way of managing relational tensions, integration implies relationship partners have an awareness of the tensions and can talk about them so as to find ways to creatively integrate and manage relational tensions.

All told, dialectics presents a rather complicated view of close relationships. This unwieldy depiction is also why it is a "perspective" and not a more precise theory. Nonetheless, dialectics' emphasis of the changing nature of relationships as well as its understanding of the various contradictions and tensions individuals experience makes it a logical approach to which many can easily relate.

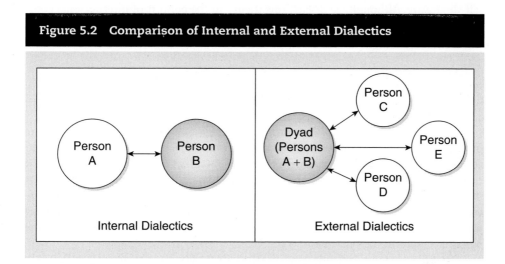

Figure 5.2   Comparison of Internal and External Dialectics

Internal Dialectics	Corresponding External Dialectics
Autonomy–Connection. Desiring some independence but also desiring a union with your partner	*Inclusion–Seclusion.* Desiring to have strong friendship and family networks but also desiring alone time with your partner
Openness–Closedness. Desiring to be completely open and honest but also desiring to have some private thoughts and feelings	*Revelation–Concealment.* Desiring to tell your family and friends relational information but also desiring to have some private information
Predictability–Novelty. Desiring a stable relationship but also desiring some excitement and spontaneity	*Conventionality–Uniqueness.* Desiring to have a traditional relationship but also desiring a unique relationship

Table 5.2   Comparison of Internal and External Dialectics

COMMUNICATION PRIVACY MANAGEMENT THEORY

In many ways, Petronio's (2002) communication privacy management theory (CPM) builds upon each of the three previous theories. Like PT, CPM is concerned with the dilemma of how and what a communicator should say. Like SET, CPM recognizes the power of maximizing rewards and minimizing costs in making decisions. And, like dialectics, CPM recognizes that managing tensions is the central way relationships are sustained. The basic premise of the theory is that people create decision-making rules to help them determine when to reveal and when to conceal private information.

Sandra Petronio developed the theory after 25 years of researching the process of self-disclosure. Although we discuss this theory in the context of interpersonal communication, Petronio views CPM as a macrotheory, as it also can be applied in group and organizational settings. Her theory moves beyond a focus of just self-disclosure to a focus on disclosure in general. Moreover, she argues that disclosure can only be understood in terms of privacy; the two concepts are interdependent.

Principles of CPM

Petronio and Durham (2008) outlined six principles of CPM. The first is the **public--private** dialectical tension. As we just discussed, a dialectical tension refers to competing demands in a relationship. In the case of CPM, the major tension is between revealing and concealing private information. When on a job interview, for example, should you tell the interviewer you had a difficult relationship with your previous supervisor? That might be the honest answer to the question about why you are leaving your present position. But if you reveal the rocky relationship with your boss, will it make the potential employer hesitant to hire you?

The second major principle concerns the nature of **private information** (Petronio & Durham, 2008). Because CPM derives from research into self-disclosure, the theory defines private information as information inaccessible to others. It may be about you, but the information can also be about a team member, a friend, or even about an entire organization. For example, you might have information about a new product under development at your workplace that the company does not want known to competitors. According to Petronio (2002), the central feature of private information is possession. That is, private information is something you own, and because you own it, you have the right to control it. The theory suggests that individuals with private information make decisions about with whom to share information, as well as what they share, when they share it, where they share it, and how they share it.

Next, CPM suggests these decisions about sharing private information are regulated by particular **privacy rules** (Petronio & Durham, 2008). Our decisions about sharing private information are informed by five decision criteria, outlined in Table 5.3. First, privacy rules are developed based on **cultural criteria**. As we discuss in Chapter 6, cultures have varying values, beliefs, and ways of communicating. As such, an individual's culture is likely to influence decisions about what should or should not be revealed. Second, **gender criteria** plays a role in privacy rules. Petronio suggests men and women have been socialized to have differing understandings of disclosure; thus, they may make different decisions when confronted with the tension of whether to share private information. Third, personal variations in **motivational criteria** are used in developing privacy rules. In Chapter 4, we described message design logics (MDLs), which are individual beliefs about the function of communication. Using MDLs as an example, a person with an expressive MDL is likely to be motivated to share more information than would a person with a conventional MDL, simply because of their individual beliefs about the purpose of communication. Of course, **contextual criteria** also influence privacy rules. Team members attending an off-site retreat at a resort might feel more inclined to share private information than would the same team members at a weekly department meeting. Finally, individuals weigh the **risk–benefit criteria** when considering whether they should disclose private information. Much like what was explained by SET, individuals assess potential rewards and costs of disclosure. For example, knowing that, like yourself, a coworker is also an adult child of an alcoholic, you might decide that sharing your own family history with the coworker might have benefits in terms of cohesion and increased understanding that might overshadow any possible risks.

Much like a fence around your home or even that little plastic bar you use to separate your groceries while in the grocery store checkout lane, the fourth principle focuses on **boundaries** (Petronio & Durham, 2008). The metaphor of a boundary is meant to provide a visual representation of two sides; on one side people keep information to themselves, and on the other side people share private information. Personal boundaries are those that contain individual information (e.g., Bob is the only one who knows he was fired from his last job), and collective boundaries are those that contain shared information (e.g., Bob and Carol both know Bob was fired from his last job). Once an individual shares information, the ownership of the information changes, as do the decision rules about privacy. The boundary has shifted, and managing the information becomes more complex.

Building on the notion that multiple people might have to maintain a boundary, the fifth principle of CPM is **boundary coordination**, which refers to the ways collective boundaries are maintained (Petronio & Durham, 2008). Petronio (2002) explains that boundary coordination takes place through boundary linkages, boundary ownership, and boundary permeability. First, **boundary linkages** refer to alliances between the owners of the information. Such alliances might be intentional, as when an individual accused of a crime shares incriminating information with a lawyer. That link is easily maintained because of attorney–client privilege. However, boundary linkages might also be unintentional. Imagine that another individual overhears this confession. The person who has overheard the information is now a part of the alliance. In this case, coordination is likely difficult, as the people in the alliance might have competing risk–benefit rules for disclosure.

Boundary ownership refers to the rights and responsibilities borne by the owners of the information (Petronio, 2002). The clearer the privacy rules are to the shared owners of the information, the more likely the information will be managed consonantly. Thus, when an individual intentionally creates a boundary linkage, she or he is also likely to indicate the rules for disclosure ("Don't tell Harry that I forgot to order the supplies!"). Not surprisingly, the rights and responsibilities are more problematic with unintentional linkages, especially if the individual who shared the information is unaware of the unintended recipient. How many times have you gossiped about someone and realized that someone else may have overheard you? Do you approach the person and say, "please don't repeat this," or do you take the risk that he or she didn't hear what you said?

Boundary permeability refers to how much information is easily passed through the boundary (Petronio, 2002). Some boundaries are permeable (easy to cross), and others may be impregnable (difficult, if not impossible, to cross). To borrow a popular phrase from the classic television series *Seinfeld*, impregnable boundaries are "in the vault." To illustrate, an individual might feel fairly comfortable in disclosing to colleagues what she had for dinner the night before, and other colleagues are likely to reciprocate. This represents a permeable boundary. However, that same individual might be much less comfortable sharing information with colleagues about a disastrous dinner date with another colleague that turned into a romantic fiasco. Of course, when the information is located within a collective boundary, the notion of permeability may be more problematic. This leads to the final principle of CPM.

Petronio (2002) recognized that the management of boundaries is not always a smooth process. Accordingly, she developed the notion of **boundary turbulence**, which occurs when the rules for privacy management are not clear. (Refer to Table 5.3 on privacy rules.) Imagine Lance tells Maggie about a forthcoming merger at work. Lance is a White male who believes information is power, and so his privacy rules dictate keeping this information private. Maggie, on the other hand, is an African-American female who believes people have the right to know about issues that might affect them. Her cultural, gender, and individual motivation criteria lead to a privacy rule that would suggest this information should be shared. In this case, differing privacy rules might cause problems with managing the information. Other causes of boundary turbulence are privacy violations, ethical dilemmas, differing expectations, and misconceptions about ownership.

Table 5.3 Privacy Rule Criteria

Criteria	Example
Cultural	Many African Americans value assertiveness and openness in sharing information.
Gender	In the United States, women are socialized to disclose more than men.
Motivational	Introverts may be less likely to share information than extroverts.
Contextual	Working in a cubicle might make an individual less likely to share information than working in a private office.
Risk–Benefit	In an environment of "don't ask, don't tell," being ambiguous about your sexual orientation might minimize risks.

Taken together, these six principles articulate the complexities associated with information management. The theory "allows us to better understand what individuals disclose, what they keep private, and how private information is handled among people" (Petronio & Durham, 2008, p. 320). CPM provides a detailed analysis of a universal problem: What should (or shouldn't) I say?

SUMMARY AND RESEARCH APPLICATIONS

This chapter provided an overview of four theories of interpersonal communication. PT explains and predicts strategies individuals use to maintain "face," or sense of desired public image. Useful in personal as well as business and educational contexts, PT has explored how supervisors use humor in order to protect employees' face needs (Chefneux, 2015), how employees handle unethical requests from colleagues (Valde, & Miller Henningsen, 2015), and competitive behavior of adult female friends (Dunleavy & Zelley, 2013). SET predicts individuals initiate and maintain relationships so as to maximize personal outcomes; at the same time, however, expectations and alternatives play a role in individuals' ultimate satisfaction and whether they stay in the relationship. Examples of SET include research explaining the various methods employees use to resign from their positions (Klotz & Bolino, 2016) and how managerial coaching is perceived as a reward that influences employee behavior (Kim & Kuo, 2015). The dialectical perspective suggests that sustaining interpersonal relationships requires communication to manage the necessary but contradictory tensions inherent in all relationships. It has been useful in exploring challenges faced by home hospice nurses during end-of-life care (Gilstrap & White, 2015), as well as strategic decision making among top management when launching a new venture (Costanzo & Di Domenico, 2015). Finally, CPM articulates a way of understanding the reasons for, and the challenges associated with, the decision to reveal or conceal private information, such as decisions to share personal health information at work (Westerman, Miller, Reno, & Spates, 2015) or to share otherwise personal information during workplace training (Thory, 2016). One burgeoning area of research is individuals' decisions to share private information on social networking sites (e.g., Romo, Thompson, & Donovan, 2017).

KEY TERMS

Autonomy–connection 85
Avoidance 80
Bald-on-record 81
Boundaries 89
Boundary coordination 89
Boundary linkages 89
Boundary ownership 89
Boundary permeability 90
Boundary turbulence 90
Change 84

Comparison level 83
Comparison level of
  alternatives 83
Contextual criteria 89
Contradictions 85
Conventionality-
  uniqueness 86
Corrective facework 80
Costs 83
Cultural criteria 88

Cyclic alteration (spiraling
  alteration) 86
Dialectical tension 85
External dialectic 86
Face 78
Face-threatening act 79
Facework 79
Gender criteria 88
Inclusion-seclusion 86
Integration 86

CASE STUDY 5: BAD MOVE

Jason was a man with a plan. Immediately after graduating from college, he created his own cleaning company. He started off cleaning houses doing all of the dirty work by himself, but over time, he grew his company to include commercial and retail cleaning, and he employed almost three dozen employees. The business was lucrative, and by the time he was 32, he sold the company for a hefty profit. He knew he wasn't ready to retire, but it was nice to have a chunk of change that allowed him to be picky about his next career move.

Within 6 months, he heard from one of his old fraternity brothers, Seth. Seth had followed the traditional route after college; he got a job with a small firm and spent his time moving from company to company trying to make it up the corporate ladder. By his early 30s, he was fed up and frustrated with corporate life.

"Bro, I am so done with this crap," Seth told Jason. "It's soul sucking. Seriously, every day I go in and do something pointless, not because it should be done, but because some overpaid drone needs to check a box somewhere."

Jason couldn't help but smirk. "That's why I opted out, man. Be your own boss. Then if you have an idiot for a manager, it's your own damn fault."

Seth groaned. "Woulda, shoulda, coulda. I wouldn't even know where to start. How did you even come up with the idea to create your own business?"

"You know me, dude. I'm a nonconformist. I knew that corporate life wasn't for me, so I started thinking about a business with a built-in demand. One look at our old fraternity house, and it became very clear to me," Jason laughed.

"What are you going to do next," Seth asked.

"I dunno. Maybe travel the world and see what strikes my fancy," Jason replied.

"Why don't you come visit me in Tampa? I'll buy you a beer or two and maybe you can lay some wisdom on me."

"It'll take more than two beers, and I am not laying anything on you, but sure, sounds like fun," Jason responded.

A few weeks later, Jason headed down to Tampa, and he and Seth hung out on the beach and brainstormed about business ideas. Over time, Seth became convinced that starting a cleaning company in Tampa made sense—not only were there plenty of homes, stores, and offices that needed to be cleaned, but the area had plenty of hotels that might magnify the business opportunities. Jason wasn't convinced. First, he had been there and done that with the cleaning industry. Second, he suspected that the area was already saturated with cleaning companies because of its reputation as a vacation destination.

Seth, however, had latched on to the idea and wasn't about to let it go. Rather than starting as a "one man show," as Jason had, Seth wanted to start with a full staff. He had the expertise to develop a website and marketing plan, he had a lot of professional contacts, and he wanted to jump into the market with guns blazing. He also wanted Jason to stick around and serve as a consultant to help him to bring the business up to speed. Jason was a bit dubious about it all, but he wasn't actually investing any money into the venture, only time and expertise, and he wanted to help out a friend.

It was a rocky start. They had a few contracts for housecleaning, and they got an office in a strip mall in return for cleaning the other tenants' spaces. They hired four employees on that basis, but since they weren't actually being paid for cleaning the commercial space, there was not much money coming in.

Jason learned that Seth was more of a talker than a doer. He also learned that Seth's "professional contacts" were friends who did not have decision-making authority to hire a cleaning company. Every time Jason tried to schedule a meeting with Seth in order to develop a strategy, Seth would tell him not to worry.

"Bro, it's under control. No worries," he would assure him.

But Jason was frustrated—he wanted to know exactly to whom Seth was talking and what sorts of results he might expect. Seth, however, wasn't willing to share that information. "I'm networking," Seth would say. "The only way to grow this business is networking."

Over time, Jason was spending more and more time in their small office, while Seth was out drumming up business. "How the hell did I end up sitting in an office all day," Jason wondered. "I was

the one who knew that I wasn't an office person, and yet, here I am!"

Things began to come to a head when Jason found out from a mutual friend that Seth was actually out partying with his buddies and not selling their new business idea. Jason immediately called Seth's cell, which went right to voice mail.

"Seth," Jason yelled. "Gimme a call immediately! We really need to talk about this business of yours."

Seth never called back, but the next day he came into the office and sought to reassure Jason.

"Look, Jason, I know things aren't going the way you would like, but I really need you," Seth explained. "Without your expertise, there is no way this can happen. I know you don't need me and my business, but I need you. Please, would you just stick it out for another month? One more month, and you can go back to travelling the world."

Jason had no reason to stick it out other than his friendship with Seth. But Seth seemed ready to work.

"One month," Jason replied. "But that is ONLY if we spend the next few hours mapping out a game plan, which includes who you will be speaking with and what you will be talking about. No more partying with friends. That is NOT how you are going to grow this business."

"Totally," Seth agreed. "Just . . . uh . . . don't tell anyone else that it's only going to be a month, okay? The workers seem to really respect you, and I don't want them to mutiny before we get everything straight."

During the remainder of the day, Seth was focused, and he agreed with all of Jason's suggestions. Jason left at the end of the day satisfied that the business could work, and that he would be out of it in just a few short weeks.

Within a week, however, things went back to the way they had been before. Jason had

(Continued)

(Continued)

prepared the payroll, and he needed Seth to sign the checks. But Seth seemed to disappear for days at a time, leaving Jason to try to explain to the employees why they were not being paid.

The final straw was when the same mutual friend who had informed Jason that Seth was out drinking with buddies contacted him again and told Jason that Seth was bragging that he was "living the dream." According to the mutual friend, Seth gloated that "I've got one guy doing all the work, and he isn't even getting paid, and I've got a bunch of illegals doing the cleaning, so they can't complain if they don't get paid!"

Jason paid the employees out of his own pocket, went back to his hotel and packed his belongings, and left Florida. The next day, Jason started getting voice mails and texts from Seth. Jason tapped Seth's number, then tapped "block caller" on his phone.

Questions for Consideration

1. What politeness strategies did Jason use with Seth? What politeness strategies did Seth use with Jason? Use politeness theory to explain why or why not these were appropriate.

2. Using social exchange theory, consider the friendship between Seth and Jason. Identify the rewards and costs for each person. Using the concepts of comparison level and comparison level of alternatives, why did Jason end the friendship?

3. Identify any internal and external dialectics that appear in the story. What strategies were used to manage these tensions? What strategies might have been better?

4. What private information and privacy rules exist in this story? How was boundary coordination used by the various characters? Did anyone violate boundary ownership? If so, who, and how did they do so?

5. What ethical issues emerge from this case? How might insight from any of the theories help navigate these challenges?

6. Do any of the interpersonal communication theories provide a better explanation than the others? Why do you believe this to be the case? What additional factors might have been included to make a different theory or combination of theories better at explaining the situation?

CULTURE

Although a beloved icon in the United States, the Walt Disney Company opened Euro Disney in 1992 (renamed Disneyland Paris in 1995) to widespread criticism. The company was taken to task for cultural imperialism; the French press, in particular, accused the company of mass producing American values and replacing European customs and traditions with American consumer culture (Forman, 1998). For the first several years, the park was considered a flop. Yet by 2008, there were over 15 million visitors annually, and in 2013, the resort was listed as France's number-one tourist attraction, surpassing the Eiffel Tower and the Louvre (Frommer's, 2013). What explains the turnaround? Jay Rasulo, former Euro Disney CEO and current chairman of Walt Disney Parks and Resorts, asserted that the newfound success required intercultural awareness: "When we first launched, there was the belief that it was enough to be Disney. Now we realize that our guests need to be welcomed on the basis of their own culture and travel habits" (Prada & Orwall, 2002, p. A12). Retail giant Walmart faced similar difficulties when it tried expanding to Germany, South Korea, and Japan. However, failure to pay attention to culture and local business practices wound up costing the company hundreds of millions of dollars. In Japan, for example, low prices are associated with cheap quality, so the "Every Day Low Prices" slogan actually deterred discerning shoppers (Holstein, 2007). E-commerce giant eBay has also struggled with culturally differences. In China, for instance, building emotional trust between buyers and sellers is the most critical part of the transaction, even more so than price (Gaussorgues, 2014). Whereas eBay's platform provides a rating system for users to give feedback, that isn't enough of an exchange to build trust in China. Instead, they prefer to shop on sites with synchronous chat applications that facilitate negotiations between sellers and customers (like Alibaba's Taobao).

Learning Objectives

After reading this chapter, you will be able to do the following:

1. Explain and identify examples for each of Hofstede's five primary cultural dimensions

2. Discuss the process of accommodation through convergence or divergence

3. Explain how the threshold for anxiety and uncertainty can either impair or motivate communication

4. Predict intercultural conflict due to cultural differences in conflict management

5. Compare and contrast major theoretical approaches to intercultural communication

6. Provide systematic understanding of a professional situation by applying theories of intercultural communication

Understanding the dynamics of cross-cultural and intercultural communication is critical in today's multicultural society and global economy (Ting-Toomey, 1992). Within the United States, multicultural communities continue to expand and flourish. Privately, international travel is relatively easy and common; in the corporate sector, global competition and cooperation is the norm. Although the proliferation of cross-cultural and intercultural communication is probably not new to you, the implications of, difficulties with, and strategies for improving these exchanges is profound, particularly considering the high failure rate of such interaction.

CULTURE DEFINED

Recognizing the diversity of today's personal and professional landscape is one thing, but what exactly is culture? We embrace Collier's (1989) notion of **culture** as one's identification with and acceptance into a group that shares symbols, meanings, experiences, and behavior. Cross-cultural communication and intercultural communication expand on this notion. **Cross-cultural communication** is the comparison of two or more cultural communities (Ting-Toomey, 1991a); for example, comparing conflict styles of U.S. managers with those of Korean managers. Somewhat differently, **intercultural communication** involves the actual interaction between members of different cultures; for instance, examining what happens when a German executive reprimands a Chinese subordinate.

Using these definitions, we have selected four theories that examine broadly defined notions of culture and emphasize how culture shapes and is shaped by communication. First, Hofstede's cultural dimensions provide a typology useful for assessing cultural differences across social contexts. Next, we look at communication accommodation theory as a way of predicting when individuals will or should adapt to or diverge from another cultural group. Third, we consider anxiety/uncertainty management theory. Finally, face-negotiation theory addresses how cultural differences with face influence conflict management.

HOFSTEDE'S CULTURAL DIMENSIONS

Geert Hofstede is a Dutch management researcher who developed an inductive theory of culture. Specifically, he gathered statistical data from 100,000 employees of IBM around the world to determine the values on which cultures vary (Hofstede, 1980). In the process, he surveyed workers from 50 countries and three regions. His analysis resulted in five dimensions with which to differentiate and rank cultures (Hofstede, 1980; Hofstede, 1991; Hofstede & Bond, 1984). Each dimension is described as a continuum, with distinct cultures classified somewhere along the continuum.

Individualism–Collectivism

Hofstede's (1980) first dimension is individualism–collectivism. This dimension addresses how people define themselves and their relationships with others. Cultures that fall on the **individualism** side of the continuum share four characteristics (Triandis, 1995). First, such cultures consider the individual to be the most important entity in any social setting. Think about some common phrases you have heard in the United States (a highly individualistic culture). When asked to do something beyond one's responsibilities, an American is likely to ask, "What's in it for me?" In explaining why an individual is ending a romantic relationship, the person might say, "I was putting more into it than I was getting out of it." In short, in individualistic cultures, the focus is on the self before all other relationships.

Second, individualistic cultures stress independence rather than dependence (Triandis, 1995). Recall the description of face needs in Chapter 5. Positive face is the desire to be appreciated and liked. Negative face is the desire to be free from impositions. Ting-Toomey (1988) argued that people from individualistic cultures tend to place relatively more emphasis on negative face needs compared with individuals from collectivistic cultures; there is a cultural preference to be free from imposition, which is in essence a desire to be independent.

Third, individualistic cultures reward individual achievement (Triandis, 1995). To illustrate, U.S. organizations frequently use merit pay and employee recognition programs. These programs focus on recognizing particular individuals and their performance, raising them above other employees in the organization. Likewise, individual achievement tends to accompany the value of competition. In individualistic cultures, competition is viewed as a good thing. This is not always the case in collectivistic cultures.

Finally, individualistic cultures value each individual's uniqueness (Triandis, 1995). In such cultures, standing out from the crowd is highly valued, whereas in collectivistic cultures, standing out from others is a source of embarrassment. Consider the variations in two cultural proverbs (Mieder, 1986). The American proverb "the squeaky wheel gets the grease" implies you will receive rewards by distinguishing yourself from others; you ought to speak up and be noticed. The Japanese proverb "the tallest nail gets hammered down" implies punishment is associated with being different—you are better off being the same as others.

Thus far we have talked at length about individualism but have not addressed collectivism in detail. **Collectivism** refers to a social system based on in-groups and out-groups. In collectivistic cultures, groups (relatives, clans, organizations) are the central way of understanding relations between people; identity is understood solely through group membership.

There are also four characteristics associated with collectivism (Triandis, 1995). First, in collectivistic cultures the views, needs, and goals of the group are more important than any individual views, needs, or goals. For many Americans, the idea of kamikaze pilots or suicide bombers makes no sense. Yet, in collectivistic cultures, the needs of the group supersede the needs of the individual. In these sorts of systems, dying for the good of a group makes sense.

Second, obligation to the group is the norm in collectivistic cultures; behavior is guided by duty, not by individual pleasure or rewards (Triandis, 1995). This focus on duty over pleasure is apparent in mate selection. In individualistic cultures, people are "free" to marry the mate of their choice. In collectivistic cultures, acceptance of the potential mate by the family is of central importance (Dion & Dion, 1993).

Third, in collectivistic cultures, the self is defined in relation to others, not as distinct from others (Triandis, 1995). Jandt's (2004) example best illustrates this point. Imagine a person from Colombia (a more collectivistic culture) coming to the United States. In the United States, a common question for the visitor would be "What do you do for a living?" because Americans are understood by their individual accomplishments. In Colombia, however, the first question asked of this same person would likely be "Who are you related to?" Knowing a person's "connections" enables strangers to place that person into particular groups; knowing where a person comes from is the same as knowing who that person is.

Fourth and finally, those from collectivistic cultures focus on cooperation rather than competition (Triandis, 1995). This characteristic manifests in particular communication patterns in collectivistic cultures. Collectivistic cultures tend to use a **high-context communication** style (Hall, 1976). A high-context message privileges relational harmony over clarity or directness; messages tend to be indirect, circular, or unspoken so as not to offend. It is assumed the receiver will actively seek to understand what is really meant. By contrast, a **low-context communication** style, characteristic of individualistic cultures, values direct, explicit expression of ideas. In low-context communication, the meaning is in the message, and sometimes "the truth hurts."

We have presented a number of details unique to individualism and collectivism, but individualism and collectivism exist together in all cultures—they are, in essence, two sides of the same coin. Certain cultures, however, tend to operate at one end of the continuum or the other. We turn next to the second dimension of culture as described by Hofstede (1980), uncertainty avoidance.

Uncertainty Avoidance

We talked about the concept of **uncertainty** in Chapter 3. As a cultural dimension, **uncertainty avoidance** refers to the extent to which "people within a culture are made nervous by situations which they perceive as unstructured, unclear, or unpredictable" (Hofstede, 1986, p. 308). Those cultures that seek to avoid ambiguity are known as high-uncertainty-avoidance cultures. Typically, cultures high in uncertainty avoidance maintain strict codes of behavior and support a belief in absolute truths. For instance, in high-uncertainty-avoidance cultures, the workplace is typified by rules, precision, and punctuality (Jandt, 2004). The preference for a business meeting would be a structured agenda, which would be rigidly followed (Lewis, 2000).

Cultures low in uncertainty avoidance tend to accept ambiguity and lack of structure more easily (Hofstede, 1986). Individuals in low-uncertainty-avoidance cultures are more inclined to take risks, innovate, and value "thinking outside of the box." Clearly, American culture is a low-uncertainty-avoidance culture. In the workplace, individuals from low-uncertainty-avoidance cultures tend to work hard only when needed (Jandt, 2004). Rules are often rejected or ignored, and punctuality has to be taught and reinforced.

Power Distance

The third dimension uncovered by Hofstede (1980) is power distance, or the extent to which people with little power in society consider inequity normal and acceptable. Cultures with **high power distance** accept power as a scarce resource; power differences are natural and inevitable. In these sorts of cultures, there is greater centralization of power and a great importance placed on status and rank. In the workplace, high-power-distance cultures tend to have a large number of supervisors, a rigid system that classifies each job along a hierarchy, and decision making only among those at the high end of the hierarchy (Adler, 1997). There also tends to be a wide salary gap between those high and low in the hierarchy (Jandt, 2004).

Cultures with **low power distance** value the minimization of power differences (Hofstede, 1980). Although hierarchy might exist, people higher in the hierarchy are not assumed to be superior to people lower in the hierarchy; people at all levels reach out to people at all other levels. Moreover, people lower in power believe that through motivation and hard work they can achieve power (Hofstede, 1980). In the workplace, low-power-distance cultures view shared decision making with subordinates as empowering (Jandt, 2004).

The United States falls on the lower end of this power distance spectrum but is not extremely low. A pervasive management style in the United States is that of "status-achievement," meaning status can be earned "via hard work, personal ambition, and competitiveness . . . and displayed effectively and proudly (e.g., by driving expensive cars or having the spacious corner office)" (Ting-Toomey, 2005, p. 75). And when you consider the following statistics, it appears the United States is becoming increasingly higher in power distance. According to 2013 Bloomberg financial data, CEO salary for Fortune 500 CEOs had increased 1,000% since 1950 (Smith & Kuntz, 2013). In 1980, the average salary of a CEO was 42 times that of the average worker. After the "great recession" and stock market collapse of 2008–2009, CEO salaries took a dive but quickly bounced back. By 2015, top CEOs made 300 times as much as the average worker (Mishel & Davis, 2015). These figures mirror statistics indicating the difference between the "haves" and "have-nots" is growing in the United States; the rich are growing richer, and the poor are not sharing the wealth. The extent to which American citizens believe this power differential is acceptable and normative demonstrates an acceptance of increasingly higher power distance.

Masculinity–Femininity

Hofstede's (1980) fourth dimension focuses on the relationship between biological sex and what is considered sex-appropriate behavior. **Masculine cultures** use the reality of biological sex in the creation of distinct roles for men and women. In masculine cultures, men are expected to be assertive, ambitious, and competitive; women are expected to be supportive, nurturing, and deferent. Translating these values to the workplace, countries with a masculine orientation believe managers are supposed to be decisive and assertive (Jandt, 2004). More important, women have a difficult time achieving workplace equality; they are given lower wages, less stable work, and few opportunities to advance (Kim, 2001).

The United States is a masculine country. Although women are making inroads in organizational life, there is still a significant wage gap (Brown & Patton, 2017), and the glass ceiling remains a reality (Ezzedeen, Budworth, & Baker, 2015). Moreover, women are often expected to conform to masculine norms if they hope to succeed at work (Brands, 2015).

By contrast, **feminine cultures** have fewer rigid roles for behavior based on biological sex (Hofstede, 1980). Men and women are equally permitted to be assertive or deferent, competitive or nurturing. Instead of rigid sex roles, the focus in feminine cultures tends to be on the facilitation of interpersonal relationships and concern for the weak (Jandt, 2004). In the workplace, feminine cultures manifest consensus seeking and a preference for quality of life over material success. To illustrate, consider Sweden, a highly feminine culture. In Sweden, the law allows both men and women to balance parenthood and employment. At the birth or adoption of a child, parents are jointly eligible for 480 days of paid, child-rearing leave ("Gender Equality in Sweden," 2013).

Long-Term and Short-Term Orientation

Hofstede's (1980) original research stopped after the first four dimensions. Responding to accusations of a Western bias to his work, Hofstede collected additional data with the assistance of Chinese scholars and ultimately added a fifth cultural dimension. Grounded in Confucian thinking, Hofstede (1991, 2001) called this dimension the orientation toward long term versus short term. A **long-term orientation** is associated with thrift, savings, perseverance, and the willingness to subordinate one's self to achieve a goal. In cultures with a long-term orientation, employees typically have a strong work ethic and keep their eyes toward the achievement of distant goals (Hofstede, 2001). A **short-term orientation** centers on a desire for immediate gratification. Individuals in these cultures tend to spend money to "keep up with the Joneses" and prefer quick results to long-term gain (Hofstede, 2001). Employees seek immediate pay and benefits and are less willing to sacrifice in the short run to achieve in the long run.

Dimensions Combined

Table 6.1 plots eight countries or regions on each of the five dimensions (Hofstede, 2001). Note that just because two countries are similar in one dimension does not mean they will be similar in another. Moreover, recognize that the rankings described are generalizations about each culture; it should come as no surprise that individual variations exist within each culture. Finally, in many countries, including the United States, different groups in the same culture might rank quite differently within a given dimension. For example, although the dominant U.S. culture is individualistic, researchers believe that African Americans and Hispanics tend more toward collectivism (e.g., Hecht, Collier, & Ribeau, 1993).

Table 6.1   Rankings of Select Countries or Regions on Hofstede's Dimensions

	Individualism–Collectivism	Uncertainty Avoidance	Power Distance	Masculinity–Femininity	Long-Term and Short-Term
Arab countries	Both	Moderate	High	Moderate masculinity	Not available
Italy	High individualism	Moderate	Moderate	Extreme masculinity	Short term
Japan	Both	Extremely high	Moderate	Extreme masculinity	Long term
Mexico	Moderate collectivism	High	High	Extreme masculinity	Not available
South Korea	High collectivism	High	Moderate	Moderate femininity	Long term
Sweden	Moderate individualism	Extremely low	Very low	Extreme femininity	Both
United States	Extreme individualism	Low	Moderate	High masculinity	Short term
Venezuela	Extreme collectivism	Moderate	High	Extreme masculinity	Not available

COMMUNICATION ACCOMMODATION THEORY

Have you ever caught yourself slipping into a southern drawl or using *y'all* while speaking to a native Texan? Maybe you have found yourself speaking in fast, clipped tones when talking with a New Yorker, or upon returning from a European vacation, friends point out that you suddenly sound more like Kate Middleton than Kate Hudson. Do you speed up while talking with some colleagues but slow your speech when speaking with others? Communication accommodation theory (CAT) can explain many of the changes in your speech and language use.

Originally conceived as speech accommodation theory (Giles, Mulac, Bradac, & Johnson, 1987) and later refined as communication accommodation theory (Giles & Coupland, 1991), CAT provides an informative platform from which to understand how and why we adapt our communication when we interact with others. Essentially, Giles and colleagues argue that when interacting with others, individuals will accommodate their speech and language patterns, either by matching their partners' speech or by differentiating their speech and language use. In this section, we explain Giles and colleagues' notion of accommodation through both convergence and divergence.

Communicating Social Identity Through In-Groups and Out-Groups

Giles and Coupland (1991) assumed individuals belong to a wide variety of social groups based on ethnicity, gender, race, and religion. Moreover, they maintained that these groups shape each person's collective identity. For example, "most ethnic minority groups in the United States have tended to form communities, however small, where they have other people of similar heritage to sustain their ethnic values, socialization practices, and culture" (Vivero & Jenkins, 1999, p. 9). Similarly, your marital status (e.g., married), your political alignment (e.g., Republican), your career (e.g., public relations director), and your ethnicity (e.g., Irish American) all represent social groups that influence the way you perceive yourself and others perceive you.

Like it or not, human beings categorize information to simplify and create understanding. One way in which we commonly categorize others and ourselves is through these social identity groups; these clusters are divided into in-groups and out-groups. **In-groups** are social affiliations to which an individual feels he or she belongs (Giles & Coupland, 1991). **Out-groups** are those social affiliations to which a person feels he or she does not belong. In the workplace, for example, you may go to happy hour with members from your team or department but would feel out of place socializing with members of another department. Similarly, if you play on a company softball league, your teammates may become an in-group, even if you had not interacted previously.

In-groups and out-groups are important for understanding CAT. According to Giles and Coupland (1991), language, speech, and nonverbal messages all communicate one's in-group and out-group status. For example, if you have been around a group of teenagers recently, you may feel very much part of the out-group because your poor command of slang (language) and lack of body piercings (nonverbal artifacts) clearly differentiate you from them. When your teenage son mumbles, "NONYA," in response to your simple question of "Where are you going tonight?" he has differentiated himself (a hip teen) from you (a stodgy middle-aged parent). Instead of simply saying, "It's none of your business," his use of Twitter slang leaves you wondering what the heck he is talking about, thereby creating a gap between his generation and yours.

The use of slang to create in-group and out-group status applies to the workplace as well. Each profession has its own set of jargon, or specialized language that not only gives precision to words and meanings but also helps create and maintain a distinct in-group. Thus, jargon includes those individuals who have similar training and experience and excludes everyone else. A member of your company's information technology (IT) department may use computer jargon that intimidates the nontechnology minded. For instance, when Karen calls her company's IT department with a question about a problem she is having with a website password, the help desk manager asks her, "What's your ISP?" Karen has no idea what an ISP is, much less which one she is using. In this instance, the help desk manager may use the jargon unintentionally when communicating with out-group members such as Karen and employees from other departments simply out of habit. Conversely, the manager may intentionally rely on jargon so as to intimidate the out-group members or to promote one's own credibility. Because she doesn't know what her ISP is, Karen may feel inferior, or she may perceive the help desk manager as possessing complex and invaluable information. Karen may even feel frustrated or annoyed because members of the help desk can't seem to explain things in plain English. Importantly, then, jargon is both inclusive and exclusive and should be used cautiously with out-group members.

Accommodation Through Convergence or Divergence

Individuals regulate their speech and conversational patterns either in an effort to assimilate with or to deviate from others (Giles & Coupland, 1991). And as Giles and Gasiorek (2014) argue, this ability to adjust "is a fundamental part of successful interaction" (p. 155). When a person wants to be viewed as part of an in-group, CAT predicts this person will accommodate by **convergence**. That is, you will alter your speech and behavior so that it matches that of your conversational partner. Speech includes word choice, pronunciation, pitch, rate, and even gestures such as smiling and gaze. For instance, elementary school teachers often converge their speech, using more expressive registers, slower speaking rates, and shorter words or phrases to accommodate their young pupils. When individuals match their speech, they convey acceptance and understanding. Interpersonal attraction also leads to convergence (Giles et al., 1987). That is, the more a person is likable, charismatic, and socially skilled, the more likely you are to try to match his or her communication patterns.

Conversely, there are times when individuals don't want to be associated with a certain group or do not find a person interpersonally attractive; sometimes you want to differentiate yourself from a particular crowd. In this instance, you will alter your speech through **divergence**. Rather than match your partner's communication patterns, you will seek to make your speech different. Deliberately diverging from the speech of your partner signals disagreement or rejection. A kindergarten teacher may use a more stern tone when disciplining the class for misbehavior. Similarly, you may overhear your 16-year-old neighbor conversing in strings of expletives with her friends simply as a way of countering adult authority. In addition to expressing disagreement or rejection of a speaker, divergence also illustrates one's cultural identity (e.g., maintaining a Scottish accent despite living in the United States) or differences in one's status (e.g., a physician's use of elaborate medical terminology when talking with a patient).

Extending the Theory: Maintenance and Nonaccommodation

Convergence and divergence are not the only options for approaching in-group/out-group interaction. Extending the theory, Giles and colleagues advanced two additional ways of managing, or failing to manage, such interactions (Giles, Willemyn, Gallois & Anderson, 2007). Maintenance simply is the absence of adjustment. Perhaps the out-group member is unaware of the perceived social distance between himself or herself and the in-group. Or maybe the out-group member doesn't care or isn't able to make the adjustment. Somewhat different, **nonaccommodation** includes over- and underaccommodation—that is too much or too little adjustment to make a successful interaction. Much like Goldilocks who had to try three of everything to get it "just right," attempting to regulate one's interaction in real time, just enough to show social affiliation or be understood can be challenging. Importantly, Giles and Gasiorek (2014) remind us that nonaccommodation is a subjective evaluation. You may appreciate a physician's attempt to simplify vocabulary while your friend may view it as condescending. In the first case, the physician's attempt to simplify vocabulary is viewed as convergence, but in the second case, it is viewed as overaccommodation.

Who Accommodates to Whom?

It is worthy to note differences in **accommodation** across groups because these differences say a great deal about the importance of perceived status, authority, and cultural and social identity within our multicultural society. In her review of research, Larkey (1996) reported that when looking at race, ethnicity, and sex in the workplace, Euro American male employees typically maintain; that is, they maintain their communicative style regardless of conversational partner because it is commonly defined as the "standard" in both the United States and much of Europe.

Conversely, minority employees (including women and members of racial and ethnic minorities) typically are expected to converge to this "standard" to achieve status within the organization. Persistent convergence may create cognitive dissonance for minority members by placing them in a dilemma; maintaining their cultural and social identity is sacrificed when using the mainstream speech patterns that are expected and rewarded.

Pitfalls of Accommodation

Notably, accommodation is not always appropriate or effective (Giles & Coupland, 1991). When in doubt, individuals rely on social norms to inform their decision to

Table 6.2 Consequences of Accommodation

	Positive Effects	Negative Effects
Convergence	Increased attraction; social approval; increased persuasion	Incorrect stereotypes of out-group; perceived condescension; loss of personal identity
Maintenance	Upholds personal identity	Apparent lack of interest or effort; perceived as overly rigid
Divergence	Asserts power differences; increased sympathy	Perceived disdain for out-group; increased psychological distance

accommodate or not. Norms are implicit expectations that guide social behavior; thus, we must rely on our perceptions of social appropriateness when determining whether to converge or diverge. Table 6.2 provides some consequences of accommodation. Note both positive and negative consequences for both types of accommodation.

Accommodation and Leader-Member Exchange

The notion of accommodation has many practical implications. One particular link might be made between the notion of accommodation and a theory called leader–member exchange (LMX). Developed by Graen and associates (Dansereau, Graen, & Haga, 1975; Graen & Uhl-Bien, 1995), LMX theory recognizes that leadership consists of an interpersonal relationship between a superior and a subordinate and that not all relationships are created equally; within organizations there are also in-groups and out-groups. Because of limited time and resources, supervisors cannot exert the same amount of energy with every employee. Accordingly, relationships between superiors and subordinates can be placed on a continuum. At one end are **leader–member exchange** relationships. LMX relationships, considered to be in-group relationships, are characterized by mutual trust, social support, and liking. There is much more interaction between organizational members in an LMX relationship than in other types.

At the other end of the continuum are **supervisory exchange** relationships (SX relationships). Interaction between the supervisor and subordinate is defined entirely by the roles they perform and the contractual obligations provided by the organization. In short, SX relationships are out-group relationships; they are impersonal, with little superior–subordinate interaction taking place.

At the midpoint of the continuum are middle-group relationships. Not surprisingly, these relationships involve elements of both LMX and SX relationships. Interaction is often impersonal, but there are occasional provisions of social support. Moderate amounts of trust and liking occur between the supervisor and the subordinate. Individuals in the middle-group are often aware they are not in the in-group, however.

The practical implications of these varying types of relationships are profound in terms of organizational outcomes. LMX relationships are associated with higher employee job satisfaction, greater satisfaction with the manager, and higher organizational commitment (Nystrom, 1990; Vecchio, Griffeth, & Hom, 1986). Subordinates in these types of relationships also evidence more innovative behaviors and greater organizational citizenship (e.g., helping others with heavy workloads, providing assistance without being asked, listening to the problems of others, and going out of their way to assist new employees). The converse is also true (Manzoni & Barsoux, 2002). Those who have SX relationships with their supervisors report lower job satisfaction, less satisfaction with their managers, and decreased organizational commitment, and they engage in more nonconforming behaviors (e.g., taking undeserved breaks, being absent without notifying others, spending time on personal conversations, violating company rules, and complaining).

Obviously, LMX relationships are beneficial to an organization. What determines the type of relationship that will develop between any given manager and employee? Research points consistently to two factors. First, simple **liking** tends to have an impact.

Dockery and Steiner (1990) found that liking was most associated with perceived similarity; the more perceived similarity between the manager and the employee, the more likely an LMX relationship. Accordingly, perceived similarity in terms of attitudes about family, money, career, strategies, goals, and education is beneficial to LMX relationships. Such attitudinal similarity is more important than demographic similarity (e.g., age, sex, race). Linking CAT to the development of an LMX relationship, one simple way an employee can develop an LMX relationship with his or her supervisor is to converge with him or her.

Second, performance has an impact. But the causal route on performance isn't clear; does high employee performance lead to an LMX relationship, or does an LMX relationship lead to high employee performance? Both explanations make sense; it is likely that high-performing individuals will receive more trust and respect from their supervisor, but it is also true that people given trust and respect might perform at higher levels. Nevertheless, it seems that when a supervisor perceives an employee as highly skilled, the supervisor is more likely to develop a leader–member exchange relationship. Unfortunately, the link between LMX relationships and performance is not as clean as researchers might like. One study found that poorly performing employees who were in the in-group still received high-performance ratings regardless of their actual performance, whereas the ratings of out-group employees were more consistent with actual performance (Duarte, Goodson, & Klich, 1993). More recently, researchers (Dunegan, Uhl-Bien, Duchon, 2002) found that certain contingencies, such as intrinsic task satisfaction, high task ambiguity and low conflict, improve the LMX/performance link.

All told, CAT explains and predicts the experience of convergence and divergence in interpersonal communication. The more we like a person or perceive ourselves as part of an in-group, the more likely we are to adapt and match our speech patterns. The more we want to communicate our difference, status, or unique cultural identity, the more likely we are to differentiate our speech from our partner's. Communicators must be aware, however, that accommodation is not always effective or well received and can have implications for workplace relationships.

ANXIETY/UNCERTAINTY MANAGEMENT THEORY

The third culture-based theory featured in this chapter is anxiety/uncertainty management theory (AUM). Developed and refined by William Gudykunst (1985, 1993, 1995, 2005) and clearly influenced by uncertainty reduction theory (see Chapter 3), AUM predicts that communication effectiveness and intercultural adjustment is a combined result of reducing intercultural anxiety and uncertainty. The key difference between uncertainty reduction theory and anxiety/uncertainty management theory is context. Whereas URT focuses on interpersonal encounters, AUM focuses on intercultural (or intergroup) encounters wherein people from different cultural backgrounds interact. Specifically, AUM posits that mindful awareness of intercultural anxiety and uncertainty motivates intergroup participants to manage the reduction of this apprehension. Developed over nearly 2 decades and still a work in progress, the theory employs 47 axioms and numerous theorems. In this section, we present AUM's key principles and predictions, while recognizing that our summary is a simplified version of Gudykunst's theory.

Although AUM has undergone many refinements over the last 3 decades, one central assumption is that at least one person in an intercultural encounter is a **stranger** (Gudykunst, 2005). Similar to the notion of in-groups and out-groups as discussed with communication accommodation theory, AUM theory views cultural strangers as out-group members, while the cultural natives are in-group members. You don't have to be in a foreign country to experience feeling like a stranger. Moving from a suburban subdivision to an urban neighborhood, shopping for specialty meats or herbs in an ethnic market, leaving the military to join a civilian lifestyle, or ordering custom furniture from an Amish carpenter might all be examples of feeling like a stranger in a strange land.

A second assumption of AUM theory is that when a stranger interacts with a cultural in-group member, uncertainty and anxiety abound. Although related, uncertainty and anxiety are distinct concepts according to AUM. Congruent with uncertainty reduction theory, AUM theory maintains that cognitive uncertainty leaves individuals unable to explain or predict their own or their partners' behavior in intercultural situations (Gudykunst, 1993). Gudykunst assumed strangers and in-group members always feel some degree of uncertainty when faced with a new interpersonal, intergroup situation. Different from uncertainty reduction theory, however, AUM argues that when the exchange is between people of different groups or cultures, individuals become hypersensitive to cultural differences.

Not all uncertainty is damaging. Gudykunst (1993) reported that individuals vary in their minimum and maximum thresholds for uncertainty. Too much uncertainty will leave you unable to make useful predictions about your partner's behavior, while too little uncertainty leads to overconfidence and opens the door for misinterpretations. If you can appropriately discern and reduce your uncertainty about your interaction partner's behavior, however, you've successfully achieved **attributional confidence** (Gudykunst & Hammer, 1988). Think of an uncertainty threshold like job stress; too much stress leaves the employee feeling overwhelmed and powerless, while too little stress leads to a lack of effort and boredom. However, the right amount of stress (termed *eustress*) motivates the employee to perform to his or capability.

In addition to uncertainty about why and how intergroup partners will act, **anxiety** is also present in intercultural encounters. Related to but distinct from uncertainty, anxiety refers to an emotional state of apprehension, worry, or fear of negative consequences (Gudykunst & Hammer, 1988). For example, anxiety may become magnified in an intercultural interaction because in-group members don't want to appear to be biased or prejudiced against cultural strangers. As with uncertainty, anxiety also operates with a threshold of minimum and maximum limits. Too much apprehension about interactions with cultural strangers leads to a reliance on stereotypes; in other words, too much anxiety shuts down people's ability to think critically about the situation, forcing them to use simplistic schema. Conversely, having too little anxiety is associated with a lack of motivation to communicate. Stated differently, if you don't have any reservations about the consequences of your actions, you may not be motivated to interact at all. Griffin (2006) provides the classic example of the "ugly American" tourist. Travelers who don't take the time to consider how they will be perceived by locals are likely to come across as rude and insensitive, whereas tourists concerned with appearing incompetent are more likely to make efforts to blend in with the natives.

Presented in Table 6.3, AUM's 47 axioms can be more easily described by categorizing them as seven general factors that predict the extent to which a person will experience anxiety and uncertainty in predicting a cultural stranger's behavior in intergroup communication (Gudykunst, 2005). Subsumed within each factor are numerous predictions that forecast the increase or decrease in anxiety and uncertainty during intergroup interactions.

AUM predicts it is only when this anxiety and uncertainty are appropriately discerned and reduced that effective communication can occur. According to Gudykunst (1995), all messages must be interpreted for meaning to be conveyed. **Effective communication** occurs when "the person interpreting the message attaches a meaning to the message that is relatively similar to what was intended by the person transmitting it" (p. 15). In other words, when misunderstandings are minimized, the person receiving the message interprets the meaning in a way congruent with the meaning intended by the sender.

Imagine the following intercultural business exchange adapted from Becker (2012). Alexandra, an American businesswoman, meets with Karthik, a potential business partner in Singapore, to discuss developing a new product for use in Southeast Asia. After a lengthy meeting, they agree to research the feasibility of the new product and then go into production. Assuming they're on the same page, the pair never discusses what they mean by "research." To Alexandra, research means contracting a market research firm to conduct phone surveys over a 4-week period, analyzing the data, and making adjustments to the proposal before going to production. To Karthik, research means asking some friends for their opinion. They leave the meeting believing they're in agreement, but clearly effective communication has not occurred.

According to AUM, the key to communication effectiveness is **mindfulness** (Gudykunst, 2005; Miller & Samp, 2007). Mindful communication suggests thoughtful, conscious behavior rather than relying on stereotypes or knee-jerk reactions to a situation. Being mindful allows us to engage in anxiety and uncertainty management because we are discerning the situation, reflecting on our communication, and striving to increase our effectiveness. Recall the predictors of anxiety and uncertainty listed in Table 6.3. Engaging in mindfulness for each of these predictors helps reduce anxiety and uncertainty, "which in turn brings out positive communication outcomes such as communication effectiveness and intercultural adjustment" (Ni & Wang, 2011, p. 272). **Intercultural adjustment**, therefore, is a secondary outcome of positively reducing anxiety and uncertainty, whereby the cultural out-group member feels emotionally secure, socially appropriate, and communicatively competent (Gudykunst, 2005).

Although anxiety/uncertainty management theory may appear overwhelming, at least with regard to the impressive volume of axioms and predictions about intercultural communication effectiveness, remember that intercultural communication itself is a complicated, dynamic process. With a clear focus on using mindfulness to help individuals reduce anxiety and uncertainty when interacting with cultural strangers, AUM makes a concerted effort to capture this phenomenon in a way that is both comprehensive and readily applicable.

Table 6.3   Predictors of Anxiety and Uncertainty in Intercultural and Intergroup Interactions

Self-concept	An individual's self-concept (including self-esteem, personal identity, and social identity) affects anxiety and uncertainty. More specifically, AUM predicts that when an individual's self-concept is threatened, his or her intercultural anxiety increases, and he or she is less likely to make accurate predictions about the cultural stranger. AUM posits the opposite when intercultural interactions uphold an individual's self-concept. That is, the more one's intergroup dealings support one's view of self, the less anxiety and uncertainty, thereby increasing the individual's ability to predict strangers' behavior.
Motivation to interact with strangers	A person's need for predictability, group inclusion, and identity sustainability influences anxiety and uncertainty. In other words, AUM proposes that as an individual's ability to predict a cultural stranger's behavior increases, anxiety and uncertainty are reduced. Conversely, AUM suggests that the greater a person's need for group inclusion, the greater one's anxiety and uncertainty, thereby making accurate predictions about behavior less likely.
Reactions to strangers	Empathy, tolerance for ambiguity, and rigidity of intergroup attitudes influence anxiety and uncertainty. Specifically, AUM predicts that empathy and the ability to tolerate ambiguity lessen anxiety and improve the ability to make accurate predictions about behavior. Conversely, AUM predicts that the more rigid one's attitudes about strangers, the greater one's anxiety and uncertainty, thereby making accurate predictions about a stranger's behavior improbable.
Social categorization of strangers	Positive expectations, perceived similarities, and intergroup knowledge reduce anxiety and uncertainty, increasing one's ability to predict strangers' behavior accurately. In particular, AUM forecasts that positive expectations, perceived similarities, and an increase in intergroup knowledge will reduce anxiety, thereby increasing the ability to make accurate predictions of actions. Conversely, AUM predicts that anxiety will increase when one expects negative behavior, perceives few similarities, and has little intergroup understanding.
Situational processes	Perceived in-group power and the cooperative–competitive nature of tasks influence anxiety and uncertainty, making it more likely to predict strangers' behavior accurately. Specifically, AUM predicts that as in-group members increase in number or perceive they have power, anxiety about the cultural stranger lessens. Likewise, when intergroup interactions focus on cooperative tasks, anxiety lessens. *(Continued)*

CHAPTER 6 • CULTURE   **111**

Table 6.3	(Continued)
Connections with strangers	Attraction, interdependence, and the quantity and quality of contacts with strangers lessen individuals' anxiety and reduce uncertainty, making it more likely to predict strangers' behavior accurately. In other words, AUM predicts that as one's social attraction to and interdependence with strangers increase, anxiety and uncertainty decrease. Likewise, AUM proposes that spending more time with strangers reduces anxiety and uncertainty.
Ethical interactions	AUM predicts that showing respect and dignity for others, as well as engaging in moral inclusiveness with strangers, reduces anxiety and minimizes uncertainty, making it more likely to predict strangers' actions with accuracy.

CONFLICT FACE NEGOTIATION THEORY

In Chapter 5, we discussed the importance of "face" with regard to interpersonal communication (IPC) and politeness theory (PT). That is, individuals typically try to balance their own positive and negative face needs while also attending to their partner's face needs. Within the context of intercultural communication, the concept of face and social identity emerges again. This time, however, Ting-Toomey (1988, 1991b, 2005, 2017) uses face to explain and predict the cultural differences associated with conflict management. Specifically, Ting-Toomey's research has illustrated differences between individualistic and collectivistic cultures' face concerns and face needs. More specifically, differing face needs influence one's approach to conflict. Conflict face negotiation theory (FNT) explains cultural differences in conflict as the result of combining differing face needs and conflict styles.

Combining Face With Cultural Orientation

FNT begins with an understanding of face. As presented in Chapter 5, **face** is the desired self-image an individual wants to present to others (Brown & Levinson, 1978, 1987; Goffman, 1967). Recall that face includes two dimensions: positive and negative. **Positive face** includes the need to be liked, appreciated, and admired; **negative face** emphasizes the desire to act freely without constraints or imposition from others. Face is not a one-way concept; face also includes the recognition that those around us have their own face needs. Awareness of others' face needs (both positive and negative) is known as having face concern. (See Chapter 5 for a complete discussion of face.)

Discussed earlier in this chapter, Hofstede's (1980) research categorized cultures along several dimensions. Central to FNT are the dimensions of individualism–collectivism, high context–low context, and power distance as described earlier in this chapter (see Ting-Toomey, 2017). FNT posits that members of individualistic, low context cultures primarily focus on negative face—that is, they prefer to present themselves as confident, self-directed, and independent (Ting-Toomey, 1988). Conversely, members of collectivistic, high context cultures primarily emphasize positive face, presenting themselves as likable, cooperative, and interested in building relationships. Similarly, members of low-power-distance cultures prefer to view individuals as equals, whereas members of high-power-distance cultures accept and rely on hierarchies and status differences (Ting-Toomey, 2005).

Together, Ting-Toomey (2005) predicts these cultural differences affect face management, and differences in face management lead to different communication patterns. Moreover, these communication differences can lead to misinterpretation and disagreement. Consider the example of an American executive who compliments a Japanese business partner's fluency in English in front of other Japanese coworkers (Cupach & Imahori, 1993). The American believes his or her actions to be face enhancing—that is, giving someone a compliment is viewed as boosting one's face. To the Japanese, however, such a compliment is actually face threatening—by singling out one individual, the cooperative emphasis is damaged. Even the best-intended messages, then, can lead to misunderstanding and intercultural conflict.

Toward a Global Understanding of Conflict Management

As you might imagine, conflict is of great interest to communication scholars and is a widely studied phenomenon. With regard to FNT, conflict is defined as either the perceived or actual incompatibility of values, expectations, processes, or outcomes between two or more individuals (Ting-Toomey, 1994). Among North American relationships, five conflict styles commonly emerge: avoiding, accommodating, competing, compromising, and collaborating (Kilmann & Thomas, 1977; Rahim, 1986; Thomas & Kilmann, 1974). These researchers likely did not think about the conflict styles in terms of being particular to "North Americans" (where they are most often tested) or cultural exclusion. As will become clear, however, these five approaches to conflict appear to exclude significant components of a collectivistic orientation.

According to Kilmann and Thomas (1977), these five conflict styles vary on two dimensions: assertiveness (concern for self) and cooperation (concern for other). Those practicing **avoidance** lack assertiveness and cooperation; they withdraw from or seek to evade conflict altogether. As such, there is little concern for self or others. Individuals with an **accommodating** style cooperate with others but demonstrate little assertiveness—typically conceding to their partner's requests. Conversely, those **competing** in a conflict situation are highly assertive but lack cooperation; they push their viewpoints on others, sometimes to the extent of sacrificing the relationship altogether. A person with a **compromising** style has moderate concern for self and others; this individual is somewhat assertive and fairly cooperative. Compromising typically involves a willingness to give up some demands to gain others. Finally, individuals with a **collaborating** style have a high regard for self and others, making the person very assertive and also very cooperative. Collaboration occurs when one actively seeks to create new solutions that meet both partners' interests without having to make the sacrifices involved with compromise.

Note that conflict style is not a fixed trait; instead, it is a person's preferred response to conflict in a given situation. You can alter your conflict style depending on the partner involved and the circumstances at hand (Cupach & Canary, 1997).

Although Ting-Toomey (1988, 1991b) acknowledged the body of North American research showing support for the five previously mentioned conflict styles, she also argued these styles primarily represent a Western view of conflict. Ting-Toomey proposed that a global understanding of conflict management is remiss without examining issues of face. Consequently, her research extends the Western understanding of conflict management by viewing conflict styles on dual dimensions of **self-face concern** and **other-face concern**. Simply put, this means individuals must consider their own positive and negative face needs (self-face concern) as well as their partner's positive and negative face needs (other-face concern). Additionally, Ting-Toomey's (2017) research suggests that both **mutual-face concern** and **communal-face concern** must be considered. Mutual face involves the recognition of both self- and other-face needs, while communal face concern focuses on managing in-group identity needs when challenged by an out-group. Together, FNT predicts a causal relationship between culture, face, and conflict style. Conflict is particularly salient for intercultural communication because, during conflict, both parties can easily lose both positive and negative face through face-threatening acts (see Chapter 5).

Indeed, research using FNT not only shows links between culture and face management but also illustrates that when culture and face are combined, individuals can predict another's conflict management style (see Oetzel & Ting-Toomey, 2003; Ting-Toomey, 1988, 1991b). After studying students' conflict responses in China, Japan, South Korea, Taiwan, and the United States, eight responses to conflict emerged (Ting-Toomey & Oetzel, 2002; see Figure 6.1). Although the terminology varies slightly, the first five conflict responses mirror those identified previously (see Kilmann & Thomas, 1977): avoid, oblige (accommodate), dominate (compete), compromise, and integrate (collaborate). When considering self-face concern and other-face concern, three additional styles emerged: emotional expression, passive aggression, and third-party help.

The **emotionally expressive** style refers to an affective response to conflict as opposed to a cognitive response (Ting-Toomey, & Oetzel, 2001). That is, emotional expression emphasizes a person's desire to react to his or her feelings or "gut reaction." A person who relies on a **passive-aggressive** style surreptitiously attempts to make his or her partner feel guilty. Passive aggression is more active than avoiding the situation altogether but less active than openly addressing the conflict; the passive-aggressive individual only drops blameful hints of the problem. Finally, the tendency to rely on **third-party help** means the person is more comfortable asking a person outside of the relationship to help manage the conflict. For example, within the context of business communication, Asians often use such intermediaries to help preserve face (Ting-Toomey, 1992).

Americans typically use confrontational and dominating conflict strategies with a stronger win–lose orientation to preserve self-face (Ting-Toomey, 1992). Conversely, Asians prefer conflict avoidance in an effort to maintain mutual face. More precisely, Taiwanese and Chinese rely more heavily on a compromising conflict style; when working with in-group (Japanese) members, the Japanese also rely on conflict avoidance.

Notably, however, the Japanese mirror Americans' more dominating conflict style when dealing with out-group (non-Japanese) associates. This ability to switch between styles depending on in-group/out-group affiliations may help explain Japanese competence when communicating in global business relationships.

All told, Ting-Toomey's (1988, 1991b, 2005, 2017) FNT offers a more holistic view of conflict, particularly within the context of cultural communication. According to her causal model, one's cultural orientation (individualism–collectivism and power distance) coupled with self- and other-face concerns predict one's likely repertoire of conflict responses. Intercultural conflict—that is, perceived disagreement between members of different cultures—may arise as a direct result of these cultural differences.

Figure 6.1 Eight Global Conflict Management Styles

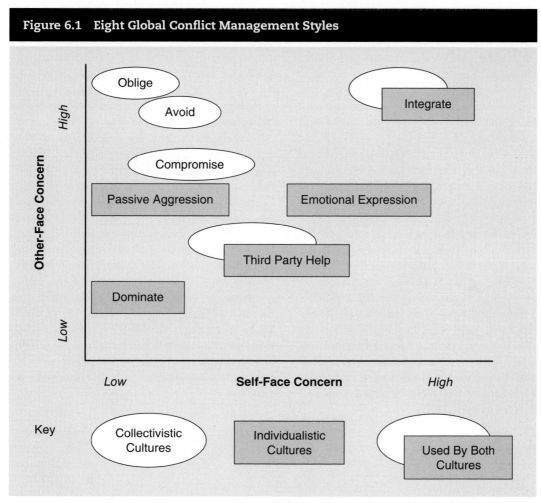

Source: From "Cross-Cultural Face Concerns and Conflict Styles: Current Status and Future Directions," by S. Ting-Toomey and J. Oetzel. In W. B. Gudykunst and B. Mody (Eds.), *Handbook of International and Intercultural Communication* (2nd ed., pp. 143–164), © 2002 by SAGE. Reprinted by permission of SAGE.

SUMMARY AND RESEARCH APPLICATIONS

We discussed four ways of examining culture and communication in the workplace. First, Hofstede's five cultural dimensions provide systematic understanding of communication differences across cultures. This model has been used successfully to examine global differences in customer services experiences (Rodriguez, Joseph, Dedmon, & Steinberg, 2016), differences in health reporting between Eastern and Western cultures (Tang & Peng, 2015), and even the extent to which these cultural dimensions permeate global organizations' social media profiles (Lo, Waters, & Christensen, 2017). For example, Lo et al. (2017) found that although Global 500 companies' Facebook landing pages are fairly consistent, when they dug deeper into the individual elements of "About Us," company "Updates," and "Media," cultural differences emerged in line with Hofstede's cultural dimensions.

Next, Giles and Coupland's (1991) communication accommodation theory predicts an individual's desire to join the in-group will lead to attempts at convergence, while one's wish to remain an out-group member will result in divergence. Recent research on nonaccommodation has emerged in a wide variety of contexts such as elder-care (Cavallaro, Seilhamer, Chee, & Ng, 2016), stepparents and stepchildren (Speer, Giles, & Denes, 2013), and excessive police stops (Giles, Linz, Bonilla, & Gomez, 2012). Also related to in-group status are LMX relationships in the workplace. In-group members are more likely to convey organizational disagreements using face-to-face communication with supervisors, whereas out-group members were more likely to use e-mail to convey their difference in opinion (Turnage & Goodboy, 2016).

Third, we reviewed anxiety/uncertainty management theory. Gudykunst (1985, 2005) sought to provide a comprehensive understanding of how communication effectiveness can be increased by mindfully reducing intercultural anxiety and uncertainty. Social media may increase individuals' cross-cultural adaptation. For example, Rui and Wang (2015) found that international students who used social network sites to communicate with native students reported a reduction in uncertainty. Conversely, when international students communicated with other international students at the host university, uncertainty was not reduced. The researchers speculated that international students' communication with native students is akin to Gudykunst's notion of making "connections with strangers" as a way to reduce uncertainty, if not anxiety.

Finally, face negotiation theory offers a transcultural approach to conflict management. Even in single-nation, multiethnic contexts such as the U.S., cultural differences in conflict management appear (Ting-Toomey et al., 2000). For example, Asian Americans reported using the avoidance strategy more than African Americans and Euro-Americans. Similarly, Hispanic and Asian Americans report using more third-party strategies than African Americans. More recently, research has examined the role of emotions in cross-national, cross-cultural conflict styles (Zhang, Ting-Toomey, & Oetzel, 2014). When comparing conflict in the United States compared with China, American participants' expression of guilt correlated with use of the obliging style, but for Chinese participants, guilt corresponded with avoidance.

KEY TERMS

Accommodating 113	Attributional confidence 109	Collectivism 99
Accommodation 106	Avoidance 113	Competing 113
Anxiety 109	Collaborating 113	Compromising 113

CASE STUDY 6: THE TROUBLE WITH TOURISTS

Historic Philadelphia is a booming travel destination. Among the many sites tourists visit while in one of the nation's oldest cities is the Granovetter Church, a partially restored building nearly 300 years old, noted for being a secret meeting place of the early founders of the United States. In 2017 alone, nearly 1.5 million people visited the political and religious landmark, with an estimated one in five hailing from a foreign country. The sheer number of visitors, as well as the number of tourists who spoke languages other than English, combined to create significant challenges for the volunteers who provide guidance and interpretation to visitors. Unlike the nearby Independence National Park, which is run by the National Park Service, the Granovetter Church is still a congregation of the Presbyterian Church of the United States of America. All touring is done in coordination with a group of volunteers, who are managed by an oversight committee of the Philadelphia Presbytery.

During a general meeting of volunteers, it became apparent the volunteers were having increasing trouble with meeting the needs of international visitors, particularly with Japanese visitors to the park. Volunteers had difficulty with explaining the general concerns and rules for behavior in what was, in essence, a place of worship. Further conversation among the volunteers implied that aggressive tour leaders were often the root of the problem. Such was the case with many tour leaders from an organization called Marzu Tours.

Marzu Tours frequently burst into the church with bullhorn in hand, talking in Japanese while an English-speaking interpretive presentation was in progress. The group would push and shove to remain together throughout the presentation, interrupting, and interfering with existing tour groups. Moreover, the Marzu Tour leaders would wander through the building on their own, often requiring a volunteer to

(Continued)

(Continued)

run to prevent the tour from entering a sacrosanct area. Other tour operators and visitors frequently complained about these groups.

After years of avoiding the problem, Mark Hastings, the chair of the oversight committee, determined direct confrontation of the problem was inevitable. He began the process of trying to contact the director of Marzu Tours. His efforts led him to Yushiko Sato, a female employee of the company. Mark decided the best approach would be to present his complaint in a straightforward manner, even though he was actually quite frustrated and angry after wasting so much time with bureaucracy and red tape while trying to find the right person to talk with.

"Ms. Sato, we at Granovetter Church are having trouble with some of your tour guides," Mark began. "They do not wait their turn for admittance, they do not follow our rules for where they can go, and they seem to push their groups in front of other groups during the tours."

"I am so sorry," Yushiko replied with a great deal of sincerity. "I will bring this to the attention of our director."

Mark hung up the phone, satisfied that the problem would be resolved and impressed with the service he had received from Yushiko. However, several months later he was still receiving complaints about the company from the volunteers. He retraced his steps and called Yushiko Sato again. This time, he asked to speak to her director.

"That is a little difficult," Yushiko replied.

Mark was frustrated by the stonewalling. "This is a problem with a fairly simple solution!" he shouted.

"Mr. Hastings, you cannot change the Japanese. The Japanese are different," Yushiko calmly explained, with just a touch of condescension.

Mark refused to take the bait. "All of our visitors are important to us; the Japanese are not more important than others, I just want to level the playing field," Mark responded with what he thought was great patience. "Can we perhaps set up a meeting to discuss this in person?"

"I will see what we can do," Yushiko replied.

Two weeks later, Mark still had not heard back from Yushiko, so he called her yet again. He was as clear and firm as he could be. She agreed to have an in-person meeting the following week. Mark was a little bit late for the meeting due to an unexpected road closure leading out of the city to the Marzu Tours office in the suburbs. He was shocked when he actually met Yushiko, who appeared to be very young and immature. The contrast between her innocent appearance and her clear distaste for his late arrival was intriguing. It was also very obvious she was a low-level employee. He realized the issue wasn't that she *would* not address the problem of her company's tour guides but that she *could* not do so; she didn't have the authority.

Mark concluded the meeting by thanking Yushiko for her concern. He had given up on working with the company and decided his volunteers would simply need better training to deal with Japanese tourists. To his bewilderment, Yushiko suggested Mark meet the local director of the company. "Finally!" he thought. "Maybe now we'll get somewhere!"

Questions for Consideration

1. How might the troubles with the tourism company be explained by Hofstede's dimensions of culture? Make sure to look at both Japanese and American cultures.

2. Did either Yushiko or Mark ever accommodate? How? With what effect?

3. Relate AUM's seven predictors of anxiety and uncertainty to the case. Which predictors seem to be the greatest contributors to the problem

at Granovetter Church? How might Gudykunst advise both Mark and Yushiko so they can engage in more mindful communication?

4. To what extent did Mark and Yushiko recognize each other's face needs during the conflict? What conflict strategies did they use? Were the strategies consistent with the predictions of face negotiation theory?

5. What ethical challenges arise when interacting with members of another culture, such as in the case study? Which theory or theories might help mitigate these challenges?

6. Do any of the theories emerge as better than the others? Why do you believe this to be the case? What situations might surface that would make a different theory or theories better at explaining the situation?

The location, history, and events of this story are entirely fictional. The Granovetter Church does not exist and is not based on any real building.

CHAPTER SEVEN

PERSUASION

Since the mid-1930s when Dale Carnegie first published his best-selling book *How to Win Friends and Influence People*, the notion of how to persuade others has been both a popular and profitable subject. Concurrently, with the rise of mass media and the pervasiveness of propaganda used in both World Wars, the study and understanding of mass-mediated persuasive messages became critical to understanding political and social change. Today, the importance of understanding the power of persuasive messages is greater than ever given the rise of social media. "When you create more media channels, you'll create more advertising. Today Americans (and most folks in modernized countries) are bombarded with advertisements. I'm talking about a tsunami of commercials, print ads, Brand labels, Facebook Ads, Google Ads, ads on your phone or anything a business can produce to get your attention and compel you to buy. Digital Marketing experts estimate that most Americans are exposed to around 4,000 to 10,000 advertisements each day" (Marshall, 2015, ¶1). Clearly, we are inundated with messages of persuasion and influence in all aspects of our lives—relational, social, political, and economic. Accordingly, we believe having an understanding of how persuasive messages work (or don't work!) is central for surviving in today's advertising and media-blitzed society.

PERSUASION DEFINED

Persuasion is typically defined as "human communication that is designed to influence others by modifying their beliefs, values, or attitudes" (Simons, 1976, p. 21). O'Keefe (1990) argued there are requirements for the sender, the means, and the recipient to consider something persuasive. First, persuasion involves the intent to achieve a goal on the part of the message sender. Second, communication is the means to achieve that goal. Third, the message recipient must have free will (i.e., threatening physical harm if the recipient

Learning Objectives

After reading this chapter, you will be able to do the following:

1. Determine which route, arguments, or peripheral cues were used in a persuasive message

2. Describe how the interplay of attitudes, normative beliefs, and perceived behavioral control is critical in persuading people to change their behavior

3. Explain refutational preemption and identify examples of counterpersuasion efforts

4. Clarify the interplay between narrative rationality, narrative fidelity, and the logic of good reasons in creative persuasive narratives

5. Compare and contrast major theoretical approaches to persuasion

6. Provide systematic understanding of a professional situation by applying persuasive theories

doesn't comply is usually considered force, not persuasion). Accordingly, persuasion is not accidental—nor is it coercive. It is inherently communicational.

Many theories in this chapter are concerned with shifts in attitude, so it is important to make clear what we mean by that term. An **attitude** is a "relatively enduring predisposition to respond favorably or unfavorably" toward something (Simons, 1976, p. 80). We have attitudes toward people, places, events, products, policies, ideas, and so forth (O'Keefe, 1990). Because attitudes are enduring, they are neither fleeting nor based on whims. Yet at the same time, attitudes are *learned* evaluations; they are not something people are born with. As such, attitudes are changeable. Finally, and perhaps most importantly, attitudes are presumed to influence behavior; although, as we will see later, this influence is not as strong as we might presume.

In this chapter, we present four theories of persuasive communication. Although portrayed as theories of persuasion, each of these viewpoints can be applied to a wide variety of communication contexts. From well-crafted public relations campaigns designed to foster positive attitudes about a company to strategically forewarning a partner he is about to hear something that might upset him, the theories presented highlight the varied ways to develop persuasive messages. The four theories we discuss in this chapter are the elaboration likelihood model, the theory of planned behavior, inoculation theory, and the narrative paradigm.

ELABORATION LIKELIHOOD MODEL

Turning to our first theory of persuasion, the elaboration likelihood model (ELM) views persuasion primarily as a cognitive event, meaning the targets of persuasive messages use mental processes of motivation and reasoning (or a lack thereof) to accept or reject persuasive messages. Developed by Petty and Cacioppo (1986), ELM posits two possible routes, or methods, of influence: centrally routed messages and peripherally routed messages. Each route targets a widely different audience. Accordingly, ELM emphasizes the importance of understanding audience members before creating a persuasive message.

Slow and Steady: The Central Route to Persuasion

Petty and Cacioppo's (1986) model depicts persuasion as a process in which the success of influence depends largely on the way the receivers make sense of the message. As mentioned earlier, ELM presents two divergent pathways one can use when trying to influence others. The more complex of the two paths is known as the **central route**, also referred to as the elaborated route. Centrally routed messages include a wealth of information, rational arguments, and evidence to support a particular conclusion. For example, during each election season, political hopefuls engage in speeches, debates, and roundtable discussions; each message is filled with elaborated and presumably rational information regarding the candidate's viewpoints, platform, and political history.

Centrally routed messages are much more likely to create long-term change for the recipient than are peripheral messages (discussed later); however, not all individuals are capable of receiving centrally routed messages. ELM argues that centrally routed messages succeed in long-term change only when two factors are met: the target must be highly motivated to process all the information given, and the target must be **able** to process the message cognitively. For example, if you are not willing to sit through a 2-hour televised debate between presidential candidates, then ELM suggests you do not have the motivation required to process an elaborated message in this instance. Alternatively, imagine you are motivated to watch the candidate's debate, but the politicians' messages are so filled with complex issues of international policy that you do not understand them. In this case, ELM suggests that despite your motivation, the ability to understand the highly specific and intricate messages offered is not present. The theory states that without *both* motivation and ability, an elaborated message is of little value.

Types of Elaborated Arguments

It should be apparent that understanding one's audience is critical when choosing the appropriate route; it is also imperative to understand the audience when constructing an **elaborated argument** (Petty & Cacioppo, 1986). In other words, it isn't enough to view your audience as motivated and able when considering the central route of persuasion. You must also consider how the audience members will likely react to the quality and arrangement of the arguments presented. Elaborated arguments can be measured as strong, neutral, or weak.

Strong arguments create a positive cognitive response in the minds of receivers while also positively aligning receivers' beliefs with those views of the persuader (Petty & Cacioppo, 1986). Strong arguments inoculate the audience against counterpersuasion and are most likely to create long-term attitude change that leads to predictable behavior. Repetition is thought to enhance the persuasive effect of strong arguments; conversely, interruptions will diminish their effectiveness. Neutral arguments generate a noncommittal cognitive response from the receiver. In other words, no attitude change occurs, and the ambivalent receiver may instead turn to peripheral cues, or shortcuts, to persuasion. Finally, weak arguments produce a negative cognitive response to the persuasive message. This negative response will not only prevent attitude change but may, in fact, have a reverse or boomerang effect, thereby reinforcing the opposing point of view.

Taking a Shortcut: The Peripheral Route to Persuasion

Noted earlier, elaborated messages are ineffective when targeted participants are neither capable nor interested in the information (Petty & Cacioppo, 1986). Although the persuader might prefer an involved audience so as to produce enduring change, it is unreasonable to expect every persuasive target to be motivated or skilled enough to understand the barrage of influential messages put forth each day. As a result, when motivation or ability is missing from the target audience, the persuader can use the **peripheral route** to persuasion. Peripheral messages rely on a receiver's emotional involvement and persuade through more superficial means. Consider the ASPCA ads that feature images of neglected and abused animals. A montage of dirty and injured animals is shown with a background of sad music. These ads are not meant to logically persuade someone to donate to the ASPCA, they are meant to tug on the heart strings.

Thus, ELM predicts that when the audience is unmotivated or unable to process an elaborated message, persuaders should focus on quick and easy ways to produce change. One significant drawback is that the peripheral route leads only to short-term change, if any change at all.

Types of Peripheral Cues

Cialdini (1993, 1994) identified seven common cues of a peripheral message: authority, commitment, contrast, liking, reciprocity, scarcity, and social proof.

With the first peripheral cue, the persuader uses the perception of **authority** to convince the audience to accept the beliefs or behaviors presented. Parents often use this peripheral cue with their children: "Clean up your room because I said so!" This message may influence children to straighten the covers and hide the toys in the closet before Grandma's visit, but it probably won't create long-term neatness.

Peripheral messages that rely on **commitment** emphasize a person's dedication to a product, social cause, group affiliation, political party, and so on (Cialdini, 1993, 1994). For example, some people publicly announce their commitment to a certain group or cause. They attend rallies; run for office; or wear pins, hats, and other logos that symbolize the affiliation (Canary, Cody, & Manusov, 2008). Similarly, wearing a polo shirt that displays your company's corporate logo demonstrates some amount of dedication to the organization. Other people demonstrate their commitment more privately, for example, by sending anonymous donations to political campaigns or charitable organizations. However, "people usually feel greater commitment to a cause if they are publicly committed to it" (Canary et al., 2008, p. 369).

One very common sequential procedure that underscores the commitment principle is the foot-in-the-door tactic (Cialdini, 1994). Here, a persuader convinces you to do something small first, like wear a campaign button. Then the persuader asks to put a campaign sign in your yard. Next, the persuader may ask you to make a donation or to host a reception. The strategy is to convince you to agree to a small, seemingly innocuous request first. Once you agree and commit yourself to the campaign, it becomes harder to refuse larger requests because there is a threat of appearing inconsistent with your commitment.

Persuading through **contrast**, or using contrast effects, requires the communicator to set up uneven points of comparison (Cialdini, 1993, 1994). For example, asking a coworker if she could do you a "giant favor" and then contrasting the statement with a simple request ("Would you text me if FedEx drops off a package while I am in a client meeting?") sets up a disparity. By inflating the coworker's expectations for the "giant favor" requested and then contrasting it with a simple favor, it is more likely to result in compliance. Retail salespeople also use this contrast principle by "reducing" prices or by showing customers the most expensive item first (because anything else will seem cheaper in comparison).

Liking messages stress affinity toward a person, place, or object (Cialdini, 1993, 1994). That is, if we like you, we will like your ideas. Many companies often rely on such messages of liking in their advertisements. By using basketball sensation Kevin Durant to sell Nike shoes or pop star Selena Gomez to sell Coke products, these companies expect that if you like Durant or Gomez, you will also like their products (and will—they hope—buy them).

Messages of **reciprocity** try to influence by emphasizing a give-and-take relationship (Cialdini, 1993, 1994). For example, it is easier to persuade your sister-in-law to babysit your children if you have done something similar for her. Advertisers also use reciprocity: "Buy these steak knives in the next 10 minutes, and we'll throw in a free cutting board!" Here, the advertiser tries to influence the receiver by throwing in some extras. If you do this for us, we'll give you a freebie. Similarly, **scarcity** is a peripheral message that preys on people's worry of missing out on something. This "Quick! Get it before they're all gone!" approach creates a sense of urgency for receivers. Home shopping channels, department stores, car dealers, and furniture stores all rely on this strategy by imposing time limits on the sale of items; presumably, you won't be able to purchase the deluxe salad spinner after the sales event expires. Realtors also use this approach; alerting prospective buyers that an offer has been placed on a property creates a sense of urgency and may start a bidding war. A house that was "of interest" now seems that much more appealing when it may disappear from the market.

Finally, the peripheral cue of **social proof** relies on the age-old notion of peer pressure (Cialdini, 1993, 1994). Although you might mistakenly believe only teenagers succumb to the "everyone's doing it" mentality, adults are also swayed by messages of social proof. Within the workplace, for instance, many corporations participate in charity drives such as with the Red Cross or the United Way. Here, employees who participate in blood drives or fund-raising are given pins to wear or balloons to display, thereby gaining influence by putting subtle pressure on other employees to "get on board."

If unaware of these techniques in the past, you should now be able to identify these seven peripheral cues—they are everywhere! Again, however, it is important to stress that these peripheral messages emphasize fleeting emotional responses and are not likely to create long-lasting change.

Types of Peripheral Messages

As with centrally routed arguments, peripheral messages can be evaluated as positive, neutral, or negative (Petty & Cacioppo, 1986). Positive peripheral messages are those perceived favorably by the audience and create a positive affective state. Positive peripheral messages have a chance at yielding weak, positive changes in attitude. For example, if you are a fan of *Full Frontal with Samantha Bee* and Bee publicly endorses Candidate X over Candidate Y, you may feel more positively about Candidate X. However, a change in attitude does not necessarily predict a change in behavior. For instance, you may believe voting is an essential civic duty for American citizens, yet you may not vote in your local primary election because you don't think you are knowledgeable of the candidates. Here, we see incongruence between a belief (voting is important) and behavior (failing to vote).

Neutral peripheral messages leave receivers feeling emotionally ambivalent; they really don't know or care about the cue used to capture their interest (Petty & Cacioppo, 1986).

If you don't know who Samantha Bee is or don't really care about her political views, then her endorsement of Candidate X will not create any attitude change—nor is it likely to influence your voting behavior. Finally, negative peripheral messages produce negative or disapproving emotional responses within the receiver. If you can't stand *Full Frontal*, then Samantha Bee's ad endorsing Candidate X will likely irritate you. Thus, you are now left with a negative impression of Candidate X because of this person's "association" with an actor or TV show you find objectionable.

ELM makes very clear predictions, summarized in Figure 7.1. The theory predicts that if receivers are motivated and able to consider an elaborated message, persuaders should rely on strong, factually based arguments. Arguments can backfire if they are

Figure 7.1   Elaboration Likelihood Model

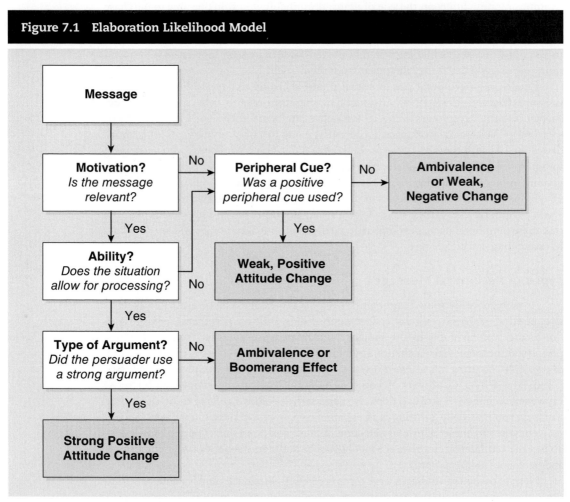

Source: *Communication and Persuasion* (p. 4) by R. E. Petty and J. T. Cacioppo, 1986, New York, NY: Springer-Verlag.

weak or poorly presented, however. Conversely, persuaders should focus on emotionally based peripheral messages if receivers cannot or will not consider an elaborated message. Persuaders must recognize that using a peripheral route guarantees no long-term change. Instead, effects, if any, will be minimal and fleeting.

THEORY OF PLANNED BEHAVIOR

ELM gives clear advice if you are trying to persuade someone to think or feel a particular way about an organization, a person, an idea, or a product. But what if your goal is to move beyond attitude change to actually changing someone's behavior? What if you want someone to buy your product, act on your proposal, or comply with instructions? Our second theory, the theory of planned behavior, may provide a template for how to persuade people to change their behavior.

Theory of Reasoned Action

The roots of the theory of planned behavior can be traced to an earlier theory, the theory of reasoned action, developed by Martin Fishbein and Icek Ajzen in the 1960s (Fishbein & Ajzen, 1975). Fishbein was frustrated by the body of persuasion research at the time; although the notion of an attitude had been well developed, studies could not provide evidence linking attitudes and behavior. Simply being *in favor* of a particular political candidate doesn't guarantee votes for him or her, and supporting the notion of environmental conservation does not necessarily lead to consistent recycling behavior. Fishbein, who later worked with Ajzen, recognized that something likely mediates the relationship between an attitude and behavior.

First, Fishbein and Ajzen (1975) assumed all behavior is intentional: We don't accidentally behave in a particular manner; we have reasons for doing so. The idiot who cut you off on your drive to work this morning likely did so because he was in a hurry. The coworker who leaves work early may be doing so to care for a sick child. The assumption that there are reasons for all of our actions led Fishbein and Ajzen to develop the notion of **behavioral intention**, which simply means you plan to act a particular way.

The next step for these authors was to determine what creates behavioral intention. Fishbein and Ajzen (1975) believed there are two predictors of behavioral intention: attitudes and normative beliefs. We have discussed attitudes already; *attitude* is defined as the sum of beliefs about something. The theory of reasoned action states that our attitudes are made up of two components: our evaluation of the object and our belief strength. Take, for example, your attitude toward technology. Would you be lost without your cell phone? Are you the type of person who needs to get the newest gadget as soon as it is released? Or are you a late adopter, someone who only uses technology after it has been established and there is no getting around using it? Different people evaluate technology differently. Some absolutely love technology, others hate it, and still more think technology is great when it helps you and horrible when it malfunctions. These variations reference your evaluation of the object, but your belief strength must also be taken into account. Do you feel very strongly that your life is better because of your iPhone, or are your positive feelings fairly weak? Your attitudes provide one indication of your behavioral intent.

According to the theory of reasoned action, the second predictor of behavioral intention is **normative beliefs**, which are your perceptions about what others in your social network expect you to do. Notably, behavioral intention is not formed by beliefs about all others in our social network but only our valued others. A disliked associate is unlikely to persuade us to behave in a particular way, but a respected colleague is likely to have that power. In addition to the value you place on others in your network, the theory suggests you must also consider the motivation to comply with these others. Some people are conformists and likely to succumb to peer pressure because of their people-pleasing ways. Others rebel, intentionally doing the opposite of what even valued others expect of them. Returning to our example of technology, if your boss wants you to keep your cell phone on 24 hours a day "just in case," your intention to do so will be influenced by how much you value your boss (and your job!) and how motivated you are to comply.

The determination of behavioral intention is achieved by looking at the relative weights of the two predictors. In some cases, attitudes might be weighted more strongly, and in others normative beliefs will be weighted more strongly. In order to persuade someone to act a particular way, then, the persuader has to send a message to affect the proper predictor. Consider trying to convince a technophobe to give up her old flip phone and buy a smartphone. If attitudes are very strong and normative beliefs are not, then a message should be sent to address attitudes ("Wouldn't you like to be able to be a part of the family group chat?"). If the opposite is true, you should focus your message on complying with valued others ("Mom, your doctor said you should have a smart phone so you can store your medical information."). Finally, the persuader can try to change the relative weights of the attitudinal and normative components. If, for example, normative beliefs are weighted more than an attitude, you can try to reduce the strength of the normative beliefs ("It's your life; you need to decide what's important for you.").

Adding to the Theory

Although research has provided some strong support for the tenets of the theory of reasoned action, Ajzen (1988, 1991) extended the theory by adding a third major predictor, changing the name to the theory of planned behavior. Ajzen recognized that sometimes we might intend to behave a certain way, but our plans are not carried through because we don't have control over the situation. Like attitudes and normative beliefs, **perceived behavioral control** is also comprised of two elements: self-efficacy and controllability. **Self-efficacy** refers to an individual's belief that she or he can actually perform the behavior. Many adults over the age of 60 consider the speed and frequency of teenagers' text messaging abilities something they couldn't duplicate even if they wanted to! People often "talk themselves out" of doing something because they fear they won't be successful. In short, you need to believe you can truly do something in order to develop the intention to do so. The second component, **controllability**, recognizes that sometimes things are simply out of our control—or are at least perceived

Figure 7.2 Theory of Planned Behavior

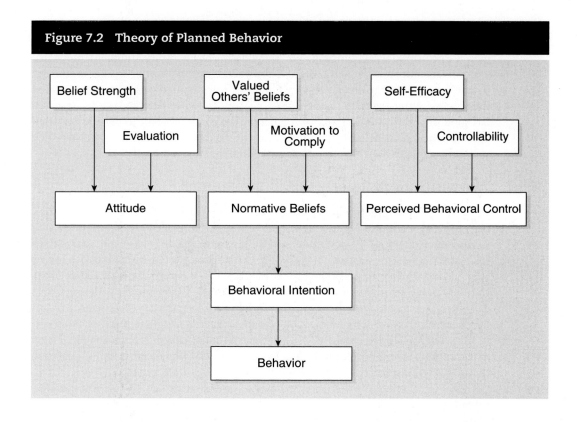

that way. You might intend to purchase a new smart phone, but a power outage might shut down the store, or demand for the new phone might exceed supply. Figure 7.2 pulls all of these components together.

The theory of planned behavior provides an explanation for why campaigns that focus only on providing information are unlikely to have any behavioral effect. Simply changing someone's attitude is not enough. If your goal as a persuader is to convince someone to act in a particular way (e.g., buy your product, donate blood, or engage in fewer arguments), you need to provide attitudinal, social norm, and controllability incentives.

INOCULATION THEORY

Thus far, we have discussed theories that give advice about how to persuade someone. But what if your goal is to persuade someone *not* to be persuaded? Given the plethora of persuasive attempts that surround us on a daily basis, knowing how to resist persuasion is also a useful tool. McGuire's inoculation theory (1961) presents a way to understand how resistance to persuasion might be achieved. Using a medical metaphor,

McGuire argued that like a vaccine that prevents you from getting a disease, particular messages might "inoculate" you from attacks on your beliefs. Specifically, an **inoculation** message presents a weaker form (i.e., a "small dose") of a contrary argument, much like a vaccine includes a weakened form of a virus. Once exposed to this weaker argument, people are less likely to change their attitudes when presented with a stronger form of the argument; they have, in essence, developed a formidable defense system. Research has supported this assertion, indicating people are more resistant to persuasion when an inoculation process takes place than when original beliefs were simply bolstered by stronger evidence (Banas & Rains, 2008; McGuire & Papageorgis, 1961).

Developing the Concept

McGuire's original theory focused solely on what he called "cultural truisms" (McGuire, 1962), such as "you should brush your teeth after every meal" and "mental illness is not contagious." Critics challenged this focus, suggesting these noncontroversial issues did not provide an adequate test of how well people will resist persuasive efforts about controversial subjects (Ullman & Bodaken, 1975, as cited in Banas & Rains, 2008). In recent years, a communication scholar named Michael Pfau and his colleagues have examined how inoculation theory might work in broader persuasive contexts, particularly in terms of health communication (Godbold & Pfau, 2000), political communication (An & Pfau, 2004), employees' organizational commitment (Haigh & Pfau, 2006), and corporate advocacy (Burgoon, Pfau, & Birk, 1995). The result is that inoculation theory has "almost limitless application" (Banas & Rains, 2008, p. 1).

Pfau (1997) suggests there are two major components to an inoculation message: threat and refutational preemption. First, **threat** is a necessary component of any inoculation effort. Note that threat is not the same as fear appeal. Instead, threat simply involves a forewarning of a potential persuasive attack on beliefs, making sure the target of the persuasive effort is aware of his or her susceptibility to the attack. According to Pfau, making you aware of a threat should motivate you to defend your attitudes or beliefs. For example, Wong (2016) investigated the effectiveness of inoculation theory in generating resistance to persuasive messages attacking the safety and effectiveness of the human papilloma virus (HPV) vaccine. To stimulate perceived threat, he had participants read a message that stated the following:

> Despite your positive attitude and feelings towards the HPV vaccine, there exists out there many reports and stories by the media and various interest groups aimed at attacking your attitude and feelings on the issue, and there is a real possibility that you will come into contact with these arguments in the near future, some of which will be so persuasive that they may cause you to question your attitude and feelings toward getting the HPV vaccine. (Wong, 2016, p. 130)

The threat need not be a strong warning; Banas and Rains (2008) found that even low levels of threat provided inoculation.

The second component of an inoculation effort is **refutational preemption**. Not only should targets receive information about potential threats, but the inoculation message should also anticipate the counterpersuasive effort by raising specific challenges and then contesting them. In the study by Wong (2016) described previously, two news reports and two messages from the Centers for Disease Control and Prevention (CDC) served as refutational preemption. The news reports interviewed doctors about the questions and concerns they have heard raised by parents and the media, with the doctors reassuring the viewing audience of the safety and the effectiveness of the vaccine. The messages by the CDC reinforced these arguments by describing the safety of vaccines in general, and the HPV vaccine specifically.

Research consistently shows that "matching" the content of refutations exactly to what actually occurs in the counterargument is unnecessary; any preemptive refutation seems to bolster the inoculation effect (Banas & Rains, 2008). In the study just described, Wong (2016) found that the messages focused on the safety of vaccines in general were just as effective as the messages focused on the HPV vaccine in particular. The bigger question appears to be how strong the preemptive arguments need to be. Using the vaccine analogy, how much "disease" in the vaccine protects the recipient, and how much is too much? McGuire (1964) argued that inoculation efforts should be "threatening enough to be defense-stimulating, but not so strong as to overwhelm" (p. 202). In testing this issue, Compton and Pfau (2004) concluded that even weak refutations provide protection.

Inoculation theory provides clear advice for professional communicators challenged (or who think they may be challenged) by "bad press." Consider the efforts of the soda industry. In 2013, there were no "sin" taxes focused on reducing the consumption of pop or other sugary drinks. As of 2017, over 9 million Americans live in an area that taxes soda (Belluz, 2017). The goals of such efforts are twofold: to address the rising obesity

Table 7.1	Inoculation Campaign Against Proposed Sweetened Beverage Taxes
	Example
Threat	"Some politicians still don't think we can choose what's best for our families without new laws, regulations, or taxes telling us what to buy."
Refutational preemption	"Getting serious about obesity starts with education, not laws and regulations." "Look around your grocery store lately? There are more choices and more information than ever before. New kinds of beverages. Different portion sizes. Calories right up front."
Conclusion	"The fact is, it's not the government's job to grocery shop for my family. It's mine."

epidemic in the United States and to provide a means to reduce budget shortfalls in an uncertain economy. The industry leaders (Coca-Cola and PespsiCo) have partnered with the American Beverage Association (ABA) to make sure the public is not persuaded to vote in favor of these tax increases, however. It's estimated the ABA has spent over $100 million in efforts to prevent the public from being persuaded to tax soft drinks, including nearly $10 million in San Francisco during 2016 alone. Table 7.1 depicts the argument presented in one advertisement called "Your Cart Your Choice," which clearly demonstrates an inoculation effort.

NARRATIVE PARADIGM

Whereas ELM emphasizes the importance of strong, logical arguments for persuading a motivated and able audience, the narrative paradigm stresses the effectiveness of influence through narration—that is, persuasion through storytelling (Fisher, 1984, 1987). Using a more subjective theoretical orientation, Fisher (1984, 1987) argues that human beings are fundamentally storytelling creatures; therefore, the most persuasive or influential message is not that of rational fact but instead a narrative that convinces us of "good reasons" for engaging in a particular action or belief.

Consider advertising. Are the most memorable ads those that inundate the audience with facts about the products, or are they those that craft a memorable story? Think about the ad featuring the employee for a cereal company; in the ad, the employee, Diana Hunter, says that when she stops into a store on her way home from work people think they smell cookies. The employee responds, "Oh, no, you just smell me. I just got out of work. That's Honey Bunches of Oats." Rather than describing the qualities of the cereal, the ad immediately captures not only the essence of the product but also the positive feelings about the cereal held by the people who make it. A number of companies have established long-standing narrative campaigns, such as the Dos Equis "Most Interesting Man in the World" ads, or Progressive Insurance's series featuring the character Flo. In a clever marketing move, Sprint hired Paul Marcarelli, the face of Verizon's long-term ad campaign ("Can you hear me now?"), to front Sprint instead, providing a continuation of the long-term campaign (albeit with a surprise twist!).

Current marketing experts understand that "the real power of strategic storied advertising is in its ability to build strong, enduring brands" (Randazzo, 2006, p. 13). It is these stories that "give brands their unique identity and personality, which in turn create an emotional bond between the consumer and the brand" (p. 13).

Not all narrative advertisements are long-term campaigns, however. One of the most successful ads of 2016 was the Sandy Hook Promise Ad called "Evan" (you can view it on YouTube). The ad seems to depict a high school love story. In watching the story, viewers "miss" the warning signs of violence displayed by a background character. By intentionally "misdirecting" the audience, the ad provides a powerful and visceral message that shows—rather than tells—people how easy it is to be unaware of troubling signs of tragic threats.

As we explain subsequently, Fisher's (1984, 1987) view of communication contrasts much of a Western emphasis on rational decision making. Yet, by juxtaposing a narrative worldview with a rational worldview, we hope you will give some thought to this strikingly different way of considering communication and influence.

Fisher's Narrative Assumptions

Five assumptions drive Fisher's (1987) explanation of the narrative paradigm. First and foremost, Fisher proposed that what makes humans unique and distinct from other creatures is our ability and drive to tell stories. Narration does not refer to "fictive composition whose propositions may be true or false" (p. 58); instead, a **narrative** includes the symbolic words and actions people use to assign meaning. Fisher evoked the Greek term *mythos* to explain human communication primarily as a collection of stories expressing "ideas that cannot be verified or proved in any absolute way. Such ideas arise in metaphor, values, gestures, and so on" (p. 19). According to this view, not even the keenest expert knows everything about his or her area of specialization; there is an element of subjectivity in even the most "logical" of messages. Instead, your values, emotions, and aesthetic preferences shape your beliefs and actions. As such, individuals relay messages and experiences through stories in an attempt to capture these subjective experiences.

Second, the narrative paradigm suggests that because individuals' lives and understanding of reality are centered on these subjective narratives, people need a way to judge which stories are believable and which are not (Fisher, 1987). Here, Fisher argued that individuals use **narrative rationality**—a logical method of reasoning by which a person can determine how believable another's narrative is. Narrative rationality relies on **good reasons** as the basis for most decision making. As opposed to relying solely on argumentative logic, good reasons allow us to validate and accept (or reject) another's narrative based on the perceived truthfulness and **consistency**. Thus, the twin tests of narrative fidelity and coherence are two ways to help make this narrative judgment of "good reasons."

When a persuasive narrative appears truthful and congruent with our own values, culture, character, and experiences, we say there is **narrative fidelity** (Fisher, 1987). Importantly, to accept a narrative, the recipient must perceive the narrative's fidelity first; without fidelity, coherence is irrelevant. Assuming the test of fidelity is met, the second criterion is that of **narrative coherence**. Fisher outlined three standards of coherence: structural, material, and characterological. *Structural coherence* refers to a story's flow and arrangement. Is the story conveyed sequentially, logically, and without contradictions? Or does it bounce around or contain inconsistencies that make it hard to follow? *Material coherence* refers to the extent to which this story matches or is consistent with other stories already accepted by the receiver. Finally, and perhaps most importantly, *characterological coherence* involves the credibility or believability of the story's "characters."

A related third assumption is that what a person accepts as a good reason is based on that individual's culture, character, history, values, experience, and the like

(Fisher, 1984, 1987). In other words, what appears to have coherence and fidelity to one person may not appeal to another who comes to the narrative relationship with a different set of values and experiences.

Fourth, the narrative paradigm proposes that "rationality is determined by the nature of persons as narrative beings" (Fisher, 1987, p. 5). Rather than conceiving of reason as rooted only in fact and logical argument, Fisher argued that rationality—and therefore persuasion—stems from humans' ability to create a coherent story. Thus, piling on the facts about a political candidate's legislative record isn't what is persuasive for voters; what will influence constituents is a candidate's ability to share his or her experiences via narrative.

Finally, the narrative paradigm presumes the world as humans know it is based primarily on sets of both cooperative and competing stories (Fisher, 1987). Individuals must use the logic of good reasons to choose among these narratives, thereby creating and re-creating their social reality. Because "human communication . . . is imbued with mythos—ideas that cannot be verified or proved in any absolute way" (p. 19), Fisher believed individuals must rely on narratives as the creation and re-creation of a common understanding. The narratives we choose can fundamentally affect our life.

Study in Contrasts: Comparing Narrative and Rational Paradigms

Mentioned earlier, the narrative paradigm contrasts with much of Western thought, including the emphasis on the rational paradigm. Table 7.2 presents the contrast between the narrative paradigm and the rational paradigm. Specifically, Fisher (1987) argued that **logos**, or purely rational argument, has been unfairly privileged as the ultimate measure of rationality. For example, he cited Aristotle's preference for persuasion and intellectual arguments grounded first and foremost in logos. As previously discussed, the narrative paradigm assumes little in our social worlds can be understood as purely fact; everything around us is shaded with the subjectivity of individual values and experiences. As such, "rationality is grounded in the narrative structure of life and the natural capacity people have to recognize coherence and fidelity in the stories they experience and tell to one another" (p. 137). Consequently, Fisher posited that mythos (narratives) and **pathos** (emotional appeals) are more meaningful to humans and, therefore, more persuasive.

Importantly, the narrative paradigm does not exclude logic (Fisher, 1987). Instead, Fisher (1987) argued that no rhetorical proof (credibility, emotion, or reason) should be regarded as superior to other forms of rhetorical proof. Fisher also maintained humans should move away from dualistic approaches (i.e., that we are either rational or narrative) and embrace more integrated perspectives (i.e., that we are both rational and narrative).

According to the narrative paradigm, then, human communication and our understanding of "reality" relies heavily on narration. What's more, Fisher (1987) believed narrative is a more effective means of influence than traditional forms of logic based on reasoning. However, only when a narrative exhibits good reasons and narrative coherence will it be convincing enough to permeate a receiver's consciousness and become translated into a change in action.

Table 7.2 Comparing the Narrative and Rational-World Paradigms

Narrative Paradigm	Rational-World Paradigm
1. Human beings are storytellers.	1. Human beings are rational.
2. Communication, persuasion, and decision making are based on the logic of good reasons.	2. Communication, persuasion, and decision making are based on sound arguments.
3. What one accepts as "good reasons" is determined individually by a person's culture, character, experiences, and values.	3. Strong arguments adhere to specific criteria for soundness and logic (e.g., using the premise-inference-conclusion model).
4. Rationality is based on one's awareness of how consistent and truthful a story appears when compared with one's own (and others') lived experiences.	4. Rationality is based on the accuracy of information presented and on the reliability of the reasoning processes used.
5. People experience the world as a series of stories from which to choose. As we make these choices, we create and re-create reality.	5. The world and reality can be viewed as a series of logical relationships revealed through reasoned argument.

Organizational Storytelling

Lest the narrative paradigm seem too intangible for practical use, consider the influence of organizational storytelling. Barker and Gower (2010) argue that integrating good storytelling in diverse, multicultural work environments has tremendous benefit to the organization and its workforce. They contend that "stories serve a persuasive communication function for organizations by representing personal, interpersonal, and corporate perspectives" (p. 304). The e-commerce retail giant, Zappos, has shown great success with organizational storytelling, both internally by using narratives to communicate organizational values to employees and externally with customers (Greenberg, 2013). In their extensive review of literature on organizational storytelling, Barker and Gower (2010) cite numerous examples of the power of organizational narratives. From using narratives to convey organizational culture (Barker, Rimler, Moreno, & Kaplan, 2004), to encouraging organizational learning (Lämsä & Sintonen, 2006), to promoting employee expertise (McLellan, 2006), to conveying authenticity in organizational leadership (Driscoll & McKee, 2007), the narrative paradigm has numerous applications for leaders of organizational development.

SUMMARY AND RESEARCH APPLICATIONS

This chapter examined four theories of persuasion. ELM argues that persuaders must carefully consider their audience before crafting a message. Receivers must be motivated and able to process objective, elaborated messages. When audience members are unmotivated or unable to process such messages (or both), peripheral cues should be used. ELM has been successful in explaining a variety of persuasive efforts, including campaigns to influence people to read nutrition labels. Dong (2015) found that centrally routed messages (statistics presented by a dietician) were more persuasive when an audience member self-identified as being health conscious, whereas peripheral messages (a celebrity sharing her shopping method, which includes reading nutrition labels) was more persuasive to those who reported lower levels of health consciousness.

In our second approach, the theory of planned behavior takes persuasion a step further, stating three concepts can predict an individual's behavior: attitude, normative beliefs, and controllability. A wide range of actions have been studied using this theory, including the likelihood that someone will post selfies on social networking sites (Kim, Lee, Sung, & Choi, 2016), willingness to intervene when a friend is the victim of relational violence (Lemay, O'Brien, Kearney, Sauber, & Venaglia, 2017), and college students' intentions to cheat on exams (Chudzicka-Czupała et al., 2016).

Third, inoculation theory provides a means to argue proactively in support of a position by sending preemptive messages that include forewarning of the threat and refutations to anticipated arguments. The theory's application has wide reach, including public relations' research demonstrating that inoculation messages are a viable proactive strategy in crisis communication (Kim, 2013) and also work to prevent people from falling prey to conspiracy propaganda (Banas & Miller, 2013). Inoculation theory has also been used to craft resistance messages applicable to public health communication professionals. From trying to uphold one's exercise motivation (Dimmock et al., 2016), to studying the efficacy of alcohol media literacy interventions among school students (Gordon, Howard, Jones, & Kervin, 2016) to protecting positive attitudes toward the HPV vaccine (Wong, 2016), inoculation theory is frequently employed either as a means of discouraging behaviors that negatively affect public health or of protecting positive health behaviors in the face of temptation to do otherwise.

Our fourth and final theory, the narrative paradigm, looks at persuasive messages through a descriptive lens. That is, persuasion isn't so much a rational process as it is an emotional one based on storytelling. Narratives must have coherence and the logic of good reasons to be influential. In addition to the benefits of organizational narratives discussed earlier, the narrative paradigm has been used to analyze the effectiveness of college recruiting materials (Burns, 2015), as well as to explain the powerful role of personal narratives among Alcoholics Anonymous members in their efforts to achieve and maintain sobriety (Lederman & Menegatos, 2011).

KEY TERMS

Able   123
Attitude   122
Authority   124
Behavioral intention   127
Central route   122

Characterological
    coherence   133
Commitment   124
Consistency   133
Contrast   124

Controllability   128
Elaborated argument   123
Good reasons   133
Inoculation   130
Liking   124

CASE STUDY 7: MILLION-DOLLAR MANIPULATION

Trina had always loved her job at the Columbus AIDS Confederation (CAC). She was part of a small nonprofit that served economically disadvantaged people who had been diagnosed with HIV/AIDS. As a case worker, Trina provided one-on-one support for her clients, helping them cope with their diagnosis and assisting them with developing a plan of care. A big part of her job was to facilitate her clients' access to community resources that might help them, whether it was housing, nutrition, or medical care. It was important work, and she loved her coworkers, her clients, and the CAC.

As a small nonprofit in a relatively large urban area, the CAC was almost always struggling to meet a sizable pool of potential clients given a modest (at best) budget. The organization had just five social workers, an executive director, and an administrator on staff. The executive director, Mohammad Bacho, not only had to oversee the work that was being done by the organization, he also had to do fundraising, marketing, and community outreach. As a licensed social worker, he also occasionally met with clients when needed, especially to cover the vacations and sick days of the social workers on staff. And, of course, there was the ongoing tension of working with the board of trustees. This tension particularly became an issue when Albert Brothman rose to chairman of the board for the CAC. Brothman was a successful CEO who managed a multi-million-dollar company based in Columbus. His demeanor was a bit brash for the "people-first" mindset typical in the nonprofit sector; Brothman was confident to the point of arrogance and aggressive to the point of bullying.

The first board meeting with Brothman at the helm did not go well. Brothman challenged Mohammad's leadership skill, questioned his fund-raising numbers, and criticized Mohammad's care for clients. As an executive director of a nonprofit, Mohammed was skilled at the delicate balance of reassuring board members while simultaneously fighting for the integrity of the nonprofit. He remained calm and simply asked the board to help him to live the mission of the organization. Little did he know that his modest request would have such troubling consequences.

At the next month's board meeting, Brothman announced that he had finalized a deal with BRcd Enterprises, a pharmaceutical company that was seeking to develop a new protease inhibitor for HIV/AIDS. BRcd had promised to donate $1 million to the CAC, which was a large

(Continued)

and potentially transformational gift. Mohammad was excited but also concerned. What was the catch? He didn't have to wait long to find out.

BRcd had already filled out its Investigational New Drug Application with the FDA and had completed Phase 1 clinical trials for the new protease inhibitor. The Phase I Trials, which were conducted on healthy volunteers, indicated that the drug was safe. The company was about to launch Phase II, which focuses on the effectiveness of the drug. For this phase, they needed to study people who had been diagnosed with HIV/AIDS. And they wanted the CAC to do the recruiting for them.

Mohammad knew that such a request had the potential of being unethical; the ethical code of the National Association of Social Workers was clear about conflict of interest. However, he also knew that his social workers had a great deal of integrity, and he could trust them to practice ethically. He called a staff meeting the day after the board meeting.

"I've got some really great news, and I have a small request," Mohammad began. "The really great news is that we have received a $1 million gift."

Trina and her colleagues couldn't help themselves. They cheered and high-fived each other. "That is incredible, Mohammad!" Trina exclaimed. "How did you manage that?" she asked.

"It wasn't me. It was Mr. Brothman. Apparently, he's got some connections to a pharmaceutical company, and he convinced them to make the gift."

"Wait, what? A pharmaceutical company?" Gavin asked. "What would a pharmaceutical company want with us?"

"Just like us, they are committed to serving people with HIV/AIDS," Mohammad explained. "They just wanted to put their money where their mouth is."

"Huh. Well, that's pretty awesome. I'm down with that," Darryl exclaimed. The other social workers mumbled their acceptance as well.

"So that was the great news, what's the small request? Would you like us to start purchasing all of our supplies at Brothman's company?" Tiffany asked. The group chuckled at her facetious comment, knowing that none of them could afford the high-end products Brothman's companies sold.

"No," Mohammad said solemnly, immediately dampening the enthusiasm of the group. "No, but this is serious. Listen, as part of the deal with the pharmaceutical company, Brothman did make a promise, and I want you to hear it from me first, and I want to make sure you understand that I have the same strong ethical commitments that you do. The pharmaceutical company, BRcd, is seeking approval from the FDA for a new HIV/AIDS drug. They are about to launch the Phase II study, and they are looking for participants for the drug trial."

"Please tell me . . ." Gavin began.

Mohammad held up his hand to hold off the question. "I informed the board that we would not violate our ethical standards as social workers. I explained conflict of interest to them, and I reminded them that many of our clients are vulnerable, and it would be inappropriate to try to persuade them to take part in the study. The board agreed. They have merely asked that we post information about the drug trial in our offices, and if we think it is appropriate, that we disseminate information about the study to any suitable clients. We will not directly solicit participants."

The social workers were mollified but still concerned. Their jobs were to advocate for their clients, not pander to the needs of a donor.

"Look, we don't exactly have many million-dollar donors beating down our door. Beggars can't be choosers, right? I'm convinced we can accept this money without compromising our integrity," Mohammad reassured.

Within a month, the money had come in, a poster about the clinical trial was displayed in the CAC lobby, and each social worker was given a handful of pamphlets about the study to distribute to any appropriate clients.

Four weeks later, Mohammad answered his office phone to a very irate chairman of the board. "Bacho, I thought I was clear with you about this BRcd deal. They gave us money. We give them subjects for their drug trial. I can see that we got the money. Why the hell don't they have any subjects for their damn study?" Brothman shouted.

"Mr. Brothman," Mohammad began. "You know that we are bound by the ethical guidelines of our profession. We simply cannot coerce our clients to take part in a study."

"I'm not talking about coercion, Bacho, I'm talking about persuasion. BRcd needs 100 people for their study, and they need them as soon as possible. Every delay means that your clients don't have another potential drug that can help them. Work harder at getting subjects."

Mohammad hung up the phone and considered how to best create a win/win solution. He decided to craft an e-mail to his staff, which read as follows:

Dear Colleagues:

We do important work at the CAC. Most of you may not think about it, but just a few years ago I was one of you; I was out in the field, doing my best to help people that society wants to ignore. I remember one of my clients, Rosa. Rosa was 26 when she was diagnosed with HIV. Unfortunately, she wasn't diagnosed until after she had 3 children, and two of her children subsequently were diagnosed with HIV. Like many of our clients, Rosa was a substance abuser, and her willingness to be treated for HIV varied depending on her sobriety. It would be easy to judge Rosa, but that's not our job. Our job is to do our very best for the

Rosas out there and to work tirelessly to make sure that her kids have a chance for a healthy life, too.

I know that you are doing everything you can for your clients. It's great that we at the CAC provide the support that we do, but isn't the real end goal to try to prevent people from needing our support? Don't we want a future where we aren't attending the funerals of our clients, or worse yet, kids who didn't deserve to deal with the issues they have to deal with?

Yes, we have come a long way in the drug treatments we have available to people with HIV/AIDS, but don't we want to stop treating the disease and start curing it?

We have the opportunity to contribute to finding a cure for HIV/AIDS. You have the information pamphlets provided by BRcd. Please consider talking about the opportunity to be a part of the study with your clients.

Yours in Service, Mohammad

Within 5 minutes of the e-mail being sent, Trina was on the phone with Tiffany. "Did you see Mohammad's e-mail?" she fumed. "Can you believe this? I thought he said that we didn't have to solicit participants!" she fumed.

"Hmmm. I didn't read it that way at all. I trust Mohammad. If he wants me to talk to my clients, I will. I mean, I won't be pressuring them, just informing them about an opportunity," Tiffany replied.

"Are you kidding me?" Trina was aghast. "I am not going to be controlled by some money-grubbing pharma company! My integrity is worth more than a million dollars."

Tiffany sighed. "Trina, Mohammad has reassured us again and again that he won't compromise our integrity. Finding volunteers

(Continued)

(Continued)

for the study is a good thing. Things aren't so black and white."

"Uh, yes they are. There is right, and there is wrong! This is wrong, Tiffany. BRcd should just find participants the same way every other pharma company does. And I'm going to let Mohammad know that it is wrong." Trina hung up, exasperated.

Trina was so angry she didn't know what to do with herself. After pacing her living room for a half an hour, she sat down at her computer and began typing. First, she wrote a letter of resignation. Then, she wrote a letter to the National Association of Social Workers (NASW), detailing what she perceived to be a violation of ethical behavior and requesting a professional review of Mohammad Bacho, and another letter to the state licensing board, asking for the same. Finally, she wrote an e-mail to her former colleagues at the CAC.

Dear Tiffany, Gavin, Darryl, and Shanae:

I want to let you know that I have resigned from my position at the CAC, and I have filed a professional complaint with the NASW and the state licensing board. I have worked with each of you for at least 5 years (and Tiff, we have worked together for 12!), and I have always been proud to be a part of a group of caring and committed social workers. I cannot in good conscience continue my employment there given the questionable ethical conditions at the CAC.

I know you—all of you. I know that you are outstanding professionals who are dedicated to doing the very best for our clients. I know you are honorable and honest and hardworking. Please do not fall prey to the questionable "deal" negotiated by the chairman of the board, Albert Brothman, and please don't be

persuaded by Mohammad's reassurances that he wants us to behave ethically. First, he swore to us that we did not have to directly solicit participants for the drug trial. Then, he asked us to "talk" to our clients about the opportunity. What's next? Have us drive our clients to the study? Make sure they're taking the study meds? Think about it. This is not just a little thing he is asking, he is asking us to violate our own code of ethics. As social workers, we are dedicated to service and the right to self-determination. We cannot use our position of power to manipulate people into doing something that might not be in their own best interests.

All my Best.

Trina

Questions for Consideration

1. What peripheral strategies did Mr. Brothman use? Why didn't these strategies work? What peripheral strategies did Mohammad use when talking with the social workers? Would a central route work better? Why, or why not?

2. How do Trina's attitudes and normative beliefs affect her behavioral intention to solicit participants for the study? How does perceived behavioral control come into play for her? Now contrast these elements with Tiffany's attitudes, normative beliefs, and behavioral intentions.

3. How did Trina use inoculation theory to try to persuade her fellow social workers?

4. Mohammad decided to send an e-mail to his staff using a narrative. Why do

you think he did so? What elements of the narrative would be persuasive to the social workers? Why do you think so?

5. What ethical challenges emerged with Brothman's behavior? What about with Mohammad's? Do any of the theories provide insight that might help to resolve or exacerbate these ethical tensions?

6. Which persuasion theory seems to explain the situation better than the others? Why do you believe this to be the case? What situations might surface to make a different theory or theories better at explaining the situation? What theories could you combine to make for an even better explanation of the encounter?

…LIC ('slaw

pain in the abdome

COLISEUM, see col…

COLLABORATE (ko

to work jointly, espec

or scientific work.

COLLABORATION (-

united labour.

COLLABORATOR (-lab

…e who assists another

literary or scientific wo…

…APSE (ko-laps'), n.

…gether; sudden

…LIC (kol'ik), n.

CHAPTER EIGHT

GROUP COMMUNICATION

Whether you work for a publishing company, a retail organization, or a Fortune 500 corporation, U.S. businesses are increasingly adopting a "team" structure. To succeed as a communication professional, understanding *how* groups work, as well as the principles and pitfalls of group decision making, is crucial to your career. In this chapter, we explain a broad range of group theories—from those that focus specifically on group decision making to those that emphasize the ways group communication creates the norms for group behavior.

GROUP COMMUNICATION DEFINED

Popular understanding implies a group is simply a collection of people. Scholars studying group communication are more precise when using the term *group*, however. According to scholars, a **group** refers to a system of three or more individuals who are focused on achieving a common purpose and who influence and are influenced by each other (Rothwell, 1998). A group is different from an **aggregate**, which is simply a set number of individuals—say, the people standing at a bus stop or the people on an elevator. Moreover, a group is distinct from an organization. Organizations typically involve formal hierarchies (e.g., CEO, director, manager) and structured channels of communication (e.g., annual performance reviews, employee newsletters). In contrast, a group's structure and patterns of communication typically emerge through interaction (Rothwell, 1998).

Because of the increased use of team-based structures in organizations, it is also of interest to articulate the nature of a **team**. In an organizational setting, a team is an ongoing, coordinated group of people working together (Dyer, 1987). Teams are typically self-directed and self-regulating, meaning typical chains of organizational command are suspended; teams are empowered to complete a task

Learning Objectives

After reading this chapter, you will be able to do the following:

1. Articulate the four functions and three types of communication identified in the functional approach to decision making

2. Recommend strategies to prevent groupthink

3. Articulate how adaptive structuration theory illuminates the group decision-making process

4. Explain the development of a rhetorical vision using symbolic convergence theory

5. Compare and contrast major theoretical approaches to group communication

6. Provide systematic understanding of a professional situation by employing theories of group communication

from start to finish. Not all groups are teams (if control is primarily external, for example), but all teams meet the qualification of being a group.

Group communication is distinct from other types of communication because all groups must balance **task communication** (communication focused on achieving the instrumental goal the group is trying to achieve) with **socioemotional communication** (communication focused on developing, maintaining, and repairing the relationships between group members). Put simply, the more time the group members spend on the task, the less their focus on relationship needs, and vice versa. Because group members likely have different orientations toward the importance of these two activities, balancing task communication and socioemotional communication is often quite challenging and usually leads to group members enacting group roles. A **group role** refers to a pattern of communicative behaviors performed by one individual in light of expectations held by other group members. Typically, group roles are classified as task-oriented roles, maintenance-oriented roles, and disruptive roles, which are roles that meet individual versus group needs. For example, the isolate is someone who withdraws from participating in the group, the zealot is someone who tries to convert all group members to his or her belief system, and the stage hog monopolizes the conversational floor and prevents others from expressing their thoughts and opinions (Rothwell, 1998).

This chapter emphasizes understanding the communication that takes place within groups and teams. The four theories we present vary in focus. First, functional group decision making centers on the tasks communication achieves in the decision-making process. Continuing with a focus on decision making, the second theory, groupthink, provides a mechanism for explaining poor or ineffective group decision making. Adaptive structuration theory also considers decision making, but it offers a broader perspective on group communication, focusing on how the communication process itself creates the norms for interaction. Finally, symbolic convergence theory explains the development of a group consciousness, including shared emotions, motives, and meanings.

FUNCTIONAL GROUP DECISION MAKING

Although groups have a number of purposes, one of the central purposes is decision making. Gouran and Hirokawa (1983, 1986, 1996) are the key researchers associated with developing the functional approach to group communication. A **function** refers to what communication does. For example, an apology serves the function of relationship repair, and a joke can serve the function of tension release. As such, the functional approach to decision making focuses less on what is actually said and more on what the communication in groups *does*; how does it function?

Gouran and Hirokawa began theory development by asking the basic question, "Why do some groups make good decisions while others make bad ones?" (Hirokawa, see Miller, 2002, p. 219). Their model argues that the answer to this question has to do with whether or not the group has successfully accomplished five functions, which they call *requisite functions* (Gouran & Hirokawa, 1983, 1996). These functions are highlighted in Table 8.1.

The first function is **problem analysis** (Gouran & Hirokawa, 1983). This means the group must take a realistic look at the nature, extent, and likely causes of the problem. This function also necessitates all members are clear about what they are trying to accomplish. A thorough analysis often involves information gathering. As an example, let's consider a group convened to address the larger organization's continued budget shortfall. The functional group decision-making theory suggests the group should spend a significant amount of time analyzing the actual gap between essential and realized revenues, the implications of the budget shortfall, and the possible causes for the short-fall. Were there too many expenditures? Slow growth in sales? Or is it just a normal downturn in the economy, which might bounce back? The answers to these questions are important because recognizing the root cause and implications of the problem deter-mines the form the solution should take.

The second function is to **determine minimal standards** or characteristics of an acceptable solution (Gouran & Hirokawa, 1996). Returning to our example, the group members studying the budget shortfall need to be clear about their goals (e.g., are they an advisory group that can only make recommendations, or are they an actual decision-making group?). Typically, this function requires group members to develop criteria; these criteria, or standards, will be used to evaluate possible solutions. Thus, our example group should also determine the requirements for a solution. Some sample criteria might include the following: budget cuts shouldn't exceed more than 5%, the implementation of the solution must be achievable within 6 months, and the solution must support the organization's mission.

The third function is to **identify alternatives**. Here, group members brainstorm to generate many possible solutions, maximizing the likelihood that a good solution is ulti-mately chosen (Gouran & Hirokawa, 1983). **Brainstorming** requires group members to come up with as many solutions as possible while following these rules: don't evaluate ideas; don't clarify ideas; encourage zany ideas; expand on others' ideas; record all ideas with no reference as to who contributed; and encourage participation from everyone (Putnam & Paulus, 2009).

Fourth, the group must **evaluate** the possible solutions (Gouran & Hirokawa, 1983, 1996). To accomplish this, group members must assess the possible solutions generated in the previous function; specifically, the members must compare the possible solutions with the criteria they developed in the second function. Both positive and negative char-acteristics of the proposed solutions should be considered before selecting the solution that best meets the group's goals (Gouran & Hirokawa, 1983). Returning to our example decision-making group, the chosen solution will likely be altered if the group deter-mined the problem was slow sales growth rather than overexpenditure. The fifth and final function is **selecting** the best alternative based on the analysis of available options completed in function four.

Functional group decision-making theory states that all five functions need to be accomplished to maximize the likelihood of an effective decision and that no one function is more important than another. Hirokawa (1994) acknowledged, however, that a spe-cific problem might make a particular function more or less challenging to accomplish. For example, because some problems are particularly obvious, problem analysis is relatively easy. Other problems might naturally have many possible solutions; here, generating alternatives might be a time-consuming endeavor. Perhaps more important than task complexity, however, are group members' awareness of and ability to reflect on their process, recognizing that process is just as, if not more, important than the product itself (Gouran & Hirokawa, 1996).

Despite appearance of a logical order to the requisite functions, research suggests it doesn't matter whether they are completed in a particular order; it only matters that the functions are completed (Hirokawa, 1994). Nevertheless, Hirokawa (1994) found that groups tackling complex problems tend to follow a similar path. Specifically, the pattern suggests that an analysis of the problem tends to happen first but that the group then cycles back and forth between problem analysis and identifying alternatives. Once criteria are established and the group is satisfied with the proposed alternatives, they move on to evaluation and selection.

Finally, functional group decision-making theory makes particular claims about communication in groups. The theory argues that "communication is a social tool used to accomplish effective decision-making" (Hirokawa & Salazar, 1999, p. 169). As such, it proposes that human beings actively construct group experience based on their communication. Gouran and Hirokawa (1986) specifically delineated three types of communication in small groups. **Promotive communication** is geared toward one of the requisite functions. **Disruptive communication** diverts, retards, or frustrates the ability of the group to achieve the requisite functions. Disruptive communication might include social communication. Finally, **counteractive communication**, or messages that return a disrupted group back to the requisite functions, is likely to be most important for group decision making.

Table 8.1 Five Functions of Decision Making	
Function	**Means of Achievement**
Problem analysis	Focus on the nature, extent, and likely causes of the problem. Be careful to differentiate between problems and symptoms of problems.
Determine standards	Identify what an ideal solution would "look like." What are absolutely necessary elements, and what would be ideal but not necessary?
Identify alternatives	Generate a large number of possible solutions: Quantity matters more than quality at this point.
Evaluate	Evaluate each alternative using the established goals.
Select	Based on the evaluation of alternatives, group members select the "best" alternative, the alternative that best fulfills the characteristics and criteria established.

Relatively narrow in scope, the functional perspective focuses solely on task communication associated with group decision making. It is the promise of improved group success that makes this theory a significant practical application for communication, business, and other professions.

GROUPTHINK

Whether or not you know the details of the theory, it's likely you've heard the term *groupthink*. Developed by Janis (1972), the notion of groupthink has bridged the gap from the realm of academics into popular culture. We performed a Google search of the term and found more than one million hits, with the term referenced in major newspapers, magazines, trade journals, and even blogs. Clearly the concept is being used—but is it being used the way Janis intended?

Groupthink is a dysfunctional "way of deliberating that group members use when their desire for unanimity overrides their motivation to assess all available plans of action" (Janis, see Miller, 2002, p. 193). As such, groupthink was designed to explain and predict how bad decisions are made by groups. At its core, the notion of groupthink represents a failure of the group to demonstrate critical thinking. When groups "go along to get along," the end result of the decision-making process is likely to be less effective than if group members question the information at hand, being careful to look at the problem from a variety of perspectives.

Antecedent Conditions

Janis (1982) articulated three **antecedent conditions** to groupthink. According to Janis, these preexisting conditions make groupthink more likely. Note that the existence of the antecedent conditions does not guarantee groupthink. Instead, Janis calls these "necessary but not sufficient" conditions. The antecedent conditions are high cohesion, structural flaws, and situational characteristics.

First, **cohesion** refers to the degree of connection, or sense of solidarity, between group members (Janis, 1982). Because groupthink emphasizes the preservation of group harmony, a high degree of cohesion is necessary for groupthink to occur. Yet Janis's notion that cohesion might engender bad decision making is novel. Think about your own work experiences; in how many "team-building" activities have you taken part? If you are a full-time student, how many of your classes have started with "icebreakers" so the class members might feel more connected to each other? Typically, workplace cohesion is viewed positively, but Janis warns cohesion might make people reluctant to "rock the boat"; yet rocking the boat might be necessary to make the best possible decision.

The second antecedent condition, **structural flaws**, refers to problems with the way the group is organized (Janis, 1982). Janis identified four specific structural flaws, any one of which might lead to groupthink. First, *group insulation* means the group is somehow isolated from the larger world. Perhaps they meet so frequently with each other and so infrequently with others outside the group that they are disconnected from the larger system. Perhaps the group hasn't had direct experience with the problem at hand.

This insulation might lead to an inability to process adequately all of the information necessary to make an effective decision. The second structural flaw is *biased leadership*. If the leader already has his or her mind made up or has a personal stake in the decision, group members might defer to the leader simply because of the power differential, regardless of whether the leader's solution is good. Third, *a lack of procedural norms* can lead to groupthink. Not having a process in place for how to make a decision can happen either because the group has not taken the time to create the process or because the group fails to follow the process. In either case, following a standard process can prevent the group from inadvertently missing a key component of the decision-making process. Last, too much *homogeneity* is problematic. Homogeneity refers to similarity; group members who are very similar—in background, values, or beliefs—are less likely to challenge each other's ideas.

The third and final antecedent condition is **situational characteristics** (Janis, 1982). In short, groupthink is more likely to occur in times of high stress. This high stress might come from pressures outside the group. Groups that work in the pharmaceutical industry experience stress from Federal Drug Administration requirements. Television network executives experience pressure from advertisers. Sometimes external forces place undue pressure on the group through operating constraints, threats, or legal requirements. High stress might also come in the form of time pressures; the more rapidly a decision has to be made, the less likely all possible solutions have been adequately studied.

Stressors don't always come from outside the group, however (Janis, 1982). Groups that have experienced recent failures may lose confidence in their decision-making ability, and the loss of confidence might create a self-fulfilling prophecy. The final category of situational characteristics is moral dilemmas; if group members feel the viable alternatives represent ethical challenges, they are more likely to fall prey to groupthink. Consider a situation where a group can come up with only three solutions to a problem, but two of the three are deemed ethically inappropriate—the group is likely to pursue the third option, regardless of how good it might be.

Again, these three antecedent conditions are necessary, but not sufficient, for groupthink. In other words, all three conditions must be present to some degree for groupthink to occur; however, these circumstances alone don't guarantee groupthink. Instead, Janis (1982) argued you have to examine how the group operates to observe symptoms of the groupthink process.

Symptoms of Groupthink

Janis (1982) identified eight symptoms grouped into three categories: overestimation, closed-mindedness, and pressure toward uniformity. The first classification of symptoms, **overestimation of the group**, occurs when group members have an inflated view of the group's abilities. Two specific symptoms to look for are an illusion of invulnerability (a belief that the group won't or can't fail) and a belief in the inherent morality of the group (because the group is good, the decisions the group makes have to be good). Note that both of these symptoms are representative of unwavering confidence in the group and its abilities. As such, group members might not feel it necessary to analyze critically the decisions being made.

The second category of groupthink symptoms includes **closed-mindedness** (Janis, 1982). These symptoms demonstrate polarized thinking, which means viewing the world in extremes. Things are perceived either as good or bad, right or wrong. If they are good, they are wholly good; if they are bad, they are wholly bad. If a decision is right, it must be completely right. Two specific instances of this category are stereotyping out-groups and collective rationalization. First, *stereotyping* out-groups refers to the process of demonizing other groups and their leaders. In the United States in 2017, both major political parties have engaged in stereotyping out-groups. On the left, conservatives have been deemed racist, misogynistic, and deplorable, and Donald Trump is compared to Hitler and Mussolini. On the right, the mainstream liberal media cannot be believed, Democrats have been labeled "libtards," and Democratic politicians are called smug, arrogant, and anti-American. When other groups are portrayed as uncompromisingly bad, it is easier to ignore information that might challenge that belief. *Collective rationalization* means that the group members tend to justify their decisions by talking themselves into it. As an example, consider a group that spends only 5 minutes coming up with a solution and 25 minutes discussing why they are right in making the decision. Rather than critically analyzing the decision, group members come up with a litany of reasons to defend why it's a good decision.

The third and final symptom of groupthink is organized around the notion of **pressure toward uniformity** (Janis, 1982). When groupthink occurs, it is not only because the group members have an inflated view of themselves or because they demonstrate polarized thinking; it is also because individual group members actively suppress critical thinking. Self-censorship means group members tend to keep their mouths shut when experiencing doubts. Often they feel as though everyone else is "on board" with the decision, so they are afraid to go out on a limb with their concerns. This tendency also highlights the illusion of unanimity, which means group members perceive a consensus, even if one hasn't been reached. As such, silence tends to be interpreted as consent. In fact, self-appointed mind guards are careful not to present any contrary information, even if they know it exists; in other words, a self-appointed mind guard engages in self-censorship. If someone actually does question the decision, a group experiencing groupthink will often place pressure on dissenters; challenges to the group are squashed.

To prevent groupthink, Janis (1982) recommends group members take the following steps: encourage critical evaluation; avoid having the leader state a preference; set up several independent subgroups to study the problem and propose solutions; discuss what is happening in the group with people outside of the group; invite outsiders into the group; assign someone to be a devil's advocate; monitor the group for the symptoms; and take time between the initial decision and the confirmation of the decision to analyze the decision critically.

Table 8.2 presents an overview of the antecedents and symptoms of groupthink. As you can see, Janis (1982) identified a large number of factors present before the group begins deliberating, as well as factors recognizable while the group is deliberating. Groupthink itself—the tendency to avoid critical thinking so cohesion can be maintained—occurs somewhere in between antecedent conditions and the symptoms.

Table 8.2 Antecedents and Symptoms of Groupthink

Antecedents	Groupthink	Symptoms
Cohesion		*Overestimation of group*
		• Illusion of invulnerability
		• Belief in morality
Structural flaws		*Closed-mindedness*
• Insulation		• Stereotypes
• Biased leadership		• Collective rationalizations
• No procedural norms		
• Homogeneity		
Situational characteristics		*Uniformity pressures*
• High stress		• Self-censorship
• Time pressure		• Illusion of unanimity
• Recent failures		• Self-appointed mindguards
• Moral dilemmas		• Direct pressure on dissenters

ADAPTIVE STRUCTURATION THEORY

Originally proposed as a general theory of social interaction (Giddens, 1979), structuration theory served as a springboard for Poole and McPhee (McPhee, 1985; Poole, 1985, 1988; Poole & McPhee, 1983) to explain group and organizational communication processes. At the core of structuration theory is the notion of structure. Structures are not physical entities but, in essence, patterns of relationships and patterns of interaction; they provide guidelines for behavior. Poole (1988) argued that structures are featured characteristics of organizations: "Division of labor, organization of workflow, arrangement of people into hierarchical positions, the use of budgets all are the hallmarks of the organization, and all involve the imposition of structure" (p. 1).

According to Poole (1988), structures serve five primary functions in groups and organizations: they provide a means for coordination and control, they assist members in defining their identities in the organization, they provide a means to monitor member performance, they help the organization to relate to its environment, and they serve a symbolic function, indicating to group members and outsiders the nature of the organization. Despite the importance of structures in groups and organizations, Poole's theory contends that structures are not as permanent as you might think; like any strong relationship, they require constant maintenance and repair. Specifically, communication is the means by which structures are developed, maintained, and changed. This process is known as structuration.

Assumptions of Structuration Theory

There are two major assumptions of structuration theory. First, the theory assumes humans are actors who make choices (Giddens, 1979). This assumption, also called **agency**, means people have free will in terms of their communicative behavior. The second assumption is that groups and organizations are produced and reproduced through structures in interaction (Giddens, 1979). This assumption requires people to understand what Giddens means by the terms *structure*, *production*, and *reproduction*.

As indicated earlier, structure is not a physical entity but a set of rules and resources used by a group in order to meet its goals. **Rules** are *how* the group should accomplish its goals. Think of rules as either formal or informal prescriptions for how to do things. A formal rule might be a company policy that everyone must show up by 8:00 a.m., and an informal rule might be that group members believe decisions are made by consensus. Resources are the properties organizational members rely on to get things done. Two types of resources are available to members. **Allocative resources** are material forms of assistance, such as time and money. **Authoritative resources** are interpersonal characteristics of group members, such as cohesion, experience, and status.

With the understanding that structures (rules and resources) are central to group life, we turn to the second premise of the theory, that groups are produced and reproduced through structures in interaction. Through their behavioral choices, group members create (produce) structures. To illustrate, group members who act as though time is more important than money will create a structure (i.e., a rule) that making rapid decisions is more important than making cost-effective decisions. The effect of this structure lives on, however. Future group members can refer back to this rule and then prioritize their decision making so that time efficiency is more important than fiscal conservation. As such, they have reinforced (or reproduced) the rule initially created. Through interaction, the structure is produced and reproduced; individuals have created it, but they are also constrained by it.

This notion that group members' action (agency) both creates and constrains interaction is known as the **duality of structure**. Note that the theory is firmly committed to pragmatism; human beings have complete free will with regard to their behavior. However, structuration theory suggests the notion of structure is intertwined with human action, providing a subtle force or influence. Ellis (1999) characterized agency and structure as "braided social entities" (p. 127). Throughout the process of structuration, human beings have the choice to change the rules or adjust the resources available to them in their interaction, but they feel pressured by the constraints of previous actions. Moreover, these activities often occur at low levels of consciousness. Group members are not always aware of structures, nor are they aware of their ability to change structures.

Adaptive Structuration Theory

Recall that Poole, Seibold, and McPhee used Giddens's structuration theory as a basis for their theory, which they called adaptive structuration theory (AST).

AST builds on the original theory by adding two concepts that make it applicable specifically to group communication. First, they believed structures are often borrowed from larger groups (Poole, Seibold, & McPhee, 1985, 1986). For example, a work group may appropriate, or borrow from, the structures of the larger corporation, such as the organizational culture. As such, the group is not starting from scratch but relying on the structures already available to them prior to interaction. Similarly, organizations can appropriate larger societal structures, such as individualism, patriotism, or capitalism. This behavior would be considered appropriation from society.

Second, AST assumes all social interactions include elements of communication, morality, and power (Poole et al., 1985, 1986). The communication element dictates how organizational members operate within a given set of meanings or understandings. As such, their language choices are important. A worker might use particular words such as *competitive* or *innovative* as symbolic reflections of the rules of the group. The idea of morality means group norms about what is and is not acceptable behavior affect the agency, or actions, of group members. Finally, *power* refers to implicit power structures (e.g., equality, or hierarchy, or authority) that affect the interactional choices made by group members.

Adaptive Structuration and Group Decision Making

The first two theories of this chapter focus on decision making in groups, and adaptive structuration theory also discusses the decision-making process. An adaptive structuration approach to decision making centers on the extent to which given structures influence the process groups use to problem solve and make a determination for action. For example, Poole and Roth (1989) investigated the paths groups took in their decision-making efforts. They identified three distinct paths. The **unitary path** is taken when a group uses the same process to generate solutions, regardless of the type of problem. For example, group members might use functional group decision making not only when deciding how to address a financial crisis but also when deciding what to order for lunch or determining the quarterly meeting schedule. As such, the single way to make decisions has become a rule for action.

In the **complex cyclic path** group members cycle through the types of activities identified by functional group decision making, but they do so in a circular fashion (Poole & Roth, 1989). For example, the group members might first seek to identify the problem, might talk about solutions, and then might go back and reinterpret the problem. This path involves a lot of discussion, and it often requires revisiting the rules and resources available to the group.

The final path is the **solution-orientation path** (Poole & Roth, 1989). In this pattern, group members make little or no effort to investigate the problem. Rather, group members assume they understand the problem and immediately seek a solution that will satisfy group members. The focus in this pattern is not on process but on resolution. As such, the rules and resources center on efficiency and results.

Adaptive Structuration and Virtual Teams

Beyond its ability to explain the development of group norms and decision-making structures, adaptive structuration theory has also emerged as one of the most frequently used explanations for what happens in virtual teams (Schiller & Mandviwalla, 2007). AST allows scholars to understand how multiple outcomes can result from the implementation of technology in the decision-making process. According to DeSanctis and Poole (1994), advanced information technologies themselves influence the production and reproduction of structure. That is, the features of the technology used by virtual teams influence the types of rules and resources available to the group members. For example, imagine a virtual team is using a particular group decision support system (GDSS) that allows for anonymous comments. Because of this feature, team members feel free to post "honest" feedback to ideas, rather than needing to concern themselves with the politics of organizational hierarchy or coalitions. As such, the social structure that emerges would be quite different from the social structure produced by a virtual team that did not have that technological option.

The major way AST contributes to our understanding of virtual groups is by providing a mechanism to understand how and why the technology necessary for geographically dispersed groups influences the way the group functions. DeSanctis and Poole (1994) identify five group interaction dimensions influenced by communication technologies. These dimensions are described in Table 8.3.

AST states that group members have the power to create the nature of their own group through the rules they create and modify in their interaction. This theory also recognizes, however, that previous rules become structures that impinge on the group's communication in the future, such that members feel pressure to abide by the rules and resources they have already created.

Table 8.3 Dimensions of Technology's Structures

Dimension	Description
Decision process	The way a decision is made; examples include consensus, simple majority, and authority rule
Leadership	Whether a leader (or leaders) is appointed or emerges and the type of leadership that develops (e.g., authoritative, democratic)
Efficiency	The way time is handled, including whether group interaction is shorter or longer than it would be if technology were not being used
Conflict management	The extent to which interaction is orderly or chaotic; the extent to which group members seek to resolve conflict and, if so, which conflict resolution strategies they select
Atmosphere	The formality of the interaction and the extent to which interaction is structured or unstructured

SYMBOLIC CONVERGENCE THEORY

The final group theory we discuss is symbolic convergence theory (SCT). Although considered a general theory of communication, SCT was developed within the traditions of group communication and has been applied most frequently to this context (Bormann, 1982). Like adaptive structuration theory, SCT is based on the notion that group members cooperatively create and sustain a shared consciousness, including shared meaning, through interaction. Specifically, SCT focuses on two aspects of group communication: the creation of a group identity and the ways group identity influences norms for behavior.

Central Concepts of SCT

As with many theories, a number of concepts are critical for understanding the explanation of group communication provided by SCT. The most important concept is a fantasy theme. The term *fantasy* can be misleading. According to SCT, *fantasy* does not refer to something desired or something fictional; rather, it refers to a creative understanding of events that fulfills a psychological or rhetorical need (Bormann, 1982).

A fantasy theme starts with a **dramatizing message**—such as a joke, anecdote, innuendo, pun, figure of speech, double entendre, or metaphor, among other things (Bormann, 1996). Importantly, these messages do not refer to present happenings; instead they reference events that have happened in the past or that are anticipated for the future. Moreover, dramatizing messages always include some level of emotional revelation, typically including both a surface level and a deeper level (Bales, 1970). Imagine Trevor, the youngest member of his work team, has recently solved a seemingly impossible problem. When walking into his next team meeting, Kyle playfully waves an imaginary magic wand and calls him Harry Potter ("What magic spell did you dig out to solve this one?"). This message serves the surface function of tension release but also serves the deeper function of recognizing the value of Trevor's work. Sometimes these messages are sent and then immediately dropped, but if the rest of the group responds to the dramatizing message, a **fantasy theme** has emerged.

Continued embellishment of the fantasy theme can result in a **fantasy chain** when the fantasy theme is developed through group interaction and enters group consciousness (Bormann, 1982). If, for example, the "Harry Potter" theme develops and is built on by other group members, a fantasy chain has emerged. At a later meeting, group members might refer to an incompetent supervisor as a "muggle" or might joke about the magic spells needed to accomplish a project on time.

According to symbolic convergence theory, building fantasy chains results in group cohesion, a process termed **symbolic convergence** (Bormann, 1982). In other words, the emergence of a fantasy chain transforms the group from a collection of individuals to an identifiable group with a group consciousness. Consider the Harry Potter fantasy chain. Imagine a subsequent meeting that includes the original work team as well as other organizational members not part of that team. Again, Kyle mentions their secret weapon, "Harry," and all of the original team members laugh—they understand the reference. The individuals who were not a part of the original team may feel left out, however, because they don't understand the joke. Bormann, Cragan, and Shields (1994) argued that when people have a shared fantasy theme, they have come to share a consciousness that can be set off by a commonly agreed upon symbolic cue. Much like an inside joke, only those who were a part of creating the fantasy theme to which the inside joke refers will respond appropriately.

Any given group might have numerous fantasy chains. That is, the same group that chains the Harry Potter fantasy theme might also use sports metaphors when referring to business situations ("You really hit that one out of the park, Jane" or "It's third and long, and we have to go for it if we're gonna win"). In addition, the group might have a stock story about a team member who failed to follow procedure and lost his job. New members might be told the story as a cautionary tale, and current members might be sanctioned by being told, "Don't be a Don!" The ways fantasy chains combine within a group leads to a **rhetorical vision**. A rhetorical vision is a unified way of viewing the world. Consider the three fantasy chains just described: Harry Potter, sports, and sanctions against violating rules. All three fantasy chains share a common way of viewing the world. All three suggest the world is clearly divided: right and wrong, good and evil, winners and losers. If you are on the side of good, you play hard and win; if you are on the side of evil, you will lose. This rhetorical vision provides a set of implicit norms for group behavior.

In addition, the process of symbolic convergence affects decision making (Bormann, 1996). For instance, building a sense of common identity and shared meaning fosters group members' creativity in decision making. Moreover, group consciousness and shared motivation also influence assumptions and preferred processes by which decisions are made. In fact, Bormann contended that group members might create fantasy themes about the decision-making process itself.

Figure 8.1 provides a visual representation of the process of symbolic convergence. Starting at the upper left-hand side of the diagram, a group member sends a dramatizing message. If others in the group interact as a result of that message, a fantasy theme has emerged. If and when group members embellish that fantasy theme, a fantasy chain results. When studying a group, observers can examine the fantasy chains to uncover the underlying rhetorical vision that provides the group with a sense of cohesion and implicit norms for behavior.

The discussion of SCT thus far implies the theory is concerned only with events internal to a group. One of the strengths of the theory, however, is that it links groups to other social systems, such as a larger organization or social movement (Poole, 1999). For example, a rhetorical vision might start in a group and spread to other parts of an organization. Conversely, the rhetorical vision of a larger organization might restrict the types of fantasy themes generated within a group.

Figure 8.1 The Symbolic Convergence Process

SUMMARY AND RESEARCH APPLICATIONS

In this chapter, we discussed four distinct theories of group communication. Our first theory, functional group decision making, delineates specific tasks or functions group members need to complete to make an effective decision. Although it sounds simple enough, poor group decision making still plagues the workplace. Gouran (2010, 2011) has more recently emphasized the role of rationality and leadership within group decision making while attempting to identify what factors most often compromise a group's ability to complete the requisite functions. Individual and collective ignorance of the task requirements, procedures, and roles, along with

ego, hierarchy, and poor leadership contribute to the difficulties workgroups face (Gouran, 2010).

Next, groupthink provides a means for understanding why group members make poor decisions through a particular focus on cohesion, structural faults, and situational constraints (Janis, 1982). The theory has been used to explain extremism and polarization in American politics (Willis, 2017) as well in the "courage" required of subcabinet officials to make difficult political decisions (Kelman, Sanders, & Pandit, 2016). Our third approach, adaptive structuration theory, focuses on how structures, or enduring patterns of relationships, develop based on group interaction and how these structures in turn constrain group interaction. Barrett and Stephens (2017) incorporated AST as a framework for understanding change within a healthcare organization as coworkers transitioned to electronic records. This technological change initially influenced colleagues' social interactions and attitudes in a negative direction, however, this reversed as workers adapted to the technology.

Finally, SCT suggests that particular types of messages called fantasy themes contribute to a rhetorical vision and sense of group identity. An examination of these fantasy themes and how they might combine provides a rhetorical vision that provides the principles by which the group operates. Social media provides another powerful mechanism by which groups can create, share, and elaborate on fantasy themes. In recent research that included Facebook interactions between team members, two complementary and competing rhetorical visions emerged (Zanin, Hoelscher, & Kramer, 2016). In some cases, the themes increased a sense of belonging and identification, where in other instances, they created divided loyalties between those who felt included in the themes and those who felt left out. Zanin et al. (2016) offered suggestions by which SCT might benefit from more research on group divergence on fantasy themes.

KEY TERMS

Agency   151
Aggregate   143
Allocative resources   151
Antecedent conditions   147
Authoritative resources   151
Brainstorming   145
Closed-mindedness   149
Cohesion   147
Complex cyclic path   152
Counteractive
    communication   146
Determine minimal
    standards   145
Disruptive communication   146
Dramatizing message   154

Duality of structure   151
Evaluate and select   145
Fantasy   154
Fantasy chain   154
Fantasy theme   154
Function   144
Group   143
Group role   144
Groupthink   147
Identify alternatives   145
Overestimation of the
    group   148
Pressure toward
    uniformity   149
Problem analysis   145

Production   151
Promotive communication   146
Reproduction   151
Rhetorical vision   155
Rules   151
Situational characteristics   148
Socioemotional
    communication   144
Solution-orientation path   152
Structural flaws   147
Structure   151
Symbolic convergence   154
Task communication   144
Team   143
Unitary path   152

CASE STUDY 8: THE GIFTED GROUP

A new leader brought renewed enthusiasm to the Brunswick County Conference & Visitors Bureau (BCCVB), the official tourism promotion agency for Brunswick County, Pennsylvania. Under her leadership, the bureau underwent both programmatic and physical expansion.

(Continued)

(Continued)

Shortly after the BCCVB relocated its offices and visitor center to a newly constructed building, the executive director decided to create a gift center committee. The purpose of the committee was to devise a plan for a visitor gift center shop—something the BCCVB had never had—in which a variety of merchandise bearing the Brunswick County logo could be sold to visitors.

The committee consisted of the following five BCCVB staff members: John Maher, communication assistant; Laura Doherty, office manager; Nannette Kearny, membership director; Lisa Berman, assistant director; and Donald Johnson, corporate sales manager. The newly formed group was highly cohesive; they had worked together for more than 5 years, and they were all committed to the vision of the visitor's bureau developed by the executive director. The committee was given 3 weeks, meeting as often as they deemed necessary to devise a plan detailing how the BCCVB would establish a visitor center gift shop. The time frame was difficult to achieve given that the group members still had to perform the duties of their regular jobs, but all of the members were committed to doing so.

The first meeting turned out to be a "meeting of the minds" to establish a consensus as to how the group would move forward. Because of their cohesion, committee members were sociable, gregarious, and comfortable working with one another. As a result, members spent a good 15 minutes at the onset of the meeting catching up with one another. Donald, the group clown, decided that an important first step was to come up with a name for the committee, and he decided the group members should be known as the "gifted group." This name led to much laughter and joking that it would be the first time Donald had ever been called "gifted" in his life.

Lisa Berman also participated in this social interaction but took naturally to a leader-type role when it came time to discuss business matters.

She made an effort to focus the committee's attention to the matter at hand—the gift shop—and enabled the group to transition from social-related to more task-related communication. At that point, the committee began discussing the overall idea of a gift shop and how to devise a plan to initiate such a venture. The group quickly came to a rather dramatic realization following this discussion: Nobody on the committee had any retail or gift shop experience. Committee members, undoubtedly discouraged by this realization, became reluctant to move forward. The meeting closed, however, with John recommending that each member research visitor center gift shops before the next gathering. Donald and Nanette initially disagreed with the proposal, saying they didn't have time to do so. Nannette asked Laura if she would be willing to do the research, and Laura quickly complied. However, Lisa pointed out that if each person did a little research, no one person would be overburdened. She persuaded the group members to take on the task as a whole.

At the second meeting, each committee member arrived with an impressive arsenal of visitor center gift shop research. Again, the first 10 or 15 minutes were devoted to socializing. And again, Lisa had to work to get people back on task. At first, Donald fought with Lisa for control of the meeting. He continued joking around, calling one of the organizational members not on the committee "special Ned." When Lisa tried to get the group back on task again, Nanette responded, "Hey, not everyone can be considered gifted," and the group continued laughing. Lisa tried to remain light hearted because she wasn't the official leader, but she was frustrated that others were wasting time. She remarked, "We won't continue to be considered gifted if we don't get this done." Donald teased, "Uh oh, teacher is mad. Are you gonna keep us after school if we don't hit the books?" At this, everyone laughed, including Lisa.

Finally turning to the job at hand, the meeting entailed a thorough investigation of each member's materials and a lengthy discussion about how the group would use the research to proceed. The committee decided to compile the research that related most directly to the BCCVB and to set a calendar indicating how, armed with such information, they would move forward with subsequent meetings. Collectively, the committee established a heavy meeting schedule, with a meeting scheduled every day for the remainder of the 2-week time frame.

Each meeting flowed in a manner very similar to that of the first and second meetings. The first 10 or 15 minutes of every meeting, even as the deadline drew near, were set aside for social interaction. Donald would joke around, and the others would follow his lead. Then, the committee would either progress naturally toward the task at hand, or Lisa Berman would comment about moving forward or getting down to business, and eventually the group would do so.

Toward the end of the second week, group energy was sagging. Everyone had been devoting a significant amount of time not only to the meetings but to "homework" each tackled in between the meetings. At this point, John's role shifted from group member to group cheerleader. He encouraged others when they became frustrated or tired. He reminded everyone that although the short time frame meant they weren't running a marathon, the work they were doing wasn't a sprint either. Donald responded, "What, we're doing the 800 meter?" Nanette retorted, "Well, hell, that's my problem, I'm out of shape!" John joined in, saying, "Actually, the hurdles were always my specialty! But yes, it is an 800-meter race; we need to keep a rapid pace, but we can't all-out sprint the whole time."

After the 3 weeks were over, the group presented their final proposal to the executive director. Following the meeting, Laura presented all of the members a track jersey with the words "The Gifted Group" written across the chest.

Questions for Consideration

1. Using the functional model, was the decision on how to establish the gift shop likely to be effective? Why, or why not? Describe how and when each function emerged.

2. What antecedents of groupthink are present? What symptoms of groupthink are present? What could the group do to prevent groupthink from occurring?

3. Using adaptive structuration theory, what structures did the group create? Make sure to consider both rules and resources. Also, consider how the rules and resources might have been different if the group had used more technology in their group decision-making process.

4. Discuss the elements of symbolic convergence as related to the group. How do you think symbolic convergence might have affected the decision-making process? How might symbolic convergence theory and groupthink influence each other?

5. What ethical issues arise when considering this group's (or any group's) communication?

6. Do any of the theories emerge as better than the others? Why do you believe this to be the case? What situations might surface that would make a different theory or theories better at explaining the situation?

CHAPTER NINE

ORGANIZATIONAL COMMUNICATION

"The single biggest problem with communication is the illusion that it has taken place."

—George Bernard Shaw

One of the most intriguing paradoxes of corporate life is how often organizational members stress the importance of communication yet how few of these members exhibit effective organizational communication. In Chapter 1, we argue that popular culture tends to oversimplify the communication process. Nowhere is this more evident than in the organizational setting.

ORGANIZATIONAL COMMUNICATION DEFINED

According to Feldner and D'Urso (2010), modern approaches to organizational communication center on the extent to which meaning is created between individuals in an organizational setting, between individuals and organizations, and between organizations and societies. Rejecting the oversimplified idea that an organization exists as a "container" in which communication occurs, organizational communication scholars instead focus on communication as a process rather than an event. Specific communication processes of interest to organizational communication scholars include the development and maintenance of workplace relationships, the socialization of new organizational members, the development of organizational cultures, the ways organizations and organizational members exert and resist power, the ways communication processes create organizational structures, and the ways organizational structures alter communication processes.

Learning Objectives

After reading this chapter, you will be able to do the following:

1. Define organizational communication and discuss how organizational communication differs from a management approach to organizational culture

2. Explain how a system's perspective provides a framework for understanding organizational communication

3. Compare and contrast Deal and Kennedy's four cultures approach to Schein's three levels of organizational culture

4. Recognize the four stages of organizational assimilation

5. Describe the differences in the four levels of control highlighted by OIC theory

6. Use the concept of a dou' interact to understand ' communication proce organization

7. Compare and contr theoretical appro organizational c

SYSTEMS METAPHOR

Much of organizational communication relies on a systems metaphor. The core of the systems metaphor is a focus on the interdependence that develops whenever people interact with each other. A **system** is a group of individuals who interrelate to form a whole (Hall & Fagen, 1968). Examples of systems are a family, a work group, and a sports team. Any time that a group of people has repeated interaction with each other, they represent a system. Systems are embedded in a hierarchy, with systems existing within other systems (Pattee, 1973). Accordingly, a subsystem is a smaller part of the group as a whole: the defensive line of a football team or the accounting department of an organization. A suprasystem is the larger system within which the system operates: The National Football League (NFL) is a suprasystem for any individual football team, and the industry of an organization is a suprasystem for that organization.

Systems approaches involve more than simply focusing on these sorts of interrelationships, however. Systems theories hinge on **nonsummativity**, or the idea that the whole is greater than the sum of its parts (Fisher, 1978). Think of your favorite sports team. Some sports teams have few superstars, but when they work together, they win a lot of games. On the other hand, some teams have "big-name" athletes, but as systems, these teams are not successful. From a systems perspective, individuals in and of themselves don't make or break the system. Instead, the system as a whole might work together to create more than what might be accomplished by those individuals alone. This ability to achieve more through group effort than individual effort is positive **synergy** (Salazar, 1995). Of course, occasionally negative synergy occurs, meaning the group achieves less than the individual parts would suggest. Nevertheless, the point of nonsummativity is that you cannot understand a system by looking only at its components, as a system is more than just its individual parts.

A major reason nonsummativity takes place is because of **interdependence** (Rapoport, 1968). Interdependence means all system members are dependent on all other system members; if one group member drops the ball—literally or figuratively—the organization as a whole is unlikely to achieve its goals. Many of you probably have had this experience at work, because there are few professional positions in which an individual operates completely independently. In the example of a magazine, the failure of an advertising sales rep to meet his or her deadline means the editor can't determine how many pages an issue will have, which means a writer doesn't know whether his or her story will run in that issue, and also that the production people can't do preproduction. Every member of a system is dependent on every other member.

Another principle central to systems approaches is **homeostasis** (Ashby, 1962). Homeostasis refers to the natural balance or equilibrium within the system. From a systems perspective, homeostasis is not meant to imply change doesn't happen. Instead, it is the tendency for a given system to maintain stability in the face of change. This effort at stability can be either functional or dysfunctional for the system. On the one hand, a successful system that achieves homeostasis is likely to continue to be successful. However, imagine a system that has a great deal of conflict, which impedes the system's ability to achieve its goals. Homeostasis would suggest that efforts to reduce the conflict might only engender more conflict, because conflict is the "natural" balance of that group. Thus, a systems approach recognizes that when a system experiences a novel situation, whether positive or negative, its members will somehow adjust to maintain stability, whether that stability is positive or negative.

A final systems concept of interest in the study of organizational communication is **equifinality**. Equifinality suggests multiple ways to achieve the same goal (von Bertalanffy, 1968). Let's say a production group is challenged with the goal of increasing revenue by 10%. They can do so by selling more product, increasing the price of the old product, reducing manufacturing costs of the old product, developing a new product, or reducing the workforce needed to make the product, among other things. In short, there are multiple paths the organization might take to achieve its goals. In addition, at any given time, there are multiple goals the organization can address. If the organization is not only trying to increase revenue but also trying to increase employee morale, it might choose to develop new products, which would simultaneously increase revenue and morale. The organization might decide morale is more important than revenue, however, and focus on that rather than revenue.

Organizational communication theories tend to rely on a systems metaphor (and its associated concepts) to describe the activities of organizations. Still, perhaps because organizational communication scholars are interested in both micro issues (such as interpersonal communication in organizations) and macro issues (such as how organizational communication shapes society), a broad range of philosophical and methodological commitments are evident in organizational communication theory. Some scholars use a social scientific approach to try to make predictions regarding workplace satisfaction or productivity. Others take an interpretive approach, with a focus on organizational storytelling or narratives. Still others take a critical approach, looking to uncover the extent to which organizational communication practices empower or marginalize organizational members or publics.

This chapter focuses on four theories of organizational communication: organizational culture, organizational assimilation, organizational identification and control, and Weick's organizing theory. The first, organizational culture, provides a language for understanding how and why organizations develop values, beliefs, behavioral norms, and ways of communicating. The second, organizational assimilation, focuses on how individuals become socialized into an organization, with a recognition of the role of organizational culture. The third, organizational identification and control, also builds on the notion of culture and assimilation, with a particular focus on how power is enacted in organizations. Finally, Weick's organizing theory puts communication processes at the heart of the ultimate success or failure of an organization.

ORGANIZATIONAL CULTURE

Few of the concepts covered in this book are more popular than the notion of **organizational culture**. Bookshelves are overflowing with tomes like *The Corporate Culture Survival Guide* and *Diagnosing and Changing Organizational Culture*. Before discussing any specific approaches to organizational culture, however, it is important to note there are at least two competing perspectives on organizational culture: approaches that view culture as something an organization *has* and approaches that view culture as something an organization *is* (Smircich, 1983).

The first approach is exemplified by Deal and Kennedy (1982, 2000), who argued that organizations become high performing when they have a strong organizational culture. These authors identified four central elements to culture: values, heroes, rites and rituals, and the cultural network. **Values** underscore the organization's core beliefs, for example, how the organization treats clients, suppliers, stakeholders, and employees. **Heroes** are the people who best represent or personify these values, such as the late countercultural visionary Steve Jobs of Apple or the notoriously frugal investment tycoon, billionaire Warren Buffett. **Rites and rituals** are public performances that demonstrate the organizational values. The most obvious of these rituals are entry rituals, such as an academic convocation to welcome incoming students or a dinner for new employees. Finally, the **cultural network** is the informal communication processes within the organization, including stories, jokes, and gossip.

Given these components, Deal and Kennedy (1982) identify four organizational cultures based on the degree of risk the organization is willing to take (low versus high) and the type of feedback and reward system it has (rapid versus slow). Table 9.1 identifies how these qualities interact to form the four cultures.

The *work hard–play hard culture* is characterized by action, fun, quick feedback, and small risks (Deal & Kennedy, 1982, 2000). Organizations of this type encourage volume and speed, but the activity has high levels of certainty. Stress comes from the pace at which one works, not from the work itself, and is very team-oriented. This type of culture is typical among sales and manufacturing organizations. From real estate, to cars, to McDonald's, the work hard–play hard culture relies on a "find a need and fill it" philosophy (Deal & Kennedy, 2000, p. 113). *The tough-guy macho culture* is one of high stakes, fast feedback, with the potential for high rewards or huge losses. People who thrive in this type of culture rely on constant feedback and are often temperamental in their demands. In fact, this type of culture values superstars rather than team players. Not surprisingly, the tough-guy macho culture is often found among advertising agencies and the entertainment industries, as well as law enforcement and medical professions, where lives are on the line. Employees in *a process culture* typically can't easily measure *what* they do, and feedback is slow, so they focus instead on *how* work is done. The work is stable and consistent, and documenting details is important. Highly regulated industries often fall into this realm, such as financial services, education, government agencies, insurance, and pharmaceuticals. Finally, the *bet-the-company* culture is exemplified by high-stakes gambles that take years to pay off. Unlike the work hard–play hard culture, stress here is a low-level constant, and being deliberate is the name of the game. Oil companies, who invest billions of dollars on a drilling operation, and capital goods manufacturers, who spend years researching and developing new products, are examples of this type of culture.

As should be evident, Deal and Kennedy's (1982, 2000) approach focuses on qualities of an organization that a manager can develop or change. The second approach to organizational culture, described by Smircich (1983), instead focuses on the processes of

Table 9.1 The Four Organizational Cultures

Feedback and Reward		Risk	
		Low	**High**
	Rapid	Work hard–play hard culture	Tough-guy macho culture
	Slow	Process culture	Bet-the-company culture

communication that create, sustain, and constrain interaction within the organization. To illustrate this perspective, we focus on the work of Schein. Schein (1985, 1992) described the elements that comprise an organizational culture and how organizational cultures assist individuals in making sense of their experiences. According to Schein (1992), *culture* refers to a pattern of shared assumptions that have been invented, discovered, or developed by a given group and are taught to new members as the correct way to perceive, think, and behave. Although this definition seems to imply organizational members are consciously aware of organizational cultures, Schein argued this is not always the case; frequently organizational members are not aware of the cultural assumptions they hold. Moreover, culture emerges from interaction and continuously develops, although it is resistant to change.

Schein's (1992) model includes three levels of culture: artifacts, values, and assumptions. Although all three make up a culture, he believed the third level, assumptions, is at the crux of organizational culture and that the first two levels, artifacts and values, may simply reflect the more abstract and subconscious assumptions shared by organizational members.

Level 1: Artifacts

Similar to Deal and Kennedy's components of a strong culture, Schein's (1992, 2010) notion of *artifacts* refers to the observable evidence of culture. Artifacts may take the form of physical entities, such as architecture, dress, and documents, but they also consist of patterns of behavior. These patterns of behavior can take the form of rituals, acronyms, forms of address, approaches to decision making, and management style. Table 9.2 lists some examples of artifacts.

Although artifacts are, by definition, observable, interpreting what they mean may not always be obvious (Schein, 1992, 2010). For example, imagine an organization that develops a pattern of using formal titles among organizational members. According to Miller (2003), such a behavioral artifact might mean the organization is very formal. On the other hand, it might simply mean organizational members hold each other in high esteem and wish to show each other respect. Or it might be

Table 9.2 Cultural Artifacts and Behaviors

Artifact/Behavior	Examples
Architecture	Open floor plan, cubicles; offices with windows; size of offices; rented suites versus owned campus
Technology	Up-to-date versus archaic computer systems; availability/type of Internet connection, e-mail, tablets, smartphones
Dress	Business attire versus casual attire; uniforms, casual Fridays; dress codes
Forms of address	Titles used versus first names; differences in address by hierarchical level
Decision-making style	Autocratic versus participatory; rapid versus slow; conservative versus risk taking
Communication patterns	Formal versus informal; friendly versus distant; use of acronyms, unique terms, myths, stories; rituals

Source: Miller, *Organizational Communication, 3rd ed.* © 2003 Wadsworth.

an indication that organizational members dislike each other and seek to maintain distance. Thus, while this level of culture is readily apparent, it does not provide much substance to an understanding of organizational culture. Attention must be turned to higher levels for such understanding.

Level 2: Values

The second level of culture is organizational members' espoused values, defined as preferences about what "ought to happen" (Schein, 1992, 2010). These preferences represent shared beliefs about how things should work. By nature, values are intangible, but organizational members are typically able to articulate them. Organizational leaders are frequently the source of values; for instance, research shows the values held by the founder of a company strongly influence the values described by other employees (Morley & Shockley-Zalabak, 1991). Certainly, literature suggests leadership is, by definition, the ability to shape members' perceptions of the task and the mission of the organization (Barge, 1994). Accordingly, it's not surprising organizational members are persuaded to adopt the values of organizational leaders.

Still, simply because a leader articulates a value system does not make it so. Championed values are not always authentic values, as evident when the ideals expressed do not match behavior (Schein, 1992, 2010). Consider, for instance, two organizations that claim to value innovation. When scrutinizing the artifacts of the first organization, observers notice the company encourages risk and gives employees time to experiment. Failures are not punished; in fact, the company encourages employees to talk about failures, because one person's failure might be the solution to another person's problem. A significant portion of the annual budget is earmarked for research and development. In this case, the artifacts seem to support the value of innovation. At the second company, however, failure is not an option; people who fail are reprimanded. The organization is resistant to change and has very rigid systems to implement even the smallest change. Little of the budget is slated for research and development, and employees are kept so busy maintaining the current product or service that they have virtually no time to develop any new ideas. In fact, employees have facetiously created the following company slogan: "We don't innovate; we duplicate." Clearly, these artifacts do not seem to suggest innovation is actually practiced. The point is that espoused values are not always identical to the actual values of the organization; just because it appears in the mission statement does not mean it reaches the level of everyday practice.

Level 3: Assumptions

The final level of culture is the most difficult to identify because it is often taken for granted by organizational members. *Assumptions* refers to the viewpoints organizational members hold about the world, including perceptions, thoughts, feelings, and beliefs. These assumptions are subconscious because they have been reinforced over and over again as the organization faces challenges. Assumptions lie at the heart of organizational culture because such presumptions are made uniformly throughout the organization (Schein, 1992, 2010).

Specifically, organizations develop assumptions about the nature of reality, time, space, human nature, and human relationships, among other things (Schein, 1992, 2010). These concepts are profound philosophical commitments, such as the "right" way for people to interact with each other, whether human beings are by nature good or evil, and whether truth is singular (i.e., there is one absolute "truth") or conditional (e.g., some things are true at some times in some places for some people).

Although this notion sounds complex, such assumptions have a substantial effect on organizational life. Consider two different employment programs for former prisoners. A fundamental assumption of one program might be that people are capable of changing. Such an assumption will affect the everyday decisions made because organizational members will spend energy seeking to develop and reward individuals rather than punish them for past infractions. Yet a different organization might assume the best predictor of future behavior is past behavior. In this case, organizational members are likely to view individuals who have made mistakes as risky prospects likely to repeat those mistakes.

According to Schein's (1992, 2010) model of organizational culture, an analysis of assumptions could assist organizational members in generating a coherent blueprint for how the organization should operate, yet this postulation is not always the case. Some organizations might simultaneously hold seemingly conflicting assumptions. For example, employees of a Catholic institution of higher learning may be challenged by incompatible assumptions; assumptions the Catholic Church makes about "truth" may contrast the assumptions some of the university's academic disciplines hold about "truth." Such contradictory assumptions might cause problems for members seeking to behave in concert with organizational assumptions. How the organization reconciles these inconsistent assumptions determines the overarching organizational culture.

Schein (1985, 1992, 2010) proposed three levels of culture: artifacts, values, and assumptions. Although there may be surface inconsistencies within and across these levels, a careful analysis of the patterns that emerge will give observers an understanding of the organizational culture. These cultures are created by employees, with particular emphasis placed on the influence of those at the highest levels in the organization. Accordingly, organizational cultures both aid and constrain organizational communication.

ORGANIZATIONAL ASSIMILATION

Many of us have learned very quickly that we don't "fit" with a particular organization. You might find, for example, you are a blue jeans kind of person in a three-piece-suit kind of world. Or you might find an organization's values (e.g., slow and steady wins the race) don't mesh with your personality (e.g., Type A). We've just finished discussing what organizational cultures are and how we might identify a particular organization's culture. Taking this a step further, Jablin (1987, 2001) created **organizational assimilation** theory as a way to explain how individuals become integrated into the culture of an organization.

Jablin (2001) argued the process of being socialized into an organization is complex and takes place over years. Moreover, the process of assimilation can be planned, for example, through a potential employee's active researching of a company or formal

Table 9.3 Stages of Assimilation

Stage	Description
Vocational anticipatory socialization	Developing a set of expectations and beliefs about the nature of work and work settings Examples: I should be paid for my work; The people I work with will be my close friends.
Anticipatory socialization	Learning about a particular vocation, position, and organization Examples: Renee's sister routinely works 10-hour days in advertising; Jared did an informational interview with a PR manager at DanCo.
Encounter/Entry	Joining the organization and making sense of its culture Example: Unlike my last job, people at DanCo are expected to speak up at meetings.
Metamorphosis	Transitioning from outsider to insider, understanding roles, and negotiating roles Example: We work hard and don't complain—it's just what we do here at DanCo.

training procedures. But assimilation is often unplanned. Coworkers' interaction styles might not be intended to send messages about the organizational culture, but the new organizational member might perceive these messages regardless.

The theory identifies four stages organizational newcomers go through before becoming full members of an organization. These stages are summarized in Table 9.3.

Vocational Anticipatory Socialization

Before we ever get our first job, we learn about the nature of work. We watch our parents leave us in the morning and return to us in the evening, oftentimes frazzled and grumpy. We listen to our teachers tell us that we've done a good job or that we have not worked hard enough. We have laughed at the incompetence of Michael Scott on *The Office* or cringed at the cruelty of the bosses in the movie *Horrible Bosses*. We've had part-time jobs and even full-time jobs, and we have listened as our professors tell us what it's really like to be a journalist, or a PR rep, or a manager. In short, we spend years collecting information about the nature of work, yet much of what we learn is distorted, biased, or just plain wrong. Jablin (2001) describes a host of studies indicating the media overrepresent managerial and professional work and underrepresent low-prestige jobs. People are often stereotyped by race and sex. Moreover, the nature of communication in the workplace is distorted, with much of the conversation focused on socializing, giving orders, or giving advice. All these notions of work are brought together in **vocational anticipatory socialization**, or the expectations and beliefs about work we bring with us as we begin to assimilate into an organization.

Anticipatory Socialization

The second stage of organizational assimilation theory is **anticipatory socialization**. Here, individuals gather information about a specific vocation, position, or organization. This stage includes the process of choosing an organization, interviewing, and preparing to enter the organization. Jablin (2001) argued that in many cases individuals retain unrealistic and inflated notions of the organization because organizations typically communicate only their positive aspects. These unrealistic expectations are often problematic, as organizational members find it difficult to meet these expectations once on the job. Clearly, during this phase the organizational newcomer starts to become socialized into the organization before he or she ever works in the organization.

Encounter

The third phase is one of high uncertainty and anxiety. In the **encounter** phase, the organizational newcomer enters the workplace and begins to learn the normal work patterns and expectations of the organization. As described in Chapter 3, there are many ways people reduce uncertainty, including observation and asking questions. Typically, the organizational newcomer relies on coworkers and his or her supervisor for uncertainty reduction. The individual in this stage frequently undergoes a "culture shock" as she or he compares expectations with the reality of the new workplace and disillusionment as she or he lets go of old values and behaviors.

Metamorphosis

The final stage of assimilation, **metamorphosis**, reflects the movement of the individual from an outsider to an insider. During this stage, the newcomer and the organization exert mutual influence in the process of developing a "fit" between the organization and the employee. Here, the newcomer internalizes values and behaviors in order to fulfill organizational expectations (known as **socialization**) while at the same time seeks to have an impact on his or her role and work environment (known as **individualization**). Imagine you have begun working at an organization that rigidly follows the rules of the employee handbook. You have reached metamorphosis if you still allow the handbook to guide your behavior, but you also use inconsistencies and missing areas of the handbook to achieve your goals. In this case, you have been socialized to rely on the handbook, as is the organizational culture, but you have adapted the culture to your own needs by taking advantage of the handbook's limitations to get what you think you need to accomplish your job.

The next theory, organizational identification and control, takes this notion of organizational assimilation a step further by articulating the hidden aspects of becoming a member of an organizational culture.

ORGANIZATIONAL IDENTIFICATION AND CONTROL

As indicated in Chapter 8, organizations are increasing their use of team-based structures to improve quality, engender creativity, and increase employee involvement (Deetz, Tracy, & Simpson, 2000). Although these are the *stated* goals of work teams, research suggests team-based structures also serve another purpose: control over employees (Barker, 1999). Consequently, organizational identification and control (OIC) theory centers on the way an individual's connection to the organization influences behavior and decision making in team-based structures (Barker, 1999). Three main concepts tie the theory together: identification, control, and discipline.

Identification

OIC's first major concept, **identification**, refers to the sense of oneness with or belongingness to an organization; when individuals experience identification, they define themselves in terms of the organization (Mael & Ashforth, 1992). Identification happens most frequently in the metamorphosis stage of organizational assimilation, as described earlier in the chapter. Evidence of identification happens when you listen to organizational members speak. Often, they will say things such as, "We don't operate that way here" or "We launched a new product today." In these cases, the organizational member is adopting the persona of the organization—she or he may have had little to do with the new product, but there is a sense of pride in and ownership of the product because of identification. This process of identification plays a central, yet subtle, role in how organizations control their employees.

Control

Quite simply, "an organization needs control to get things done" (Miller, 2003, p. 210). OIC suggests there are, however, several forms of control an organization might use. Based on Edwards's (1981) delineation, an organization may exert control through three traditional methods. **Simple control** involves direct, authoritarian control. If a manager makes threats (e.g., "do this, or you'll get fired") or places conditions on an employee (e.g., "you can leave early if you finish the Kegway project"), she or he is using a classic way of controlling employees by simply directing the employee as to what can or should be done.

The second method of control is slightly more subtle. **Technological control** involves the use of technology to manage what can and can't be done in the workplace (Edwards, 1981). A factory assembly line is a perfect example; employees must go exactly as fast as the assembly line is moving—no faster and no slower (as the classic episode of *I Love Lucy* in the candy factory illustrated). Employees on an assembly line can only take prescribed breaks, as well, because the whole line must be shut down if one person takes a break. A more contemporary example of this type of control is the limitation of computer technology. How often have you been told by someone, "The computer program won't let us do that"? The technology you have access to and the ways technology works serve as a means of organizational control.

The third kind of control is **bureaucratic control** (Edwards, 1981). Undoubtedly, you are familiar with the term *bureaucracy*, and it is usually associated with negative perceptions. Edwards, however, was referring to the vision of bureaucracy first articulated by Max Weber, a German sociologist. Writing at the turn of the 20th century, Weber argued that modern organizations are served best by a hierarchical system of rules, with rewards and punishments drawn from those rules. That hierarchy is evident in contemporary organizations through company policies and formal procedures. Employee handbooks and other such formalized rule systems are the clearest example of bureaucratic control.

These three forms of control are the ways power has typically been exerted in organizations. In developing OIC, however, Tompkins and Cheney (1985) suggested that changes in organizations during the latter part of the 20th century have shifted the way control is wielded. With the growing use of team-based organizations and organizations grounded in participation and empowerment, Tompkins and Cheney identified two additional types of control: unobtrusive and concertive.

First, **unobtrusive control** is based on shared values within the organization. Put simply, in the modern organization, management's job is to create a vision and mission for the organization. When organizational members make decisions based on the vision or credo of the organization, they are not making those decisions because they are forced to but because they believe in the mission of the organization—they identify with the organization. Thus, the commitment to organizational values controls employees.

Similarly, the second type of control is based on interpersonal relationships and teamwork (Tompkins & Cheney, 1985). More obvious than unobtrusive control, concertive control happens when coworkers develop mechanisms to reward and control behavior that influences the team. For example, Barker (1999) suggested group members can discipline nonconforming coworkers through criticizing directly, monitoring, being silent, and exerting social pressure, among other things. As with simple control, concertive control is obvious and direct. It is not, however, a managerial function in this system but happens among hierarchical equals. Because of this, it is often described as a hidden form of control. Table 9.4 provides an overview of the types of control.

Discipline

Pulling together the concepts of identification and control, Barker (1999) and colleagues (see also Tompkins & Cheney, 1985) suggested **discipline** is achieved through a sense of responsibility to the work group because members identify with their organization and because they share common values and a vision for the organization. When individuals are faced with a decision, they will rely on organizational values to make that decision—there is no need for top-down management directives. If an individual is not behaving in concert with organizational values, work group members tend to censure that individual.

Notably, according to OIC theory, superiors need not do the disciplining themselves; the norms for behavior generated by the organizational mission and values coupled with the identification of organizational members work together to maintain organizational control. Thus, the creation of organizational missions and visions might have the explicit function of driving the organization's business, and work teams might provide a mechanism for employee empowerment, but these initiatives also serve the implicit function of controlling employees.

Table 9.4   Organizational Identification and Control

Type of Control	Examples
Simple	• Commands • Threats
Technological	• Assembly lines • Removing computer games from workplace machines
Bureaucratic	• Employee handbooks • Employment contracts
Unobtrusive	• Identification with organizational values • Decision making based on organizational mission
Concertive	• Monitoring of other team members' performance • Coworker pressure on nonconforming members

ORGANIZING THEORY

The previous theories in this chapter have linked communication processes to organizational processes. The fourth and final perspective, Weick's (1969) organizing theory, takes this link one step further by stating that communication *is* the organization. Instead of viewing organizations as containers in which communication occurs, Weick argued communication is what constitutes an organization. Instead of examining an organization (a noun), Weick examined the process of **organizing** (a verb).

With roots in Darwin's theory of evolution, information theory, and systems theory, organizing theory assumes organizations exist in an **information environment** (Weick, 1969). Rather than focusing on the physical environment, Weick's theory is concerned with the massive amounts of information organizations have available to them, from internal and external sources. Organizations depend on information to accomplish their goals, and the Herculean challenge of processing it all.

In addition to issues of quantity, managing the information environment is difficult because much of the information organizations deal with is unpredictable. The term **equivocality** references the ambiguity of information available to organizations (Weick, 1969). Messages are equivocal to the extent there may be multiple understandings of the information. Equivocality is different from the concept of uncertainty. When individuals are uncertain about a message, they can gather more information to reduce uncertainty. However, when individuals find a message to be equivocal, they do not need additional information; instead, they must decide which one of multiple interpretations is the best fit. Consider the example of Kristine, who has to decide how to invest her money. The state of the economy is equivocal; some financial planners argue that real estate will pick up, and so she should invest in property, whereas others suggest that because real estate is recovering so slowly, Kristine should invest in the stock market. Gathering more information is likely only to add to the equivocality. In the end, she has to interpret the state of the economy for herself, but her interpretation is only one of many.

According to Weick (1969), one way to reduce equivocality is to rely on **rules** (also called recipes). The term *rule* most often refers to guidelines for behavior, and Weick's use of the term is consistent with this conceptualization. Typically, organizations have rules, or guidelines, for analyzing both the equivocality of a message and how to respond to it. These rules are developed to make a process more efficient and are generally based on past successes. There are many obvious examples of rules, such as rules for whom to contact to accomplish certain tasks, rules about specific forms to be used, and rules about processes to be followed. Rules can also be less formalized, too. For example, an organization might have had past success with increasing profits by reducing packaging costs for its products. Accordingly, the next time corporate earnings are in question, the standard response is to seek to reduce packaging costs: Cost reduction has become a rule.

Rules don't always work, and there isn't always a rule for every situation. Organizing theory suggests a second way to reduce equivocality is for organizational members to engage in communication cycles known as double interacts (Weick, 1969). Double interacts are suited for instances of high equivocality because they require organizational members to develop interdependent relationships in the process of communicating.

Recall the concept of nonsummativity discussed earlier: The whole is greater than the sum of its parts. Weick's theory is grounded in systems principles, and so he argued greater involvement among organizational members can produce greater results in reducing equivocality.

A **double interact** consists of an act, a response, and an adjustment (Weick, 1969). An act is a communication behavior initiated by one person or group of people. The receivers of the message communicate in return, which is considered a response. This two-way exchange of messages is most typically used to understand the communication process. Weick proposed genuine communication requires a third step, an adjustment to the information originally received. This adjustment can take several forms. It might be a confirmation that the information has been understood. If the information is still equivocal, the adjustment might be additional information gathering.

To illustrate, the marketing department of a major manufacturing company has created a new product to be sold exclusively at Walmart. They approach production with the new idea, but members of the production team respond by telling marketing the configuration they have sold cannot be produced on the current assembly lines. Marketing amends the proposal so the customer receives the specialty product, and the production department can use existing equipment and materials: act, response, adjustment.

At the beginning of this section, we stated Weick (1969) was more concerned with the process of organizing than with the entity of an organization. Double interacts are the process of organizing; according to Weick, they are the links that hold an organization together. Weick also believed, however, that organizing is an evolutionary process. Much like Darwin's theory of evolution, which suggests organisms become extinct if they can't adapt to their environment, organizing theory maintains organizations that don't adapt to their environment will collapse. Accordingly, Weick (1969) proposed a three-stage process of **sociocultural evolution** for organizations.

The first stage of sociocultural evolution is **enactment**. Enactment occurs when members of an organization take note of equivocal information in their information environment. Recall that equivocal information can be interpreted in multiple ways. Recognizing multiple interpretations and putting into practice a mechanism for making sense of the information are at the heart of enactment.

The second stage is **selection**. In seeking to reduce equivocality, organizational members must choose how to respond. As described earlier, organizational members can choose between rules, or standard guidelines for how to respond, and a double interact, which is a communication process that allows members to adapt solutions to the problem.

The third stage is **retention**. Retention is a form of organizational memory. What was done and how it was done is stored, formally or informally, so organizational members can refer to it again. Notice what is happening here; even if organizational members go through a double interact to reduce equivocality, in this stage, the double interact is retained as a new rule or guideline for behavior in the future. Accordingly, retention should be used sparingly. Figure 9.1 provides a visual illustration of sociocultural evolution.

Figure 9.1 Weick's Model of Organizing

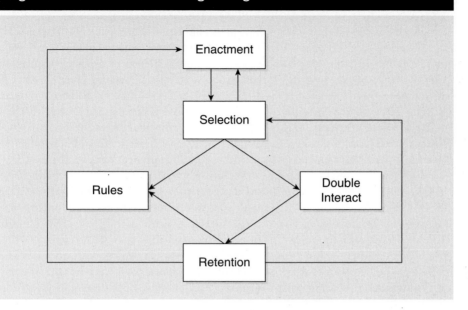

To complete the analogy with Darwin's theory of evolution, Weick's (1969) theory of organizing posits that organizations exist in a complex information environment. This environment is complex because organizations have to deal with equivocal information. Organizations that don't adapt to equivocality, whose members don't use double interacts to resolve new forms of ambiguity, will not survive and flourish. In short, change is the key to organizational success, and change occurs through the process of communicating.

SUMMARY AND RESEARCH APPLICATIONS

This chapter introduced four theories of organizational communication. We first looked at organizational culture, using two distinct theories to illustrate this concept: Deal and Kennedy's strong culture approach, which identifies four types of organizational cultures, and Schein's model of organizational culture, which suggests three levels of culture: artifacts, values, and assumptions. Deal and Kennedy's approach has been applied within the context of training clinical social workers to help them recognize organizational fit and prevent burnout (Steiner & Cox, 2014).

Schein's model proposes that assumptions are at the heart of organizational culture, and his model has been applied to a new paradigm of business development called corporate sustainability (see Baumgartner, 2009). Specifically, an organization can only become socially, environmentally, and economically viable with a strong organizational culture that supports these sustainable values. Hogan and Coote (2014) tested Schein's model of culture among law firm principals and found that firms' artifacts, norms, and innovative behaviors influenced values and, subsequently, firm performance. Second, organizational assimilation theory details four stages of socialization into a new organization. In a qualitative study of millennial (also see Chapter 4) employees, Jarvis (2016) found that these newcomers' communication styles significantly affected their ability to assimilate to organizational expectations. Her findings suggest that information sharing via detailed instructions, mentors, and intradepartmental socialization during the encounter/entry phase are of critical importance when onboarding this generation of employees to maximize the possibility of assimilation and minimize turnover.

Next, organizational identification and control proposes that when organizational members identify with the values of an organization, they can be controlled through self-discipline and peer pressure. For example, Dutch researchers found that peers' use of concertive control helped to explain why employees, in public and private sectors, often did not take advantage of the generous work-life balance policies (ter Hoeven, Miller, Peper, & den Dulk, 2017). Use of jokes and reprimands between colleagues served as powerful signals about when and how often one should use flexible arrangements so as not to leave coworkers overburdened. Finally, Weick's theory of organizing argues organizations and their members must process equivocal information in order to succeed. Recent research has applied Weick's notion of organizing and equivocality to complex learning environments with high equivocality, such as within a medical humanities course (Ledford, Saperstein, Cafferty, McClintick, & Bernstein, 2015). Ledford et al. found that classroom use of microblogs facilitated the three phases of organizing: enactment, selection, and retention. Results also showed that using technology was an effective means to manage the equivocality that came with the subject matter.

KEY TERMS

Anticipatory socialization   169
Bureaucratic control   171
Concertive control   172
Cultural network   164
Discipline   172
Double interact   174
Enactment   174
Encounter   169
Equifinality   163
Equivocality   173
Heroes   164
Homeostasis   162

Identification   170
Individualization   170
Information environment   173
Interdependence   162
Metamorphosis   170
Nonsummativity   162
Organizational
   assimilation   168
Organizational culture   163
Organizing   173
Retention   174
Rites and rituals   164

Rules   173
Selection   174
Simple control   171
Socialization   170
Sociocultural evolution   174
Synergy   162
System   162
Technological control   171
Unobtrusive control   171
Values   164
Vocational anticipatory
   socialization   169

CASE STUDY 9: LOSING HOPE

For more than 80 years, Hope Medical Center had serviced its local residents as a privately run, not-for-profit community hospital. However, with the rapidly escalating cost of medical care, last year, Hope's board of directors agreed that, for the hospital to survive, it was in their best interest to partner with the Greater Valley Hospital Alliance (GVHA)—a for-profit hospital management group. Under GVHA's management, resources could be used more efficiently, the hospital would have more financial security, and patients and doctors alike would have access to other facilities in GVHA's network of hospitals. GVHA had promised that Hope's daily operations would remain untouched after the merger. When announced in the local newspaper, nearby residents and the hospital staff enthusiastically supported the partnership.

Stella Brindle had worked for Hope for the last 8 years in its community relations department. She helped publicize the hospital's services, success stories, and awards. She also helped the hospital raise money, and she was particularly proud of her work directing the most recent fund-raising campaign that helped finance the hospital's pediatric unit renovations. Stella was excited by the merger; by sharing resources, she believed the partnership would free her from some of the more tedious job duties and allow her team to focus more on fund-raising and developing the hospital's services.

Additionally, Stella's team had spearheaded an initiative called the Beacon of Hope, a mission statement and motto for all employees. Called the Beacon for short, its purpose was to "inspire all members of the Hope community to realize what it means to be truly exceptional caregivers." The Beacon had emerged after the American Medical Association named Hope as "the nation's most compassionate hospital." The director of community relations, Devin Au'berge, wanted to formalize this standard of care and assigned Stella to lead the Beacon initiative.

With support from the entire hospital community, the Beacon was to serve as a code of conduct for all physicians, nurses, staff members, and volunteers. Stella ran a number of focus groups and sought input from various stakeholders. As a result, Hope employees were quite proud of the Beacon and what it stood for. The mission statement appeared prominently on all of the hospital's promotional materials, and a framed copy hung in each patient's room. The hospital gift shop even sold a variety of items with the Beacon's logo. Hope's physicians were invited to use the Beacon in their patient office areas, and the Beacon logo was stitched on all hospital lab coats and scrubs.

Despite the Beacon initiative's success and the initial community support for merging with GVHA, however, tough times were on the horizon for Hope. Six months into the merger, Stella and many other employees had serious regrets about joining the GVHA network. When initially proposed by the board, Hope employees were led to believe that a partnership with GVHA would have minimal impact on their day-to-day tasks. The CEO of GVHA even told hospital staff that "a partnership would not disrupt the wonderful community culture of Hope Medical Center." However, only days after the deal was signed, this promise seemed moot. First, a bright red and purple GVHA banner was hung, overshadowing

(Continued)

(Continued)

the Beacon. Next, GVHA administrators sent an e-mail informing Hope employees that as part of the GVHA network, Hope employees must wear the GVHA-approved uniforms or lab coats. Although seemingly a trivial issue, Stella and the rest of the community relations team were upset. Not only were they being forced to wear a uniform, but the demand also meant the Beacon logo could no longer be worn because it wasn't "consistent" with the other GVHA hospitals.

Transformations appeared in the gift shop, too. The Beacon merchandise was still there but on a back shelf where it was hard to see. And several weeks after that, Stella noticed changes to the hospital's website. The Beacon was no longer featured prominently; instead it was a tiny link, buried halfway down the page. Stella was confused; normally, her department managed the website and all changes were made as a team. Yet, no one in community relations knew anything about the changes. When Stella called GVHA to find out about the new website, she was told, "Oh, you don't need to worry about maintaining your site anymore. We'll do all of that for you so you have more time to work on fundraising." Stella felt conflicted. On one hand, no one in community relations liked the tedious task of constantly updating the website; however, she wished the team would have been asked, or at least informed, about this change.

The changes weren't just about logos and merchandise. Hope had always prided itself on its family-like atmosphere where all of the doctors, nurses, and staff members knew each other by first name. The cafeteria and elevators were typically jovial places because people would chat with each other. Since the merger, however, physicians and nurses could be required to work at several of GVHA's hospitals, depending on which hospital had the most need. This meant there was an ongoing influx and exodus of medical personnel and more unfamiliar faces.

Although always busy, the pace at Hope now felt more intense as doctors dashed from room to room trying to see all of their patients before driving to another location.

Community relations started receiving complaints—first from the nurses, then from the doctors, and even from patients. A letter to the editor was published in the local newspaper, criticizing Hope for "going commercial." Reported medical mistakes had risen since the partnership, and patient satisfaction had declined. Stella's boss, Devin, asked the community relations team to start categorizing these complaints. After a month, Devin prepared a report and called a meeting with the board of directors. She showed them all of the data along with her conclusion: Hope was losing what had made it such an exceptional hospital. The medical staff felt more overworked than ever, while patients felt like numbers, rather than people. The whole philosophy behind the Beacon had become overshadowed by GVHA's businesslike atmosphere. The board was at a loss. If the hospital's record of medical mistakes was too high, or if too many patients filed complaints, GVHA would void their contract and withdraw hospital funding. Clearly, something had to be done, but what?

Questions for Consideration

1. Compare and contrast the culture of Hope Medical Center (before the merger) with that of GVHA. Make sure to describe the artifacts, values, and assumptions apparent in both organizations. Using Deal and Kennedy's four cultures, which type of culture has Hope historically had? Based on Schein's theory, can the cultures of Hope and GVHA coexist? Why, or why not?

2. Using organizational assimilation theory, describe the stages of Stella's adjustment (or failure to adjust) to the "new" hospital after the GVHA merger. Do you believe metamorphosis will occur? Why, or why not?

3. What types of organizational control did Hope Medical Center use before the partnership? Compare this with the types of control GVHA uses to manage its hospital network.

4. Using organizing theory, what evidence is there of the use of double interacts?

What might sociocultural evolution predict will happen to Hope?

5. What ethical issues arise with the merger? Do any of the theories provide insight into helping manage these ethical tensions?

6. Do any of the theories emerge as better than the others? Why do you believe this to be the case? How could the story be altered so as to make a different theory or combination of theories better at explaining the situation?

CHAPTER TEN

MEDIATED COMMUNICATION

Is your LinkedIn profile up to date? How often do you tweet? Do you know what time it is if you don't have your smartphone? Are you more likely to watch TV shows and movies on a television or on a tablet? There are a bewildering array of communication technologies available to us, with new platforms being launched nearly every month and old platforms slowly becoming obsolete (AOL anyone?). With so many communication channels available to us, being a competent communicator requires selecting the appropriate method to share a particular message. This chapter focuses on **mediated communication** channels—how mediated channels become popular as well as how and why we use them.

WHAT IS SOCIAL MEDIA?

When we use the term *media*, we typically are referring to large organizations responsible for producing the content we see on television and in the movies; the recordings we listen to on the radio and on our MP3 players; and the books and periodicals we read in print, on a Kindle, or on the web. By contrast, the term *social media* refers to "digital technologies that allow people to connect, interact, produce and share content" (Lewis, 2010, p. 2). These media forms vary in nature and purpose and include blogs, microblogging sites like Twitter, wikis, social networking websites like Facebook and LinkedIn, podcasting, video and photo sharing sites such as YouTube and Instagram, and discussion forums. Social media are considered distinct from traditional media because social media are based on user-generated content (versus "institutional content") and because the costs of creating and disseminating the content are either free or relatively inexpensive.

The original focus of social media was on its ability to assist individuals with achieving their personal goals (Vorvoreanu, 2009). However, more and more frequently people are pushing for the use

Learning Objectives

After reading this chapter, you will be able to do the following:

1. Explain social media and discuss how social media differ from mass media

2. Articulate which qualities of an innovation will make it more likely to be adopted

3. Explain how social network analysis explains the production and reproduction of memes

4. Apply the concept of ambiguity to match a communication message to the appropriate communication channel

5. Identify the gratifications sought by using particular media forms

6. Compare and contrast major theoretical approaches to mediated communication

7. Provide systematic understanding of a professional situation by employing principles of individual and social approaches to communication

of social media to achieve professional, rather than personal, goals. This is particularly evident in the realm of public relations; PR scholars such as Avery, Lariscy, and Sweetser (2010) claim "virtually no organization can afford to neglect its social media presence" (pp. 198–199). In part, this is because social media allow for one group or individual to easily persuade other groups or individuals (Blossom, 2009). Yet there is little evidence social media are different from any other channel available to communicators.

A critical understanding of the role of social media in our lives requires us to understand the nature of mediated forms of communication. The first theory we discuss, diffusion of innovations, seeks to explain how and why particular new communication technologies develop and grow. Next, we explain social network theory, which helps to understand the web of connections we develop through social media. Third, we describe media richness theory, which focuses on the choices a communicator must make about the proper channel for disseminating particular messages. Finally, we discuss uses and gratifications theory, which centers on the choices audience members make in order to fulfill their needs.

DIFFUSION OF INNOVATIONS

Why do we all know DVDs and BluRay for our at-home movie viewing, but we have little memory of LaserDisc? Other than public displays of affection, what else does PDA stand for, and why don't we use them anymore (answer: personal digital assistant)? Is Facebook dead now that your grandmother has a page? Rogers's (2003) diffusion of innovations theory provides a framework for understanding why some inventions become popular and others never really catch on. An **innovation** is an idea, practice, or object perceived as new. Although we often think of innovations in terms of technology, Rogers was careful to make sure innovations are understood in the broadest sense possible. His own academic background was in agriculture, and his earliest research focused on farmers' use of a new weed spray. Since the development of his model in the early 1960s, diffusion of innovations has been used to understand everything from the spread of particular medical technologies to the adoption of educational practices. Moreover, Rogers was clear in his belief that what is considered innovative varies by place and community. For example, video chatting through Facetime or Skype might not be new to you, but for some groups of people and in some parts of the world, seeing someone live while you talk with him or her might seem very futuristic indeed.

Innovation Decision Process

Rogers (2003) identified six stages through which a person, group, or organization progresses in deciding whether to adopt an innovation. The first stage is known as the **knowledge stage**; here, the potential adopter becomes aware of the innovation and its potential uses. Second, the **persuasion stage** occurs when the potential adopter goes beyond mere awareness of the innovation and actively seeks information about it. She might do an Internet search, with careful attention to product reviews, or she might talk to people in her social network to assess their perspective of the innovation. The third stage is the **decision stage**, during which the potential adopter weighs the benefits and costs of the innovation and chooses either to adopt the innovation or to reject it.

Of course, if the innovation is rejected, the process ends here, but if the innovation is adopted, the process continues with the fourth stage. The **implementation stage** occurs when the adopter puts the innovation into use. Not surprisingly, this stage might include a lot of uncertainty and frustration. The adopter has to figure out how the innovation works in general, which specific features are useful and which are less than useful for his or her specific needs, and how to incorporate the innovation into an everyday routine. One important part of implementation is called **reinvention**, wherein the adopter "repurposes" the innovation. For example, voice mail was developed so callers could leave a message if the phone was not answered. However, many people call themselves and leave a message to create an audio reminder for themselves.

The fifth stage is the **confirmation stage**. During this stage, the adopter reconsiders his or her adoption of the technology. Is it worth it? Does it do what the person had hoped it would do? If the answer is yes, the person has finally entered the **adoption stage**. If not, the person discontinues his or her use of the innovation. Discontinuance can take two forms. **Replacement discontinuance** occurs when an innovation is replaced with either a new version or an older version. Using a newer innovation makes sense, but why use an older technology? There are many reasons, including pragmatic; many people prefer faxing information rather than sending a scanned document because there are no worries about sending unencrypted information online. The second type of discontinuance is **disenchantment rejection**, or abandonment, which is when the adopter simply stops using the innovation. For example, after the iPhone was introduced, many people abandoned their PalmPilots and other PDAs.

Why Some Innovations and Not Others?

Of course, not every innovation succeeds. Rogers (2003) was concerned not only with the process of adopting an innovation but also with the essential question of why some innovations are adopted and others are not. He identified five qualities that influence the rate and likelihood of an innovation being adopted. The first is **relative advantage**. Simply put, the innovation has to be better at achieving the goals for performance than other, competing technologies. There are a number of ways an innovation might be considered "better." It might be faster, cheaper, easier to use, more effective, or just be "cooler" than other options. For example, for years Apple products were perceived as having an "it" factor that made them cooler than other brands. That image has started to fade recently (see Chen, 2013).

The second factor that influences the adoption of an innovation is **compatibility**. The extent to which an innovation is consistent with a potential adopter's values, lifestyle, or experience makes it a more attractive option. Consider, for example, a new mother who is philosophically opposed to genetically modified food. If she finds out a new product is made from grain grown using genetically engineered seeds, she is not going to purchase that product. On a more basic level, you are not going to purchase software that is only compatible with a Macintosh if you already own a PC.

Third, potential adopters consider **complexity**, which refers to the level of difficulty in understanding or using the innovation. For example, if the learning curve for a new technology is perceived as too steep, that technology will not be used, regardless of the benefits it might provide. On the other hand, an individual doesn't have to actually understand how television broadcasts work if the television set itself is easy to use; if you can plug it in, turn it on, and figure out how to change channels without reading a lengthy technical manual, the innovation is likely to be adopted.

Trialability is the next factor that influences the rate and likelihood of adoption. The extent to which potential adopters can "try" the innovation before making a decision can expedite the decision-making process. Whether test-driving a new car or a computer, trying on a new style of clothing, getting a sample pack of a potential new prescription, or sitting in on a graduate class before applying to the school, people are much more likely to adopt an innovation if they have had the opportunity to try it out before being required to purchase it.

The last factor is **observability**. People are much more likely to adopt an innovation if they actually see the innovation in public or if the results of the innovation are visible. If everyone else seems to be using a new technology it becomes much more appealing to those who are not ("Seriously, Mom, I am the only person at school without one."). Similarly, if the innovation's impact is obvious ("Wow! You look great! What new fitness routine are you using?"), people will be more inclined to adopt it.

Time and Diffusion

You have probably heard the old question "If a tree falls in the woods and no one hears it, does it make a sound?" A similar question can be asked regarding the diffusion of innovations. That is, if an innovation is available and no one adopts it, can it have an impact? The answer is no. Even if an innovation exhibits the five qualities just described, ultimately people determine the success or failure of its adoption. The third major contribution diffusion of innovations makes to our understanding of how communication media develop and grow is through a focus on critical mass. **Critical mass** refers to the notion that if a sufficient number of people adopt the innovation, additional adoption of the innovation becomes self-sustaining, assuring future growth (Markus, 1987).

At issue is the **rate of adoption**, or the relative speed with which an individual (or group or organization) adopts the innovation. Rogers (2003) classified people into five categories, from those most likely to embrace the innovation rapidly to those who may never adopt the innovation. Figure 10.1 displays categories of people in the innovation adoption process. **Innovators** are the first group of any social system to adopt an innovation. They tend to be younger, high in social class, and categorized as risk takers socially connected with other innovators, even if they live in different regions of the world. The next group of people are **early adopters**. Unlike innovators, early adopters tend to be connected with others more locally. However, they tend to be opinion leaders who have a greater influence on other members of the social system. As such, they play a central role in the diffusion of innovations, since their opinions are respected, and they assist others with their uncertainty about the innovation. The **early majority** is the next group of individuals. Although they do not serve as role models or opinion leaders, they carefully deliberate over the adoption of the innovation, and it is their decision to adopt that allows the diffusion of the innovation to reach a critical mass. The fourth group is called the **late majority**. These individuals tend only to adopt an innovation because of peer pressure; they tend to be skeptical of innovations and unwilling to take risks. Finally, the **laggards** rarely, if ever, adopt the innovation. Typically, older and more traditional in beliefs, laggards are not only mistrustful of new ideas, products, or services, they also are leery of innovators and early adopters.

Returning to the notion of critical mass, the process whereby people adopt the use of interactive media is different from the adoption of other types of innovations (Markus, 1987). Interactive media such as the telephone, text messaging, or Facebook entail **reciprocal interdependence**; that is, even if innovators or early adopters have the technology, they need others to adopt the technology in order to receive the maximum benefits. Think about it: What good is having the ability to text on your phone if other people cannot receive your texts? Accordingly, early adopters must actively persuade others to adopt the technology, resulting in a steep increase in the adoption rate. Look at Figure 10.1 again. The first half of the bell curve demonstrates that the rate of adoption is not a straight line but more like a slightly flattened "S" curve.

Diffusion of innovations theory depicts the process whereby new media technologies are adopted in society. The theory details the decision-making process that

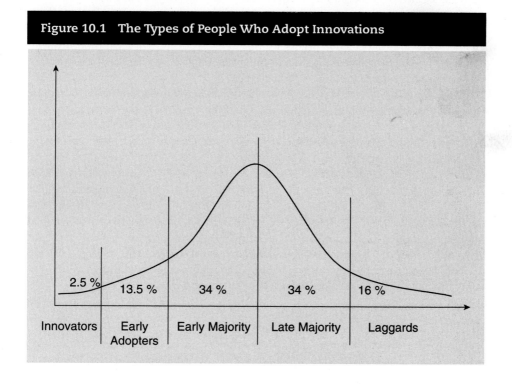

Figure 10.1   The Types of People Who Adopt Innovations

individuals use in the adoption process and qualities that make a given innovation more likely to be adopted. Finally, the theory classifies people in terms of their likeliness to adopt an innovation, with early adopters playing an important role in persuading others to adopt the innovation.

SOCIAL NETWORK ANALYSIS

In Chapter 9 we introduced you to systems perspectives, which focus on how groups of people interrelate to form a whole. Systems perspectives are used to understand many contexts for communication, although they are used most often to understand organizational communication. Likewise, network analysis has historically been associated with an organizational context, but the growth of social media has led a number of scholars to implement network analysis to understand the relationship patterns of social media users.

In the 1980s, Fabergé Organics shampoo had a popular commercial featuring Heather Locklear, who was so excited about using the shampoo that she told two friends about it . . . and they told two friends . . . and so on and so on until the screen was filled with people who had heard about the shampoo from one of their friends. In 2012, the same concept was used by the AIDS Council, who developed a public service announcement for Foursquare that focused on safe sex: When you have sex with someone, you are not only having sex with them, you are having sex with everyone they have ever had sex with . . . and so on (because Foursquare identifies "where you have been," the commercial talked about how many other people had "been there already"). Both of these ads feature one of the central concepts of social network analysis: All of us are connected to others, who are connected to others, leading us to "six degrees of separation" from all others around the world (although apparently the popularity of Facebook has now led us to four degrees of separation; see Barnett, 2011).

According to Monge and Contractor (2001), "Communication networks are the patterns of contact between communication partners that are created by transmitting and exchanging messages through time and space" (p. 440). Network analysis involves mapping out those patterns, with a special focus on the types of links between members, the roles members play in the network, the mode or channel by which messages are exchanged, and the content of the messages. At its most basic level, consider your own Facebook network. How many friends do you have? How many of your own friends are also friends with other people on your friends list? How often do you actually message or respond to each of the people on your friends list? Do you primarily share personal information, professional information, or both? How many people do you also talk with using other channels of communication? Social network analysis allows you to develop a picture of how individuals, groups, and organizations are connected with each other to better understand structures of influence and the spread of ideas.

Network Properties

Four attributes of networks are considered in a social network analysis (Miller, 2003). The first is the **network mode**. Put simply, the network mode involves the channel or channels used by network members. Consider people who work for the same organization but in two different locations; they may have phone and e-mail contact but may never have actually met each other face-to-face. An understanding of which channels are used in the network is important, as each channel has strengths and weaknesses (which we talk about when we discuss media richness theory). The second is the **content** of messages. Gilpin (2010), for example, did a network analysis of the social media content posted by the supermarket chain Whole Foods. She found the content could be classified as focusing either on the core identity of the company or on the well-being of its customers. The third network property is **density**, or the number of interconnections among network members. Highly dense networks involve many connections between network members, such as those between a group of college friends, whereas a less dense network is one of few connections between members. Consider, for example, the informal or social connections between coworkers. Although there may be significant connections among coworkers when considering task-related communication, the coworkers might not have many social connections, making the social network a low-density network. Believe it or not, a lack of a social network among coworkers has been found to negatively predict productivity, so understanding network density can be very important (Litterst & Eyo, 1982). The final consideration is the **level of analysis**. When conducting a social network analysis, is the focus on the individuals in the network, particular groups of organizational members (e.g., departments in an organization or cliques in a friendship circle), or connections among and between organizations?

Properties of Network Links

In addition to considerations of the properties of the network itself, social network analysis also requires uncovering the nature of the connections between network members (Monge & Contractor, 2001). Seven potential links can be assessed: **strength** (the frequency, intimacy, or intensity of the connection), **direction** (the extent to which the link is reciprocal between network members), **symmetry** (whether the two people connected share the same type of relationship with each other), **frequency** (how often the two people communicate with each other), **stability** (the existence of the link over time), **mediation** (whether the connections between network members exist because of a common link), and **multiplexity** (the extent to which two network members are linked together by more than one relationship or type of communication). To illustrate, consider the simple network depicted in Figure 10.2. You can see that network members A, B, C, D, and E seem to have a dense network likely to also be strong, direct, symmetrical, frequent, stable, and demonstrate multiplexity—they are perhaps people who both work together and socialize with each other. Now consider the relationship between B and E; despite being in the same dense network, they are connected only because A, C, and D serve as mediators. One can easily imagine that, at one time, B and E might have been directly connected, but their link faded over time. Finally, consider F's relationship with K. The arrow goes in only one direction, perhaps indicating that K's work requires input from F, but F does not require feedback from K to do her job.

Figure 10.2   Exemplar Social Network Graph

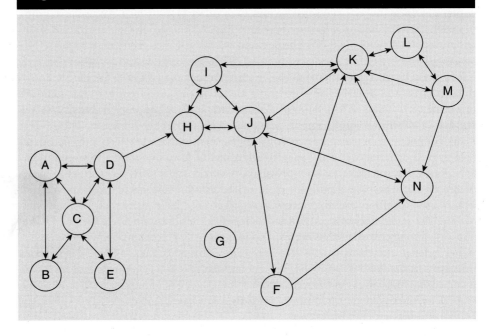

Figure 10.2 includes only a single arrow between network members, but a thorough network analysis might involve multiple types of arrows to demonstrate the different modes of communication between network members. For example, you might have a black arrow to depict face-to-face communication, a blue arrow to depict e-mail, a red arrow to depict Facebook, a green arrow to depict the phone, and so forth. In addition, you might have an unbroken arrow to illuminate links for professional communication and a dashed arrow to show links for social communication. A complete social network analysis is very complex, sometimes requiring 3-D imagery. We encourage you to search online to view images of social network analyses to see the intricacy such work requires.

Network Roles

Social network analysis also requires a consideration of the roles each member plays in the network. Network members are considered **nodes,** since networks are not always comprised of individuals. Five types of roles have been uncovered (Monge & Contractor, 2001). An **isolate** is a node that belongs in a network but has no links. In Figure 10.2, G is an isolate: He or she might work for an organization but does not communicate with others in the organization. Although this sounds improbable, it could be that G's role is a boundary spanner who connects with members of other organizations. A **gate-keeper** is a node that controls the flow of information between one part of the network and another. Consider D in Figure 10.2; he or she is the sole link between members on the left-hand side of the network and those on the right-hand side. A **bridge** is a member of more than one group. J, for example, is a part of the H-I-J group and a member of the J-K-N-F group. A **liaison** has connections with two or more groups that would otherwise not be linked. However, liaisons are not nodes of either of those groups. H, for example, is a liaison for the A-B-C-D-E network and the J-K-N-F network. Finally, a **star** is a node that is highly central to the network. Consider K in Figure 10.2. She or he has six network links, more than anyone else in the network.

In the case of a single organization and talking about individuals, the roles just described make sense, as it is easy to consider individuals playing each role. However, in more sophisticated and extensive social network analyses, we need to recognize that the nodes might be entire organizations. In this case, we need to also consider **hubs**, which are highly dense networks embedded within a larger network. To simplify this notion, consider the Internet as a network. A few heavily used websites, such as Google, Facebook, and YouTube would be considered hubs, whereas very specialized websites might be closer to isolates—they might be password protected and not hyperlinked from any other website.

Implications for Understanding Social Media

Recall that the purpose of social media theory is to uncover the patterns of connections within a system. More than just identifying "who talks to whom," a social network analysis can allow us to uncover large-scale trends in ideas and influences. For example, Kelly (2008) has mapped the blogosphere, uncovering the connections between news (and faux news) sites. Sedereviciute and Valentini (2011) developed a method for PR practitioners to uncover organizational stakeholders through mapping social media content. Similarly, De Nooy and Kleinnijenhuis (2013) created a mechanism to study patterns of support and attack in the political communication arena.

The concepts described earlier (network properties, network links, and network roles) are most often used to investigate the structure of a social network. However, scholars also use social network analysis to investigate **semantic networks**, which particularly focus on the content of the communications (Gilpin, 2010). In this way, researchers can understand the spread of **memes**—ideas, behaviors, or practices that spread from one person to another in a network (Dawkins, 1989). Consider the spread of the ALS ice bucket challenge, the "eat it or wear it" videos, and the #saltbae memes in recent years. Social media not only connect each of us in six (or four!) degrees of separation, they also allow for the production and reproduction of significant social trends.

MEDIA RICHNESS THEORY

The decline and ultimate end of Taylor Swift and Calvin Harris's relationship was on public display through their tweets. And, according to an article in *Vogue*, Katy Perry claimed Russell Brand texted her that he wanted a divorce. In Aziz Ansari's book *Modern Romance*, Ansari provides statistics indicating that the majority of young adult relationships end via digital media, with up to 20% occurring over social media. Most of us have the empathy to realize these might not have been the best media choices to sever a relationship. However, in the professional world, sometimes the choice is less obvious. For example, is it okay to conduct layoffs via e-mail? Media richness theory, developed by Daft and Lengel (1984), recognizes that as new communication technologies develop, the decision about the best way to send a message becomes more complex.

What Is a Rich Medium?

The central argument of media richness theory is that communication professionals should match the communication channel to the content of the information (Lengel & Daft, 1988). **Media richness** refers to the information-carrying capacity of the medium. One determines the richness of the media by assessing four characteristics: speed of feedback (related to synchronous or asynchronous capacities), ability to personalize the message, availability of multiple cues, and language variety (Daft & Lengel, 1986). Face-to-face interaction is considered the most "rich" medium. Imagine an organizational training session. A face-to-face trainer can quickly adjust the session if he or she sees that employees do not understand a particular process ("Okay, let me try another way to explain how this new software program is different from the old program"). The trainer can recognize individuals in the group and craft messages to those individuals ("José, your department won't need to be concerned about this next application"). The trainer can use words, facial expressions, gestures, pauses, eye contact, and a host of other possible nonverbal cues in the session. Finally, the trainer can change the vocabulary or jargon usage depending on with whom he or she is talking. Contrast this with a much less rich medium: a digital video. Imagine a group of employees sitting in a room watching a recorded training session. If the employees do not understand something on the recording, little can be done; the recording cannot be changed in the moment to adapt to audience confusion. Moreover, given production expenses, the recording likely would be

Table 10.1 Media Richness	
Richer Media	**Face-to-face**
↑	Video conferencing, social networking, interactive websites
	Telephone
	E-mail
	Texting, instant messaging, microblogs
	Video or audio recordings
↓	Memos, letters
Leaner Media	Bulk mail, brochures, pamphlets, flyers

produced for all employees and wouldn't be tailored to particular groups or individuals or to their backgrounds or experiences. As such, it would be considered a "lean" medium. Table 10.1 identifies media from most to least rich based on these characteristics.

How Ambiguous Is the Message?

Of course, the main idea of the theory is that the medium should match the message. As such, the second major consideration is the nature of the message that needs to be sent. Daft and Lengel (1984, 1986) were influenced by the work of Karl Weick (see Chapter 9), so they focused on the notion of ambiguity. **Ambiguity** refers to the possibility of multiple interpretations. If the goal of communication is understanding (as Daft and Lengel assumed), then ambiguous messages are those that run a greater risk of being misunderstood. Imagine you are an employee of an organization facing financial crisis. The senior management team of your organization has decided that, rather than layoffs, they will reduce employee benefits. You might have many questions about such a decision. Will this affect all employees? Is it a permanent decision, or will benefits be returned once the crisis is over? Will the elimination of these benefits really solve the financial problems, or might there still be layoffs sometime in the future? Can individuals choose which benefits are reduced? After all, health care might be a major concern to some employees, and retirement benefits might be of greater concern to others. In short, this sort of situation is highly ambiguous. Not surprisingly, according to media richness theory, the more ambiguous the message, the richer the medium should be in communicating that message. In the situation just described, media richness theory would suggest using a town hall meeting or even small group meetings to explain the decision and to answer questions; a memo would not be an appropriate choice. On the other hand, using e-mail or a memo might be a perfectly suitable method for announcing the meeting itself, as the time and date of a meeting is not particularly ambiguous.

As asserted earlier, communication effectiveness is assumed to occur because of a match between the ambiguity of the message and the richness of the media. A highly ambiguous message communicated using a lean media form is likely to exacerbate uncertainty and create misunderstanding. Conversely, using a very rich medium to communicate fairly straightforward information is a form of overkill, potentially wasting time and money and possibly contributing to a sense of information overload. Can you imagine having a personal conversation about every bit of information you deal with on an everyday basis? It would be exhausting! As it is, you likely delete some e-mails and texts without reading them because of information overload.

Some scholars have challenged media richness theory because the theory implies there is an objective richness to particular media that does not vary based on individual or organizational variations. After all, we all know people who pick up the phone for even the simplest of questions, whereas others prefer e-mail exchanges. Similarly, organizations have differing cultures related to the preferred ways of communication. However, scholars have found that above and beyond such variations, there are objective differences in the ability of various communication channels to communicate particular types of messages (Trevino, Lengel, & Daft, 1987). As such, a skilled communicator needs to consciously consider media richness in the communication process.

USES AND GRATIFICATIONS THEORY

Uses and gratifications theory (UGT) represents a somewhat different means by which to analyze and explain the use of mediated communication. Rather than look at the media choices made by a message sender, UGT focuses on *why* a receiver uses particular media forms. Specifically, UGT maintains that because humans have options and free will, individuals will make specific decisions about which media to use and when to use them (Katz, Blumler, & Gurevitch, 1973). The choices and decisions you make are based on personal needs and values you wish to fulfill. Thus, you can select among various media for **gratification** of your individual needs.

Three primary assumptions drive our discussion of UGT. First, Katz et al. (1973) believed audience members actively use various media to fulfill certain needs or goals. Thus, media usage isn't passive, involuntary, or coerced. Instead, media technologies represent numerous options available to fulfill a person's social or psychological needs and values. Indeed, the increase in communication technologies available to people in the 21st century only boosts the viability of the notion of choice (Ruggiero, 2000). In this way, UGT suggests media use is active and goal driven based on individuals' needs.

Second, **mass communication** isn't something that happens to you; nor do the media do anything to you. There is no magic spell cast by media owners to coax you into viewing their programming. Instead, UGT maintains a person must identify his or her need and make a media choice (Katz et al., 1973). Individuals *choose* to surf the Internet, tweet, or put together a Pinterest board. In this regard, the term *media effects* is misleading. Katz et al. (1973) did not believe in the simple "straight-line effect" whereby a given medium causes people to think or behave differently. According to Katz et al., audience members choose a medium and allow themselves to be swayed, changed, and influenced—or not. You choose to view a YouTube video and watch; YouTube doesn't turn itself on and watch you.

Third, media outlets compete with other available means of satisfying personal needs (Katz et al., 1973). Stated differently, there are many ways to fulfill individual needs. If you feel frazzled after a hectic day at work, you may fulfill your need to relax and unwind by watching a sitcom (mass media) or escaping to the movies. Alternatively, you may meet your needs by taking a run in the park, practicing yoga, or soaking in a warm bath with a glass of wine. Thus, the mass media represent only a handful of alternatives available to you. Next, we present reasons individuals use the media and how media exposure can gratify various social and psychological needs.

Why Do We Watch What We Watch?

McQuail (1987) identified four broad classes of motivations that include several subcategories. For example, we can use the media for entertainment purposes. Under the umbrella term of *entertainment* are some specific subtypes; individuals can relax, escape from daily problems, feel some form of excitement or emotional catharsis, pass time, or simply enjoy an artistic pleasure. You may relax by listening to satellite radio while on your commute home from a long day at the office. You may have watched *The Ring* to experience an eerie thrill or *Casablanca* to experience a romantic heartbreak. Your children may watch *Dora the Explorer* on DVD while riding in the backseat of your car to prevent boredom. Similarly, you may turn on a TV sitcom as a diversion from the daily grind. Table 10.2 provides an overview of gratifications.

Second, media outlets and content are used to provide information (McQuail, 1987). This media function presents individuals with opportunities to learn about current and historical events, to obtain advice, and to feel secure or satisfy curiosity by acquiring general knowledge. Thus, you may turn on news radio for the weather, traffic updates, and local sports scores. You probably have watched or read about local, national, and world news to find out what is going on in your neighborhood as well as in the world. You may read an advice column for investment strategies or etiquette protocols. You may use the Internet to scour real estate web pages and research the dimensions of your dream home.

Third, people use the media to reflect, reinforce, or contrast their personal identity (McQuail, 1987). In other words, individuals can choose among various media and media content to gain insight into or assist in the development of their own attitudes or beliefs. For example, you might watch Dr. Phil to hear how others struggle with relationship issues. Likewise, a person often acquires a deeper sense of self by comparing, and perhaps contrasting, one's self with characters portrayed in various media. For instance, you are probably familiar with the hit show *The Big Bang Theory*. Although you may find the characters of Sheldon, Leonard, Raj, and Howard to be hilarious with their lack of social skill, you also are apt to compare your own experiences and attitudes with theirs. Are you that self-centered? That neurotic? That immature? That insecure? We hope

Table 10.2 Gratifications

Gratification	Examples
Entertainment	• Listening to a Barry White CD to set a romantic mood • Watching *Psycho* to experience a thrill • Watching YouTube videos because you have nothing else to do
Information	• Seeking advice about practical matters, such as how to cook a turkey (Food Network) • Finding out the weather so you know what to wear to work
Personal identity	• Reading *Vogue* or *Esquire* so you know how to dress and be considered stylish • Putting together a Pinterest board to share your passions
Personal relationships and social interaction	• Listening to the Sports Radio Network on your drive to work so you can talk about it with your coworkers • Watching *America's Got Talent* every week to bond with your family

not! But that is exactly the point of the show—to present extreme personalities audience members can at once relate to and simultaneously ridicule for their triviality.

A fourth and final reason is that people turn to various media for personal relationships and social interaction (McQuail, 1987). Media exposure can help individuals learn about or connect with others through comparisons of interpersonal relationships and social situations. Certain media can even serve as a substitute for real-life relationships by offering companionship. Wednesday morning watercooler gossip about the latest twist on *The Voice* creates a sense of community. Following the (sometimes harebrained) parenting decisions on *Black-ish* allows viewers to compare and commiserate about their own family foibles. Reading a magazine article titled "How to Tell if He Is Really Into You" or a newspaper interview with someone who successfully developed a relationship by "swiping right," may provide readers with an opportunity to consider their own dating disasters.

UGT maintains people have many options from which they deliberately select to meet personal needs. The question, then, is not what impact the media have on us, but, rather, why people choose the media forms they do and what gratifications they receive from their choices.

SUMMARY AND RESEARCH APPLICATIONS

In this chapter, we presented an overview of four theories of mediated communication. First, we described the diffusion of innovations: the process by which people decide to adopt a new media technology, the characteristics that make a new media technology more appealing, and the categories of people most and least likely to adopt the new technology. For example, Oliveira, Thomas, Baptista, and Campos (2016) found that compatibility, perceived technology security, performance expectations, innovativeness, and social influence had both direct and indirect effects on the decision to use mobile payment technologies, as well as the intention to recommend the technology. Next, Gloor, Fronzetti Colladon, Grippa, and Giacomelli (2017) used a social network analysis to compare the e-mails of managers who voluntarily quit versus those who decided to stay over the course of 5 months. They found that managers who quit had less network centrality, and the content of their e-mails demonstrated less engagement than the mangers who decided to stay. Third, media richness theory provides advice for choosing particular media to send different types of messages, and is helpful in understanding media choices within organizations, such as communication preferences between superiors and subordinates (Salmon & Joiner, 2005; Shepherd & Martz, 2006). Pazos, Chung, and Micari (2013) successfully used media richness theory to predict employees would be more likely to use instant messaging for simple tasks (e.g., requesting or supplying information) than for more complex tasks (e.g., to problem solve or resolve a disagreement). Finally, UGT focuses on the choices receivers make. It argues audience members are active and use media forms that provide them with the individual gratifications they seek. As an example, researchers uncovered four gratifications for sharing photos online: seeking and showcasing experiences, technological affordances, social connection, and reaching out (Oeldorf-Hirsch & Sundar, 2016). They concluded that the uses and gratifications for online photo sharing cannot be separated by posting versus viewing photos but instead by the experience that these activities foster conjointly.

KEY TERMS

CASE STUDY 10: CASINO CONTROVERSY

When the Pennsylvania Gaming Control Board approved applications for the development of two casinos within the city limits of Philadelphia, controversy immediately ensued. Before the state had unveiled the approved casino locations, anyone could pick up a newspaper or watch a newscast and see something about the much-awaited casino proposal. These stories emphasized that the casinos would bring jobs and tourism to the city. Suburban residents like June Johnson were thrilled because casino revenue would (at least theoretically) help lower the state's escalating property taxes, and the city's union contractors were eager for the opportunity to bid on the development contracts.

However, these initial news stories never considered the local concerns that would surface, such as traffic congestion and crime. When the announcement hit that the casinos would be built next to residential areas, local homeowners and small business owners were furious.

Karen Moyer, 52, was a long-time resident and homeowner of the neighborhood adjacent to where the casinos were proposed. Worried about declining home values and the quality of the neighborhood, Karen organized a political action group called CasiNO!Philly. Karen made use of all of her network connections to get people involved with the group; she not only posted on her own Facebook page, she posted on the pages of local businesses, local schools,

(Continued)

(Continued)

and other local nonprofit groups. She created a website and posted information such as newspaper articles about the casino proposals along with contact information for the politicians who had supported the initiative. The website also featured an electronic board where registered users could post comments and organize meetings. She started following the Twitter accounts of local politicians and members of the Gaming Control Board, tweeting responses to them with the hashtag #CasiNO!Philly. As the action group's membership grew, CasiNO!Philly began tweeting about potential protests and rallies around historical tourist attractions like Independence Hall and the National Constitution Center. The aim was to attract as much media attention as possible, thereby creating negative publicity for the casino proposals.

CasiNO!Philly's social media outreach was strong, but it didn't actually become successful until one of the members of the action group contacted Karen with an idea. Warren Trembly was a 16-year-old skateboarder who attended a cyber-charter school with a focus on new media technologies. Warren introduced Karen to an application called Loke, which provided real-time navigation information to users through their smartphones, also identifying where other network members were at any given time. The app allowed members of the network to see all current CasiNO!Philly activities near the user's current location, as well as all other members' current locations. Warren convinced a core of the activists to start using it to coordinate their efforts, and soon nearly a third of the people who identified with the effort downloaded and used the app.

The coordinated effort worked. Philadelphia newspapers, news radio stations, and TV news stations reported on virtually every protest, which they could easily find because of the information available on Loke. Bloggers wrote about it. The TV news stations even began covering the protests live. The *Philadelphia Times* ran a series of news features examining nearby Atlantic City and its neighborhood collapse due to an increase in robberies, vandalism, and prostitution. A popular local radio talk show held several programs focusing on residents' opinions of the state's proposal. The hashtag #CasiNO!Philly trended nearly daily in the social media stats for Philadelphia.

With all of this momentum, CasiNO!Philly members took their plight to the city council where they successfully lobbied to have a referendum put on the city's mayoral election ballot. The referendum would give Philadelphia voters a say as to whether or not they wanted casinos in their districts. If passed, the referendum would also prevent slot machines and gaming parlors from being built within 1,500 feet of homes, places of worship, civic centers, public parks, playgrounds, pools, or libraries.

As the election approached, Karen Moyer's city councilman, Chad DeMario, changed his position on the issue. Initially, when the state first proposed that casinos be developed in Philadelphia, Chad supported the measure. However, after several televised protests, he changed his position and helped pass the referendum.

Not to be outmaneuvered, the casino investors' group ran a full-page advertisement in the Sunday *Philadelphia Times* right before the November election. The ad promised their organization would strive to maintain the integrity of the existing neighborhoods while elevating the city's status as a tourist destination. Election Day arrived, and after all the votes were counted, the referendum passed by a slim margin. The issue of finding the "perfect" location for Pennsylvania's casinos was tossed back to the state legislature. Pleased, Karen Moyer updated CasiNO!Philly's website to read "CasiNO!Philly Wins Media Jackpot! No Casinos Here!"

Questions for Consideration

1. Discuss the adoption of Loke using the diffusion of innovations approach. What qualities of the innovation made it likely to be adopted? How might the CasiNO!Philly members be ranked in terms of the qualities of individuals in the adoption process? How did the group reach critical mass?

2. Describe the properties of the networks and network links Karen and CasiNO!Philly evidenced.

3. Explain the differences in media richness between the CasiNO!Philly group and the casino investor group. What advice would you give to the casino investors if they want to make their message less ambiguous?

4. According to UGT, individuals make choices about how they use various media to fulfill different needs. What choices did CasiNO!Philly make? How about the casino investors' group?

5. What ethical concerns arise in this scenario? Do any of the theories offer ways in which to manage these ethical issues?

6. Do any of the theories emerge as better than the others? Why do you believe this to be the case? What situations might surface that would make a different theory or theories better at explaining the situation?

CHAPTER ELEVEN

MASS COMMUNICATION

"The past decades have witnessed thousands of empirical studies into the cognitive, emotional, attitudinal, and behavioral effects of media on children and adults" (Valkenburg & Peter, 2013, p. 221). Results suggest that exposure to TV, movies, music, and other media forms is associated with childhood obesity, sexual activity, use of tobacco products, drug and alcohol use, low academic achievement, and attention-deficit/hyperactivity disorder (St. George, 2008). Whew! With such negative consequences, why do we continue to allow the media into our lives? Perhaps it is because such a dismal view oversimplifies our complex relationship with the media. For many of us, the media provide both personal and professional opportunities for development. After all, *Sesame Street* really can teach our children, and the opportunity to surf the web can simplify our quest for information. Moreover, despite the commonly held view of negative media effects, scholarly research often conflicts with popular beliefs and even contradicts other scholars' work. Intellectual and political debate remain over *who* are most affected, *to what extent* these individuals are influenced, and *why* some people are more affected than others. In this chapter, we present four of the most influential and often controversial theories that attempt to explain and predict media use and media effects: agenda-setting theory, cultivation theory, social cognitive theory of mass media, and encoding/decoding theory. First, however, we discuss exactly what we mean by mass media.

CHARACTERISTICS OF MASS MEDIA

Mass communication and mass media are decidedly different from mediated communication and social media. Mediated communication includes all messages in which there is a device, third party, or electronic mechanism that facilitates communication between the sender and receiver. By contrast, **mass communication** "is a process

Learning Objectives

After reading this chapter, you will be able to do the following:

1. Discuss the five characteristics of mass communication/mass media

2. Describe and apply the elements of framing to current news stories

3. Explain the process of cultivation via mainstreaming, resonance, and symbolic double jeopardy

4. Relate the process of observational learning and modeling to media violence

5. Differentiate between three ways of reading messages, using preferred, negotiated, or oppositional codes

6. Compare and contrast major theoretical approaches to mass media

7. Provide systematic understanding of a professional situation by applying theories of mass communication

in which professional communicators use technology to share messages over great distances to influence large audiences" (Pearson, Nelson, Titsworth, & Harter, 2008, p. 3). Note the source could be an announcer, reporter, writer, and so on, while the technology used to mediate the mass message could include fiber optics, satellites, cable, radio waves, and printing presses to name a few. In turn, the **mass media** include organizations responsible for using technology to send mass messages to the public. Mass communication and the mass media are intertwined; without organizations and agencies to create, produce, and transmit the message content, reaching a mass audience would be difficult. If all of these distinctions seem confusing, remember this: all mass communication is mediated but not all mediated messages are mass communication.

McQuail (2010) identified five key characteristics of the mass media that have stood the test of time, despite advances in technology and the decrease in some mediums. First, and noted in Chapter 10, the mass media are able to reach an enormous amount of people instantly or almost instantly with information, entertainment, or opinions. However, while the mass communication sender can promptly reach a large audience, feedback from these receivers back to the source is typically much, much slower. For example, if you want to comment on an article written in your local print newspaper or favorite magazine, you need to write a letter or send an e-mail to the editor. The letter may or may not be read, published, or otherwise acknowledged. Likewise, if you want to complain about "lewd" content on a supposed family friendly TV show, you must write, e-mail, or attempt a phone call. Again, the show's producer may or may not receive, read, or otherwise acknowledge your message. With emerging and interactive media technologies, this slow feedback process is not always the case (think about texting your vote to *America's Got Talent* or *The Voice*). Nonetheless, the quality of feedback the audience can provide is often much less rich than in interpersonal communication.

A second characteristic offered by McQuail (2010) argues that the media continue to inspire universal fascination. Again, the popular technologies may change (from sitting around the radio listening to Abbott and Costello to watching streaming video via Netflix), but people's preoccupation with shared stories continues. Likewise, a third feature of mass media is that it can rouse, in equal measure, hope and fear in audiences. Think about the U.S. presidential election of 2016; it seems almost everyone in the United States watched endless news coverage on television, posted on Facebook, and tweeted their feelings about the candidates—some celebrated the victory of President Trump while others watched his ascendency to the presidency with despair.

The fourth property of mass media noted by McQuail (2010) concerns the relationship between the media and other sources of societal power. Unlike other types of communication noted in this book, the mass media influence and are influenced by the four sources of social power identified by Mann (2012): economic, ideological, military, and political power. Most mass media are funded by advertising. By emphasizing consumerism, either directly through advertisements or indirectly through product placement, sponsoring a national sporting event, or drawing attention to characters' dress, hairstyles, and homes, the media can encourage our shopping and spending habits. To illustrate, research indicates that the more young adults watch or read about celebrity culture and lifestyles, the more materialistic they are (Lewallen, Miller, & Behm-Morawitz, 2016).

In terms of ideological power, most Americans can agree that a key term associated with the 2016 American presidential election was "fake news." What is fascinating is what people consider to be fake news; it seems that one's political ideology influences what people view as "fake." Although predating the election, Garrett, Weeks, and Neo (2016) found that biased news site use promotes inaccurate beliefs, leading to partisan belief gaps. Put in simpler terms, the media outlet that one chooses to watch can lead to very different beliefs about the political world.

Indeed, consider the role of the media during political campaigns. According to CBS news, candidates for the presidency in 2016 spent $6.8 billion in their efforts to win the election—more than the $6 billion per year that Americans spend on cereal, the $5.4 billion they spend on pet grooming, or the $5.4 billion they spend on legal marijuana (Berr, 2016). Interestingly, this figure is down from the 2012 election, but that doesn't mean that the media played a diminished role. Trump bought fewer television ads than predicted, in part because he "benefited from huge amounts of free press" (Berr, 2016, ¶3). We may not like those negative attack ads squeezed in between our primetime TV viewing or the news (real or fake) that appears on our Facebook feeds, but clearly it is influential.

Economic power also influences and is influenced by the media. Boomgaarden, van Spanje, Vliegenthart, and De Vreese (2010) found that media coverage strongly influenced public perceptions of the national economy. Further, the lack of scrutiny with which commercial journalists reported on subprime mortgages and the housing rise and fall in the United States is believed to have influenced the public's opinions about the safety of home loans and subsequent panic when the bubble burst, contributing to the market collapse (Longobardi, 2009).

Finally, McQuail's (2010) fifth characteristic of the media is the assumption that it is a source of enormous power and influence. For instance, the media influence social reality—that which we perceive to be true. The 6 o'clock evening news provides viewers with information, but that information is edited, and other stories are omitted. The news stories presented may or may not be complete, accurate, or reliable. After the Boston Marathon bombing in 2013, the FBI criticized the Associated Press, the *Boston Globe*, the BBC, CNN, Fox News, and other news organizations for hastily and inaccurately reporting that a Saudi suspect had been apprehended well before any suspects were arrested (Williams, 2013). In a rush to be first with breaking news, imprecise, misleading, or incorrect stories can result, thereby creating unintended consequences. The alleged "Saudi suspect" turned out to be an injured witness, who due to the false reports, ended up receiving threatening e-mails, forcing him to leave his home (Chaudary, 2013). The point here isn't to demonize news organizations; rather, it is to highlight the power the media have.

The theories featured in this chapter focus on the media's power and influence—the ways and the extent to which various media influence receivers. Again, the four theories are agenda-setting theory, cultivation theory, social cognitive theory of mass communication, and encoding/decoding theory. According to these theories of mass communication influence, although mass media can't make us watch, read, or listen, when we do participate as audience members, we are transformed in some way.

AGENDA-SETTING THEORY

McCombs and Shaw (1972; McCombs, Shaw, & Weaver, 2014) were among the first communication scholars to test and support their ideas of media influence within the realm of political news. Before their study of the 1968 presidential campaign, it was widely held that the news media simply reflected the public's interests, covering issues about which audience members already knew or wanted to understand in more detail. In this way, many assumed the news media simply act as mirrors of public interest. According to this viewpoint, extensive coverage of the size of the crowds at Trump's rallies was because the American viewing public wanted to learn about it.

McCombs and Shaw (1972), however, had a hunch that something wasn't quite right with the "news media as a reflection of society" theory. Instead, they argued that public opinion is actually shaped, in part, *by* media coverage—particularly with regard to political news and campaigns. Rather than the news media simply providing a reflection of the public's interests, McCombs and Shaw posited the reverse equation—that is, the public mirrors what is presented by the news media. In other words, McCombs and Shaw conceived the news media present audiences with an **agenda** for what events the public should consider as important—this view is known as **first level (or primary) agenda setting**.

McCombs and Shaw (1972) tested this first level agenda-setting function of the news media, relying on two key assumptions. First, they argued that the news media have an agenda. That is, the news media tell audiences what "news" to consider as important. However, the media's agenda is somewhat limited. That is, the primary agenda-setting function proposes that news media provide "not *what* to think . . . but what to think *about*" (emphasis added; Cohen, 1963, p. 13).

Second, McCombs and Shaw (1972; McCombs et al., 2014) posited that people's **need for orientation** influences the extent to which the agenda-setting function shapes public thought. This need for orientation depends both on a topic's relevance as well as on a person's uncertainty about a given issue. McCombs and Shaw argued that most people need such assistance when trying to understand and evaluate the complex world of politics. Consequently, audience members who need help determining political realities come to rely on news media to point out topics of importance. For example, in 2017, the city of Philadelphia levied a beverage tax on all sweetened drinks—from juice, to sports drinks, to soda (locally known as the "soda tax")—as a means of increasing revenue to fund the city's early childhood education initiatives, public library renovations, and city park maintenance (Aubrey, 2017). As this legislation was introduced, debated, and passed, the city's residents, merchants, and beverage workers likely had a high need for orientation. How much will this tax increase my family's grocery bill? Or a college student's meal plan? How will this tax affect consumer spending, vender revenue, and manufacturing? How will profits of the tax be spent? Is such a tax even legal? Whereas, people living just outside the city limits and who don't work or regularly visit the city likely wouldn't have a need for orientation. They don't care much about the issue because it really didn't affect them.

Returning to McCombs and Shaw (1972), they drew on these assumptions and used media coverage of the 1968 presidential election as an opportunity to study agenda-setting theory. They predicted a causal relationship between the news media's coverage of the candidates (Richard Nixon and Hubert Humphrey) and subsequent voters' perceptions. In other words, McCombs and Shaw hypothesized that voter perceptions of Nixon and Humphrey and their campaign election issues would form *after* and *based on* the content of campaign coverage presented within various media outlets.

To test their prediction, McCombs and Shaw (1972) used two central criteria for measuring the media's agenda: **length** and **position** of a news story. Newsprint and broadcast news media (such as TV or radio) contain limited space or time for reporting a given story. Furthermore, on TV and radio, time is money. Similarly, for newspapers and news magazines, space is money; like TV and radio, advertisers and subscribers support the publications to the extent that not every news story can possibly be reported in any one publication.

What McCombs and Shaw (1972) found, and what other researchers have continued to support through numerous studies of the subject (see McCombs et al. 2014), is a clear link between what the news media present to audiences and what the audiences perceive of the issues reported. Although their initial study could only find a correlation, not causality (see Chapter 2 for a discussion of causation), subsequent researchers were able to support the causal relationship through experimental research studies (e.g., Iyengar, Peters, & Kinder, 1982). In other words, these researchers found that what the news media present as important is then perceived by the public as important. This causal notion of agenda setting is further developed through framing.

"Framing" the News and Second Level Agenda Setting

The news media's success in telling viewers and readers "what to think about" stems from how the media frame issues (McCombs & Shaw, 1972). Much like an art gallery director's choice of which frame to place around a given painting, the media have been shown to frame news events. Whereas the gallery director chooses a frame that highlights or deemphasizes certain features of the painting, perhaps nuances in color or angular shaping of objects, news media **gatekeepers**—the handful of news editors who set the agenda—also select, emphasize, elaborate, and even exclude news stories or parts of news stories to create a certain effect for the audience. As Griffin (2003) reported, "75% of stories that come across a news desk are never printed or broadcast" (p. 394). This is probably a good thing because it is estimated the average person can only follow three to five ongoing news stories at a time. However, when considering the large number of news stories, or parts of news stories, left on the editing room floor, it may give you pause to wonder what *has* been left out. If you are interested, Project Censored, associated with the media literacy organization Media Freedom Foundation, identifies "the News that Didn't Make the News" every year. Although it is difficult to know which stories or aspects of stories have been excluded, a savvy reader or viewer can take a critical examination of the news event presented. Table 11.1 provides an overview of **framing** through the processes of **selection**, **emphasis**, **elaboration**, and **exclusion**.

We should note that although agenda setting focuses on the gatekeeping ability of the media, other people besides journalists, editors, and broadcasters can influence the media agenda. Public relations professionals, lobbyists, advertisers, and even the president of the United States can influence what the media cover as news (Eshbaugh-Soha, 2013; Huckins, 1999; Peake, 2001). Accordingly, media professionals might, either consciously or unconsciously, frame news coverage, but it can also be deliberately manipulated by other parties.

Framing also brings us to the theory's growth by extension and addition of **second level agenda-setting**, or **attribute agenda setting** (Ghanem, 1997; McCombs & Evatt, 1995; McCombs et al., 2014). Whereas first-level agenda setting focuses on the

Table 11.1   Framing the News

Process	Example in Action
Selection: What stories are chosen?	• "Since the 2001 terrorist attacks on the United States, covering the type of violence inspired by al-Qaeda and the Islamic State (IS) has become a staple of the news media's repertoire. Collectively, this reporting increases the public's sense of vulnerability: An evil is out there, unpredictable and ferocious, sure to strike again." (Seib, 2017, ¶2)
Emphasis: What focus or tone is taken?	• "Cellphone videos of screaming victims; details of first responders' hectic efforts; "Was it terrorism?" guesswork; speculation about the perpetrator" (Seib, 2017, ¶1)
Elaboration: What details are included to round out the story?	• "Western reporting about IS-inspired terrorist attacks almost always, explicitly or implicitly, notes a connection to Islam." (Seib, 2017, ¶6) • "The news media do not cover all terrorist attacks the same way. Rather, they give drastically more coverage to attacks by Muslims, particularly foreign-born Muslims—even though those are far less common than other kinds of terrorist attacks." (Kearns, Betus, & Lemieux, 2017, ¶4)
Exclusion: What aspects of the situation are not reported?	• "The complexities of terrorism and Islam. Who are these people who murder so wantonly? Why do they do it? And, most importantly, how might such attacks be stopped?" (Seib, 2017, ¶4) • "Islam usually disappears from the news until the next tragedy, even though approximately 80 percent of Muslims live outside the Arab world in countries of rising importance such as Indonesia, Pakistan and Nigeria." (Seib, 2017, ¶8) • "Coverage should also address state-sponsored extremism, most notably Saudi Arabia's well-funded promotion of Wahabbist Muslim ideology. This fundamentalist doctrine is intrinsically separatist and lends itself to militancy. It provides a purported theological rationale for treating moderate Muslims—as well as non-Muslims—as enemies." (Seib, 2017, ¶9)

media telling audiences what to think about through length and position of a selected story, expansion of the theory led to the investigation of second-level agenda setting. Second-level agenda setting proposes that the manner in which stories are framed influences audiences' attitudes and *how* to think about the issues covered (Ghanem, 1997). That is, the manner in which a frame is prepared—how and what features of a story are selected, emphasized, elaborated, and excluded—affects public opinion about that issue. There has been extensive research on the influence of second-level agenda setting, ranging from the attitudinal effects of political advertising (Golan, Kiousis, McDaniel, 2007), to coverage and framing of the mass shooting in Aurora Colorado (Holody & Daniel, 2017), to coverage and framing of the BP oil spill (Kleinnijenhuis, Schultz, Utz, & Oegema, 2015). Emerging research on agenda setting theory is also investigating a third-level: the interplay of how social networks (horizontal media) and traditional (vertical) media interact to influence public opinion (McCombs et al., 2014).

Obviously, the news media do not affect every issue or every audience member, and those who are affected will not necessarily be affected in the same way. As McCombs and Bell (1974) argued, even with the media's ability to influence, our thoughts, opinions, and actions are not predetermined by the news media's agenda. Certain issues are more likely to influence audience thought, and certain individuals are more likely to be influenced by these issues. Aligning with McCombs and Shaw's (1972; McCombs et al., 2014) assumption of need for orientation, the media are particularly effective in creating public interest in political issues, such as stories about the candidates and their campaign strategies. Similarly, social issues such as human rights violations, chronic disease, and teen violence also seem to create a high need for orientation.

Agenda-setting theory states that gatekeepers selectively determine an agenda for what's news. By selecting, excluding, emphasizing, and elaborating certain aspects of the news, public opinions are inevitably shaped and influenced. Thus, the news media influence their audiences to think about selected issues in a certain light.

CULTIVATION THEORY

Like agenda setting, cultivation theory also emphasizes media effects. Unlike agenda-setting theory, which has been used to study the framing of news within a variety of media, the origins of cultivation theory focus almost exclusively on one medium: TV (Gerbner, 1998; Gerbner, Gross, Morgan, & Signorelli, 1980; Signorelli, Gerbner, & Morgan, 1995). Specifically, George Gerbner and colleagues have spent nearly 5 decades specifically examining the portrayal of violence on TV. These researchers argue the inescapable violent content of TV programming influences audiences' view of social reality. Specifically, cultivation theory predicts viewers who watch lots of TV will overestimate the occurrence of real-life violence, thereby perceiving the world as a "mean and scary" place. Before explaining cultivation theory's causal thesis in more detail, we explain several assumptions.

First, cultivation theory assumes TV has become central to American life and culture (Gerbner, 1998). Nearly 99% of Americans have at least one TV in their home and watch, on average, 5 hours of live TV programming each day. Couple this with the fact that 50% of people also have streaming services such as Netflix or Hulu, and the result is that people are consuming over 10 hours of media content every day (Koblin, 2016). Because of its ubiquity, Gerbner believes TV has become the principal source of stories and storytelling in the United States. Whereas neighbors and family members used to gather around the dinner table, sit on the front porch, or stand on the street corner sharing stories about what happened during the day or recounting the local gossip, individuals and families now watch endless hours of police procedurals, and watercooler gossip is centered around who got kicked off the reality show du jour. Thus, Gerbner maintains TV has usurped personal conversation, books, religion, and any other medium as the primary source for storytelling and that the stories being told are not "from anyone with anything relevant to tell. They come from a small group of distant conglomerates with something to sell" (Gerbner, 1998, p. 176).

Second, cultivation theory assumes TV influences audience perceptions of social reality, thereby shaping American culture in terms of how individuals reason and relate with others (Gerbner, 1998). In other words, through TV's selective and mass-produced depiction of current events, stories, dramas, comedies, and the like, only certain aspects of social life are presented. Gerbner does not suggest TV programming seeks to persuade audiences to think or act in a particular way; instead, he argues that the repetitive representation of commercialized social life is what audiences come to expect and believe as more or less normative.

A final assumption is that TV's effects are limited (Gerbner, 1998), meaning TV is not the only factor—or necessarily the greatest factor—that affects an individual's view of social reality. Although this statement of "limited effects" sounds like backpedaling, Gerbner et al. (1980) argued that the consistency of TV's effect is more telling than its magnitude. In other words, the effects of TV may not be huge, but they are consistently present and do make a significant difference in the way people think, feel, and interact.

Starting With Violence

Although cultivation theory is now focused on issues other than violence, Gerbner and colleagues were originally interested in the extent to which TV fostered a "mean and scary world" thanks to the frequency of violent programming. First, Gerbner and colleagues (Gerbner et al., 1980; Signorelli et al., 1995) have defined violence as the "overt expression of physical force (with or without weapon, against self or others) compelling action against one's will on pain of being hurt and/or killed or threatened to be so victimized as part of the plot" (p. 280). This definition includes cartoon violence, comedic or humorous violence, and so-called accidental violence. Notably, the definition excludes more ambiguous messages such as verbal assaults, threats, and inconsequential gestures, such as sticking out one's tongue or giving someone the finger.

Using this definition of violence, Gerbner and his associates (Gerbner et al., 1980; Signorelli et al., 1995) then created the **violence index**, an objective research instrument that uses content analysis to measure the prevalence, frequency, and role of characters involved in TV violence (for an overview, see Chapter 2). Researchers have assessed violence annually and have studied more than 50 years of TV programming. Year after year, they have repeatedly found that the prevalence, frequency, and role of TV violence during daytime (8:00 a.m. to 2:00 p.m.) and primetime programming (8:00 p.m. to 11:00 p.m.) differ little. In fact, more than half of primetime programs contain violent content, with about five violent acts per episode; children's programs are worse, averaging 20 violent acts per hour. Heroes and villains alike engage in equal amounts of violence.

Not only does research indicate TV shows are markedly violent, cultivation research also illustrates an imbalance with regard to who is victimized (Gerbner, 1998). Specifically, the victims of TV violence are disproportionately of minority backgrounds; African American, Latino, underprivileged, elderly, disabled, or female TV characters are more likely to be victims of violence than are White, middle-class male characters. Moreover, Gerbner's 30-plus years of research shows these same minority groups are vastly underrepresented during primetime. For example, Tukachinsky, Mastro, and Yarchi (2015) conducted a content analysis of the most frequently viewed television shows over a 20-year period. They concluded that there was a severe underrepresentation of Latinos, Asian Americans, and Native Americans. Moreover, media portrayals of these groups were stereotypical. In other words, a **symbolic double jeopardy** exists in which minority persons are significantly less visible on TV than in real life, and these minority TV characters are much more likely to be portrayed as victims of violence. Not surprisingly, then, minority audience members worry the most about being victimized as a result of TV viewing.

What Effects? For Whom?

The media do not affect everyone; cultivation theory predicts individuals' social attitudes change as their TV viewing increases. In other words, the more TV you watch, the more likely you are to view the world in a way consistent with TV reality. Gerbner et al. (1980) separated heavy viewers, or "television types," from light viewers. Television types average 4 or more hours of TV viewing each day, whereas light viewers report watching 2 hours of TV or less each day. As predicted, television types erroneously believed their chances of being involved with violence were 1,000 times greater than crime statistics suggest; these viewers overestimated criminal and police activity and were more likely to agree with statements such as "most people will take advantage of you if they could" (Gerbner et al., 1980). Gerbner called this phenomenon the **mean-world syndrome**, whereby heavy viewers significantly overestimate real-life danger. Figure 11.1 depicts the differences between heavy and light TV viewers. Televised reality doesn't match actual reality, and heavy viewers are partially influenced by TV reality, whereas light viewers are not. Interestingly, research indicates light viewers select certain programs to watch and then turn the TV off, whereas heavy viewers tend to graze, watching whatever shows catch their attention (Gerbner, 1998).

How Else Is Reality Distorted?

In addition to a focus on violence, more recent research using cultivation theory has focused on differing perceptions of other social issues as a consequence of

Figure 11.1 Heavy Versus Light TV Viewers' Attitudes

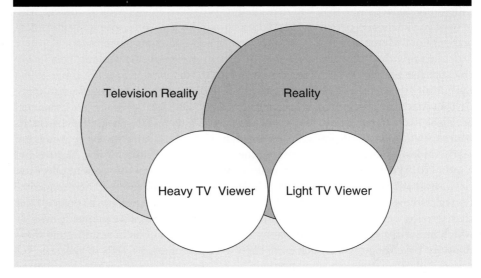

Television Reality

Reality

Heavy TV Viewer

Light TV Viewer

watching TV. For example, an increasing number of studies have focused on media images of women and how the media influence individuals' perceptions of "healthy" or normal body image. Nabi (2009) assessed the frequency of viewing physical makeover programs and found heavy viewers of such programs were more dissatisfied with their appearance and expressed greater likelihood of undergoing plastic surgery than light viewers of this type of programming. Others have looked at the relationship between media images and general beliefs about obesity and disordered eating (Gentles & Harrison, 2006; Hesse-Biber, Leavy, Quinn, & Zoino, 2006).

Moving beyond the effects of TV, still other researchers have looked successfully at other media forms for cultivation effects. To illustrate, Park (2008) found frequent exposure to print advertisements for drugs to treat depression was associated with a distorted sense of the likelihood an individual would develop clinical depression. Vergeer, Lubbers, and Scheepers (2000) found heavy newspaper viewing of ethnic crime was associated with a greater perceived threat by ethnic minorities. Still, other scholars have begun investigating whether cultivation can take place through movies, video games, and even virtual reality experiences.

How Does Cultivation Take Place and With What Effect?

Finally, cultivation theory research suggests viewers' attitudes are cultivated in two ways: mainstreaming and resonance (Gerbner, 1998). **Mainstreaming** implies viewers—heavy viewers in particular—develop a common view of social reality based on their frequent exposure to the repetitive and dominating images, stories, and messages depicted on TV. Thus, these television types are likely to perceive the world in ways that parallel TV's theatrical portrayal of life—as more corrupt, more crime ridden, more attractive, more sexualized, and so on.

Resonance is the second way cultivation is thought to occur (Gerbner, 1998). Resonance involves congruency between viewers' own violent experiences and those they see on TV. In other words, when individuals who have actually faced acts of violence in their own lives then watch violent TV programming, they are forced to replay their own life situations again and again. The TV violence reinforces, or resonates, with their personal experiences and only serves to amplify their suspicion of a mean and scary world while rejecting the vision of a life without such aggression. Similarly, if a person feels as though he or she has been victimized in other ways (being discriminated against because of sex, physical appearance, affectional preference, and so forth), viewing such actions on TV amplifies feelings that such behavior is the norm.

Cultivation theory assumes the power of TV is ubiquitous and that its primary message (violence) doesn't reflect reality in any consistent way. Moreover, TV programming negatively affects heavy viewers by creating a distorted attitude about people and the world. While the theory's main focus has emphasized TV violence, the same principles of cultivation have been extended to other domains, such as media's influence on young adults' perceptions of homosexuality (Calzo & Ward, 2009), the relationship between videogamers' acceptance of racial stereotypes (Behm-Morawitz & Ta, 2014), early adolescents' media use and attitudes about sex (Malacane & Martins, 2017), and body image ideals (Van Vonderen & Kinnally, 2012).

SOCIAL COGNITIVE THEORY OF MASS COMMUNICATION

Bandura's (1977, 1986, 1994, 2001) social cognitive theory of mass communication, originally developed as an extension of social learning theory, has been widely used to study the media's influence on behavior, particularly to understand the relationship between media use and violent behavior. In contrast to cultivation theory's prediction that heavy television viewing distorts people's attitudes and perceptions of social reality, social cognitive theory posits that the media play a significant role in influencing behavior through observational learning. We discuss several assumptions of social cognitive theory next.

First, whereas social learning theory can apply quite broadly—from learning how to break up with a romantic partner to learning how to perform CPR—Bandura's development of social cognitive theory demonstrates specific concern with mass media's influence on cultural ideology. Like Gerbner, Bandura (2001) was particularly concerned with the mass media's ubiquity and social construction of reality, arguing that "heavy exposure to [television's] symbolic world may eventually make the televised images appear to be the authentic state of human affairs" (p. 282). In other words, the mass media, and TV in particular, are tremendously influential in shaping our view of what is "normal."

A second assumption of social cognitive theory is one's ability to self-reflect (Bandura, 2001). Stated differently, humans are not only actors but also self-examiners of their behavior. This metacognitive activity can be both rightful as well as faulty. You can have accurate self-reflections about the appropriateness of your behavior at the office holiday party, just as you can have wildly distorted ones. The quality of the self-reflection depends in part on the deductive reasoning process, information used in the assessment, and one's own biases.

Beyond the cultivating power of the mass media and humans' self-reflective abilities, Bandura's (1977) most central claim is that "most human behavior is learned observationally through modeling: from observing others one forms an idea of how new behaviors are performed, and on later occasions this coded information serves as a guide for action" (p. 22). In other words, you can learn plenty about relationships, social norms, and acceptable behavior simply by taking note of what others do (and of the consequences) in particular situations. Bandura also maintained that learning through vicarious, observational **modeling** saves individuals time and embarrassment from using a behavioral trial-and-error approach; "learning would be exceedingly laborious, not to mention hazardous, if people had to rely solely on the effects of their own actions to inform them what to do" (p. 22).

This notion of learning through vicarious observation contrasts with classical learning theory. According to classical learning, humans learn primarily through the trial and error of doing, by improving on their own actions, not through observational modeling. Intuitively, however, Bandura's (1977, 1986) idea of learning through observation makes sense. For example, even if you are not a parent right now, you probably have learned quite a bit about raising children from observation—from reflecting on your own parents' child-rearing methods, as well as by watching friends, siblings, and TV parents interact with their children. Thus, social cognitive theorists believe you can learn quite a bit by watching what others do (and don't do) and by noting others' reactions to your behaviors. You can then decide which behaviors to emulate and which to overlook.

Four Processes of Observational Learning

Certainly, not every child who watches *Looney Tunes* or *SpongeBob* lashes out and hits other kids over the head, just as not every adult who watches *Big Little Lies* or *Scandal* is having an affair. Other factors come into play. Guided by four processes or "subfunctions," social cognitive theory maintains observational learning is more than monkey see, monkey do (Bandura, 2001). Rather, modeling is based on attention, retention, reproduction, and motivational processes. Figure 11.2 provides an overview.

Attention Processes. Using social cognitive theory, you can't learn much if you don't actually observe and pay attention to a particular behavior. Thus, selective attention to a given situation is critical. Bandura (1977, 2001) noted an **attention process** is determined by both the observer's characteristics and the arrangement of intended behaviors. In other words, the observer needs to be attentive, and the actions in question need to be worthy of notice. Obviously, TV stations and other mass media outlets want to make money. To do so, they need audiences. Programmers, scriptwriters, advertisers, and even actors need viewers' attention. Bright colors, rapid edits, the use of popular songs, dazzling special effects, violence, and sex are just a few of the ways the media seek to gain our attention.

Retention Processes. Learning through observational modeling is not inherently a negative process. In fact, learning by observing has many positive aspects. For example, you can learn how to cook by watching *The Chew* on ABC. Social cognitive theory posits humans can learn without actually engaging in a particular behavior if they can visually and verbally store the images to which they have attended (Bandura, 1977, 2001). In other words, the **retention process** allows you to learn from the observed behaviors.

That said, the modeling process is more complicated than simply watching and mirroring another's behavior. Instead, observational learning is a cognitive process wherein individuals observe, organize, remember, and mentally rehearse behavior (Bandura, 1977). "Observers who code modeled activities into either words, concise labels, or vivid imagery learn and retain behavior better than those who simply observe or are mentally preoccupied with other matters while watching" (p. 26).

Behavioral Reproduction Processes. It only makes sense that to engage in a modeled behavior, one must have the motor skills necessary to reproduce the activity in question. You might attend to and remember how to tie a chicken before roasting, but if you do not have the strength, coordination, or motor skills necessary, you will not be able to replicate the behavior with much success. As Bandura (1977) noted, in the **reproduction process,** individuals can typically execute a fairly accurate demonstration of a new behavior through modeling; they then refine the action through self-corrective adjustments based on feedback and focused demonstrations of behavioral segments only learned in part. Additionally, social cognitive theory maintains that "modeling is not merely a process of behavioral mimicry, as commonly misconstrued. . . . Subskills must be improvised to suit varying circumstances" (Bandura, 2001, p. 275). Think about learning how to parallel park. You might have practiced successfully in an empty parking lot, using orange cones, rather than automobiles, as markers. Now think about parallel parking between real cars in a congested downtown area during rush hour or on a decline with a crying baby in the backseat. The essential principles of parking and mechanics of the behavior are virtually the same; however, the conditions in which the behavior occurs can influence your ability to complete the task. Thus, you must assess and adjust the behavior based on the circumstance.

Motivational Processes. The last piece of observational learning related to social cognitive theory is motivation (Bandura, 1977, 2001). To go from observation to action requires the ability to replicate the behavior as well as the desire, or motivation, to use the learned action. The **motivation process** is inspired by three types of incentives: direct, vicarious, and self-produced (Bandura, 2001). **Direct motivation** is more likely when you perceive you will be rewarded as a consequence of modeling an observed behavior. If, however, you perceive you will be punished as a result, your motivation to use the behavior diminishes. **Vicarious motivation** occurs when individuals "are motivated by the successes of others who are similar to themselves" (p. 274). Conversely, people are typically deterred when they see negative consequences for their peers. Finally, with **self-produced motivation,** individuals rely on their own personal standards, engaging in observed activities they find personally worthwhile and refusing to participate in those activities of which they disapprove.

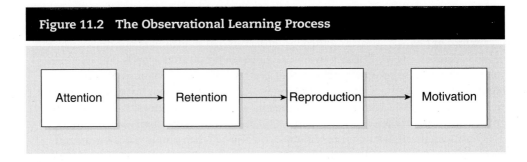

Figure 11.2 The Observational Learning Process

Attention → Retention → Reproduction → Motivation

Dual Paths of Influence

Thus far, we've focused on what Bandura (2001) terms a **direct path of influence**. That is, the media influence viewers directly, from creating attention-getting messages, to enabling behavior, to providing incentives to replicate actions so the viewer changes her or his behavior. A second route, the **socially mediated path of influence**, can also link mass media to behavior—through social networks. In the socially mediated path, "media influences are used to link participants to social networks and community settings" (p. 285). Through these social connections, individuals receive guidance, incentives, and social support, making behavioral change more likely. For example, religiously watching *Dr. Phil* may not provide enough motivation for you to change your dead-end job or stand up to an exploitative relative. However, *Dr. Phil* also has resources, newsletters, and strategies on the show's website. Here, people can connect with a community of people with similar problems, get advice from experts, and receive referrals to therapists, ultimately providing the motivation necessary to change their lives. In this case, the media's influence is facilitated by participation in a related social network.

Modeling and Media Violence

As a theoretical construct, observational learning represents an impartial process; it is not inherently negative or positive. As Bandura (1977) argued, observational learning is simply a primary means by which humans learn. When applied within the realm of mass communication, however, research shows such modeled learning can be hazardous, particularly for viewers of media violence (Bandura, 1986). Television is one mass medium in which violent action is both common and frequently rewarded. After all, Superman doesn't save Metropolis from Lex Luther by holding a sit-in.

Remember that for observational learning to occur, the first step is to gain attention. Violent content can be easily found in both entertainment programs and on TV newscasts. In both cases, Bandura (1986) argued violent acts grab viewers' attention. Aggressive behaviors such as kicking, punching, stabbing, shooting, and biting are also easy to remember and reproduce, the second and third steps in the modeling process. Finally, positive motivation is easily introduced when fictitious characters as well as real-life heroes are rewarded (or not punished) for their aggression.

According to social cognitive theory, if viewers know how to do something, they are more likely to do it, particularly when they have positive incentives, such as getting 15 minutes of fame or getting peers' attention and respect. However, the relationship between observation and motivation is a critical determinant in the modeling process. It is not simply the observation of violence that leads one to engage in violent behavior; it is the positive reward associated with aggressive action that entices one to model observed behaviors (Bandura, 1977, 1986; Bandura, Ross, & Ross, 1963; Huesmann, Moise-Titus, Podolski, & Eron, 2003). If violent behavior is denounced, viewers are less likely to copy the aggression. Note it is not enough that "bad guys" are punished on television; many of the "good guys" are rewarded for using violence to triumph over the bad guy. Indeed, as Bandura (1986) argued, "Given that aggressive life styles are portrayed as prevalent, socially acceptable, and highly functional, it is not surprising that viewing violence is conducive to aggressive conduct" (p. 292).

Social cognitive theory predicts the mass media have significant influence because humans learn observationally through a four-step process: attention, retention, motor reproduction, and motivation. For communication scholars, media producers, parents, and viewers, social cognitive theory adds a new level of complexity to TV and media. That is, if individuals are exposed to media aggression that is easily replicable and socially rewarding, viewers, particularly young audience members, are more likely to turn to such violence themselves. Much like cultivation theory, social cognitive theory has also emphasized the effects of media violence. However, recent research has applied the theory to other domains, such as the use of social media to encourage "fitspiration," a blend of fitness and thinness ideals, whereby the goal is to model, quite literally, these thin and fit values (Simpson & Mazzeo, 2017).

ENCODING/DECODING THEORY

At the same time American scholars were focusing on the extent to which the mass media affect their audience, scholars in other parts of the world were investigating the same issue but with a different focus. You may remember that in Chapter 2 we described the social scientific and humanistic approaches to understanding communication. We also mentioned a third perspective called a critical approach. Theories that take a critical perspective seek to uncover the extent to which communication processes create and reflect differences in power (Craig, 1999). The goal of such theories is to raise awareness of inequities. One critical approach that addresses media effects was created by British sociologist Stuart Hall. Most commonly called encoding/decoding theory, it is also called cultural studies, preferred reading theory, and reception theory.

Assumptions of Encoding/Decoding Theory

Four assumptions set the foundation for understanding encoding/decoding theory (Hall, 1973). First, Hall calls the focus of his work **cultural studies** rather than media studies because he believes the media are simply one mechanism for the development and dissemination of cultural ideologies. An **ideology** is a mental framework used to understand the world; it includes language, concepts, categories, and images we use to make sense out of our experiences (Hall, 1986). Typically, ideologies work at a low level of consciousness. Because we live in a particular culture, we tend not to notice cultural ideologies; it is akin to asking a fish to describe water. For fish, water just is. The same is true of ideologies; they are taken-for-granted truisms. Hall believes the media tend to produce messages that support the **dominant ideology**, meaning a view of the world that supports the status quo. For example, an essential U.S. ideology is the power of the individual. Americans believe a single person can make a difference in the world. Now consider successful U.S. novels and films such as the *Hunger Games* and *Divergent*. On the surface, both series are female empowerment action yarns. However, underneath the surface,

> [b]oth "Divergent" and "The Hunger Games" are fundamentally works of propaganda disguised as fantasy or science fiction. They're not propaganda on behalf of the left or the right, exactly, or at least not the way we generally use those words in America. They are propaganda for the ethos of individualism, the central ideology of consumer capitalism, which also undergirds both major political parties and almost all American public discourse. It's an ideology that transcends notions of left and right and permeates the entire atmosphere with the seeming naturalness of oxygen in the air. (O'Hehir, 2014, ¶2)

O'Hehir (2014, ¶5) concludes that both films are "designed to remind us how grateful we should be to live in a society where we can be 'ourselves,' where we can enjoy unspecified and entirely vague freedoms."

Hall argues mass media messages are a cultural production because they provide a means to create, challenge, reproduce, or change cultural ideologies. According to Hall (1986), the process whereby our cultural ideologies are reinforced is called **articulation**.

The second assumption of encoding/decoding theory is that the meaning of a message is not fixed or determined entirely by the sender (Hall, 1973). In the process of **encoding** or creating a message, the sender typically develops a message using the signs and symbols of a cultural ideology. However, Hall suggests the interpretation, or **decoding**, of the message is not guaranteed. Consider the 2017 Pepsi ad featuring Kendall Jenner joining a protest movement and handing a police officer a Pepsi. Many viewers believed the advertisement trivialized the Black Lives Matter movement. The ad was quickly removed, and the company posted a statement saying "Pepsi was trying to project a global message of unity, peace, and understanding. Clearly we missed the mark and apologize" (Victor, 2017, ¶2). Here is a clear case of variations in decoding.

Third, encoding/decoding theory assumes all messages are encoded using an ideology (Hall, 1973). That is, there is no such thing as "value-free" communication. Although we might not immediately perceive the meaning system embedded into a television show, song, or movie, Hall assures us that "every language—every symbol—coincides with an ideology" (Becker, 1984, p. 72). Because we are not likely to see the presence of ideologies we endorse, however, we do not often recognize the power built into the messages.

Finally, encoding/decoding theory is grounded in the belief in an active audience. Hall believes audience members can challenge the ideologies embedded in the messages they receive (Hall, 1973). Despite the level of optimism inherent in this belief, Hall does not believe recognizing and wrangling over ideology is easy. After all, it is much easier to become an unthinking recipient of media content than it is to critically confront who benefits and who loses from particular beliefs. Because he comes from a critical tradition, however, he encourages people to do so.

"Reading" a Message

In order to encourage a critical analysis of what we encounter in the media, the central idea of encoding/decoding theory is that even though the media present us with messages that support the dominant ideology, media consumers do not have to interpret the messages in this way (Hall, 1973). Hall describes three ways to interpret—or *read*—a message. To illustrate these ways of interpreting the message, consider President Donald Trump's campaign slogan, "Make America Great Again!" The slogan was first used by Ronald Reagan during his 1980 presidential campaign. Trump began to use it in November 2012, immediately after Barack Obama won re-election. At that time, he filed an application with the U.S. Patent and Trademark office for exclusive rights to the slogan for political purposes. The slogan was emblazoned on hats, on television commercials, and on his website. Keeping the slogan in mind, let's return to a consideration of the ways to interpret a message.

Encoding/decoding theory says the first way an audience can interpret a message is by engaging in a **preferred reading** (Hall, 1973). In this case, the receiver of the message uses the **dominant code** (i.e., the dominant ideology) to interpret the content of the message. That is, the receiver understands and accepts the values and beliefs embedded in the message; this type of reading is considered easy and natural. In the case of the slogan "Make America Great Again!" most U.S. citizens readily understand the sentiment. One essential aspect of American ideology is American exceptionalism, which suggests that America's history and institutions make it superior to other countries, especially to Europe (Tyrrell, 2016). The slogan clearly and explicitly links the current state of the United States to this notion of superiority, suggesting simultaneously that being "great" is the natural state of the country, but that at present, the country is not living up to its potential.

In contrast, some receivers use the **negotiated code**. When using the negotiated code, the receiver accepts the dominant ideology in general but engages in some selective interpretation in order to better fit his or her view of the world (Hall, 1973). "Essentially, the receiver only accepts the preferred meanings that he/she wants to accept, while 'misunderstanding' the meanings incompatible with his/her lifestyle" (Platt, 2004, p. 4). Individuals who read the slogan from a negotiated code might believe that America never lost its superiority; they might be part of the population that survived and even thrived during the economic downturn of 2008–2010. As such, they might buy into American exceptionalism without considering the economic hardships that others experienced. Alternatively, some might negotiate a meaning that suggests that America is great, but so too are other countries. Anyone who has eaten in Italy, wondered at the scenery of Iceland, or shopped in Tokyo can attest that there are some pretty great aspects of other places.

Finally, receivers might use the **oppositional code**, in which the receiver recognizes the ideological bias in the message (Hall, 1973). Individuals who use the oppositional code identify the preferred reading, but they deconstruct the message and reconstruct it from a different point of view. Many Americans questioned the nostalgia associated with Trump's slogan. "For Trump's base of white, working-class men without college degrees, this message resonates: This used to be a great country for them, and now they are hurting. But for most Americans, the good old days weren't actually that good, and the 'greatness' Trump talks about was delivered on the backs of large swaths of the American public. When Trump promises to 'Make America Great Again,' we should ask: Great for whom? Certainly not for women, or Americans of color, or children, or gay men, or religious minorities. In the bygone days that Trump harkens back to, it wasn't so great to be anything but a straight white Christian male." (Filipovic, 2016, ¶1–2). In this case, readers of the slogan interpret it as naïve at best and potentially harmful at worst.

Decoding Is the Central Process

Although Hall's theory is called encoding/decoding theory, the main thrust of the theory focuses on the decoding process. According to Hall, it is only when mediated messages are decoded that they have any meaning, and we can consider possible media effects (Hall, 1973). Hall argues most theories of mass communication ignore the decoding process because decoding tends to happen at a very low level of consciousness. He also points out that a full understanding of decoding is difficult because most people tend to confuse denotative and connotative meaning. **Denotative** meaning refers to a literal meaning; you might think about it as a dictionary definition. **Connotative** meaning refers to all associated meanings. As an example, think about the meaning of the word *terrorist*. As Procter (2004) points out, most people might believe they are interpreting the term in a purely objective way, but it is virtually impossible to separate the meaning of a concept from feelings about the concept, previous experiences associated with it, and value judgments about it. As such, it is the connotative meanings that make up an ideology. According to Hall, media effects are insidious, not necessarily because the media encode messages supportive of the status quo but because audience members who use the dominant code to read the messages over and over again eventually come to believe the dominant ideology is "not simply plausible and universal, but commonsense" (Procter, 2004, p. 67). To assist you with being able to read a media message from multiple points of view, select any text (e.g., a newscast, a magazine advertisement, a sitcom) and try to accomplish the tasks associated with each of the three codes in Figure 11.3.

Figure 11.3 Questions to Answer Using Each of the Codes

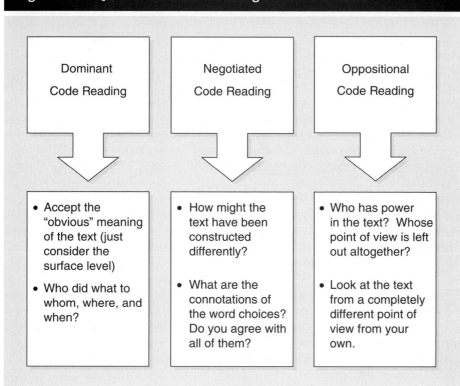

Dominant Code Reading	Negotiated Code Reading	Oppositional Code Reading
• Accept the "obvious" meaning of the text (just consider the surface level) • Who did what to whom, where, and when?	• How might the text have been constructed differently? • What are the connotations of the word choices? Do you agree with all of them?	• Who has power in the text? Whose point of view is left out altogether? • Look at the text from a completely different point of view from your own.

Oppositional Does Not Mean Against

Before concluding our section on encoding/decoding theory, it is important to be clear that the term *oppositional* does not necessarily imply someone is against dominant values or beliefs; it simply means the individual doing an oppositional reading of a message understands the dominant ideology but chooses to interpret the message differently. When messages are reinterpreted in ways not intended by the source, new ideologies are formed and can take root (Pillai, 1992). Similarly, Hall is not concerned with a personal or isolated oppositional reading; he is concerned with the use of an oppositional code among social groups, with a particular focus on minority groups, as a means for increasing power (Procter, 2004). The use of an oppositional code is likely to be viewed as deviant by those who endorse a dominant ideology, but Hall endorses as a critical approach any cultural resistance that might result in political empowerment.

SUMMARY AND RESEARCH APPLICATIONS

In this chapter, we discussed four theories of mass media—specifically, theories about how to understand the power and influence of the mass media. First, agenda-setting theory states that the news media do not tell us what to think, but they do tell us what to think about. Agenda-setting theory has been applied not only to political issues, but also to social issues. Jarlenski and Barry (2013) found that the media played an important agenda-setting role in public perceptions about the health risks of trans fat. In a different realm, Marchionni (2012) found that media coverage of human trafficking influenced public perceptions of the problem; in the United States, media coverage has focused primarily on human sex trafficking, ignoring the large number of children and adults who are forced into other labor and service positions. Accordingly, Americans are less likely to recognize the widespread problems associated with human trafficking. Our second mass media theory, the cultivation approach, suggests the social perceptions of individuals who watch large quantities of TV are skewed toward the reality presented on TV. In a study examining the relationship between TV viewing and attitudes about sexual violence toward women, researchers discovered daily television viewers were significantly more likely to accept rape myths—that is, the victim was promiscuous, she "asked for it" by wearing sexy clothing, or that women fabricate the crime after regretting their own misbehavior (Kahlor & Eastin, 2011). Heavy viewers were also more likely to believe rape accusations were false. For example, "one in four respondents indicated that 30% or more of rape accusations are false; only one in eight respondents accurately estimated the number of false accusations to be 5%" (p. 222). Just as agenda-setting theory extends beyond political news, cultivation theory extends beyond media violence. Cultivation research has found that heavy viewers have more negative attitudes about immigrants (Atwell Seate & Mastro, 2016). Likewise, heavy viewers of medical dramas underestimate the gravity of chronic illnesses such as cancer and cardiovascular disease (Chung, 2014).

Discussed third, social cognitive theory is based on learning theory, specifically the idea that when individuals are cognitively aware, motivated, and physically able, they will model their behavior after esteemed others, including people or characters shown in the media. Kapidzic and Martins (2015) found that individuals exposed to scantily clad models in magazines were more likely to select profile pictures of themselves showing their body in revealing clothing. Similarly, Martins and Wilson (2012) found girls who view social aggression on TV, such as verbally harassing or spreading gossip about a peer, are more likely to engage in these aggressive behaviors themselves. Finally, Golden and Jacoby (2017) found that girls who consumed a lot of media associated with Disney Princesses tended to engage in more stereotypical, gender-based play.

Lastly, Hall's encoding/decoding theory is also concerned with the power and influence of the media, contending the media develop, propagate, and reinforce cultural ideologies. In doing so, audience members who use the dominant code to interpret messages assume this dominant ideology is the "right" or "normal" way of viewing the world, when in fact, other interpretations exist. Perks's (2012) study of satiric and ironic comedy that implicitly pokes fun at racial differences can actually challenge the dominant ideology of racial stereotypes. She contends such critical examinations of ironic comedy can be used to promote media literacy because viewers can learn there are people who critically challenge these ideas. In a similar vein, Molina-Guzmán (2016) investigated the preferred, negotiated, and oppositional readings of the 2014–2015 media coverage of #OscarsSoWhite.

KEY TERMS

CASE STUDY 11: THE NEW (MEDIA) CULTURE WARS

Evelyn and Doug were active in their retirement. They both spent a lot of time working for their community theater group, organizing fund-raisers, building sets, and selling tickets. As full as their life was, they missed their six grand-children, who lived several states away. Their world changed when they joined Facebook; now they could see pictures of Ella's junior prom and Kyle's first efforts at t-ball. They could "like" a funny post from Andy and express sympathy when Allison came down with a stomach virus.

Although both Evelyn and Doug used the social media site, Evelyn, in particular, was a very active user. In fact, if anything, she might have been an "over liker." Whenever she saw a post

that mentioned one of her favorite merchants or products, she liked it. Whenever she saw a post from a relative or former coworker, regardless of what it was about, she liked it. And whenever she saw anything about one of her favorite plays or actors or songs, she liked that, too.

In fact, the more she "liked," the more she liked Facebook. Her news feed was filled with posts that were really interesting to her, and her social network expanded to include people she had never actually met but who shared a lot of common interests. Despite her expanding net-work, however, Evelyn remained nervous about fully using the site. She knew how to comment on posts and accept friend requests, of course,

(Continued)

but she was still nervous about using the messenger function, or how to share a story, and she had absolutely no idea how to post a photograph or video. On the few occasions she had done any of these things, she had one of her grandkids sitting next to her showing her how to do it. Despite her best efforts to pay attention, the whole thing was just too nerve wracking for her, so she just chose not to do any of those things.

One day, one of her new Facebook friends, Rose, posted a story about the proposed federal budget, which was described as eliminating all funding to the arts. Rose was horrified by this possibility, and Evelyn quickly posted a comment supporting Rose's assessment.

After that first story, it seemed like every day her friends were posting new stories about the budget cuts to the arts. Each story provided more details about the cuts, providing draconian estimates of the impact it would have on all aspects of the arts. Not only would the cuts eliminate the National Endowment for the Arts, but the cuts also affected art education at all levels. The stories suggested that even kindergartners would no longer have finger paints or paste, and that nonprofit groups associated with the arts would lose their nonprofit status.

Evelyn was outraged! What was even more shocking was that the mainstream media was not reporting on any of it. "Typical," Evelyn thought. "If it isn't sports, weather, or people killing people, why would they bother covering it?"

One day, one of her friends posted information about an online petition. To join the petition, subscribers were directed to a web link; once they clicked on the link, they were asked to provide their name, address, phone number, and e-mail address. Evelyn completed it and hit "send," grateful that she could add her voice against the senseless cuts.

Soon afterward, she noticed that her computer was not working very well. It was processing very slowly, and she was no longer able to connect to some of her favorite sites. In fact, she was having trouble connecting to Facebook!

Her world became much smaller for a time. She was stuck with her in-person friends because she could no longer follow and respond to her online friends. She was stuck reading the daily newspaper and watching the nightly news, which of course focused only on the positives of the proposed federal budget. It was 2 months before she saw Andy, her oldest grandchild. Andy started teasing her about taking a "social media break."

"Grandma, I'm kinda offended that you aren't writing 'LOL' on my very witty posts," Andy said. "What, have you moved onto Instagram or Snapchat? Or is there a new social media platform for the geriatric set?"

"I'm sure you have been as funny as usual, Andy, but I think my computer is too old. Stop smirking, I said my computer, not me! For some reason, it's running really slowly, and I can't connect to a lot of my favorite sites," Evelyn explained.

"Sounds like you have some malware, Grandma. Do you remember clicking on something right before the computer started having problems?" Evelyn thought about it. She knew that she had been actively reading stories about arts funding, but she wasn't sure what might have been a problem.

"Not really, Andy. I've been doing a lot of reading about that fool-for-a-president's budget cuts to the arts, but everything I was reading was sent to me by a friend, so I doubt that there could have been anything wrong there," Evelyn replied.

"Whoa! I thought you liked our president. What made you change your mind?" Andy asked.

"He's going to eliminate all funding to the arts! No more art classes in school! And our community theater group will lose our nonprofit status!" Evelyn fumed.

"Wait, what? Where did you hear that?"

"There are all of these news organizations that post stories on Facebook! You would think these things would be covered in the paper or on TV, but they are completely ignoring how devastating these cuts are!" she exclaimed.

"Um, Grandma, I think maybe you have been reading a lot of fake news," Andy replied. "The president couldn't cut funding for art classes in schools even if he wanted—school districts determine what gets funded and what doesn't. And I don't think he can change the tax code that easily. After I get rid of the malware, I think we need to have a little lesson in media literacy."

Questions for Consideration

1. Compare how the mainstream media framed the budget cuts with how the Facebook stories that Evelyn read framed the budget cuts. How would agenda setting explain why Evelyn was so engrossed with the Facebook stories?

2. Based on the description of Evelyn, how might her attitudes have been cultivated by the Facebook stories? Make sure to use mainstreaming and resonance in your answer.

3. Apply social cognitive theory to the case. How would it explain Evelyn's limited abilities with Facebook? How would it explain her decision to support the online petition?

4. What might be the dominant, negotiated, and oppositional code readings to the budget cuts to the arts? Which does Evelyn take, and why do you believe this to be the case?

5. What ethical issues emerge from this case? Which, if any, of the mass media theories provide insight into resolving these ethical challenges?

6. Do any of the mass media theories provide a better explanation than the others? Why do you believe this to be the case? What additional factors might have been included to make a different theory or combination of theories better at explaining the situation?

CHAPTER TWELVE

WHAT SHOULD A COMMUNICATOR DO?

In Chapter 1, we asserted that the most competent communicators understand the underlying principles of communication. We proposed that scholarly theory provides a means to obtain that understanding. We then proceeded to inundate you with 36 distinct theories, each of which introduced several new concepts, and each of which illuminated a somewhat different aspect of the communication process. Chapter 12 helps you make sense of it all. In the following pages, we identify influences and effects consistently identified in research using the theories. In the end, we genuinely believe application of the individual theories, as well as a synthesis of commonalities across the theories, can assist professionals in enhancing their communication skill.

Before drawing any conclusions, recall that competent communication means being both effective, which means achieving your goals, and appropriate, which means following social expectations for communication (Spitzberg & Cupach, 1989). Research indicates communication competence has profound effects on professional success. It is not surprising that the more communicatively competent a manager is, the more satisfied employees are with that manager (Berman & Hellweg, 1989; Steele & Plenty, 2015). More interesting is that strong relationships exist between a supervisor's communication competence and employee job satisfaction (Madlock, 2008; Mikkelson, York, & Arritola, 2015; Steele & Plenty, 2015) and organizational identification (Myers & Kassing, 1998). In fact, communication competence is a better predictor of job satisfaction than is leadership style (Madlock, 2008). As Madlock (2008) concluded, developing professionals' levels of communication competence might be the best way to increase employee satisfaction and performance while reducing absenteeism and turnover.

The theories discussed in this book provide clues about achieving communication competence in the professional setting. In this

Learning Objectives

After reading this chapter, you will be able to do the following:

1. Explain the influences and effects consistently associated with the theories studied

2. Describe commonalities across the theories studied

3. Explain how the theories studied can assist in enhancing professional communication skill

4. Articulate how understanding communication theory can aid in one's own communication competence

5. Apply individual theories to professional contexts

chapter, we highlight some conclusions we can come to about communication and the influences on communication drawn from intrapersonal/cognitive and individual/social approaches; interpersonal, intercultural, group, organizational, persuasion, and mediated communication; and mass communication theory. We encourage you to pay attention to what the theories say about being both effective and appropriate in your professional communications.

CONCLUSIONS ABOUT COMMUNICATION

As abstractions, theories don't often provide specific templates with stock phrases for those individuals seeking communication advice. They are not topographical maps that can be followed mindlessly from point A to point B. Instead, theories tend to provide general sorts of directions, relying on practitioners to fill in the details. As an analogy, think of a theory as a compass, not as a GPS. Unlike a GPS, a theory will not tell you to follow Bethlehem Pike for four lights, make a left on Dager Road at the BMW dealership, and then take the first left onto Houston Road. Rather, a theory will tell you that you should be traveling north; it is up to the driver to use his or her own creativity in figuring out the best way to go north. Nevertheless, in reviewing Chapters 3 through 11, you will note the theories seem to converge on two general decision points that commonly face communicators: whether communication should be direct or indirect (or some point in between) and whether the communication should be similar to or different from previous communication.

Direct or Indirect

The first decision point is whether communicators ought to assert directly what they are thinking or what they need. Certainly, being direct is likely to be an effective choice because there is less room for misunderstanding (e.g., going "bald on record"). The communication theories discussed in this book suggest, however, numerous influences on whether a direct strategy is also appropriate.

First, as should be clear after reading Chapter 6, different cultures hold different values about clarity and openness. This is true not only for international cultures but also for people in Generation X and those in the Millennial generation, who tend to use (and need) more direct communication (see Chapter 4). Accordingly, to maximize communication competence, you should recognize and adapt to cultural preferences for directness. Second, there are situational influences on the appropriateness of directness. Politeness theory (PT), for example, suggests those in power are more likely to be direct, and those with less power tend to use more indirect strategies. There is also a time and place for directness; expectancy violations theory (EVT) suggests context plays a role in our expectations for communication. Thus, you might expect a coworker to give a direct answer to a straightforward question during decision making (e.g., "Did the plant finish production last night?"). You might not expect a direct answer during labor negotiations (e.g., "What is the smallest increase you would accept?").

Finally, there are individual preferences for being direct. Recall our discussion of message design logics (MDLs) in Chapter 4. Individuals using an expressive MDL will value direct communication, whereas those with a conventional MDL will hold stricter expectations for being appropriate. To be a competent communicator you need to consider not only whether you think being direct might be appropriate behavior but also what the culture would expect, what the situation demands, and what your conversational partner might prefer.

Reciprocate or Compensate

The second decision point that emerges from reviewing the theories presented in this book is whether a person should communicate in a similar fashion to previous messages or whether she or he ought to behave differently. This question is at the core of numerous theories. Systems theory makes the general point that patterns of communication can be symmetrical (the same) or complementary (different). EVT projects whether a person will reciprocate or compensate based on the reward valence of the communicator and the valence of the violation. Uncertainty reduction theory (URT) predicts people are more likely to reciprocate during times of high uncertainty. And communication accommodation theory (CAT) suggests converging (behaving more like the other person) can lead to attraction, whereas diverging (behaving in a different fashion) can be a means of asserting power.

Certainly, these factors play a role in whether you choose to behave in a similar or different fashion. What if the issue isn't how you are going to act, however, but getting someone else to act in a particular manner? Beyond the specific advice offered by the theories described here, a wealth of research suggests a strong reciprocity effect (see Burgraff & Sillars, 1987; Cupach, Canary, & Spitzberg, 2009; Sillars, 1980). This means that, over time, people tend to mirror each other's behavior. Therefore, if you want someone to behave in a certain way, you should behave in the fashion you want the other person to behave. Eventually, the other person is likely to reciprocate.

CONCLUSIONS ABOUT INFLUENCES AND EFFECTS

In addition to specific questions that emerge about communication, a review of the theories presented in this book suggests many variables influence communication with numerous effects. Notably, the same variable can be both an influence and an effect. Consider your own values or beliefs. These values can influence how you choose to communicate; being a feminist, for example, might cause you to use gender-neutral language. At the same time, communication can inspire you to change your values or beliefs; someone might persuade you that using the generic *he* is exclusionary, thereby changing your beliefs about the power of language.

Throughout this book, 14 variables emerge as consistent explanations of areas that influence or are affected by the communication process. Table 12.1 provides an overview, but we briefly explain each concept and its importance, providing advice along the way.

Table 12.1 Concepts Appearing in Multiple Theories

Influence or Effect	Theories Identifying the Influence or Effect	
Cohesion, connection, and in-groups	AUM (Chap. 6) CAT (Chap. 6) Cultural dimensions (Chap. 6) Dialectics (Chap. 5) DOI (Chap. 10) Groupthink (Chap. 8)	LMX (Chap. 6) Networks (Chap. 10) OAT (Chap. 9) OIC (Chap. 9) SCT (Chap. 8) URT (Chap. 3)
Context	AST (Chap. 8) Attribution theory (Chap. 3) AUM (Chap. 6) CPM (Chap. 5)	EVT (Chap. 3) Groupthink (Chap. 8) Organizing theory (Chap. 9)
Expectations	Attribution theory (Chap. 3) Cultural dimensions (Chap. 6) EVT (Chap. 3)	SET (Chap. 5) SRT (Chap. 4) URT (Chap. 3)
Face and self versus other orientation	AUM (Chap. 6) CPM (Chap. 5) FNT (Chap. 6)	Interactional perspective (Chap. 4) PT (Chap. 5) TL (Chap. 4)
Individual qualities	AUM (Chap. 6) Attribution theory (Chap. 2) CPM (Chap. 4) DOI (Chap. 10)	EI (Chap. 4) EVT (Chap. 3) Narrative paradigm (Chap. 7)
Interest and involvement	AUM (Chap. 6) AST (Chap. 9) Cognitive dissonance (Chap. 3)	DOI (Chap. 10) ELM (Chap. 7) Social cognitive theory (Chap. 11)
Needs	AUM (Chap. 6) DOI (Chap. 10) FGDM (Chap. 8)	PT (Chap. 5) SCT (Chap. 8) UGT (Chap. 10)
Power and control	AST (Chap. 8) CAT (Chap. 6) Cultural dimensions (Chap. 6) Encoding/decoding (Chap. 11) Interactional perspective (Chap. 4)	Networks (Chap. 10) OIC (Chap. 9) PT (Chap. 5) TPB (Chap. 7)
Relationships	AST (Chap. 8) DOI (Chap. 10) EVT (Chap. 3)	Interactional perspective (Chap. 4) Networks (Chap. 10)

Influence or Effect	Theories Identifying the Influence or Effect	
Rewards	CPM (Chap. 5) EVT (Chap. 3) SET (Chap. 5)	Social cognitive theory (Chap. 11) TL (Chap. 4) URT (Chap. 3)
Rules	AST (Chap. 8) CAT (Chap. 6) CPM (Chap. 5) Dialectics (Chap. 5)	Interactional perspective (Chap. 4) MDL (Chap. 4) OIC (Chap. 9) Organizing theory (Chap. 9)
Social networks	Agenda-setting theory (Chap. 11) Dialectics (Chap. 5) DOI (Chap. 10) LMX (Chap. 6)	Networks (Chap. 10) OIC (Chap. 9) Social cognitive theory (Chap. 11)
Uncertainty and ambiguity	Agenda-setting theory (Chap. 11) AUM (Chap. 6) Cultural dimensions (Chap. 6) Dialectics (Chap. 5)	Media richness theory (Chap. 10) OAT (Chap. 9) URT (Chap. 3)
Values and beliefs	AUM (Chap. 6) Cognitive dissonance (Chap. 3) Cultivation theory (Chap. 11) Cultural dimensions (Chap. 6) DOI (Chap. 10) Encoding/decoding (Chap. 11)	Interactional perspective (Chap. 4) MDL (Chap. 4) Narrative paradigm (Chap. 7) OIC (Chap. 9) Organizational culture (Chap. 9) TL (Chap. 4) TPB (Chap. 7)

Note: AST = adaptive structuration theory; AUM = anxiety/uncertainty management theory; CAT = communication accommodation theory; CPM = communication privacy management theory; DOI = diffusion of innovations; EI = emotional intelligence; ELM = elaboration likelihood model; EVT = expectancy violations theory; FGDM = functional group decision making; FNT = face negotiation theory; LMX = leader–member exchange; MDL = message design logics; NP = narrative paradigm; OAT = organizational assimilation theory; OIC = organizational identification and control theory; PT = politeness theory; SCT = symbolic convergence theory; SET = social exchange theory; SRT = social role theory; TL = transformational leadership; TPB = theory of planned behavior; UGT = uses and gratifications theory; URT = uncertainty reduction theory.

Cohesion, Connection, and In-Groups

The degree to which individuals are connected with others is a function of the communication experienced by those individuals. For example, symbolic convergence theory (SCT) suggests particular communication practices, called fantasy chaining, create group cohesion. Organizational assimilation theory (OAT) suggests communication practices socialize employees into becoming members of an in-group. Conversely, many theories focus on the reverse process, suggesting one's connection to an in-group will influence that individual's communication. Uncertainty reduction theory (URT), for instance, suggests shared social networks decrease uncertainty, thereby decreasing uncertainty-reducing messages. Leader–member exchange (LMX) suggests one's in-group status with a manager might increase supportive communication from that manager. And anxiety/uncertainty management theory (AUM) suggests that when in-group members perceive they have power, anxiety about communicating with cultural strangers lessens.

On the other hand, AUM also predicts too much reliance on in-group membership might actually reduce one's mindfulness, such that in-group members rely on stereotypes rather than thinking critically when communicating with cultural strangers. Similarly, organizational identification and control theory (OIC) suggests cohesion can function as a means of controlling employees. Connection is achieved through communication, but once achieved it can have both positive and negative results.

The practical implication of this recognition is an appreciation for when team-building activities are appropriate and when they are not. For example, some amount of team building is often important at the initial stages of group interaction. Team building might be avoided, however, if the group is facing a high-stress decision; such efforts might only lead to groupthink. Moreover, too much cohesion might exacerbate tensions between two groups in a workplace.

Context

Several theories identified contextual influences on communication. Expectancy violations theory (EVT), for example, states that context influences your expectations for how interactions will occur. Organizing theory proposes that the central challenge facing organizations is making sense of an equivocal information environment. Groupthink talks about the role of the situational context in the likelihood of making a poor decision. The context, then, can influence not only the nature of our communication but also our expectations for and understanding of communication. Accordingly, professionals should stop and think about the context in which communication occurs because the same message might be understood very differently in another context. For example, consider how often individuals argue that media stories present them in a negative light because their quotes were taken "out of context."

Expectations

A few theories make special note of individuals' expectations, suggesting these expectations play a role in your evaluation of communication events. To illustrate, both Hofstede's theory of cultural dimensions and social role theory suggest one's biological sex is associated with expectations for appropriate behavior. Attribution theory indicates our expectations for others influence our attributions—say, for example, when a man behaves in a manner not socially prescribed (and therefore expected). Both EVT and social exchange theory (SET) suggest your expectations determine how you evaluate your interactions with others. The practical advice for the professional communicator is to challenge one's own expectations. Knowing why you have certain expectations and making sure to maintain realistic expectations can enhance perceptions of relational and interactional satisfaction. On the other hand, the professional communicator must also make sure the recipients of messages have appropriate expectations. As inoculation theory would suggest, if you want to prevent a potentially damaging counter-persuasive effort, the best thing you can do is to forewarn receivers to expect the persuasive effort.

Face and Self Versus Other Orientation

Several theories implicitly recognize the importance of sustaining individuals' desired images. Not only is protecting one's own self needs warranted, but theories such as politeness theory (PT) and face-negotiation theory (FNT) propose communicators ought to consider others' face needs in interaction. Such efforts are likely to lead to organizational success; transformational leaders, after all, are those skilled at understanding both themselves and others. Accordingly, the advice taken from these theories is to recognize others' needs to protect their image.

Individual Qualities

As indicated earlier, understanding one's self and others is important for effective communication. Several theories explicitly address how qualities of the individual might affect the communication process. For example, expectancy violations theory (EVT) suggests that communicator characteristics (age, sex, and the like) influence your expectations for communication. Attribution theory proposes that one of the ways you answer the question "why?" is by looking for stable internal dispositions of the communicator. Finally, communication privacy management theory (CPM), on the other hand, suggests that one's own individual values and beliefs will determine the privacy rules that he or she creates. The conclusion drawn here is that you cannot presume everyone will respond in the same way to the same message or situation; you need to tailor your communication to match the qualities of the interactants.

Interest and Involvement

Regarding persuasion, the elaboration likelihood model (ELM) maintains the central route is used by people who are motivated—in other words, interested and involved. Turning to mass media theories, agenda-setting theory states a person's need for orientation and the information's relevance determine whether news media set an agenda for that individual. Social cognitive theory suggests the media must gain our attention in order to influence us to model what we see. Successful communicators cannot presume interactional partners or audience members will naturally be engaged in a given topic.

Needs

One way to engage communication partners is to recognize and seek to meet their needs. Politeness theory (PT), for example, suggests everyone has positive face needs (e.g., the desire to be liked and appreciated) and negative face needs (e.g., the desire to be free from imposition). A different view of needs is proposed by uses and gratifications theory (UGT), which states people select particular media forms to meet particular needs. Symbolic convergence posits that fantasy themes and fantasy chains meet psychological needs of the group. Finally, functional group decision making argues communication in groups must meet four functions (or achieve four needs) to make effective decisions. Professional communicators, then, ought to match particular messages to the needs of those with whom they are communicating. Note that this is receiver focused; certainly meeting one's own needs is important, but competent communication also recognizes the needs of the receiver.

Power and Control

A recurring theme among the theories discussed in this book is that communication is a central means for exerting power; power influences the type of communication used. The link between communication and power can take a macroscopic (big picture) or microscopic focus (individual interactions). On a large scale, Hofstede's cultural dimensions recognize that some cultures accept large differentials in power, whereas others don't. The extent to which a culture tolerates a high power distance influences the perceived appropriateness of particular communication strategies. Also taking a macroscopic perspective, encoding/decoding theory suggests the media's use of the dominant ideology in encoding messages socializes us into adopting that ideology. A slightly different macroscopic view of communication and power is taken by organizational identification and control theory (OIC), which centers on the hidden forms of control in organizations. OIC focuses on the role of unobtrusive (shared values) and concertive control (peer pressure) in organizational life.

Other theories focus on the role of power in more microscopic settings. Both politeness theory (PT) and communication accommodation theory (CAT) suggest people are more likely to adjust their behavior if they have less power than their interactional partner. Accordingly, you will likely engage in more politeness or will converge to your partner if you perceive this person as having more power than you. Finally, the theory of planned behavior (TPB) suggests a person's perceived power over the situation determines whether he or she will be persuaded to act in a particular fashion.

At the beginning of this section, we stated that a number of the theories presented in this book suggest communication is the means by which power is exerted. By now you should recognize that *who* gets to say things, *what* is said, and *how* it is said (or what is *not* said and *why* it is not said) are important questions for uncovering how power is understood and being carried out in any interaction. Competent communicators recognize not only obvious examples of power enactment but also less obvious examples.

Relationships

Just as different contexts call for differing types of communication, diverse relationships call for varied types of communication. To illustrate, expectancy violations theory (EVT) asserts the relationship you have with interactional partners forms your expectations for how an interaction should proceed. Moreover, outside observers may be just as likely to understand a given relationship as are the relational partners; the interactional perspective suggests all communication includes a relationship level that provides clues as to the nature of the relationship between communicators. As practical advice, communication professionals should be mindful of existing relationships (whether agreeable or poor) and monitor the relationship levels of messages to gauge how an interaction is proceeding.

Rewards

One way to understand individualistic cultures using Hofstede's cultural dimensions is to recognize that members of individualistic cultures ask, "What's in it for me?" Many theories discussed in this text explicitly recognize the power of rewards in making sense of communication interactions. Uses and gratifications theory (URT), for example, says the incentive value of an interactional partner can increase your uncertainty about him or her; the more rewarding the person is, the more likely you are to seek to reduce uncertainty. Several other predictions are associated with rewards. Expectancy violations theory (EVT) suggests the reward value of the violator determines in part whether a person will reciprocate or compensate. Communication privacy management theory (CPM) posits individuals will reveal or conceal risky behavior based on the potential rewards for doing so. Social role theory (SET) predicts people seek to maximize rewards and minimize costs in relationships; thus, lack of rewards can lead to dissatisfaction or relational termination. Accordingly, people make choices based on perceived reward power; those who have reward power will be subject to more uncertainty reduction, will have others compensate for perceived negative behaviors, will be privy to more private information, will be perceived as more attractive to relational partners, and will be emulated more often.

Rules

Several of the theories discussed in this book make reference to the rules used to guide communication practices. CPM, for example, explicitly discusses the development of rules for sharing information. Message design logics (MDL) talks about varying perspectives on rules. Individuals using a conventional MDL tend to be rule governed, individuals using an expressive MDL tend to eschew politeness rules, and individuals with a rhetorical MDL learn to bend the rules to meet their own goals. Similarly, the interactional perspective suggests individuals of different generations tend to have different views of rules. Veterans, for example, tend to strictly follow rules, whereas members of Generation X tend to reject rules, and members of the Millennial generation are more likely to ignore any rule that impinges on what they want to do.

Taking a bigger perspective on rules, two theories of organizational communication focus on how contemporary organizations might rethink reliance on rules. Organizational identification and control theory (OIC) discusses how more sophisticated forms of control rely on more implicit, subtle rules than bureaucratic forms of control. Organizing theory also disdains formal rules, suggesting relying on rules rather than creative solutions might serve as the death knell of an organization.

Social Networks

Many theories focus not only on specific relationships we have with others but on the patterns of relationships in which our lives are embedded. Most obviously, the network approach focuses on how we might understand social media through an analysis of links with others. Diffusion of innovations (DOI) also focuses on social networks; this theory suggests early adopters influence others in their network to adopt new innovations. Similarly, social cognitive theory suggests the media can have an indirect path of effects on viewers through a socially mediated process, and agenda setting theory is now investigating the ways in which horizontal media via social networks influence the agenda setting function of news media.

Uncertainty and Ambiguity

The notion of uncertainty is frequently proposed as a central motivator for human communication. URT proposes that uncertainty is uncomfortable, so we use communication to reduce it. Indeed, this notion is used within a specific context in organizational assimilation theory (OAT). Agenda-setting theory says a person's need for orientation, which includes his or her uncertainty about an issue, determines the extent of the agenda-setting effect. Media richness theory suggests richer media forms are required when the message is ambiguous. On the other hand, several theories propose a more complex relationship between uncertainty and communication; dialectics argues individuals have conflicting desires for certainty and uncertainty (in the form of the predictability and novelty dialectic). Hofstede's cultural dimensions suggest cultures vary on uncertainty avoidance, with some cultures more tolerant of uncertainty than others. Nevertheless, it seems clear that uncertainty is often perceived as problematic and can drive a person to send or seek specific messages.

Values and Beliefs

Finally, a theme that emerges consistently throughout our presentation of theories is yet another cognitive variable: people's values and beliefs. Suggested earlier in this chapter, values and beliefs have a complex relationship with communication. On one hand, a person's values and beliefs lead that individual to communicate in a particular fashion. On the other hand, communication might be the means by which you reinforce, modify, or change your values and beliefs. At least 14 of the theories discussed in this book address values and beliefs. The theories range from those focusing on individualistic approaches (MDL posits that people's beliefs about communication influence how they communicate); to persuasive settings (the narrative paradigm suggests an individual's values determine in part which stories they find reasonable); to group settings (symbolic convergence states that group members construct a rhetorical vision, which is a system of values or beliefs about how the world works); to organizational settings (Schein's model of organizational culture identifies values and assumptions as abstract ways of understanding how to operate within an organization); to mass-mediated settings (cultivation theory says heavy television viewers are "mainstreamed" into believing television reality); to cultural contexts (members of different cultures hold different values and beliefs that influence how people should communicate with members of that culture). In all cases, the advice to communication professionals is to understand others' values and beliefs and to recognize the difficulty in asking people to change them.

RETURNING TO COMMUNICATION COMPETENCE

At the beginning of this chapter, we asserted that competent communication requires one to be both effective and appropriate. After reviewing the 14 common concepts we have identified, it should be clear that achieving your goals often means considering what the receiver might view as appropriate. If we were to summarize the single biggest piece of advice culled from all the theories discussed in this book, it would be that competent communicators are those who take a receiver orientation to communication; in the pursuit of their own goals they consider what others need to hear (and how they might hear it) so they might accomplish those goals.

According to Spitzberg and Cupach (1984, 1989), the development of communication competence is contingent on three elements: motivation, knowledge, and skill. *Motivation* references your reasons for doing things; knowing what you want is the foundation for being a competent communicator. That you have taken this class and have read this book provides some indication of motivation for improving your communication skill. *Knowledge* refers to knowing how to act. It is not enough to have good intentions; one must also understand *how* to be effective and appropriate in communication. We hope the theories discussed in this book have increased your knowledge in this area.

The final component of competence is skill. *Skill* is the actual behavior. Despite the best of intentions and a wealth of knowledge, we don't always behave competently. As with any skill, however, communication skill can be developed and enhanced. Skill development requires practice, adjustment after evaluation, and being open to constructive criticism. The challenge you will face as a professional communicator is to use your motivation and knowledge as a foundation for increased skill.

SUMMARY

This chapter provided a synthesis of the theories presented throughout the text. First, we identified two decision points communicators face: whether to be direct or indirect and whether to behave in a similar or different manner compared with other communicators. These decisions were framed in the balance of the effectiveness and appropriateness needed to be a competent communicator. Then we turned our attention to 14 important variables that influence the communication process: cohesion, connection, and in-groups context; expectations; face and self-versus-other orientation; individual qualities; interest and involvement; needs; power and control; relationships; rewards; rules; social networks; uncertainty and ambiguity; and values and beliefs. Specific advice for the professional communicator was interspersed throughout the discussion of these variables.

CASE STUDY 12: ARGUMENTS AT AMAZING ADVENTURES

Selena Framingham is a 24-year-old woman from the South. She was the first in her family to attend college, and she was very proud of the fact that she paid for her entire education by earning scholarships and working summers at a theme park, Amazing Adventures. The hours were long at the theme park, but she and the other workers had a good time despite the oppressively hot weather, cranky children, and obnoxious parents. Besides, she made good money, and she had graduated debt free thanks to numerous scholarships and grants.

After receiving her undergraduate degree, Selena worked full-time doing public relations for a nonprofit company. She quickly became disillusioned with the job, and after doing this work for a little over a year, she decided that neither public relations nor the nonprofit world was a good fit for her. She decided to pursue a graduate degree and was excited to be accepted into a prestigious program. However, attending graduate school full-time was even more expensive than funding her undergraduate degree. She received a grant, which paid for part of her tuition, but she found she had to work both part-time during the semester and full-time during the summer to pay for both school and her living expenses.

Selena contacted Bonnie, one of her old friends at Amazing Adventures, and asked if she might be able to get a job at a senior level for the summer. "Gee Selena, I don't think there are any management-level jobs open, and even if there were, I don't think they would be seasonal. But let me check around and see what I can do," Bonnie replied.

Bonnie had moved up the ladder at Amazing Adventures, starting with Selena at a concession stand at the age of 18 before they were both promoted to ride operators. Bonnie had stayed with the company when Selena took the public relations job, and now she worked in the accounts payable department of the business office.

The next day, Bonnie called Selena. "Hey, would you mind working in the ticket office this summer? I know it isn't management, but I can make sure your seniority is used to calculate your pay grade. Plus, the ticket booth is air-conditioned, and best of all, there's no cleaning up involved!" Selena thought it was a good option to make a decent salary for the summer and decided to go for it.

On her first day back at work, she found a lot of the original management had left, including supervisors who had been there for a long time. Fortunately, Selena was told she would be working for Sam, whom she had known as a ride operator back in the good old days in the park. Sam had always been easy going, and she figured he would be the same laid-back guy she had hung out with in the past. While at work, Selena did everything she could to be what she considered a good employee. She typically did whatever her supervisors told her to do because she respected authority. And, if she were completely honest, she knew there were bonuses at the end of the summer if a supervisor thought you had been an exemplary employee.

Selena and Sam quickly fell into a habit. Each time he walked by her ticket booth, he would give her a different task to do, which was mainly tedious busywork. One day, he commanded, "Straighten up the maps and distribute some of them to the other ticket counters." Being the good employee she was, Selena hastily agreed and did it immediately.

On another day, Sam demanded, "The glass on these booths has fingerprints all over it.

Get the glass cleaner, and clean it up." He didn't even stop to deliver his orders; he just yelled at her as he was walking by. Again, she quickly responded to his request.

This pattern continued for over a week, and Selena began to silently fume about his behavior. "Just who the heck does he think he is?" she silently contemplated. "I've known him for over 5 years, and I'm the one with a college degree and working on my master's degree. I deserve a little more respect!" she thought. But she didn't say anything; she just did what she was told to do.

During her third week on the job, she called Sam over to her booth because she needed more change. He came over to her register with the change, as requested. When he did so, he saw several promotional cards piled to the side of the register. The promotional cards were given by local companies, and they worked as discounts to the park.

Sam challenged Selena, "What are these doing here?" Selena was confused by the question. "Sometimes people want them back after they buy their tickets. I keep a few of them in a pile and throw them out later," she responded.

Sam rolled his eyes and sighed deeply. "Selena, throw these cards out so you don't get them confused with new ones." Selena was taken aback by his request. "I have never once confused an old card with a new card," she protested.

He rebutted, "Throw them out anyway."

Without thought, Selena argued, "I would have thrown them out *eventually*, and I was going to throw them out soon anyway. I just keep them because some people want them back."

Sam responded sarcastically, "You shouldn't wait until they pile up like that, and obviously you haven't given anyone back their cards because they are sitting there in a pile."

For Selena, it was the straw that broke the camel's back. She couldn't believe Sam was nit picking about something so trivial! "Don't tell me how to do my job, Sam. I know what I'm doing. I've been here longer than you," she screamed, her temper rising.

Sam looked at her, laughed, and threw the cards in the bin underneath the register. Walking away, he didn't acknowledge Selena in any way. Selena stood there and sputtered, thinking she would complain to Sam's supervisor. However, before she could do so, a human resources representative approached her and told her she was being reassigned to a concession stand.

Questions for Consideration

1. This chapter suggests two decisions each communicator should make: whether to be direct or indirect and whether to compensate or reciprocate. Discuss both Selena's and Sam's behavior in terms of these two decisions, articulating what in each case leads you to the conclusions you draw.

2. Do you believe Selena and Sam are competent communicators? Why, or why not? What could they do to improve their communication competence?

3. What ethical challenges does incompetent communication bring with it? How does greater understanding of what communication competence entails lead to more ethical interaction?

4. Discuss how each of the following influenced Selena's and Sam's behavior:

   a. cohesion/connection/in-groups
   b. expectations
   c. face
   d. power/control
   e. relationships
   f. rewards
   g. uncertainty

GLOSSARY

Accommodating: cooperating with others but demonstrating little assertiveness—typically conceding to the partner's requests.

Accommodation: adjusting one's speech and/or conversational patterns.

Accuracy: in evaluating theory, the extent to which systematic research supports the explanations provided by the theory.

Acuity: in evaluating theory, the ability of a theory to provide insight into an otherwise intricate issue.

Adoption stage: part of the innovation decision process whereby the new technology meets the user's goals and is embraced

Agency: a belief in free will.

Agenda: coverage by mass media, which provides an indication of what events the public "should" consider as important.

Agentic qualities: stereotypically male qualities, for example, being assertive, controlling, confident, ambitious, and forceful.

Aggregate: a set number of individuals—for example, the people standing at a bus stop or the people on an elevator.

Allocative resources: material forms of assistance, such as time and money.

Ambiguity: the possibility of multiple interpretations.

Analogic communication: a message that resembles what it means. Often nonverbal.

Antecedent conditions: factors associated with group decision making that might lead to groupthink.

Anticipatory socialization: the stage of organizational assimilation during which the individual gathers information about a specific vocation, position, and/or organization.

Anxiety: an emotional state of apprehension, worry, or fear of negative consequences.

Articulation: the process whereby our cultural ideologies are reinforced.

Attention process: determined by both the observer's characteristics and the arrangement of intended behaviors. In other words, the observer needs to be attentive, and the actions in question need to be worthy of notice.

Attitude: a relatively enduring predisposition to respond favorably or unfavorably toward something.

Attribute agenda setting: also known as second-level agenda setting; the manner in which stories are framed influences audiences' attitudes and how to think about the issues covered.

Attribution: the answer to the question "why did that person behave in that fashion?"

Attributional confidence: appropriately discerning and reducing uncertainty about an interactional partner's behavior.

Authoritative resources: interpersonal characteristics of group members, such as cohesion, experience, and status.

Authority: use of the perception of power or expertise to convince the audience to accept the beliefs or behaviors presented.

Autonomy–connection: the internal dialectical tension focusing on the desire to be alone versus the desire to be in a relationship.

Avoidance: refusing to enact a behavior that might be considered face threatening.

Axiom: a fundamental truth.

Bald-on-record: making no effort to be polite.

Behavioral intention: a plan to act a particular way.

Behavioral uncertainty: uncertainty as to how someone should behave in a given situation.

Behaviorism: in psychology, a narrow focus on cause and effect.

Boundaries: a metaphor for divisions between who has access to private information and who does not.

Boundary coordination: the ways collective boundaries are maintained.

Boundary linkages: alliances between owners of the information.

Boundary ownership: the rights and responsibilities borne by owners of the information.

Boundary permeability: how much information is easily passed through a privacy boundary.

Boundary turbulence: when privacy rules are unclear, making boundary coordination challenging.

Brainstorming: a specific technique used in decision making to generate potential solutions.

Bridge: a member of more than one group.

Bureaucratic control: exerting control over employees by rules and procedures.

Central route: an elaborated route for persuasion. Succeed in long-term attitude change if the audience is motivated and able to process the message.

Change: in a dialectical approach, the assumption that a steady state is impossible to achieve.

Characterological coherence: part of narrative fidelity where the credibility or believability of the story's "characters" is assessed.

Closed-ended questions: in a survey, questions that require the respondent to use selected possible responses.

Closed-mindedness: viewing the world in extremes. For example, things are viewed either as purely good or purely evil.

Cognition: the processes of reducing, elaborating, transforming, and storing stimuli.

Cognitive: in psychology, the focus on the internal processes that occur between cause and effect.

Cognitive uncertainty: uncertainty about how someone should think or feel about a given situation.

Cohesion: the connection between group members.

Collaborating: in conflict, demonstrating a high regard for self and other. Win-win.

Collectivism: a belief that the views, needs, and goals of the group are more important than any individual views,

needs, or goals. Focuses on obligation, connection, and cooperation.

Commitment: reliance on a person's dedication to a product, social cause, group affiliation, or political party to craft a persuasive effort.

Commonsense theory: theory in use. Typically created by an individual's own personal experiences or developed from helpful hints passed on from family members, friends, or colleagues.

Communal-face concern: managing in-group identity needs when challenged by an out-group.

Communal qualities: stereotypical female attributes, for example., the expression of affection and exhibiting sympathy, helpfulness, sensitivity, nurturance, and gentility.

Communibiological approach: an approach that assumes that neurobiological temperaments and traits cause variations in the communication process.

Communication: a complex process associated with sending, receiving, and interpreting messages. Scholars disagree as to the scope of the process, whether a source or receiver orientation should be taken or whether message exchange need be successful to count as communication.

Communication competence: achieving a successful balance between effectiveness and appropriateness.

Communicator reward valence: an evaluation about the person who has violated expectations; the extent to which the violator is perceived as attractive or rewarding.

Comparison level: rewards a person expects to receive in a particular relationship.

Comparison level of alternatives: the alternatives to staying in the relationship.

Compatibility: the extent to which an innovation is consistent with a potential adopter's values, lifestyle, or experience.

Compensate: making up for someone else's behavior, for example stepping backward if someone steps forward.

Competing: in conflict, a highly assertive style that lacks cooperation. Seeking a win-lose solution.

Complementary pattern: a pattern of communication in which the sender and the receiver use differing styles of communication.

Complete observer: in an ethnography, when the researcher does not interact with the members of the culture or context.

Complete participant: in an ethnography, when the researcher is fully involved in the social setting, and the participants do not know the researcher is studying them.

Complex-cyclic path: when group members cycle through the types of activities identified by functional group decision making but do so in a circular fashion.

Complexity: the level of difficulty in understanding or using the innovation.

Compromising: in conflict, moderate concern for self and others.

Concept: an agreed-upon aspect of reality.

Concertive control: when coworkers develop mechanisms to reward and control behavior that influences the team.

Confirmation stage: part of the innovation decision process whereby the user evaluates and reconsiders whether or not the technology is worth adopting.

Connotative: associated or subjective meanings of a symbol.

Consensus: the extent to which an individual believes most people would behave in a given fashion.

Consistency: the extent to which an individual believes a target other typically behaves in a particular fashion.

Consonance: when two stimuli or pieces of information are in balance or achieve congruence.

Content: information published by a medium, such as a television show, newspaper article, or video.

Content analysis: a research method that involves creating categories for communication content and counting the number of times each category appears.

Content level: the actual symbols used in a message.

Contextual criteria: situations that encourage or dissuade one from sharing private information.

Contradictions: the essential but opposing needs experienced by relational partners.

Contrast: the use of uneven points of comparison in a persuasive effort.

Controllability: the extent to which a given action is within the actor's control.

Conventional logic: the belief that communication is rule governed and that communicators should follow those rules.

Conventionality–uniqueness: an external tension that focuses the desire to behave in ways considered normative versus wanting to emphasize their relationship's distinctiveness by doing something differently.

Convergence: altering speech and behavior so it matches that of the conversational partner.

Corrective facework: messages an individual can use to restore one's own face or to help another restore face after a face-threatening act has occurred.

Correspondent inferences: judgments about an actor's intentions when a dispositional attribution is made

Costs: lost resources.

Counteractive communication: in functional group decision making, communication that returns discussion toward one of the requisite functions.

Critical mass: if a sufficient number of people adopt the innovation, additional adoption of the innovation becomes self-sustaining, assuring future growth.

Cross-cultural communication: the comparison of two or more cultural communities.

Cultural criteria: the degree to which a person's values, beliefs, and ways of communicating, influence privacy decisions.

Cultural network: informal communication processes within an organization, including stories, jokes, and gossip.

Cultural studies: the study of the role of the mass media in producing and reproducing cultural beliefs. The media are simply one mechanism for the development and dissemination of cultural ideologies.

Culture: one's identification with and acceptance into a group that shares symbols, meanings, experiences, and behavior.

Cyclic alteration (spiraling alteration): managing a dialectical tension by fulfilling one pole or need at one time and then shifting to fulfill the other pole at a later time.

Decision stage: part of the innovation decision process whereby the users weighs pros and cons of an innovation and decides whether or not to adopt it.

Decoding: the interpretation of a message.

Deductive theory: developed by starting with a theory—or hypothesis—then gathering data to support, reject, or refine the theory.

Denotative: the dictionary-type definition of a symbol.

Density: the number of interconnections among network members.

Dependent variable: the presumed effect.

Descriptive prejudice: stereotype that women have less leadership potential than men because they lack agentic qualities.

Determine minimal standards: criteria for or characteristics of an acceptable solution.

Determinism: the belief that causes and effects can be uncovered when studying human communication.

Deviance: behavior that is counter to expectations for typical behavior.

Dialectical tension: opposing forces within relationships that must be managed.

Digital communication: a message that has no direct link between the symbol and its meaning. Often verbal.

Direct motivation: when you perceive you will be rewarded as a consequence of modeling an observed behavior.

Direct path of influence: the media influences viewers directly, from creating attention-getting messages, to enabling behavior and providing incentives, to replicating actions so the viewer changes her or his behavior.

Direction: the extent to which the link is reciprocal between network members.

Discipline: a sense of responsibility to the work group that fosters particular behaviors.

Disenchantment rejection: when individuals stop using an innovation altogether.

Dispositional factors: personal features, such as one's personality, character, or biological traits.

Disruptive communication: in functional group decision making, communication not geared toward one of the requisite functions.

Dissonance: incongruence between attitudes and behavior.

Dissonance ratio: the proportion of incongruent beliefs held in relation to the number of consonant beliefs.

Distinctiveness: the extent to which an individual believes a target other has behaved in a similar fashion across different types of situations.

Divergence: differentiating from a partner by seeking to engage in speech and behavioral patterns different from that of the partner.

Dominant code: a preferred reading; interpreting a message using the dominant ideology.

Dominant ideology: a view of the world that supports the status quo.

Double bind: the dilemma women face in leadership. If they behave in a stereotypically female manner they are viewed as ineffective. If they behave in a stereotypically male manner they are viewed as inappropriate.

Double interact: an act, response, and adjustment.

Dramatizing message: a joke, pun, figure of speech, anecdote, double entendre, or metaphor, among other things, that meets emotional needs.

Duality of structure: the idea that group members' actions both create and constrain interaction.

Early adopters: opinion leaders who play a central role in the diffusion of innovations; they embrace innovations early on and have influence on other members of the social system.

Early majority: carefully deliberate whether to adopt an innovation; their decision to adopt allows the diffusion of the innovation to reach a critical mass.

Effective communication: communication that assists the communicator in achieving his or her goals.

Elaborated argument: argument designed to be processed in the central route.

Elaboration: in addenda-setting theory, the elements selected to accompany or build on a news story.

Emotional intelligence: the ability to monitor one's own and others' emotions.

Emotionally expressive: an affective response to conflict as opposed to a cognitive response.

Emphasis: the particular slant taken by a news story.

Enactment: noticing and attending to particular information in the information environment.

Encoding: the process of putting an idea into symbolic form.

Encounter: the stage of organizational assimilation during which the individual begins to learn the norms of the organization.

Equifinality: the idea that there is more than one way to achieve the same goal.

Equivocality: ambiguity of information.

Ethnography: a research method that requires the researcher to immerse himself or herself into a particular context or culture in order to understand communication rules and meanings.

Evaluate and select: in decision making, comparing each solution to the preestablished criteria to ascertain the best solution.

Exclusion: which stories are not covered or which elements of a story are not included.

Expectancy: what an individual anticipates will happen in a given situation.

Experiment: a research method that involves control and manipulation of variables. The only method that allows for a determination of cause and effect.

Expressive logic: the belief that the purpose of communication is to express one's thoughts, feelings, or beliefs.

Extension: when new concepts or ideas are added to a theory.

Exterior locus of control: the belief that an individual does not have control over his or her behaviors; for example, the belief in fate or situational influences.

External consistency: when evaluating a theory, the extent to which the theory is coherent with other widely held theories.

External dialectic: a tension between a dyad and a larger group, including social norms.

Face: desired public image.

Face-threatening act: behaving in a way that challenges another person's face needs.

Facework: specific messages that thwart or minimize face-threatening acts.

Fantasy: a creative understanding of events that fulfils a psychological or rhetorical need.

Fantasy chain: when dramatizing messages are developed further by the group, creating an extended fantasy.

Fantasy theme: a fantasy developed through group interaction that enters group consciousness.

Feminine culture: the cultural belief that norms for behavior should not be determined by biological sex.

Field experiment: an experiment that takes place in a location where people would normally engage in particular communication.

First-level agenda setting: also called primary agenda setting; news media tell audiences what "news" to consider as important.

First-order change: changing the behaviors of individuals in a system.

Focus group: a survey method that involves questioning a small group of people at the same time.

Framing: mass media's ability to highlight aspects of news stories by selecting, emphasizing, elaborating on, and even excluding news stories or parts of news stories to create a certain effect for the audience.

Frequency: how often members of a network communicate with each other.

Function: what communication does. For example, an apology serves the function of relationship repair.

Gatekeeper: a node that controls the flow of information between one part of the network and another.

Gatekeepers: in agenda-setting theory, news editors who select which stories run.

Gender: cultural expectations for men and women. Genders are masculine, feminine, androgynous, and undifferentiated.

Gender criteria: sex role norms that encourage or dissuade one from sharing private information.

Generalization: a pattern that holds true across groups, time, and place.

Good reasons: in the narrative paradigm, that which influence us to accept a narrative. Good reasons are based on an individual's culture, character, history, values, and experience.

Gratification: what an individual seeks to gain from the use of a particular media form.

Group: a system of three or more individuals focused on achieving a common purpose who influence and are influenced by each other.

Group role: a pattern of communicative behaviors performed by one individual in light of expectations held by other group members.

Groupthink: a type of decision making that leads to poor decisions.

Hedonic relevance: the degree to which an individual believes an actor's behavior directly affects him or her.

Heroes: organizational members who best represent or personify the organization's values.

High-context communication: messages that privilege relational harmony over clarity or directness.

High power distance: cultural beliefs that accept power as a scarce resource; power differences are viewed as natural and inevitable.

Homeostasis: the natural balance in a system.

Hub: highly dense networks embedded within a larger network.

Humanistic approach: the philosophical approach to that study of communication that involves pragmatism, as well as specific theoretical and methodological commitments.

Idealized influence: serving as a role model for employees.

Identification: the sense of oneness with or belongingness to an organization.

Identify alternatives: in decision making, the process of generating possible solutions.

Ideology: a mental framework used to understand the world; it includes language, concepts, categories, and images used to make sense of experiences.

Implementation stage: part of the innovation decision process whereby the adopter puts the innovation into use.

Incentive: the extent to which an individual can provide rewards or punishments.

Inclusion–seclusion: an external tension that focuses on the desire for the dyad to be alone versus spending time with others in their network.

Independent variable: the presumed cause.

Individualism: the belief that the individual is the essential unit of society. Focuses on independence, achievement, and uniqueness.

Individualization: organizational newcomers' desire to have an impact on his or her role and work environment.

Individualized consideration: considering each individual's needs and abilities while supporting development and mentoring efforts.

Inductive theory: a theory developed by gathering data first, then drawing conclusions.

Information environment: internal and external information within which an organization exists.

In-groups: social affiliations to which an individual feels he or she belongs.

Innovation: an idea, practice, or object perceived as new.

Innovators: first group of a social system to adopt an innovation; typically risk takers socially connected with other innovators.

Inoculation: a method of preventing persuasion.

Inspirational motivation: presenting employees with a clear vision and a desirable future.

Integration: managing a dialectical tension by incorporating aspects of both poles so as to create a more fulfilling experience.

Intellectual stimulation: challenging assumptions and encouraging new approaches.

Intension: a deeper or more nuanced understanding of theoretical concepts.

Intentionality: the extent to which a definition of communication focuses on source intent or receiver interpretation.

Interaction analysis/conversation analysis: a research method that focuses on the nature or structure of interaction.

Interactive strategy: a direct means by which to reduce uncertainty whereby one goes directly to the source who has the most information.

Intercultural adjustment: a cultural out-group member feels emotionally secure, socially appropriate, and communicatively competent.

Intercultural communication: interaction between members of different cultures.

Interdependence: the notion that all system members are dependent on all other system members.

Interior locus of control: the belief that an individual has control over his or her own behaviors.

Internal consistency: when evaluating a theory, the extent to which the ideas of the theory are logically built on one another.

Internal dialectic: tensions within a dyad.

Interpretation: the understanding someone derives from a message.

Interview: an oral survey method.

Irrelevance: beliefs and behaviors that have nothing to do with each other.

Isolate: a node that belongs in a network but has no links.

Knowledge stage: part of the innovation decision process whereby a potential adopter becomes aware of an innovation and its potential uses.

Laboratory experiment: an experiment that takes place in a location other than where people would normally engage in particular communication.

Laggards: laggards rarely, if ever, adopt the innovation.

Late majority: behind the early majority and somewhat resistant to adopt an innovation; skeptical of innovations and unwilling to take risks but influenced by peer pressure.

Leader–member exchange: relationships between a supervisor and employee characterized by mutual trust, social support, and liking.

Length: how long a news story is; this could be measured in minutes or seconds (broadcast TV), column length (print), or percentage of screen used (online).

Level of analysis: in-network analysis, whether the focus is on individuals in the network, particular groups of organizational members, or on connections among and between organizations.

Level of observation: the focus of a definition of communication. The level of observation might be narrow, limiting the focus of what "counts" as communication, or broad, accepting a wide range of activities as communication.

Liaison: a node with connections to two or more groups that would otherwise not be linked.

Liking: persuasive messages that stress affinity toward a person, place, or object.

Logos: the Aristotelian focus on logic as the foundation for persuasion.

Long-term orientation: a cultural approach that is associated with thrift, savings, perseverance, and the willingness to subordinate one's self to achieve a goal.

Low-context communication: a cultural approach to communication that values direct, explicit communication.

Low power distance: a cultural belief that values the minimization of power differences.

Magnitude of dissonance: degree of discomfort produced when experiencing conflicting behaviors and beliefs.

Mainstreaming: a common view of social reality based on frequent exposure to the repetitive and dominating images, stories, and messages depicted on TV.

Manipulation: in establishing causality, research participants are exposed to varying levels of the independent variable.

Masculine culture: a cultural belief that the appropriate roles for men and women are distinct.

Mass communication: a process in which professional communicators use technology to share messages over great distances to influence large audiences.

Mass media: the organizations responsible for using technology to send mass messages to the public.

Material coherence: the extent to which a narrative is consistent with other stories already accepted by the receiver.

Mean-world syndrome: heavy television viewers significantly overestimate real-life danger.

Media: complex organizations that are the source of many mass communication messages.

Media richness: the information-carrying capacity of a medium.

Mediated communication: communication in which there is something in between the sender and receiver. Most often the mediation is a technology.

Mediation: in network analysis, whether the connections between network members exist because of a common link.

Meme: ideas, behaviors, or practices that spread from one person to another in a network.

Message design logic: a belief about how communication should work.

Metamorphosis: the stage of organizational assimilation during which the individual is fully socialized into the organization.

Mindfulness: thoughtful, conscious behavior.

Minimax principle: the assumption that people want to make the most of benefits while lessening costs.

Model: either a synonym to the term *theory*, a precursor to a theory, a physical representation of a theory, or a specific—often mathematical—application of predication.

Modeling: by observing others one forms an idea of how new behaviors are performed, and on later occasions, this coded information serves as a guide for action.

Motivational criteria: individual variations that encourage or dissuade one from sharing private information.

Motivational process: to go from observation to action requires the motivation to use the learned action. Motivation is inspired by three types of incentives: direct, vicarious, and self-produced.

Multiplexity: the extent to which two network members are linked together by more than one relationship or type of communication.

Mutual-face concern: recognition of both self- and other-face needs.

Mythos: a collection of stories expressing ideas that cannot be verified or proved in any absolute way.

Narrative: the symbolic words and actions people use to assign meaning.

Narrative coherence: a narrative that appears to flow smoothly, make sense, and be believable.

Narrative fidelity: a narrative that appears truthful and congruent with our own experiences.

Narrative rationality: a logical method of reasoning by which a person can determine how believable another's narrative is.

Need for orientation: relevance of a news story, as well as uncertainty.

Negative face: a person's desire to act freely, without constraints or imposition from others.

Negative politeness: when a speaker makes an effort to recognize another person's negative face needs.

Negotiated code: when decoding a message, the receiver accepts the dominant ideology implicit in the message but engages in selective interpretation so that the message better first his or her world view.

Network mode: the channel or channels used by network members.

Node: an individual network member.

Nonaccommodation: failure to converge or diverge.

Nonrandom sample: a sampling technique in which all members of the population do not have an equal chance of being included.

Nonsummativity: the notion that the system is more than simply a sum of its parts.

Normative beliefs: perceptions about what others in your social network expect you to do.

Normative judgment: whether a definition of communication requires success or accuracy in order for an activity to be considered communication.

Objectivity: the belief that researchers should be value free when conducting research.

Observability: the extent to which an individual can view the innovation or its effects.

Off-record: subtle hints or indirect mentions of a face-threatening topic.

Open-ended questions: in a survey, questions that allow a respondent to use his or her own words to respond.

Openness–closedness: an internal tension that centers on the desire to share information versus the desire to keep some information private.

Oppositional code: in decoding a message, the individual recognizes the ideological bias in the message. Individuals who use the oppositional code identify the preferred reading but deconstruct the message and reconstruct it from a different point of view.

Organizational assimilation: the process of being socialized into an organization.

Organizational culture: the lived experience of organizational members that consists of values, beliefs, and ways of behaving and communicating.

Organizing: the process of communication that creates an organization.

Other-face concern: demonstrating an awareness of the other person's positive and negative face needs.

Outcome value: in social exchange theory, what an individual receives from the relationship (i.e., rewards minus costs).

Out-groups: social affiliations to which a person feels he or she does not belong.

Overestimation of the group: when group members have an inflated view of the group's abilities.

Participant–observer: in an ethnography, when a researcher becomes fully involved with the culture or context but admits his or her research agenda before entering the environment.

Particularism: approach of social science whereby narrowly defined areas are incrementally studied with the belief that the whole picture will be uncovered eventually.

Passive-aggressive: surreptitious attempts to make a partner feel guilty. Passive aggression is more active than avoiding the situation altogether but less active than openly addressing the conflict.

Pathos: Aristotelian focus on emotion as a means of persuasion.

Perceived behavioral control: an inability to behave consistently with one's attitudes. Two components: self-efficacy and controllability.

Peripheral route: a route for processing persuasive messages when motivation or ability is missing. Results in short-term persuasion at best.

Personalism: the belief that an actor specifically and intentionally behaves in ways that are hurtful or helpful.

Persuasion: human communication designed to influence others by modifying their beliefs, values, or attitudes.

Persuasion stage: part of the innovation decision process whereby a potential adopter goes beyond awareness of an innovation and actively seeks information about it.

Population: everyone or everything that demonstrates a particular characteristic.

Position: the location of a news story; this could be the order it appears (broadcast news), which page or section of a newspaper, or how far "down" on a digital screen.

Positive face: a person's need to be liked, appreciated, and admired.

Positive politeness: emphasizing the receiver's need to be liked or appreciated.

Postdecision theory: focuses on how people make sense of their decisions after they have made them.

Power: the ability to influence others through rewards or punishments. Influences politeness.

Practicality: when evaluating a theory, the extent to which the theory can be used to solve real-world problems.

Pragmatism: the belief that scholars should focus on the communicative choices people make.

Praxis: the assumption that the development of a relationship is neither linear (always moving forward) nor repetitive (cycling through the same things again and again).

Predictability–novelty: an internal tension that centers on the desire to have new experiences versus the desire to manage uncertainty.

Preferred reading: decoding a message using the dominant ideology.

Prescriptive prejudice: actual evaluations of women as less effective than men.

Pressure toward uniformity: Pressure placed on group members by other group members to reach a unanimous agreement.

Prestige: the social distance between communicators. Influences politeness.

Preventive facework: strategies used to help ourselves or others avoid or mitigate face-threatening acts.

Primary research: research reported by the person who conducted it.

Privacy rules: conventions that govern decisions about sharing private information.

Private information: information that is inaccessible to others.

Problem analysis: a realistic examination of the nature, extent, and likely causes of a problem.

Production: in adaptive structuration theory, the idea that the choices group members make create a structure.

Promotive communication: in functional group decision making, communication geared toward one of the requisite functions.

Public–private: a tension between revealing and concealing private information.

Punctuation: the desire to understand the beginnings and endings and causes and effects of communication.

Qualitative: an approach to analyzing data that focuses on rich descriptions of what has been observed, interpreted, or critiqued.

Quantitative: an approach to analyzing data that focuses on numbers or statistics.

Questionnaire: a written survey method.

Random sample: technique in which all members of the population have an equal chance of being in the sample.

Rate of adoption: the relative speed with which an individual (or group or organization) adopts an innovation.

Rationalize: the ability to justify dissonance.

Receiver orientation: the position in the intentionality debate proposing that anything a receiver considers a message should be considered communication.

Reciprocal interdependence: if an innovator or early adopter has the technology, they need others to adopt the technology in order to receive the maximum benefits, for example, social media.

Reciprocate: engaging in the same behavior as someone else.

Reciprocity: influence of efforts that emphasize a give-and-take relationship.

Refutational preemption: a counterpersuasive effort that involves raising specific challenges and then contesting them.

Reinvention: when adopters change the use for, or "repurpose," an innovation

Relationship level: indicators in a message that suggest how to interpret the message and the nature of the relationship between the communicators.

Relative advantage: an innovation has to be better at achieving the goals for performance than other competing technologies in order to be adopted.

Replacement discontinuance: when individuals reject an innovation after trying it, returning to a different version of the innovation.

Reproduction: in adaptive structuration theory, the idea that the structures group members create constrain future actions, thus being reinforced.

Reproduction process: individuals' demonstration of a new behavior through modeling; beyond simply mimicry, individuals refine the action through self-corrective adjustments based on feedback and focused demonstrations of behavioral segments that have only been learned in part.

Resonance: congruency between viewers' own violent experiences and that which they see on TV.

Retention: The third step in socio-cultural evolution. In this stage, the organization stores what was done and how it was done, either formally or informally, so that members can refer to it again.

Retention process: visually and verbally storing mediated images.

Revelation–concealment: an external tension between keeping some information private within the dyad versus sharing information with the larger network.

Rewards: preferred resources (e.g., time, money, love).

Rhetorical criticism: a research method that involves describing, interpreting, and analyzing texts.

Rhetorical logic: the belief that communication is a cooperative game in which participants pursue multiple goals.

Rhetorical vision: a unified way of viewing the world.

Risk: the extent to which engaging in a face-threatening act will cause harm to another's face needs.

Risk–benefit criteria: an assessment of the rewards and costs for disclosing private information.

Rites and rituals: public performances that demonstrate organizational values.

Rules: how something should be done.

Sampling: studying only a small group of people or objects and assuming the results hold true of the entire population.

Scarcity: a peripheral persuasive message that preys on people's worry of missing out on something.

Schemata: cognitive structures for organizing new information.

Scholarly theory: one that has undergone systematic research.

Secondary research: research reported by someone other than the person who conducted it.

Second-level agenda setting: also known as attribute agenda setting; the manner in which stories are framed influences audiences' attitudes and how to think about the issues covered.

Second-order change: resolving underlying differences in perspective, most often through the process of reframing.

Segmentation: managing dialectical tensions by compartmentalizing the relationship such that certain issues coincide with one pole or need and other issues are appropriate for the opposite pole.

Selection: in the dialectical perspective, managing dialectical tensions by favoring one pole or need at the expense of the other. In organizing theory, an organization's decision to rely on either a rule or a double interact. In agenda-setting theory, news stories chosen to be printed or aired.

Selective attention: focusing solely on information that reaffirms beliefs.

Selective exposure: actively avoiding information inconsistent with previously established beliefs or behaviors.

Selective interpretation: deciphering ambiguous information so it is perceived to be consistent with established beliefs.

Selective retention: dismissing or forgetting information that creates dissonance.

Self-efficacy: an individual's belief that she or he can perform a behavior.

Self-face concern: being aware of one's own positive and negative face needs.

Self-produced motivation: when individuals rely on their own personal standards, engaging in observed activities they find personally worthwhile and refusing to participate in those activities of which they disapprove.

Semantic network: a particular focus on the content of the communications in a network analysis.

Sex: the biological differentiation between males and females.

Short-term orientation: a cultural belief in immediate gratification.

Simple control: exerting direct authority through commands.

Situational characteristics: problems with the experiences of a group that might lead to groupthink.

Situational factors: external causes for behavior that are relatively uncontrollable and determined by the environment or situation.

Social desirability: consistent with social conventions.

Social proof: persuasive messages that focus on peer pressure.

Social scientific approach: the philosophical approach to that study of communication that involves determinism, as well as specific theoretical and methodological commitments.

Socialization: the process by which an organizational newcomer internalizes the values and behaviors in order to fulfill organizational expectations.

Socially mediated path of influence: media influences used to link participants to social networks and community settings. Through these social connections, individuals receive guidance, incentives, and social support, making behavioral change more likely.

Sociocultural evolution: the process of organizational information processing. Organizations that do not go through this process will cease to exist.

Socioemotional communication: communication focused on developing, maintaining, and repairing relationships between group members.

Solution-orientation path: group members make little or no effort to investigate the problem. Rather, group members assume they understand the problem and immediately seek a solution that will satisfy group members.

Source orientation: the position in the intentionality debate proposing the only messages that should be considered communication are those a source intends to send.

Stability: the existence of a network link over time.

Standpoint: a position from which an individual views and understands the world.

Star: a node that is highly central to the network.

Stranger: out-group member.

Strength: the frequency, intimacy, or intensity of a network connection.

Structural coherence: the degree to which a narrative has a logical structure and flow.

Structural flaws: problems with the composition of a group that include homogeneity, biased leadership, and lack of decision-making norms.

Structure: patterns of relationships or interaction.

Subjectivity: the belief that meaning is unique to each person.

Succinctness: when evaluating theory, the extent to which a theory's explanation or description is sufficiently concise.

Supervisory exchange: interaction between a supervisor and subordinate defined entirely by the roles they perform and the contractual obligations provided by the organization.

Survey research: a method for studying communication that centers on how people think, feel, or intend to behave. Specific types of survey research include interviews, focus groups, and questionnaires.

Symbolic convergence: the transformation of a collection of individuals to an identifiable group with a group consciousness.

Symbolic double jeopardy: minority persons are significantly less visible on TV than in real life, and these minority TV characters are much more likely to be portrayed as victims of violence.

Symmetrical pattern: a pattern of communication in which the sender and receiver use similar styles of communication.

Symmetry: whether two people connected in a network share the same type of relationship with each other.

Synergy: the ability to achieve more through group effort than individual effort.

System: a group of people who interrelate to form a whole.

Task communication: communication focused on achieving an instrumental goal.

Team: an ongoing, coordinated group of people working together.

Technological control: exerting control over employees through the use of technology to manage what can and can't be done in the workplace.

Text/data mining: a research method that uses advanced data analysis techniques to uncover patterns in large amounts of information.

Textual analysis: a research method that studies the characteristics or patterns of a written or recorded message.

Theory: any systematic summary about the nature of the communication process.

Third-party help: asking a person outside of the relationship to help manage the conflict.

Threat: a forewarning of a potential persuasive attack on beliefs, making sure the target of the persuasive effort is aware of his or her susceptibility to the attack.

Totality: interdependence between relationship partners.

Transactional leadership: a style that seeks to achieve solid, consistent performance from subordinates through a process of bilateral exchange.

Transformational leadership: a style that seeks to inspire exceptional performance by using subordinates' ideas and actions as a catalyst for transformation.

Trialability: the extent to which potential adopters can "try" an innovation before making the decision to adopt it.

Uncertainty: the inability to explain or predict one's own or others' behavior.

Uncertainty avoidance: cultural preferences for the extent to which ambiguity is tolerated.

Unitary path: when a group uses the same process to generate solutions, regardless of the type of problem they are seeking to solve.

Unobtrusive control: exerting authority over employees by identification with an organizational mission.

Values: core beliefs.

Variable: any concept that has two or more values.

Vicarious motivation: when individuals are motivated by the successes of others similar to themselves.

Violation valence: the positive or negative evaluation of an expectation.

Violence index: an objective research instrument that uses content analysis to measure the prevalence, frequency, and role of characters involved in TV violence.

Vocational anticipatory socialization: the stage of organizational assimilation during which an individual learns what it means to work.

Working theory: generalizations made in particular professions about the best techniques for doing something.

REFERENCES

Adler, N. J. (1997). *International dimensions of organizational behavior* (3rd ed). Cincinnati, OH: South-Western College.

Ajzen, I. (1988). *Attitudes, personality, and behavior.* Chicago, IL: Dorsey Press.

Ajzen, I. (1991). The theory of planned behavior. *Organizational Behavior and Human Decision Processes, 50,* 179–211.

Alsop, R. (2008). *The trophy kids grow up: How the millennial generation is shaking up the workplace.* San Francisco, CA: Jossey-Bass.

American Academy of Pediatrics. (2017). *Media and children communication toolkit.* Retrieved from https://www.aap.org/en-us/advocacy-and-policy/aap-health-initiatives/pages/media-and-children.aspx

An, C., & Pfau, M. (2004). The efficacy of inoculation in televised political debates. *Journal of Communication, 54,* 421–436.

Andersen, J., Nussbaum, J., Pecchioni, L., & Grant, J. A. (1999). Interactional skills in instructional settings. In A. L. Vangelisti, J. A. Daly, & G. W. Friedrich (Eds.), *Teaching communication* (2nd ed., pp. 359–374). Mahwah, NJ: LEA.

Anderson, K. (1998, February). Pop-psychology as science and infomerical as journalism: ABC News sponsors John Gray's interplanetary sexism. *Sojourner: The Women's Forum, 23,* 1–2, 14–15, 44.

Ansari, A. (2015). *Modern romance.* New York, NY: Penguin Press.

Ashby, W. R. (1962). Principles of the self-organizing system. In H. von Foerster & G. Zopf (Eds.), *Principles of self-organization* (pp. 255–278). New York, NY: Pergamon.

Atwell Seate, A., & Mastro, D. (2016). Media's influence on immigration attitudes: An intergroup threat theory approach. *Communication Monographs, 83(2),* 194-213. doi:10.1080/03637751.2015.1068433

Aubrey, A. (2017, April 5). Judge takes up big soda's suit to abolish Philadelphia's soda tax. NPR. Retrieved from http://www.npr.org/sections/thesalt/2017/04/05/522626223/judges-take-up-big-sodas-suit-to-abolish-philadelphias-sugar-tax

Avery, E., Lariscy, R., & Sweetser, K. D. (2010). Social media and shared—or divergent—uses? A coorientation analysis of public relations practitioners and journalists. *International Journal of Strategic Communication, 4,* 189–205.

Axley, S. R. (1984). Managerial and organizational communication in terms of the conduit metaphor. *Academy of Management Review, 9,* 428–437.

Aylor, B., & Dainton, M. (2001). Antecedents in romantic jealousy experience, expression, and goals. *Western Journal of Communication, 64,* 370–391.

Aylor, B., & Dainton, M. (2004). Biological sex and psychological gender as predictors of routine and strategic relational maintenance. *Sex Roles, 50,* 689–697.

Bales, R. F. (1970). *Personality and interpersonal behavior.* New York, NY: Holt, Rinehart & Winston.

Banas, J. A., & Miller, G. (2013). Inducing resistance to conspiracy theory propaganda: Testing inoculation and metainoculation strategies. *Human Communication Research, 39(2),* 184–207. doi:10.1111/hcre.12000

Banas, J., & Rains, S. (2008, November). *Testing inoculation theory: A meta-analysis.* Paper presented at the annual meeting of the NCA 94th Annual Convention, San Diego, CA. Retrieved from http://www.allacademic.com/meta/p261402_index.html

Bandura, A. (1977). *Social learning theory.* Upper Saddle River, NJ: Prentice Hall.

Bandura, A. (1986). *Social foundations of thought and action: A social cognitive theory.* Englewood Cliffs, NJ: Prentice Hall.

Bandura, A. (1994). Social cognitive theory of mass communication. In J. Bryant & D. Zillmann (Eds.), *Media effects: Advances in theory and research* (pp. 61–90). Hillsdale, NJ: Lawrence Erlbaum.

Bandura, A. (2001). Social cognitive theory of mass communication. *Media Psychology, 3(3)*, 265–299. doi:10.1207/S1532785XMEP0303_03

Bandura, A., Ross, D., & Ross, S. (1963). Imitations of aggressive film-mediated models. *Journal of Abnormal Psychology, 66*, 3–11.

Barge, J. K. (1994). *Leadership*. New York, NY: St. Martin's Press.

Barker, J. R. (1999). *The discipline of teamwork: Participation and concertive control.* Thousand Oaks, CA: Sage.

Barker, R. T., Rimler, G., Moreno, E., & Kaplan, T. E. (2004). Family business narrative perceptions: Values, succession, and commitment. *Journal of Technical Writing and Communication, 34*(4), 291–320.

Barker, R., & Gower, K. (2010). Strategic application of storytelling in organizations: Toward effective communication in a diverse world. *Journal of Business Communication, 47*(3), 295–312. doi:10.1177/0021943610369782

Barnett, E. (2011, November 22). Facebook cuts six degrees of separation to four. *Telegraph*. Retrieved from http://www.telegraph.co.uk/technology/facebook/8906693/Facebook-cuts-six-degrees-of-separation-to-four.html

Bar-On, R. (2006). The Bar-On model of emotional-social intelligence (ESI). *Psicothema, 18*(Suppl), 13–25.

Barrett, A. K., & Stephens, K. K. (2017). The pivotal role of change appropriation in the implementation of health care technology. Management Communication Quarterly, 31, 163-193. doi:10.1177/0893318916682872

Bass, B. M. (1985). *Leadership and performance beyond expectations.* New York, NY: Free Press.

Bass, B. M. (1997). Does the transactional–transformational leadership paradigm transcend organizational and national boundaries? *American Psychologist, 52*, 130–139.

Bass, B. M. (1998). *Transformational leadership: Industrial, military, and educational impact.* Mahwah, NJ: Erlbaum.

Baumgartner, R. J. (2009). Organizational culture and leadership: Preconditions for the development of a sustainable corporation. *Sustainable Development, 17*, 102–113.

Baxter, L. A. (1988). A dialectical perspective on communication strategies in relationship development. In S. Duck (Ed.), *Handbook of personal relationships: Theory, research, and interventions* (pp. 257–273). Chichester, UK: Wiley.

Baxter, L. A., & Montgomery, B. M. (1996). *Relating: Dialogues and dialectics.* New York, NY: Guilford Press.

Beaton. (January 6, 2017). Top employers say millennials need these four skills in 2017. *Forbes Online*. Retrieved from https://www.forbes.com/sites/carolinebeaton/2017/01/06/top-employers-say-millennials-need-these-4-skills-in-2017/#66eae9167fe4

Beatty, M. J., & McCroskey, J. C. (2001). *The biology of communication: A communibiological perspective.* Creskill, NJ: Hampton Press.

Becker, E. F. (2012, August 6). Tip sheet: Three tips to fix cross-cultural miscommunications. *PR News* [online]. Retrieved from http://www.prnewsonline.com/tip-sheet-three-tips-to-fix-cross-cultural-miscommunications/

Becker, S. L. (1984). Marxist approaches to media studies: The British experience. *Critical Studies in Mass Communication, 1*(1), 66–80.

Behm-Morawitz, E., & Ta, D. (2014). Cultivating virtual stereotypes? The impact of video game play on racial/ethnic stereotypes. *Howard Journal of Communications, 25*, 1–15. doi:10.1080/10646175.2013.835600

Belluz, J. (June 8, 2017). The U.S. had no soda taxes in 2013. Now nearly 9 million Americans live with them. Vox. Retrieved from https://www.vox.com/science-and-health/2017/6/6/15745908/soda-tax-seattle-philadelphia-sugar-drinks

Berger, C. R. (1979). Beyond initial interaction: Uncertainty, understanding, and the development of interpersonal relationships. In H. Giles & R. St. Clair (Eds.), *Language and social psychology* (pp. 122–144). Oxford, UK: Basil Blackwell.

Berger, C. R. (1995). Inscrutable goals, uncertain plans, and the production of communicative action. In C. R. Berger & M. Burgoon (Eds.), *Communication and social processes* (pp. 1–28). East Lansing: Michigan State University Press.

Berger, C. R. (1997). *Planning strategic interaction: Attaining goals through communicative action.* Mahwah, NJ: Erlbaum.

Berger, C. R., & Bradac, J. J. (1982). *Language and social knowledge: Uncertainty in interpersonal relations.* London, UK: Arnold.

Berger, C. R., & Calabrese, R. J. (1975). Some explorations in initial interaction and beyond: Toward a developmental theory of interpersonal communication. *Human Communication Research, 1*, 99–112.

Berman, S. J., & Hellweg, S. A. (1989). Perceived supervisor communication competence and supervisor satisfaction as a function of quality circle participation. *Journal of Business Communication, 26*, 103–122.

Berr, J. (November 8, 2016). Election 2016's price tag: $6.8 billion. CBS Moneywatch, Retrieved from http://www.cbsnews.com/news/election-2016s-price-tag-6-8-billion

Blossom, J. (2009). *Content nation: Surviving and thriving as social media changes our work, our lives, and our future.* Indianapolis, IN: Wiley.

Bonito, J. A., & Wolski, S. L. (2002). The adaptation of complaints to participation frameworks. *Communication Studies, 53*, 252–268.

Boomgaarden, H., van Spanje, J., Vliegenthart, R., & De Vreese, C. (June, 2010). *Covering the crisis: Economic news and economic expectations.* Paper presented at the annual conference of the International Communication Association, Singapore.

Bormann, E. G. (1982). The symbolic convergence theory of communication: Applications and implications for teachers and consultants. *Journal of Applied Communication Research, 10*, 50–61.

Bormann, E. G. (1996). Symbolic convergence theory and communication in group decision making. In R. Y. Hirokawa & M. S. Poole (Eds.), *Communication and group decision making* (2nd ed., pp. 81–113). Thousand Oaks, CA: Sage.

Bormann, E. G., Cragan, J. E., & Shields, D. C. (1994). In defense of symbolic convergence theory: A look at the theory and its criticisms after two decades. *Communication Theory, 4*, 259–294.

Brands, R. (2015, July 15). 'Think manager, think man' stops us seeing woman as leaders. The *Guardian (U.S. Edition)*. Retrieved from https://www.theguardian.com/women-in-leadership/2015/jul/15/think-manager-think-man-women-leaders-biase-workplace

Brown, A., & Patton, E. (2017, April 3). The narrowing, but persistent, gender gap in pay. Pew Research Center. Retrieved from http://www.pewresearch.org/fact-tank/2017/04/03/gender-pay-gap-facts

Brown, P., & Levinson, S. (1978). Universals in language usage: Politeness phenomenon. In E. Goody (Ed.), *Questions and politeness* (pp. 56–89). Cambridge, UK: Cambridge University Press.

Brown, P., & Levinson, S. (1987). *Politeness: Some universals in language use.* Cambridge, UK: Cambridge University Press.

Bruni, F. (2012, December 8). Bin Laden, torture, and Hollywood. *New York Times.* Retrieved June 19, 2013, from http://www.nytimes.com/2012/12/09/opinion/sunday/bruni-binladen-torture-and-hollywood.html?pagewanted=all&_r=0

Bryant, S. E. (2003). The role of transformational and transactional leadership in creating, sharing and exploiting organizational knowledge. *Journal of Leadership and Organizational Studies, 9*, 32–43.

Burgoon, J. K. (1978). A communication model of personal space violations: Explication and an initial test. *Human Communication Research, 4*, 129–142.

Burgoon, J. K. (1994). Nonverbal signals. In M. L. Knapp & G. R. Miller (Eds.), *Handbook of interpersonal communication* (pp. 229–285). Thousand Oaks, CA: Sage.

Burgoon, M., Pfau, M., & Birk, T. S. (1995). An inoculation theory explanation for the effects of corporate issue/advocacy advertising campaigns. *Communication Research, 22*, 485–505.

Burgraff, C. S., & Sillars, A. L. (1987). A critical examination of sex differences in marriage. *Communication Monographs, 54*, 276–294.

Burns, M. E. (2015). Recruiting prospective students with stories: How personal stories influence the process of choosing a university. *Communication Quarterly, 63(1)*, 99–118. doi:10.1080/01463373.2014.965838

Busch, P., Venkitachalam, K., & Richards, D. (2008). Generational differences in soft knowledge situations: Status, need for recognition, workplace commitment and idealism. *Knowledge & Process Management, 15(1)*, 45–58.

Calhoun, L. (2008). *One cannot not communicate (unless you are the US and Iran): An interactionist perspective on the foreign policy dilemmas between the US and Iran.* Paper presented at the meeting of the National Communication Association, San Diego, CA.

Calzo, J. P., & Ward, L. M. (2009). Media exposure and viewers' attitudes toward homosexuality: Evidence for mainstreaming or resonance? *Journal of Broadcasting & Electronic Media, 53,* 280–299. doi:10.1080/08838150902908049

Canary, D. J., & Hause, K. S. (1993). Is there any reason to research sex differences in communication? *Communication Quarterly, 41,* 129–144.

Canary, D. J., & Zelley, E. D. (2000). Current research programs on relational maintenance behaviors. In M. E. Roloff (Ed.), *Communication Yearbook 23,* (pp. 305–339). Thousand Oaks, CA: Sage.

Canary, D. J., Cody, M. J., & Manusov, V. L. (2008). *Interpersonal communication: A goals-based approach* (4th ed.). Boston, MA: Bedford/St. Martin's.

Canary, D. J., Emmers-Sommer, T. M., & Faulkner, S. (1997). *Sex and gender differences in personal relationships.* New York, NY: Guilford Press.

Caruso, D. R., Mayer, J. D., & Salovey, P. (2002). Relation of an ability measure of emotional intelligence to personality. *Journal of Personality Assessment, 79*(2), 306–320. doi:10.1207/S15327752JPA 7902_12

Catano, V. M., & Morrow Hines, H. (2016). The influence of corporate social responsibility, psychologically healthy workplaces, and individual values in attracting Millennial job applicants. *Canadian Journal of Behavioural Science / Revue Canadienne des Sciences du Comportement, 48,* 142–154. doi:10.1037/cbs0000036

Cavallaro, F., Seilhamer, M. F., Chee, Y. F., & Ng, B. C. (2016). Overaccommodation in a Singapore eldercare facility. *Journal of Multilingual & Multicultural Development, 37,* 817-831. doi:10.1080/01434632.2016.1142553

Chaudary, A. (2013, May 21). Boston Marathon Saudi "suspect" speaks out. *The Islamic Monthly* [online]. Retrieved from http://www.theislamicmonthly.com/exclusive-interview-with-the-saudi-man-from-boston

Chefneux, G. (2015). Humour at work. *Language & Dialogue, 5*(3), 381–407. doi:10.1075/ld.5.3.02che

Chen, B. X. (2013, February 10). Samsung emerges as potent rival to Apple's cool. *New York Times.* Retrieved from http://www.nytimes.com/2013/02/11/technology/samsung-challenges-apples-cool-factor.html?pagewanted=all&_r=0

Chudzicka-Czupała, A., Grabowski, D., Mello, A. L., Kuntz, J., Zaharia, D. V., Hapon, N., & . . . Börü, D. (2016).

Application of the theory of planned behavior in academic cheating research–cross-cultural comparison. *Ethics & Behavior, 26*(8), 638–659. doi:10.1080/10508422.2015.1112745

Chung, J. E. (2014). Medical dramas and viewer perception of health: Testing cultivation effects. *Human Communication Research, 40,* 333–349. doi:10.1111/hcre.12026

Cialdini, R. B. (1993). *Influence: Science and practice* (3rd ed.). New York, NY: HarperCollins.

Cialdini, R. B. (1994). Interpersonal influence. In S. Shavitt & T. C. Brock (Eds.), *Persuasion: Psychological insights and perspectives* (pp. 195–218). Boston, MA: Allyn & Bacon.

Cohen, B. C. (1963). *The press and foreign policy.* Princeton, NJ: Princeton University Press.

Collier, M. J. (1989). Cultural and intercultural communication competence: Current approaches and directions for future research. *International Journal of Intercultural Relations, 13,* 287–302.

Compton, J. A., & Pfau, M. (2004). Use of inoculation to foster resistance to credit card marketing targeting college students. *Journal of Applied Communication Research, 32*(4), 343–364.

Costanzo, L. A., & Di Domenico, M. (2015). A multi-level dialectical–paradox lens for top management team strategic decision-making in a corporate venture. *British Journal of Management, 26*(3), 484–506. doi:10.1111/1467-8551.12073

Craig, R. T. (1999). Communication theory as a field. *Communication Theory, 9,* 119–161.

Craig, R. T., Tracy, K., & Spisak, F. (1993). The discourse of requests: Assessment of a politeness approach. In S. Petronio, J. K. Alberts, M. L. Hecht, & J. Buley (Eds.), *Contemporary perspectives on interpersonal communication* (pp. 264–283). Madison, WI: Brown & Benchmark.

Crawford, M. (2004). Mars and Venus collide: A discursive analysis of marital self-help psychology. *Feminism & Psychology, 14,* 63–79. doi:10.1177/0959-353504040305

Cullen, K. L., Edwards, B. D., Casper, W. C., & Gue, K. R. (2014). Employees' adaptability and perceptions of change-related uncertainty: Implications for perceived organizational support, job satisfaction, and performance. *Journal of Business and Psychology, 29*(2), 269–280. doi:10.1007/s10869-013-9312-y

Cupach, W. R., & Canary, D. J. (1997). *Competence in interpersonal conflict.* New York, NY: McGraw-Hill.

Cupach, W. R., & Imahori, T. T. (1993). Identity management theory: Communication competence in intercultural episodes and relationships. In R. L. Wiseman & J. Koester (Eds.), *Intercultural communication competence* (pp. 112–131). Newbury Park, CA: Sage.

Cupach, W. R., & Metts, S. (1994). *Facework*. Thousand Oaks, CA: Sage.

Cupach, W. R., Canary, D. J., & Spitzberg, B. H. (2009). *Competence in interpersonal conflict* (2nd ed.). Long Grove, IL: Waveland Press.

Daft, R. L., & Lengel, R. H. (1984). Information richness: A new approach to managerial behavior and organizational design. In L. L. Cummings & B. M. Staw (Eds.), *Research in organizational behavior 6* (pp. 191–233). Homewood, IL: JAI Press.

Daft, R. L., & Lengel, R. H. (1986). Organizational information requirements, media richness and structural design. *Management Science, 32,* 554–571.

Dainton, M., Aylor, B., & Zelley, E. D. (2002, November). *General and relationship-specific social support, willingness to communicate, and loneliness in long-distance versus geographically close friendships.* Paper presented at the National Communication Association annual conference, New Orleans, LA.

Dance, F. E. X. (1970). The "concept" of communication. *Journal of Communication, 20,* 201–210.

Dance, F. E. X., & Larson, C. E. (1976). *The functions of communication: A theoretical approach.* New York, NY: Holt, Rinehart & Winston.

Dansereau, F., Graen, G., & Haga, W. J. (1975). A vertical dyad approach to leadership within formal organizations. *Organizational Behavior and Human Performance, 12,* 46–78.

Dawkins, R. (1989). *The selfish gene* (2nd ed.). Oxford, UK: Oxford University Press.

De Nooy, W., & Kleinnijenhuis, J. (2013). Polarization in the media during an election campaign: A dynamic network model predicting support and attack among political actors. *Political Communication, 30*(1), 117–138. doi:10.108 0/10584609.2012.737417

Deal, T. E., & Kennedy, A. A. (1982). *Corporate cultures: The rites and rituals of corporate life.* Reading, MA: Addison-Wesley.

Deal, T. E., & Kennedy, A. A. (2000). *Corporate cultures: The rites and rituals of corporate life* (2nd ed.). New York, NY: Basic Books.

Deetz, S. A. (1994). Future of the discipline: The challenges, the research, and the social contribution. In S. A. Deetz (Ed.), *Communication yearbook 17* (pp. 565–600). Thousand Oaks, CA: Sage.

Deetz, S. A., Tracy, S. J., & Simpson, J. L. (2000). *Leading organizations through transition.* Thousand Oaks, CA: Sage.

DePaulo, B. M., Stone, J. I., & Lassiter, G. D. (1985). Deceiving and detecting deceit. In B. Schlenker (Ed.), *The self and social life* (pp. 323–370). New York, NY: McGraw-Hill.

Dervin, B. (1993). Verbing communication: Mandate for disciplinary intervention. *Journal of Communication, 43,* 45–54.

DeSanctis, G., & Poole, M. S. (1994). Capturing the complexity in advanced technology use: Adaptive structuration theory. *Organization Science, 5*(2), 121–121. Retrieved from http://pubsonline.informs.org/journal/orsc

Dieker, N. (July 26, 2016). Infographic: The absolutely ridiculous amount of content consumed every minute. *Contently.com.* Retrieved from https://contently.com/strategist/ 2016/07/26/infographic-content-consumed-every-minute -absolutely-ridiculous

Dimmock, J. A., Gagné, M., Proud, L., Howle, T. C., Rebar, A. L., & Jackson, B. (2016). An exercise in resistance: Inoculation messaging as a strategy for protecting motivation during a monotonous and controlling exercise class. *Journal of Sport & Exercise Psychology, 38,* 567–578. doi:10.1123/jsep.2016-0146

Dion, K. K., & Dion, K. L. (1993). Individualistic and collectivistic perspectives on gender and the cultural context of love and intimacy. *Journal of Social Issues, 49,* 53–59.

Dockery, T. M., & Steiner, D. D. (1990). The role of initial interaction in leader–member exchange. *Group and Organizational Studies, 15,* 395–413.

Dong, Z. (2015). How to persuade adolescents to use nutrition labels: Effects of health consciousness, argument quality, and source credibility. *Asian Journal of Communication, 25(1),* 84–101. doi:10.1080/01292986.2014.989241

Driscoll, C., & McKee, M. (2007). Restorying a culture of ethical and spiritual values: A role for leader storytelling. *Journal of Business Ethics, 73*(2), 205–217. doi:10.1007/ s10551–006–9191–5

Duarte, N. T., Goodson, J. R., & Klich, N. R. (1993). How do I like thee? Let me appraise the ways. *Journal of Organizational Behavior, 14,* 239–249.

Dunegan, K. J., Uhl-Bien, M., & Duchon, D. (2002). LMX and subordinate performance: The moderating effects of task characteristics. *Journal of Business and Psychology, 17*(2), 275-285. doi:10.1023/A:1019641700724

Dunleavy, K. N., & Zelley, E. D. (2013, November). *The face of adult female friendships: Examining the relationships between interpersonal competition and facework.* Paper presented at the National Communication Association's annual conference, Washington, DC. Retrieved from http://citation.allacademic.com

Dutihl, D. (November 29, 2012). Divorce causes: Five communication habits that lead to divorce. *Huffington Post.* Retrieved from http://www.huffingtonpost.com/2012/11/29/divorce-5-communication-h_n_2159531.html

Dyer, W. G. (1987). *Team building: Issues and alternatives* (2nd ed.). Reading, MA: Addison-Wesley.

Eagly, A. H. (1987). Sex differences in social behavior: A social-role interpretation. Hillsdale, NJ: Erlbaum.

Eagly, A. H., & Karau, S. J. (2002). Role congruity theory of prejudice toward female leaders. *Psychological Review, 109*(3), 573–598. doi:10.1037/0033–295X.109.3.573

Easton, S. S., & Bommelje, R. K. (2011). Interpersonal communication consequences of email non-response. *Florida Communication Journal, 39*(2), 45–63.

Edwards, R. (1981). The social relations of production at the point of production. In M. Zey-Ferrell & M. Aiken (Eds.), *Complex organizations: Critical perspectives* (pp. 156–182). Glenview, IL: Scott, Foresman.

Ellis, D. G. (1999). *Crafting society: Ethnicity, class, and communication theory.* Mahwah, NJ: Erlbaum.

Elsesser, K. M., & Lever, J. (2011). Does gender bias against female leaders persist? Quantitative and qualitative data from a large-scale survey. *Human Relations, 64*(12), 1555–1578. doi:10.1177/0018726711424323

Eshbaugh-Soha, M. (2013). Presidential influence of the news media: The case of the press conference. *Political Communication, 30,* 548-564. doi:10.1080/10584609.2012.737438

Ezzedeen, S. R., Budworth, M., & Baker, S. D. (2015). The glass ceiling and executive careers: Still an issue for pre-career women. *Journal of Career Development, 42,* 355–369. doi:10.1177/0894845314566943

Feldner, S., & D'Urso, S. C. (2010). Threads of intersection and distinction: Joining an ongoing conversation within organizational communication research. *Communication Research Trends, 29*(1), 4–28.

Festinger, L. (1957). *A theory of cognitive dissonance.* Stanford, CA: Stanford University Press.

Festinger, L. (1962). *A theory of cognitive dissonance.* Stanford, CA: Stanford University Press.

Filipovic, J. (March 16, 2016). The major problem with "Make America Great Again." *Cosmopolitan Magazine.* Retrieved from http://www.cosmopolitan.com/politics/a55305/make-america-great-again-donald-trump

Fishbein, M., & Ajzen, I. (1975). *Belief, attitude, intention and behavior: An introduction to theory and research.* Reading, MA: Addison-Wesley.

Fisher, B. A. (1978). *Perspectives on human communication.* New York, NY: Macmillan.

Fisher, W. R. (1984). Narration as a human communication paradigm: The case of public moral argument. *Communication Monographs, 51,* 1–22.

Fisher, W. R. (1987). *Human communication as narration: Toward a philosophy of reason, value, and action.* Columbia: University of South Carolina Press.

Folkenflik, D. (May 6, 2016). Beyond 'Sesame Street': A new Sesame Studios channel on YouTube. *NPR.* Retrieved from http://www.npr.org/2016/05/06/476913166/beyond-sesame-street-a-new-sesame-studios-channel-on-youtube

Forman, J. (1998). Mickey Mouse and the French press. *Technical Communication Quarterly, 3,* 247–258.

Forrest, S. (2004). Learning and teaching: The reciprocal link. *The Journal of Continuing Education in Nursing, 35,* 74–80.

Frey, L. R., Botan, C. H., & Kreps, G. L. (2002). *Investigating communication: An introduction to research methods* (2nd ed.). Boston, MA: Allyn & Bacon.

Frommer's. (2013). *Introduction to Disneyland Paris.* Retrieved from http://www.frommers.com/destinations/disneylandparis/0796010001.html

Gabrenya Jr., W. K. (2003). Theories and models in psychology [online]. Retrieved from http://my.fit.edu/~gabrenya/IntroMethods/eBook/theories.pdf

Gallois, C., Ogay, T., & Giles, H. (2005). Communication accommodation theory: A look back and a look ahead. In W. Gudykunst (Ed.), *Theorizing about intercultural communication* (pp. 121–148). Thousand Oaks, CA: Sage.

Garcia-Retamero, R., & López-Zafra, E. (2006). Prejudice against women in male-congenial environments: Perceptions of gender role congruity in leadership. *Sex Roles, 55*(1–2), 51–61. doi:10.1007/s11199–006–9068–1

Gardner, L., & Stough, C. (2002). Examining the relationship between leadership and emotional intelligence in senior level managers. *Leadership & Organization Development Journal, 23,* 68–78.

Garrett, R. K., Weeks, B. E., & Neo, R. L. (2016). Driving a wedge between evidence and beliefs: How online ideological news exposure promotes political misperceptions. *Journal of Computer-Mediated Communication, 21*(5), 331–348. doi:10.1111/jcc4.12164

Gass, R. H., & Seiter, J. S. (2003). *Persuasion, social influence, and compliance gaining* (2nd ed.). Boston, MA: Allyn & Bacon.

Gaussorgues, F. (2014, May 12). Why Taobao succeeds unlike eBay [Blog post]. Retrieved from https://www.saos.biz/procurement-in-china/why-taobao-succeeds-in-china-unlike-ebay

Gender equality in Sweden. (2013). Swedish Institute [online]. Retrieved from http://sweden.se/society/gender-equality-in-sweden

Gentles, K. A., & Harrison, K. (2006). Television and perceived peer expectations of body size among African American adolescent girls. *Howard Journal of Communications, 17*(1), 39–55.

Gerbner, G. (1998). Cultivation analysis: An overview. *Mass Communication & Society, 1,* 175–194.

Gerbner, G., Gross, L., Morgan, M., & Signorelli, N. (1980). The "mainstreaming" of America: Violence profile no. 11. *Journal of Communication, 30,* 10–29.

Ghanem, S. (1997). Filling in the tapestry: The second level of agenda setting. In M. McCombs, D. L. Shaw, & D. Weaver (Eds.), *Communication and democracy: Exploring the intellectual frontiers of agenda-setting theory* (pp. 3–14). New York, NY: Routledge.

Giannetti, L. (1982). *Understanding movies* (3rd ed.). Englewood Cliffs, NJ: Prentice Hall.

Giddens, A. (1979). *Central problems in social theory: Action, structure, and contradiction in social analysis.* Berkeley: University of California Press.

Giles, H., & Coupland, N. (1991). *Language: Contexts and consequences.* Pacific Grove, CA: Wadsworth.

Giles, H., & Gasiorek, J. (2014). Parameters of nonaccommodation: Refining and elaborating communication accommodation theory. In J. P. Forgas, O. Vincze, & J. László (Eds.), *Social Cognition and Communication* (pp. 155–172). New York, NY: Psychology Press.

Giles, H., Linz, D., Bonilla, D., & Gomez, M. L. (2012). Police stops of and interactions with Latino and white (non-Latino) drivers: Extensive policing and communication accommodation. *Communication Monographs, 79*(4), 407–427. doi:10.1080/03637751.2012.723815

Giles, H., Mulac, A., Bradac, J. J., & Johnson, P. (1987). Ethnolinguistic identity theory: A social psychological approach to language maintenance. *International Journal of the Sociology of Language, 68,* 66–99.

Giles, H., Willemyn, M. Gallois, C., & Anderson, M. C. (2007). Accommodating a new frontier: The context of law enforcement. In K. Fiedler (Ed.), *Social Communication* (pp. 129–162). New York, NY: Psychology Press.

Gilpin, D. (2010). Organizational image construction in a fragmented online media environment. *Journal of Public Relations Research, 22*(3), 265–287. doi:10.1080/10627261003614393

Gilstrap, C. M., & White, Z. M. (2015). Interactional communication challenges in end-of-life care: Dialectical tensions and management strategies experienced by home hospice nurses. *Health Communication, 30*(6), 525–535. doi:10.1080/10410236.2013.868966

Glaser, B. G., & Strauss, A. L. (1967). *The discovery of grounded theory: Strategies for qualitative research.* Chicago, IL: Aldine.

Gloor, P. A., Fronzetti Colladon, A., Grippa, F., & Giacomelli, G. (2017). Forecasting managerial turnover through e-mail based social network analysis. *Computers in Human Behavior, 71,* 343–352. doi:10.1016/j.chb.2017.02.017

Godbold, L. C., & Pfau, M. (2000). Conferring resistance of peer pressure among adolescents: Using inoculation theory to discourage alcohol use. *Communication Research, 27,* 411–437.

Goffman E. (1959). *The presentation of self in everyday life.* New York, NY: Doubleday.

Goffman, E. (1967). *Interaction ritual: Essays on face-to-face behavior.* New York, NY: Pantheon Books.

Golan, G. J., Kiousis, S. K., & McDaniel, M. L. (2007). Second-level agenda setting and political advertising. *Journalism Studies, 8,* 432–443. doi:10.1080/14616700701276190

Golden, J. C., & Jacoby, J. W. (2017). Playing princess: Preschool girls' interpretations of gender stereotypes in Disney princess media. *Sex Roles,* doi:10.1007/s11199-017-0773-8

Goldfarb, R. S., & Ratner, J. (2008). "Theories" and "models": Terminology through the looking glass. *Econ Journal Watch, 5*(1), 91–108.

Goleman, D. (1995). *Emotional intelligence.* New York, NY: Bantam Books.

Gordon, C. S., Howard, S. J., Jones, S. C., & Kervin, L. K. (2016). Evaluation of an Australian alcohol media literacy program. *Journal of Studies on Alcohol and Drugs, 77,* 950–957. doi:10.15288/jsad.2016.77.950

Gouran, D. S. (2010). Overcoming sources of irrationality that complicate working in decision-making groups. In S. Schuman (Ed.), *The handbook of working with difficult groups: How they are difficult, why they are difficult, and what you can do about it* (pp. 137–152). San Francisco, CA: Jossey-Bass.

Gouran, D. S. (2011). Leadership as reasoned argument in decision-making and problem-solving groups. Conference Proceedings. *National Communication Association/American Forensic Association* (Alta Conference on Argumentation), pp. 104–112.

Gouran, D. S., & Hirokawa, R. Y. (1983). The role of communication in decision-making groups: A functional perspective. In M. Mander (Ed.), *Communications in transition* (pp. 168–185). New York, NY: Praeger.

Gouran, D. S., & Hirokawa, R. Y. (1986). Counteractive functions of communication in effective group decision-making. In R. Y. Hirokawa & M. S. Poole (Eds.), *Communication and group decision making* (pp. 81–92). Beverly Hills, CA: Sage.

Gouran, D. S., & Hirokawa, R. Y. (1996). Functional theory and communication in decision-making and problem-solving groups: An expanded view. In R. Y. Hirokawa & M. S. Poole (Eds.), *Communication and group decision making* (pp. 55–80). Thousand Oaks, CA: Sage.

Graen, G., & Uhl-Bien, M. (1995). Development of leader-member exchange theory of leadership over 25 years: Applying a multilevel perspective. *Leadership Quarterly, 6,* 219–247.

Gray, J. (1992). *Men are from Mars, women are from Venus: A practical guide to improving communication and getting what you want in your relationships.* New York, NY: HarperCollins.

Gray, J. (1997, 2005). *Mars and Venus on a date: A guide for navigating the 5 stages of dating to create a loving and lasting relationship.* New York, NY: Harper Collins.

Greenberg, P. (2013). The narrative is the thing: the art of corporate storytelling. *Social CRM: The Conversation* [online]. Retrieved from http://www.zdnet.com/the-narrative-is-the-thing-the-art-of-corporate-storytelling-7000024315

Griffin, E. (2003). *A first look at communication theory* (5th ed.). New York, NY: McGraw-Hill.

Griffin, E. (2006). *A first look at communication theory* (6th ed.). New York, NY: McGraw-Hill.

Griffin, E., Ledbetter, A., & Sparks, G. (2015). *A first look at communication theory, 9th ed.* New York, NY: McGraw Hill.

Gudykunst, W. B. (1985). A model of uncertainty reduction in intercultural encounters. *Journal of Language and Social Psychology, 4*(2), 79–98. doi:10.1177/0261927X8500400201

Gudykunst, W. B. (1993). Toward a theory of effective interpersonal and intergroup communication: An anxiety/uncertainty management (AUM) perspective. In R. L. Wiseman & J. Koester (Eds.), *Intercultural communication competence* (pp. 33–71). Newbury Park, CA: Sage.

Gudykunst, W. B. (1995). Anxiety/uncertainty management (AUM) theory: Current status. In R. L. Wiseman (Ed.), *Intercultural communication theory* (pp. 8–58). Thousand Oaks, CA: Sage.

Gudykunst, W. B. (2005). An anxiety/uncertainty management (AUM) theory of strangers' intercultural adjustment. In W. B. Gudykunst (Ed.), *Theorizing about intercultural communication* (pp. 419–458). Thousand Oaks, CA: Sage.

Gudykunst, W. B., & Hammer, M. R. (1988). Strangers and hosts: An uncertainty reduction based theory of intercultural adaptation. In Y. Y. Kim & W. B. Gudykunst (Eds.), *Cross-cultural adaptation: Current approaches* (pp. 106–139). Newbury Park, CA: Sage.

Guerrero, L. K., & Burgoon, J. K. (1996). Attachment styles and reactions to nonverbal involvement change in romantic dyads: Patterns of reciprocity and compensation. *Human Communication Research, 22,* 335–336.

Guerrero, L. K., Jones, S. M., & Burgoon, J. K. (2000). Responses to nonverbal intimacy change in romantic dyads: Effects of behavioral valence and degree of behavioral change on nonverbal and verbal reactions. *Communication Monographs, 67,* 325–346.

Haigh, M., & Pfau, M. (2006). Bolstering organizational identity, commitment, and citizenship behaviors through the process of inoculation. *International Journal of Organizational Analysis, 14,* 295–316.

Hall, A. D., & Fagen, R. E. (1968). Definition of a system. In W. Buckley (Ed.), *Modern systems research for the behavioral scientist* (pp. 81–92). Chicago, IL: Aldine.

Hall, E. T. (1976). *Beyond culture.* Garden City, NY: Doubleday.

Hall, S. (1973). *Encoding and decoding in the television discourse.* Birmingham, UK: Centre for Cultural Studies.

Hall, S. (1986). Gramsci's relevance for the study of race and ethnicity. *Journal of Communication Inquiry, 10*(2), 5–27.

Handfield-Jones R., Nasmith L., Steinert Y., & Lawn, N. (1993). Creativity in medical education: The use of innovative techniques in clinical teaching. *Med Teacher, 15,* 3–10.

Hartsock, N. (1983). The feminist standpoint: Developing the ground for a specifically feminist historical materialism. In S. Harding & M. B. Hintikka (Eds.), *Discovering reality* (pp. 283–310). Boston, MA: Riedel.

Heath, R., Brandt, D., & Nairn, A. (2006). Brand relationships: Strengthened by emotion, weakened by attention. *Journal of Advertising Research, 46*(4), 410–419.

Hecht, M. L., Collier, M. J., & Ribeau, S. A. (1993). *African American communication: Ethnic identity and interpretation.* Newbury Park, CA: Sage.

Hegel, G. W. F. (1966). *The phenomenology of mind* (2nd ed., J. B. Braillie, Trans.). New York, NY: Humanities Press. (Original work published 1807)

Heider, F. (1958). *The psychology of interpersonal relations.* New York, NY: Wiley.

Heintz, K. E., & Wartella, E. A. (2012). Young children's learning from screen media. *Communication Research Trends, 31*(3), 22–29.

Hesse-Biber, S., Leavy, P., Quinn, C. E., & Zoino, J. (2006). The mass marketing of disordered eating and eating disorders: The social psychology of women, thinness and culture. *Women's Studies International Forum, 29,* 208–224.

Hickson, M., & Neiva, E. (2002). Toward a taxonomy of universals in the biology of communication. *Journal of Intercultural Communication Research, 31*(3), 149.

Hirokawa, R. Y. (1994). Functional approaches to the study of group discussion: Even good notions have their problems. *Small Group Research, 25,* 542–550.

Hirokawa, R. Y., & Salazar, A. J. (1999). Task-group communication and decision-making performance. In L. R. Frey, D. S. Gouran, & M. S. Poole (Eds.), *The handbook of group communication theory and research* (pp. 167–191). Thousand Oaks, CA: Sage.

Hofstede, G. (1980). *Culture's consequences.* Beverly Hills, CA: Sage.

Hofstede, G. (1986). Cultural differences in teaching and learning. *International Journal of Intercultural Relations, 10,* 301–319.

Hofstede, G. (1991). *Cultures and organizations: Software of the mind.* London, UK: McGraw-Hill.

Hofstede, G. (2001). *Culture's consequences: International differences in work-related values* (2nd ed.). Thousand Oaks, CA: Sage.

Hofstede, G., & Bond, M. H. (1984). Hofstede's culture dimensions: An independent validation using Rokeach's value survey. *Journal of Cross Cultural Psychology, 15,* 417–433.

Hogan, S. J., & Coote, L. V. (2014). Organizational culture, innovation, and performance: A test of Schein's model. *Journal of Business Research, 67,* 1609–1621. doi:10.1016/j.jbusres.2013.09.007

Holody, K. J., & Daniel, E. S. (2017). Attributes and frames of the Aurora shootings. *Journalism Practice, 11,* 80–100. doi:10.1080/17512786.2015.1121786

Holstein, W. J. (2007, July 27). Why Wal-Mart can't find happiness in Japan. *Fortune.* Retrieved from http://archive.fortune.com/magazines/fortune/fortune_archive/2007/08/06/100141311/index.htm

Huckins, K. (1999). Interest-group influence on the media agenda: A case study. *Journalism and Mass Communication Quarterly, 76,* 76–86.

Huesmann, L. R., Moise-Titus, J., Podolski, C. L., & Eron, L. D. (2003). Longitudinal relations between children's exposure to TV violence and their aggressive and violent behavior in young adulthood 1977–1992. *Developmental Psychology, 39,* 201–221.

Iyengar, S., Peters, M., & Kinder, D. (1982). Experimental demonstrations of the "not-so-minimal" consequences of television news programs. *American Political Science Review, 76,* 848–858.

Jablin, F. M. (1987). Organizational entry, assimilation, and exit. In F. M. Jablin, L. L. Putnam, K. H. Roberts, & L. W. Porter (Eds.), *Handbook of organizational communication: An interdisciplinary perspective* (pp. 679–740). Newbury Park, CA: Sage.

Jablin, F. M. (2001). Organizational entry, assimilation, and disengagement/exit. In F. M. Jablin & L. L. Putnam (Eds.), *The new handbook of organizational communication* (pp. 732–818). Thousand Oaks, CA: Sage.

Jandt, F. E. (2004). *An introduction to intercultural communication: Identities in a global community.* Thousand Oaks, CA: Sage.

Janis, I. L. (1972). *Victims of groupthink: A psychological study of foreign-policy decisions and fiascoes.* Boston, MA: Houghton Mifflin.

Janis, I. L. (1982). *Groupthink: Psychological studies of policy decisions and fiascoes.* Boston, MA: Houghton Mifflin.

Jarlenski, M., & Barry, C. L. (2013). News media coverage of trans fat: Health risks and policy responses. *Health Communication, 28(3),* 209-216. doi:10.1080/10410236.2012.669670

Jarvis, C. E. (2016). The impact of communication style on organizational assimilation: A qualitative inquiry exploring generation Y employees during their first year of employment with an organization (Order No. 10108827). Available from ProQuest Dissertations & Theses Global. (1793669189).

Jimenez, M. (2017). A quantitative study: The relationship between managers' emotional intelligence awareness and demographics and leadership styles. *Dissertation Abstracts International, 77,* 8-A(E).

Jones, E. E., & Davis, K. E. (1965). From acts to dispositions: The attribution process in person perception. In L. Berkowitz (Ed.), *Advances in experimental social psychology* (Vol. 2, pp. 220–266). Orlando, FL: Academic Press.

Kahlor, L., & Eastin, M. S. (2011). Television's role in the culture of violence towards women: Study of television viewing and the cultivation of rape myth acceptance. *Journal of Broadcast and Electronic Media, 55(2),* 215–231. doi: 10.1080/08838151.2011.566085

Kapidzic, S., & Martins, N. (2015). Mirroring the media: The relationship between media consumption, media internalization, and profile picture characteristics on Facebook. *Journal of Broadcasting & Electronic Media, 59(2),* 278–297. doi:10.1080/08838151.2015.1029127

Kaplan, A. (1964). *The conduct of inquiry.* San Francisco, CA: Chandler.

Kates, D. (August 23, 2016). Kids are getting too much screen time—and it is affecting their development. *National Post* [online]. Retrieved from http://news.nationalpost.com/health/kids-are-getting-too-much-screen-time-and-its-affecting-their-development

Katz, E., Blumler, J. G., & Gurevitch, M. (1973). Uses and gratifications research. *Public Opinion Quarterly, 37,* 509–523.

Kearns, E.M., Betus, A., & Lemieux, A. (March 13, 2017). Yes, the media do underreport some terrorist acts. Just not the ones most people think of. *Washington Post* [online]. Retrieved from https://www.washingtonpost.com/news/monkey-cage/wp/2017/03/13/yes-the-media-do-underreport-some-terrorist-attacks-just-not-the-ones-most-people-think-of/?utm_term=.88493239a8c9

Kelley, H. H. (1967). Attribution theory in social psychology. *Nebraska Symposium on Motivation, 15,* 192–238.

Kelley, H. H. (1973). The processes of causal attribution. *American Psychologist, 28,* 107–128.

Kelly, J. (2008). Mapping the blogosphere: Offering a guide to journalism's future. *Nieman Reports, 62(4),* 37–39.

Kelman, S., Sanders, R., & Pandit, G. (2016). "I won't back down?" Complexity and courage in government executive decision making. *Public Administration Review, 76,* 465–471. doi:10.1111/puar.12476

Kerssen-Griep, J., Hess, J. A., & Trees, A. R. (2003). Sustaining the desire to learn: Dimensions of perceived instructional facework related to student involvement and motivation to learn. *Western Journal of Communication, 67,* 357–381.

Kilmann, R. H., & Thomas, K. W. (1977). Developing a forced-choice measure of conflict-handling behavior.

The MODE instrument. *Educational and Psychological Measurement, 37*, 309–325.

Kim, E. Y. (2001). *The yin and the yang of American culture: A paradox.* Yarmouth, ME: Intercultural Press.

Kim, E., Lee, J., Sung, Y., & Choi, S. M. (2016). Predicting selfie-posting behavior on social networking sites: An extension of theory of planned behavior. *Computers in Human Behavior, 62*, 116–123. doi:10.1016/j.chb.2016.03.078

Kim, S. (2013). Does corporate advertising work in a crisis? An examination of inoculation theory. *Journal of Marketing Communications, 19*(4), 293–305. doi:10.1080/13527266.2011.634430

Kim, S. (2014). The role of prior expectancies and relational satisfaction in crisis. *Journalism & Mass Communication Quarterly, 91*(1), 139–158. doi:10.1177/1077699013514413

Kim, S., & Kuo, M. (2015). Examining the relationships among coaching, trustworthiness, and role behaviors: A social exchange perspective. *Journal of Applied Behavioral Science, 51*(2), 152–176. doi:10.1177/0021886315574884

Kleinnijenhuis, J., Schultz, F., Utz, S., & Oegema, D. (2015). The mediating role of the news in the BP oil spill crisis 2010: How U.S. news is influenced by public relations and in turn influences public awareness, foreign news, and the share price. *Communication Research, 42*, 408–428. doi:10.1177/0093650213510940

Klotz, A. C., & Bolino, M. C. (2016). Saying goodbye: The nature, causes, and consequences of employee resignation styles. *Journal of Applied Psychology, 101*(10), 1386–1404. doi:10.1037/apl0000135

Koblin, J. (June 30, 2016). How much do we love TV? Let us count the ways. *The New York Times.* Retrieved from https://www.nytimes.com/2016/07/01/business/media/nielsen-survey-media-viewing.html?mcubz=2&_r=0

Koenig, A. M., Eagly, A. H., Mitchell, A. A., & Ristikari, T. (2011). Are leader stereotypes masculine? A meta-analysis of three research paradigms. *Psychological Bulletin, 137*, 616–642. doi:10.1037/a0023557

Lam, C., & O'Higgins, E. E. (2012). Enhancing employee outcomes: The interrelated influences of managers' emotional intelligence and leadership style. *Leadership & Organization Development Journal, 33*(2), 149–174. doi:10.1108/01437731211203465

Lamke, L. K., Sollie, D. L., Durbin, R. G., & Fitzpatrick, J. A. (1994). Masculinity, femininity, and relationship satisfaction: The mediating role of interpersonal competence. *Journal of Social and Personal Relationships, 11*, 535–554.

Lämsä, A.-M., & Sintonen, T. (2006). A narrative approach for organizational learning in a diverse organisation. *Journal of Workplace Learning, 18*(1/2), 106–120. Retrieved from http://www.emeraldinsight.com/journal/jwl

Larkey, L. K. (1996). Toward a theory of communicative interactions in culturally diverse workgroups. *Academy of Management Review, 21*, 463–491.

Lederman, L. C., & Menegatos, L. M. (2011). Sustainable recovery: The self-transformative power of storytelling in Alcoholics Anonymous. *Journal of Groups in Addiction & Recovery, 6*, 206-227. doi:10.1080/1556035X.2011.597195

Ledford, C. W., Saperstein, A. K., Cafferty, L. A., McClintick, S. H., & Bernstein, E. M. (2015). Any questions? An application of Weick's model of organizing to increase student involvement in the large-lecture classroom. *Communication Teacher, 29*, 116–128. doi:10.1080/17404622.2014.1003309

Leeds-Hurwitz, W. (1992). Forum introduction: Social approaches to interpersonal communication. *Communication Theory, 2*(2), 131–139.

Lemay, E. J., O'Brien, K. M., Kearney, M. S., Sauber, E. W., & Venaglia, R. B. (2017). Using conformity to enhance willingness to intervene in dating violence: A theory of planned behavior analysis. *Psychology of Violence*, doi:10.1037/vio0000114

Lengel, R. H., & Daft, R. L. (1988). The selection of communication media as an executive skill. *Academy of Management Executive, 2*(3), 225–232.

Lewallen, J., Miller, B., & Behm-Morawitz, E. (2016). Lifestyles of the rich and famous: Celebrity media diet and the cultivation of emerging adults' materialism. *Mass Communication & Society, 19*(3), 253–274. doi:10.1080/15205436.2015.1096945

Lewin, K. (1951). *Field theory in social science: Selected theoretical papers.* New York, NY: Harper & Row.

Lewis, B.K. (2010). Social media and strategic communication: Attitudes and perceptions among college students. *Public Relations Journal, 4*, 1–23

Lewis, R. D. (2000). *When cultures collide: Managing successfully across cultures.* London, UK: Nicholas Brealey.

Light, T. (2002). *Thinking ahead about buyer's remorse.* Real-Estate ABC. Retrieved from http://www.realestateabc.com/homeguide/remorse.htm

Litterst, J. K., & Eyo, B. (1982). Gauging the effectiveness of formal communication programs: The search for the communication-productivity link. *Journal of Business Communication, 19*(2), 15–26.

Littlejohn, S. W. (1989). *Theories of human communication* (3rd ed.). Belmont, CA: Wadsworth.

Littlejohn, S. W. (2002). *Theories of human communication* (7th ed.). Belmont, CA: Wadsworth.

Lo, K. D., Waters, R. D., & Christensen, N. (2017). Assessing the applicability of Hofstede's cultural dimensions for Global 500 corporations' Facebook profiles and content. *Journal of Communication Management, 21*(1), 51–67. doi:10.1108/JCOM-04-2016-0021

Longobardi, E. (2009). How "subprime" killed "predatory." *Columbia Journalism Review, 48*(3), 45–49.

Maccoby, E. E. (1990). Gender and relationships: A developmental account. *American Psychologist, 45,* 513–520.

Madlock, P. E. (2008). The link between leadership style, communicator competence, and employee satisfaction. *Journal of Business Communication, 45*(1), 61–78.

Mael, F., & Ashforth, B. E. (1992). Alumni and their alma mater: A partial test of the reformulated model of organizational identification. *Journal of Organizational Behavior, 13,* 103–123.

Malacane, M., & Martins, N. (2017). Sexual socialization messages in television programming produced for adolescents. *Mass Communication & Society, 20,* 23–46. doi:10.1080/15205436.2016.1203436

Mann, M. (2012). *The sources of social power: Globalizations, 1945–2011* (Vol. 4). New York, NY: Cambridge University Press.

Manzoni, J. F., & Barsoux, J. L. (2002). *The set-up-to-fail syndrome: How good managers cause great people to fail.* Boston, MA: Harvard Business School.

Marchionni, D. M. (2012). International human trafficking: An agenda-building analysis of the U.S. and British press. *International Communication Gazette, 74*(2), 145–158. doi:10.1177/1748048511432600

Markus, M. L. (1987). Toward a "critical mass" theory of interactive media: Universal access, interdependence and diffusion. *Communication Research, 14,* 491–511.

Marshall, R. (September 10, 2015). How many ads do you see in one day? *Red Crow Marketing.* Retrieved from http://www.redcrowmarketing.com/2015/09/10/many-ads-see-one-day

Martins, N. and Wilson, B. J. (2012). Social aggression on television and its relationship to children's aggression in the classroom. *Human Communication Research, 38,* 48–71. doi:10.1111/j.1468-2958.2011.01417.x

Mayer, J. D., & Salovey, P. (1997). What is emotional intelligence? In P. Salovey & D. J. Sluyter (Eds.), *Emotional development and emotional intelligence: Educational implications* (pp. 3–34). New York, NY: Basic Books.

Mayer, J. D., Caruso, D. R., & Salovey, P. (1999). Emotional intelligence meets traditional standards for an intelligence. *Intelligence, 27*(4), 267–298. doi:10.1016/S0160–2896(99)00016–1

Mayer, J. D., Salovey, P., & Caruso, D. R. (2008). Emotional intelligence: New ability or eclectic traits? *American Psychologist, 63*(6), 503–517. doi:10.1037/0003–066X.63.6.503

McCombs, M., & Bell, T. (1974). The agenda-setting role of mass communication. In M. Salwen & D. Stacks (Eds.), *An integrated approach to communication theory and research* (p. 100). Hillsdale, NJ: Erlbaum.

McCombs M., & Evatt, D. (1995). Issues and attributes: Exploring a new dimension in agenda setting. *Comunicación Y Sociedad, 8,* 1-20.

McCombs, M., & Shaw, D. (1972). The agenda-setting function of the mass media. *Public Opinion Quarterly, 36,* 176–187.

McCombs, M. E., Shaw, D. L., & Weaver, D. H. (2014). New directions in agenda-setting theory and research. *Mass Communication & Society, 17,* 781-802. doi:10.1080/15205436.2014.964871

McCroskey, J. C. (2006). The role of culture in a communibiological approach to communication. *Human Communication, 9*(1), 31–35.

McGuire, D., Todnem By, R., & Hutchings, K. (2007). Towards a model of human resource solutions for achieving intergenerational interaction in organizations. *Journal of European Industrial Training, 31*(8), 592–608.

McGuire, W. J. (1961). Resistance to persuasion conferred by active and passive prior refutation of the same and alternative counterarguments. *Journal of Abnormal and Social Psychology, 63*, 326–332.

McGuire, W. J. (1962). Persistence of the resistance to persuasion induced by various types of prior belief defenses. *Journal of Abnormal and Social Psychology, 64*, 241–248.

McGuire, W. J. (1964). Inducing resistance to persuasion: Some contemporary approaches. In L. Berkowitz (Ed.), *Advances in experimental social psychology* (Vol. 1, pp. 191–229). New York, NY: Academic Press.

McGuire, W. J., & Papageorgis, D. (1961). The relative efficacy of various types of prior belief-defense in producing immunity against persuasion. *Public Opinion Quarterly, 26*, 24–34.

McLellan, H. (2006). Corporate storytelling perspectives. *Journal for Quality and Participation, 29*(1), 17–20.

McMullin, L. (2001). 1969: First broadcast of *Sesame Street*. In D. Schugurensky (Ed.), *History of education: Selected moments of the 20th century* [online]. Retrieved from http://schugurensky.faculty.asu.edu/moments/1969sesamestreet.html

McPhee, R. D. (1985). Formal structure and organizational communication. In R. D. McPhee & P. K. Tompkins (Eds.), *Organizational communication: Traditional themes and new directions* (pp. 149–178). Beverly Hills, CA: Sage.

McQuail, D. (1987). *Mass communication theory: An introduction* (2nd ed.). Newbury Park, CA: Sage.

McQuail, D. (2010). *McQuail's mass communication theory* (6th ed.). Thousand Oaks, CA: Sage.

Mieder, W. W. (1986). *Encyclopedia of world proverbs: A treasury of wit and wisdom through the ages*. Englewood Cliffs, NJ: Prentice Hall.

Mikkelson, A. C., York, J. A., & Arritola, J. (2015). Communication competence, leadership behaviors, and employee outcomes in supervisor-employee relationships. *Business & Professional Communication Quarterly, 78*, 336–354. doi:10.1177/2329490615588542

Millar, F. E., & Rogers, L. E. (1976). A relational approach to interpersonal communication. In G. R. Miller (Ed.), *Explorations in interpersonal communication* (pp. 87–203). Beverly Hills, CA: Sage.

Miller, A. N., & Samp, J. A. (2007). Planning intercultural interaction: Extending anxiety/uncertainty management theory. *Communication Research Reports, 24*(2), 87–95. doi:10.1080/08824090701304717

Miller, G. R. (1978). The current status of theory and research in interpersonal communication. *Human Communication Research, 4*, 164–178.

Miller, K. (2002). *Communication theories: Perspectives, processes, and contexts*. New York, NY: McGraw-Hill.

Miller, K. (2003). *Organizational communication: Approaches and processes* (3rd ed.). Belmont, CA: Wadsworth.

Mishel, L., & Davis, A. (2015). Top CEOs make 300 times more than typical workers. *Economic Policy Institute, Issue Brief, 399*, 1-14. Retrieved from http://www.epi.org/files/2015/top-ceos-make-300-times-more-than-typical-workers.pdf

Molina-Guzmán, I. (2016). #OscarsSoWhite: How Stuart Hall explains why nothing changes in Hollywood and everything is changing. *Critical Studies in Media Communication, 33*(5), 438–454. doi:10.1080/15295036.2016.1227864

Monge, P. R., & Contractor, N. S. (2001). Emergence of communication networks. In F. M. Jablin & L. L. Putnam (Eds.), *Handbook of organizational communication: Advances in theory, research, and methods* (pp. 440–502). Thousand Oaks, CA: Sage.

Montgomery, B. M. (1993). Relationship maintenance versus relationship change: Dialectical dilemma. *Journal of Social and Personal Relationships, 10*, 205–224.

Morley, D. D., & Shockley-Zalabak, P. (1991). Setting the rules: An examination of organizational founders' values. *Management Communication Quarterly, 4*, 422–449.

Myers, S. A., & Kassing, J. W. (1998). The relationship between perceived supervisory communication behaviors and subordinate organizational identification. *Communication Research Reports, 15*, 71–81.

Nabi, R. L. (2009). Cosmetic surgery makeover programs and intentions to undergo cosmetic enhancements: A consideration of three models of media effects. *Communication Research, 35*(1), 1–27.

Neisser, U. (1967). *Cognitive psychology*. New York, NY: Appleton-Century-Crofts.

Ni, L., & Wang, Q. (2011). Anxiety and uncertainty management in an intercultural setting: The impact on organization-public relationships. *Journal of Public Relations Research, 23*(3), 269–301. doi:10.1080/1062726X.2011.582205

Nystrom, P. C. (1990). Vertical exchanges and organizational commitments of American business managers. *Group and Organizational Studies, 15*, 296–312.

O'Hehir, A. (March 22, 2014), 'Divergent" and "Hunger Games as capitalist agitprop. Salon [online]. Retrieved from http://www.salon.com/2014/03/22/divergent_and_hunger_games_as_capitalist_agitprop

O'Keefe, B. J., & Delia, J. G. (1982). Impression formation and message production. In M. E. Roloff & C. R. Berger (Eds.). *Social cognition and communication* (pp. 33–72). Beverly Hills, CA: Sage.

O'Keefe, B. J., & Shepherd, G. J. (1987). The pursuit of multiple objectives in face-to-face persuasive interaction: Effects of construct differentiation on message organization. *Communication Monographs, 54*, 396–419. DOI: 10.1080/03637758709390241

O'Keefe, B. J. (1988). The logic of message design: Individual differences in reasoning about communication. *Communication Monographs, 55*, 80–103.

O'Keefe, B. J. (1997). Variation, adaptation, and functional explanation in the study of message design. In G. Philipsen & T. L. Albrecht (Eds.), *Developing communication theories* (pp. 85–118). Albany: State University of New York Press.

O'Keefe, B. J., & Delia, J. G. (1988). Communicative tasks and communicative practices: The development of audience-centered message production. In B. Rafoth & D. Rubin (Eds.), *The social construction of written communication* (pp. 70–98). Norwood, NJ: Ablex.

O'Keefe, B. J., Lambert, B. L., & Lambert, C. A. (1997). Conflict and communication in a research and development unit. In B. D. Sypher (Ed.), *Case studies in organizational communication 2* (pp. 31–52). New York, NY: Guilford Press.

O'Keefe, D. J. (1990). *Persuasion: Theory and research*. Newbury Park, CA: Sage.

Oeldorf-Hirsch, A., & Sundar, S. S. (2016). Social and technological motivations for online photo sharing. *Journal of Broadcasting & Electronic Media, 60(4)*, 624–642. doi: 10.1080/08838151.2016.1234478

Oetzel, J. G., & Ting-Toomey, S. (2003). Face concerns in interpersonal conflict: A cross-cultural empirical test of the face negotiation theory. *Communication Research, 30*, 599–624.

Offor, E. E. (2012). Analysis of sex stereotyping on women's positive evaluation and promotion to executive leadership roles. *Dissertation Abstracts International Section A, 73*, 260.

Oliveira, T., Thomas, M., Baptista, G., & Campos, F. (2016). Mobile payment: Understanding the determinants of customer adoption and intention to recommend the technology. *Computers in Human Behavior, 61*, 404–414. doi:10.1016/j.chb.2016.03.030

Palmer, B., Walls, M., Burgess, Z., & Stough, C. (2001). Emotional intelligence and effective leadership. *Leadership & Organization Development Journal, 22*, 5–11.

Park, J. S. (2008). The social reality of depression: DTC advertising of antidepressants and perceptions of the prevalence and lifetime risk of depression. *Journal of Business Ethics, 79(4)*, 379–393.

Parks, M. R., & Adelman, M. B. (1983). Communication networks and the development of romantic relationships: An expansion of uncertainty reduction theory. *Human Communication Research, 10*, 55–79.

Pattee, H. H. (Ed.). (1973). *Hierarchy theory: The challenge of complex systems*. New York, NY: Braziller.

Paustian-Underdahl, S. C., Walker, L. S., & Woehr, D. J. (2014). Gender and perceptions of leadership effectiveness: A meta-analysis of contextual moderators. *Journal of Applied Psychology, 99*, 1129–1145. DOI:10.1037/a0036751

Pazos, P., Chung, J. M., & Micari, M. (2013). Instant messaging as a task-support tool in information technology organizations. *Journal of Business Communication, 50(1)*, 68–86. doi:10.1177/0021943612465181

Peake, J. S. (2001). Presidential agenda setting in foreign policy. *Political Research Quarterly, 54*, 69–86.

Pearson, J., Nelson, P., Titsworth, S., & Harter, L. (2008). *Human communication* (3rd ed.). New York, NY: McGraw-Hill.

Perks, L. (2012). Three satiric television decoding positions. *Communication Studies, 63(3)*, 290–308. doi:10.1080/10510974.2012.678925

Peters, R. S. (1974). Personal understanding and personal relationships. In T. Mischel (Ed.), *Understanding other persons*. Oxford, UK: Rowman & Littlefield.

Petronio, S. (2002). *Boundaries of privacy: Dialectics of disclosure.* Albany, NY: SUNY Press.

Petronio, S., & Durham, W. T. (2008). Communication privacy management theory: Significance for interpersonal communication. In L. A. Baxter & D. O. Braithwaite (Eds.), *Engaging theories in interpersonal communication: Multiple perspectives* (pp. 309–322). Thousand Oaks, CA: Sage.

Petty, R. E., & Cacioppo, J. T. (1986). *Communication and persuasion: Central and peripheral routes to attitude change.* New York, NY: Springer-Verlag.

Pfau, M. (1997). The inoculation model of resistance to influence. In F. J. Boster & G. Barnett (Eds.), *Progress in communication sciences* (Vol. 13, pp. 133–171). Norwood, NJ: Ablex.

Pillai, P. (1992). Rereading Stuart Hall's encoding/decoding model. *Communication Theory, 2*(3), 221–233.

Platt, C. (2004). *A culture of thinness: Negotiated and oppositional decoding of eating disorder discourse by anorectics.* Paper presented at the meeting of the International Communication Association, New Orleans, LA.

Poole, M. S. (1985). Communication and organizational climates: Review, critique, and a new perspective. In R. D. McPhee & P. K. Tompkins (Eds.), *Organizational communication: Traditional themes and new directions* (pp. 79–108). Beverly Hills, CA: Sage.

Poole, M. S. (1988). *Communication and the structuring of organizations.* Unpublished manuscript, University of Minnesota, Minneapolis.

Poole, M. S. (1999). Group communication theory. In L. R. Frey, D. S. Gouran, & M. S. Poole (Eds.), *The handbook of group communication theory and research* (pp. 37–70). Thousand Oaks, CA: Sage.

Poole, M. S., & McPhee, R. D. (1983). A structurational approach to organizational climate. In L. L. Putnam & M. E. Pacanowsky (Eds.), *Communication and organizations: An interpretive approach* (pp. 195–220). Beverly Hills, CA: Sage.

Poole, M. S., & Roth, J. (1989). Decision and development in small groups IV: A typology of group decision paths. *Human Communication Research, 15,* 323–356.

Poole, M. S., Seibold, D. R., & McPhee, R. D. (1985). Group decision-making as a structurational process. *Quarterly Journal of Speech, 71,* 74–102.

Poole, M. S., Seibold, D. R., & McPhee, R. D. (1986). A structurational approach to theory-building in group decision-making research. In R. Y. Hirokawa & M. S. Poole (Eds.), *Communication and group decision-making* (pp. 237–264). Beverly Hills, CA: Sage.

Prada, P., & Orwall, B. (2002, March 12). Parlez-vous Disney? Oui, ja, yes—Mickey's bosses learn from past mistakes in opening new park in France. *The Wall Street Journal,* p. A12. Retrieved from ProQuest Central. (Document ID: 110371846).

Procter, J. (2004). *Stuart Hall.* New York, NY: Routledge.

Putnam, L. L. (1983). The interpretive perspective: An alternative to functionalism. In L. L. Putnam & M. E. Pacanowsky (Eds.), *Communication and organizations: An interpretive approach* (pp. 13–30). Beverly Hills, CA: Sage.

Putnam, V. L., & Paulus, P. B. (2009). Brainstorming, brainstorming rules and decision making. *The Journal of Creative Behavior, 43*(1), 23–39.

Rahim, M. A. (1986). *Managing conflict in organizations.* New York, NY: Praeger.

Randazzo, S. (2006). Subaru: The emotional myths behind the brand's growth. *Journal of Advertising Research, 46*(1), 11–17. doi:10.2501/S002184990606003X

Rapoport, A. (1968). The promises and pitfalls of information theory. In W. Buckley (Ed.), *Modern systems research for the behavioral scientist* (pp. 137–142). Chicago, IL: Aldine.

Reinard, J. (1998). *Introduction to communication research* (2nd ed.). New York, NY: McGraw-Hill.

Reynolds, P. D. (1971). *A primer on theory construction.* New York, NY: Bobbs Merrill.

Ritter, B. A., & Yoder, J. D. (2004). Gender differences in leader emergence persist even for dominant women: An updated confirmation of role congruity theory. *Psychology of Women Quarterly, 28*(3), 187–193. doi:10.1111/j.1471–6402.2004.00135.x

Rodriguez, E., Joseph, D., Dedmon, J., & Steinberg, H. (2016). Economic customer service, cultural differences, & the big 5 in Canada, China, India, & the United States. Allied Academies International Conference: *Proceedings of the Academy for Economics & Economic Education (AEEE), 19*(2), 18–22.

Rogers, E. M. (2003). *Diffusion of innovations* (5th ed.). New York, NY: Free Press.

Romo, L. K., Thompson, C. M., & Donovan, E. E. (2017). College drinkers' privacy management of alcohol content on Social-Networking Sites. *Communication Studies, 68*(2), 173-189. doi:10.1080/10510974.2017.1280067

Rothwell, J. D. (1998). *In mixed company: Small group communication* (3rd ed.). New York, NY: Harcourt Brace.

Rubin, R. B. (1999). Evaluating the product. In A. L. Vangelisti, J. A. Daly, & G. W. Friedrich (Eds.), *Teaching communication* (2nd ed., pp. 425–446). Mahwah, NJ: LEA.

Ruggiero, T. E. (2000). Uses and gratifications theory in the 21st century. *Mass Communication and Society, 3*(1), 3–37.

Rui, J. R., & Wang, H. (2015). Social network sites and international students' cross-cultural adaptation. *Computers in Human Behavior, 49*, 400–411. doi:10.1016/j.chb.2015.03.041

Runes, D. D. (Ed.). (1984). *Dictionary of philosophy.* Totowa, NJ: Rowman & Allanheld.

Rusbult, C. E. (1980). Commitment and satisfaction in romantic associations: A test of the investment model. *Journal of Experimental Social Psychology, 16*, 172–186.

Salant, P., & Dillman, D. A. (1994). *How to conduct your own survey.* New York, NY: Wiley.

Salazar, A. J. (1995). Understanding the synergistic effects of communication in small groups: Making the most out of group member abilities. *Small Group Research, 26*, 169–199.

Salmon, S., & Joiner, T. A. (2005). Toward an understanding of communication channel preferences for the receipt of management information. *Journal of American Academy of Business, 7*, 56–62.

Salovey, P., & Mayer, J. D. (1989). Emotional intelligence. *Imagination, Cognition and Personality, 9*(3), 185–211.

Salovey, P., Caruso, D., & Mayer, J. D. (2004). Emotional intelligence in practice. In P. Linley & S. Joseph (Eds.), *Positive psychology in practice* (pp. 447–463). Hoboken, NJ: John Wiley & Sons.

Schein, E. (2010). *Organizational culture and leadership* (4th ed.). San Francisco, CA: Jossey-Bass.

Schein, E. H. (1985). *Organizational culture and leadership.* San Francisco, CA: Jossey-Bass.

Schein, E. H. (1992). *Organizational culture and leadership* (2nd ed.). San Francisco, CA: Jossey-Bass.

Schiller, S. Z., & Mandviwalla, M. (2007). Virtual team research: An analysis of theory use and a framework for theory appropriation. *Small Group Research, 38*(1), 12–59. doi:10.1177/1046496406297035

Sedereviciute, K., & Valentini, C. (2011). Towards a more holistic stakeholder analysis approach. Mapping known and undiscovered stakeholders from social media. *International Journal of Strategic Communication, 5*(4), 221–239. doi:10.1080/1553118X.2011.592170

Seib, P. (June 3, 2017). Mainstream media fails in terrorism coverage. *Newsweek* [online]. Retrieved from: http://www.newsweek.com/mainstream-media-fails-terrorism-coverage-619883

Seifert, J. W. (2007, January 18). *Data mining and homeland security: An overview.* Congressional Research Service Report for Congress, order code RL31798. Retrieved from http://www.fas.org/sgp/crs/intel/RL31798.pdf

Shaw, H. (2013). *Sticking points: How to get 4 generations working together in the 12 places they come apart.* Carol Stream, IL: Tyndale House.

Shepherd, M. M., & Martz W. B. (2006). Media richness theory and the distance education environment. *Journal of Computer Information Systems, 47*, 114–122.

Sherry, J. L. (2004). Media effects theory and the nature/nurture debate: A historical overview and directions for future research. *Media Psychology, 6*(1), 83–109.

Signorelli, N., Gerbner, G., & Morgan, M. (1995). Violence on television: The cultural indicators project. *Journal of Broadcasting and Electronic Media, 39*, 278–283.

Sillars, A. L. (1980). Attributions and communication in roommate conflict. *Communication Monographs, 47*(3), 180–200. doi:10.1080/03637758009376031

Simons, H. W. (1976). *Persuasion: Understanding, practice, and analysis.* Reading, MA: Addison-Wesley.

Simpson, C. C., & Mazzeo, S. E. (2017). Skinny is not enough: A content analysis of fitspiration on Pinterest. *Health Communication, 32*, 560–567. doi:10.1080/10410236.2016.1140273

Sivanathan, N., & Fekken, G. C. (2002). Emotional intelligence, moral reasoning, and transformational leadership. *Leadership & Organization Development Journal, 23*, 198–204.

Smircich, L. (1983). Concepts of culture and organizational analysis. *Administrative Science Quarterly, 28,* 339–358.

Smith, E. B., & Kuntz, P. (2013, April 30). CEO pay 1,795-to-1 multiple of wages skirts U.S. law. *Bloomberg* [online]. Retrieved from http://www.bloomberg.com/news/2013–04 –30/ceo-pay-1–795-to-1-multiple-of-workers-skirts-law -as-sec-delays

Smola, K. W., & Sutton, C. D. (2002). Generational differences: Revisiting generational work values for the new millennium. *Journal of Organizational Behavior, 23,* 363–382.

Speer, R. B., Giles, H., & Denes, A. (2013). Investigating stepparent-stepchild interactions: The role of communication accommodation. *Journal of Family Communication, 13,* 218–241. doi:10.1080/15267431.2013.768248

Spitzberg, B. H., & Cupach, W. R. (1984). *Interpersonal communication competence.* Beverly Hills, CA: Sage.

Spitzberg, B. H., & Cupach, W. R. (1989). *Handbook of interpersonal competence research.* New York, NY: Springer-Verlag.

St. George, D. (2008, December 2). Media bombardment is linked to ill effects during childhood. *The Washington Post,* p. C7. Retrieved from http://www.washingtonpost.com/wp -dyn/content/article/2008/12/01/AR2008120102920.html

Staton, A. Q. (1999). An ecological perspective on college/university teaching: The teaching/learning environment and socialization. In A. L. Vangelisti, J. A. Daly, & G. W. Friedrich (Eds.), *Teaching communication* (2nd ed., pp. 31–47). Mahwah, NJ: LEA.

Steele, G. A., & Plenty, D. (2015). Supervisor–subordinate communication competence and job and communication satisfaction. *International Journal of Business Communication, 52,* 294-318. doi:10.1177/2329488414525450

Steiner, S., & Cox, K. (2014). Aligning organizational and individual culture and values. In R. A. Bean, S. D. Davis, M. P. Davey, R. A. Bean, S. D. Davis, M. P. Davey (Eds.), *Clinical supervision activities for increasing competence and self-awareness* (pp. 127–133). Hoboken, NJ: John Wiley & Sons.

Stoverink, A. C., Umphress, E. E., Gardner, R. G., & Miner, K. N. (2014). Misery loves company: Team dissonance and the influence of supervisor-focused interpersonal justice climate on team cohesiveness. *Journal of Applied Psychology, 99(6),* 1059-1073. doi:10.1037/a0037915

Strekalova, Y. A. Krieger, J. L., Neil, J., Caughlin, J. P., Kleinheksel, A. J., & Kotranza, A. (2016). I understand how you feel. *Journal of Language and Social Psychology, 36,* 61-79. DOI: 10.1177/0261927X16663255

Summers, J. (August 28, 2014). Kids and screen time: What does the research say? *NPR.* Retrieved from: http://www.npr.org/sections/ed/2014/08/28/343735856/ kids-and-screen-time-what-does-the-research-say

Tang, L., & Peng, W. (2015). Culture and health reporting: A comparative content analysis of newspapers in the United States and China. *Journal of Health Communication, 20(2),* 187-195. doi:10.1080/10810730.2014.920060

Tannen, D. (1990). *You just don't understand: Women and men in conversation.* New York, NY: Morrow.

Taylor, K. (March 10, 2014). Millennials spend 18 hours a day consuming media—And it's mostly content created by peers. *Entrepreneur Magazine.* Retrieved from https://www .entrepreneur.com/article/232062

Tennert, F. (2014). An attributional analysis of corporate reporting in crisis situations: The 2010 Toyota recall. *Journal of Communication Management, 18(4),* 422–435. doi:10.1108/JCOM-09-2012-0074

Ter Hoeven, C. L., Miller, V. D., Peper, B., & Den Dulk, L. (2017). "The Work Must Go On": The role of employee and managerial communication in the use of work–life policies. *Management Communication Quarterly, 31,* 194–229. doi:10.1177/0893318916684980

Texter, L. A. (1995). Attribution theory. In R. L. Hartman & L. A. Texter (Eds.), *Advanced interpersonal communication* (pp. 53–68). Dubuque, IA: Kendall Hunt.

Thibaut, J. W., & Kelley, H. H. (1959). *The social psychology of groups.* New Brunswick, NJ: Transaction Books.

Thomas, K. W., & Kilmann, R. H. (1974). *Thomas-Kilmann conflict mode instrument.* Tuxedo, NY: Xicom.

Thory, K. (2016). To reveal or conceal? Managers' disclosures of private information during emotional intelligence training. *Human Resource Development Quarterly, 27(1),* 41-66. doi:10.1002/hrdq.21222

Ting-Toomey, S. (1988). Intercultural conflicts: A face-negotiation theory. In Y. Kim & W. Gudykunst (Eds.), *Theories in intercultural communication* (pp. 213–238). Newbury Park, CA: Sage.

Ting-Toomey, S. (1991a). Cross-cultural communication: An introduction. In S. Ting-Toomey & F. Korzenny (Eds.), *Cross-cultural interpersonal communication* (pp. 1–7). Newbury Park, CA: Sage.

Ting-Toomey, S. (1991b). Intimacy expression in three cultures: France, Japan, and the United States. *International Journal of Intercultural Relations, 15,* 29–46.

Ting-Toomey, S. (1992, April). *Cross-cultural face-negotiation: An analytical overview.* Paper presented at the meeting of the Pacific Region Forum on Business and Management Communication, Vancouver, British Columbia.

Ting-Toomey, S. (1994). Managing intercultural conflicts effectively. In L. Samovar & R. Porter (Eds.), *Intercultural communication* (7th ed., pp. 360–372). Belmont, CA: Wadsworth.

Ting-Toomey, S. (2005). The matrix of face: An updated face-negotiation theory. In W. B. Gudykunst (Ed.), *Theorizing about intercultural communication* (pp. 71–92). Thousand Oaks, CA: Sage.

Ting-Toomey, S. (2017). Conflict face negotiation theory: Tracking its evolutionary journey. In X. Dai & G. M. Chen (Eds.), *Conflict management and intercultural communication: The art of intercultural harmony* (pp. 123–143). New York, NY: Routledge.

Ting-Toomey, S., & Oetzel, J. G. (2001). *Managing intercultural conflict effectively.* Thousand Oaks, CA: Sage.

Ting-Toomey, S., & Oetzel, J. (2002). Cross-cultural face concerns and conflict styles: Current status and future directions. In W. Gudykunst & B. Mody (Eds.), *Handbook of international and intercultural communication* (2nd ed., pp. 143–164). Thousand Oaks, CA: Sage.

Ting-Toomey, S., Yee-Jung, K. K., Shapiro, R. B., Garcia, W., Wright, T. J., & Oetzel, J. G. (2000). Ethnic/cultural identity salience and conflict styles in four US ethnic groups. *International Journal of Intercultural Relations, 24,* 47–81. doi: 10.1016/S0147-1767(99)00023-1

Tomkiewicz, J., & Bass, K. (2008). Attitudes of business students toward management generation cohorts. *North American Journal of Psychology, 10*(2), 435–444.

Tompkins, P. K., & Cheney, G. E. (1985). Communication and unobtrusive control in contemporary organizations. In R. D. McPhee & P. K. Tompkins (Eds.), *Organizational communication: Traditional themes and new directions* (pp. 179–210). Beverly Hills, CA: Sage.

Trevino, L. K., Lengel, R. H., & Daft, R. L. (1987). Media symbolism, media richness, and media choice in organizations. *Communication Research, 14*(5), 553–574.

Triandis, H. C. (1995). *Individualism and collectivism.* Boulder, CO: Westview Press.

Tukachinsky, R., Mastro, D., & Yarchi, M. (2015). Documenting portrayals of race/ethnicity on primetime television over a 20-year span and their association with national-level racial/ethnic attitudes." *Journal of Social Issues, 71,* 17–38. doi: 10.1111/josi.12094.

Turnage, A. K., & Goodboy, A. K. (2016). E-Mail and face-to-face organizational dissent as a function of leader-member exchange status. *International Journal of Business Communication, 53,* 271-285. doi:10.1177/2329488414525456

Twenge, J. (2014). *Generation me: Revised and updated. Why today's young Americans are more confident, assertive, entitled—and more miserable than ever before.* New York, NY: Atria.

Twenge, J. M., & Campbell, S. M. (2008). Generational differences in psychological traits and their impact on the workplace. *Journal of Managerial Psychology, 23*(8), 862–877.

Twenge, J. M., Campbell, S. M., Hoffman, B. J., & Lance, C. E. (2010). Generational differences in work values: Leisure and extrinsic values increasing, social and intrinsic values decreasing. *Journal of Management, 36*(5), 1117–1142. doi:10.1177/0149206309352246

Tyrrell, I. (October 21, 2016). What, exactly, is "American exceptionalism?" *Aeon* [online]. Retrieved from http://theweek.com/articles/654508/what-exactly-american-exceptionalism

Valde, K. S., & Miller Henningsen, M. L. (2015). Facework in responding to unethical communication. *International Journal of Business Communication, 52*(4), 369–403. doi:10.1177/2329488414525445

Valkenburg, P. M., & Peter, J. (2013). The differential susceptibility to media effects model. *Journal of Communication, 63*(2), 221–243. doi:10.1111/jcom.12024

Van Vonderen, K. E., & Kinnally, W. (2012). Media effects on body image: Examining media exposure in the broader context of internal and other social factors. *American Communication Journal, 14*(2), 41–57.

Vecchio, R. P., Griffeth, R. W., & Hom, P. W. (1986). The predictive utility of the vertical dyad linkage approach. *Journal of Social Psychology, 126,* 617–625.

Vergeer, M., Lubbers, M., & Scheepers, P. (2000). Exposure to newspapers and attitudes toward ethnic minorities: A longitudinal analysis. *Howard Journal of Communications, 11*(2), 127–143.

Victor, D. (April 5, 2017). Pepsi pulls ad accused of trivializing Black Lives Matter. *New York Times* online. Retrieved June from https://www.nytimes.com/2017/04/05/business/kendall-jenner-pepsi-ad.html?mcubz=2

Vivero, V. N., & Jenkins, S. R. (1999). Existential hazards of the multicultural individual: Defining and understanding "cultural homelessness." *Cultural Diversity and Ethnic Minority Psychology, 5*, 6–26.

von Bertalanffy, L. (1968). *General system theory: Foundations, development, applications* (Rev. ed.). New York, NY: Braziller.

Vorvoreanu, M. (2009). Perceptions of corporations on Facebook: An analysis of Facebook social norms. *Journal of New Communications Research, 4*, 67–86.

Wadsworth, A., Patterson, P., Kaid, L., Cullers, G., Malcomb, D., & Lamirand, L. (1987). "Masculine" vs. "feminine" strategies in political ads: Implications for female candidates. *Journal of Applied Communication Research, 15*(1/2), 77.

Wallen, A. S., Mor, S., & Devine, B. A. (2014). It's about respect: Gender–professional identity integration affects male nurses' job attitudes. *Psychology of Men & Masculinity, 15*, 305-312. doi:10.1037/a0033714

Wang, Y., & Huang, T. (2009). The relationship of transformational leadership with group cohesiveness and emotional intelligence. *Social Behavior and Personality, 37*, 379–392.

Watzlawick, P., Bavelas, J. B., & Jackson, D. D. (1967). *Pragmatics of human communication: A study of interactional patterns, pathologies, and paradoxes.* New York, NY: Norton.

Watzlawick, P., Weakland, J., & Fisch, R. (1974). *Change: Principles of problem formulation and problem resolution.* New York, NY: Norton.

Weick, K. E. (1969). *The social psychology of organizing.* Reading, MA: Addison-Wesley.

West, R., & Turner, L.H. (2017). *Introducing communication theory: Analysis and application, 6th ed.* New York, NY: McGraw Hill.

Westerman, C. K., Miller, L. E., Reno, K. M., & Spates, S. A. (2015). Sharing personal health information at work: What is appropriate and expected in organizations? *Communication Studies, 66*(3), 378-397. doi:10.1080/10510974.2015.1019157

Westermann, J. W., & Yamamura, J. H. (2007). Generational preferences for work environment fit: Effects on employee outcomes. *Career Development International, 12*(2), 150–161.

Williams, M. (2013, April 17). FBI urges media to "exercise caution" after inaccurate arrest reports. *The Guardian* [online]. Retrieved from http://www.guardian.co.uk/world/2013/apr/17/fbi-media-exercise-caution-bombings

Willis, J. (2017). Moving toward extremism: Group polarization in the laboratory and the world. In S. C. Cloninger, S. A. Leibo, S. C. Cloninger, S. A. Leibo (Eds.), *Understanding angry groups: Multidisciplinary perspectives on their motivations and effects on society* (pp. 53–76). Santa Barbara, CA, US: Praeger/ABC-CLIO.

Wong, N. H. (2016). "Vaccinations are safe and effective": Inoculating positive HPV vaccine attitudes against anti-vaccination attack messages. *Communication Reports, 29*(3), 127–138. doi:10.1080/08934215.2015.1083599

Wood, J. T. (1993). Gender and moral voice: From woman's nature to standpoint theory. *Women's Studies in Communication, 15*, 1–24.

Wood, J. T. (2015). *Gendered lives: Communication, gender, and culture (11th ed.).* Stamford, CT: Cengage Learning.

Wood, J. T., & Dindia, K. (1998). What's the difference? A dialogue about differences and similarities between women and men. In D. J. Canary & K. Dindia (Eds.), *Sex differences and similarities in communication: Critical essays and empirical investigations of sex and gender in interaction* (pp. 19–39). Mahwah, NJ: Erlbaum.

Zanin, A. C., Hoelscher, C. S., & Kramer, M. W. (2016). Extending symbolic convergence theory. *Small Group Research, 47*, 438-472. doi:10.1177/1046496416658554

Zemke, R., Raines, C., & Filipczak, B. (2013). *Generations at Work: Managing the Clash of Boomers, Gen Xers, and Gen Yers in the Workplace (2nd ed.).* New York, NY: American Management Association.

Zhang, Q., Ting-Toomey, S., & Oetzel, J. G. (2014). Linking emotion to the conflict face-negotiation theory: A U.S.-China investigation of the mediating effects of anger, compassion, and guilt in interpersonal conflict. *Human Communication Research, 40*, 373–395. doi:10.1111/hcre.12029

Zimbardo, P. G., Ebbesen, E. B., & Maslach, C. (1977). *Influencing attitudes and changing behavior.* New York, NY: Random House.

ABOUT THE AUTHORS

Marianne Dainton (MA, PhD, The Ohio State University; BA, Villanova University) is professor of communication at La Salle University in Philadelphia. She teaches communication theory, interpersonal communication, group communication, and organizational communication. Marianne's research focuses on communication that facilitates relationship maintenance. She has published in *Communication Monographs, the Journal of Social and Personal Relationships, Family Relations*, and *Communication Quarterly*, among other places. She has also published a book titled *Maintaining Black Marriage: Individual, Interpersonal, and Contextual Dynamics* (2017), numerous book chapters, and is the coeditor (with Daniel Canary) of the book *Maintaining Relationships Through Communication* (2003).

Elaine D. Zelley (MA, PhD, The Pennsylvania State University; BA, Ursinus College) is an associate professor of communication at La Salle University in Philadelphia. She teaches communication theory; interpersonal communication; organizational communication; group communication; and sex, gender, and communication. Elaine's research also focuses broadly on the communication of relationship maintenance. She is particularly interested in politeness, facework, and friendships. She has published in *Communication Yearbook* and has also coauthored several book chapters dealing with the topics of relationship maintenance, friendship, and competition.

INDEX